W9-AUG-798

DATE DUE

19

JUL 1968

AUG 1968

NOV 8 1968

SWK

MAY 08 1994   APR 29 1994

MAY 11 1995

MAY 11 1995

SOCIOLOGY IN ACTION

THE DORSEY SERIES IN ANTHROPOLOGY AND SOCIOLOGY

EDITOR

ROBIN M. WILLIAMS, JR.
Cornell University

SOCIOLOGY IN ACTION

CASE STUDIES IN SOCIAL PROBLEMS
AND DIRECTED SOCIAL CHANGE

Edited by

ARTHUR B SHOSTAK, Ph.D.
Assistant Professor of Sociology,
University of Pennsylvania

1966
THE DORSEY PRESS
HOMEWOOD, ILLINOIS

© 1966 BY THE DORSEY PRESS

ALL RIGHTS RESERVED. THIS BOOK OR ANY PART THEREOF MAY NOT BE REPRODUCED WITHOUT THE WRITTEN PERMISSION OF THE PUBLISHER

First Printing, April, 1966

Library of Congress Catalog Card No. 66-14551

PRINTED IN THE UNITED STATES OF AMERICA

M
5
545

DEDICATED to those moved by the essays herein to take action:

"The responsibility is to keep everlastingly challenging the present with the question: But what is it that we human beings want, and what things would have to be done, in what ways and in what sequence, in order to change the present so as to achieve it?"

ROBERT S. LYND, from *Knowledge for What?*

"The scientist who stands tall in his profession is actually a pygmy if he takes no responsibility for what he makes. . . . The biggest lesson of all to be learned about contemporary civilization is that nothing anyone is doing today makes any sense unless it is connected to the making of a genuine peace."

NORMAN COUSINS

PREFACE

Like you, I am curious about the possible applications of sociology to real-life problems. I have long wondered what other sociologists do professionally outside the classroom, school office, or home study—and have reluctantly come to expect little guidance in the matter from the professional meetings and journals. The rare discussion or article I have discovered has only heightened my curiosity as it has usually been of the "trumpet-call" variety (i.e., an inspired "demand" to do this or that, bereft of any account of something accomplished, or still yet, attempted).

This gap in available knowledge is all the more strange when viewed against the action-rich background of contemporary sociology. Comte and Saint-Simon, the founding fathers, were both social engineers; Durkheim and Weber championed particular social reforms; the American founding fathers were social problem-oriented; the first sociology courses in America dealt with the relief of various social pathologies, and one of the first professional journals was entitled *The Journal of Applied Sociology* (now, revealingly enough, *Sociology and Social Research*). The oddity of our current "blackout" on applied work is further compounded when contrasted with such well-known action examples as Stouffer's *The American Soldier,* or the work of the professional pollsters, or the misplaced furor over sociology in the 1954 School Desegregation Case. These examples continue to suggest that *some* sociologists *somewhere* are doing *some things* we might look into.

Aware from personal experience and the professional "grapevine" that much now *is* being done by action sociologists, and, provoked by a popular idea among colleagues that the next 20 years are likely to be known as the sociological decades, I determined some months ago to systematically learn more about the doings of fellow actionists. In conventional fashion, I initiated a literature search, hoping in vain to bring together a worthy collection of action-essay reprints. Doomed from the start, the search underlined the need for the production of a *new* kind of essay.

What is "new" about the 24 essays commissioned especially for this volume, and what is characteristic of the 14 reprints also employed, is a sharp focus on something *actually done.* My contributors, almost all professional sociologists, seek in an unusually frank and engaging fashion to "involve" us in their most recent and significant attempt to "use" sociology. Whether the essay concerns testimony on community identification in a school boundaries dispute, or project sponsorship in the hostile setting of a medical hospital, or an enthusiastic report on sociology's new use in the Peace Movement, the writers recount real occurences in the full richness of the actual experience. Human beings and events are observed here not so much through the punch holes of an IBM card as through the sensitivities of sociologically-skilled men and women.

This focus on work actually done is by no means confined only to work successfully done: such a restriction, albeit common, would be incompatible with my goal of a balanced review. Accordingly, I have asked several of the volume's sociologists to break with precedent, and review one of their unsuccessful, ill-fated action projects. These unique case studies of failure are not the usual melánge of impressionistic warnings and vague forebodings, but are actual accounts and analyses by disappointed men who "were there." If properly read, these essays can provide considerable guidance into the practitioner's *real* world, and considerable advice on successful project management.

Another unique feature of the volume concerns its deliberate, explicit *sociological* character. With rare exception, the focus is on a situational, rather than a historical analysis of behavior; on styles of interaction of men in groups, rather than on unique personal events; on efforts to change systems, rather than individuals; on society, rather than on the psyche. Unlike volumes bearing similar titles that range broadly across the various social sciences, few essays are used here from clinical psychology, cultural anthropology, institutional economics, social psychology, or the like. Eleven of the volume's 16 reprint authors are sociologists, as are 26 of the 31 original contributors. The choice was made to concentrate in depth on one discipline, thus the book's title: *Sociology* in Action.

The sound of the trumpet *is* heard in the volume's essays, but it is heard in proper perspective—as a theme built out of the composition's major movement (its action reports). Having established their *bona fides* with their action accounts, several contributors move on to offer provocative comments on the serious costs of uneven academic attention to applied work, the significant contributions theory and action make to each other, and the many existing and unfolding opportunities for applied sociology. At all times the discussion is grounded in the hard reality of actual experience; nothing is asked but what the writer has not tried—or is not now trying it—himself. No challenges are made but what the challenger has not been—or is not now challenged by the very subject—himself.

Unfortunately, it has not been possible to cover all the existing areas of action in the fashion of this volume—a lack of appropriate reprints or possible contributors helps explain the volume's omission of family sociology, industrial sociology, mass communication, mass culture, and mass leisure. For the same reasons it has not been possible to represent the very considerable work being done in applied sociology by professional sociologists of other countries. Nor has it always been possible to allow full sway to the authors of material used in exposition—tight space and time considerations explain often severe editorial cuts in reprints and new essays alike.

Nevertheless, the essays do make the point that sociology *has* much to contribute as an applied science; sociologist *are* busy professionally outside of "laboratories, libraries, and swivel chairs"; sociology *itself* has much to gain from action projects; and the people involved in action are a fascinating assortment of expert sociologists.

I have learned much in the process of assembling this anthology and I now pursue my profession with greater insight into its background, new pride in its record, higher regard for its personnel, and deeper trust in its potential. The anthology will have achieved its goal if readers leave the book interested in the applications of sociology to real-life problems, or possibly, leave it encouraged to consider careers in action sociology.

ARTHUR B. SHOSTAK

Philadelphia, Pa.
March, 1966.

ACKNOWLEDGMENTS

Particularly instrumental in my decision to prepare this anthology was the stimulation of Penn's bright and questioning student body; its considerable serious concern with practical applications of sociological insights early aroused my interest in this publication venture. The personal examples of three faculty friends served to demonstate to me the significance of current efforts in applied sociology—and the need for greater public and professional awareness of these efforts: my models here were Professor Melvin Tumin (Princeton sociologist), Professor Otto Pollak (Penn sociologist), and Professor Howard E. Mitchell (Penn Clinical Psychologist, and Director, Penn Human Resources Program). The literature search entailed in collecting essays was aided considerably by Mr. Jerome Stone, an undergraduate major in sociology. The many hours of typing and retyping were expertly handled as an afterwork extra assignment by Carol Galvelis, Emily Tarsell, Barbara Lewis, and Clare Cosgrove. Special appreciation is owed my editorial assistant, Beau-Janette B. Fleming, a personal friend and an invaluable student of human communications. Dr. Robin Williams, Jr., Sociology Consultant and Editor of the Dorsey Press, contributed much to the book's final tone and form. Finally, I would reserve a particular vote of thanks for my collaborators, men and women who graciously met my very tight deadline, accepted my vigorous editorial revisions of their work, and strove most successfully to present frank, engaging, and significant accounts of their actual "adventures" in applied sociology.

ARTHUR B. SHOSTAK

REPRINT PERMISSIONS

Reprint permission has been granted by the author and journal for the use (and indicated abridgement) of the following essays:

Bugental, J. F. T. and Robert Tannenbaum, "Sensitivity Training and Being Motivation," *Journal of Humanistic Psychlogy*, Spring, 1963.

Clinard, Marshall B., "The Sociologist and Social Change in Underdeveloped Countries," *Social Problems*, Winter, 1963.

Etzioni, Amitai, "Social Analysis as a Sociological Vocation," *American Journal of Sociology*, March, 1965 (Abridged).

Eugster, Carla, "Field Education in West Heights: Equipping a Deprived Community to Help Itself," *Human Organization*, Fall, 1964.

Goldstein, Rhoda, "The Participant as Observer," *Phylon*, Fall, 1964 (Abridged and retitled: "The Participant as Observer: Sociological Gains from Public Roles").

Halleck, Seymour L, "The Impact of Professional Dishonesty on Behavior of Disturbed Adolescents," *Social Work*, April, 1963.

Horowitz, Irving L., "The Life and Death of Project Camelot," *Trans-action*, November/December, 1965.

Key, William H., "Controlled Intervention—The Helping Professions and Directed Social Change," *American Journal of Orthopsychiatry*, forthcoming, (Abridged).

Killiam, Lewis M., "The Social Scientist's Role in the Preparation of the Florida Desegregation Brief," *Social Problems*, Fall, 1960.

Lindersmith, Alfred R, "Social Problems and Sociological Theory," *Social Problems*, Fall, 1960.

Lippitt, Ronald, "The Process of Utilization of Social Research to improve Social Practice," *American Journal of Orthopsychiatry*, forthcoming (Abridged).

Riessman, Frank and S. M. Miller, "Social Change versus the 'Psychiatric World View'", *American Journal of Orthopsychiatry*, January, 1964.

Schwartz, Morris S., "The Uses of Sociology in a Mental Hospital," *Social Problems*, Winter, 1963.

TABLE OF CONTENTS

PART ONE

PERSPECTIVE

The sociologist of the 1960's has an unprecedented opportunity to help guide constructive reforms. His traditional roles as teacher, researcher, and writer may be supplemented by such action-oriented varieties as the "Back-patter," the "Merlin," the "Broker," the "Shotgun," the "Arbitrator," and the "Self-Generator." The author of these labels, Dr. Marvin B. Sussman, defines their character and provides historical perspective on their development in the introductory essay below. His high regard for "this new breed of sociologist" helps set the tone for the entire volume.

THE SOCIOLOGIST AS A TOOL OF SOCIAL ACTION*

by Marvin B. Sussman

THE CLASSROOM and research laboratory are no longer the sole domains of the sociologist. The sociologist of the 1960's is likely to teach, research, consult, administrate, and take additional leadership responsibility in the solution of social problems. Particularly in his new role as consultant, the opportunity to influence change in social institutions and policies gives him an unprecedented responsibility.

KNOWLEDGE FOR WHAT?

One phenomenon which has escalated the development of the multiple roles of the sociologist is the closing of the gap between the discovery of knowledge and its application outside of academia. The quest for applicable knowledge is so great that discoveries barely out of the laboratory are being immediately applied to improve the health, political, social, and family systems of existing societies. This rapid transition from knowledge to practice has precipitated a growing realization by the modern university that it has a responsibility to direct the distribution and proper application of this knowledge. Increasingly, universities have taken on large research projects which, while pursuing theoretical

---

*I wish to thank Elaine Marie Stahl for her helpful suggestions in writing the final draft of this paper.

3

concerns, almost always contain practical components as well. The ultimate hope is that a bit of knowledge derived from these projects will cure a malignant disease, or solve a critical social problem such as the consequences of extended unemployment.

There was a time when the gap between the discovery of knowledge and its practical application was so extensive that the university could afford to live in splendid isolation. But as societies have become more complex and their survival has become more dependent on the harmonious arrangement of component parts, the university, like any other institution, has discovered that it cannot base decisions concerning its own destiny solely on internal considerations but has to recognize as well the external conditions which impinge on it. The university has come to recognize that it cannot remain isolated from a world of disintegrating social systems and rapid social change.

University involvement began with training and research programs in the medical and basic sciences, programs undertaken with support from both government and industry. In a society which owes its development to a science technology and is concerned with the extension and provision of adequate health care to all its citizens, these developments were logical ones.

Since World War II, it has gradually become apparent that the university was lopsided in its focus on the medical and basic sciences. When spokesmen from these respective fields indicated this and themselves asked for help from the behavioral sciences, a renaissance was engendered leading today to an era of affluence for the sociologist. The university began to encourage social science research to find solutions to health, military, industrial, economic, and family problems. The pursuit of esoteric knowledge was not discarded but was assigned a secondary place. Under this changed university orientation, the sociologist received a mandate and a new set of expectations. He has today a responsibility equal in value to that of his colleagues in the natural and physical sciences and their professions. In effect, the work system of the sociologist is presently giving him wholehearted support, a situation which is awesome and somewhat frightening because expectations are so high that success in meeting them is most unlikely.

THE SOCIAL INTEGRATION OF THE SOCIOLOGIST

A second phenomenon which has produced the new consultant role for the sociologist is the change which has taken place in the discipline during the past 40 years as it has responded to demands within and outside. During the past decade, sociologists have become highly involved and even identified with the recurrent social problems of American society. Their previous relative uninvolvement can largely be explained by the isolation of the university as a social system within the society and by the knowledge gap already mentioned. But perhaps more important in years past was the group's reaction against a "social progress" sociology which was dominant in the early 1900's and characterized American sociology until the Great Depression of 1930.

"Social progress" sociology hailed the advances of science and education as steps toward the society's achievement of its desired goals, steps approaching a higher level of functioning where critical social problems such as those of minority groups, poverty, crime, and international tensions would be solved. Sociologists active during this early period were esoteric theorists. They had competing schools, and very few conducted basic research in which they could test hypotheses and reformulate their theories. The U.S. after World War I was doing very well economically, and while there were problems such as Prohibition and the parallel increase in the incidence of crime, relatively few social problems constituted crises demanding empirical investigation for causes and consequences.

The depression of the 1930's and its attendant social ills required a hard look at what had gone wrong. When the social order breaks down, action is required immediately; it cannot wait for the findings of research. Social scientists played a very minor role in the development of social policies and programs to handle the problems of the depression. Nevertheless, the depression constituted a powerful stimulus for the development of a new empirical sociology which emphasized the need to be value- and bias-free, a sociology which abandoned the social progress theme and sought from the natural and physical sciences models useful for the study of social phenomena. Research designs were introduced, and a period of experimental sociology began, using controls and tests for validity and reliability of data now being gathered from systematic questionnaires, interviews, and observations. The use of statistics as a technique and a theory for the quantification of data became more widespread, and sociologists began to use statistics in reporting their research findings.

Armchair research was discarded in favor of a new hard-nosed empiricism. The first empirical studies investigated the consequences of the depression. In a systematic way, the researchers tabulated the social and economic conditions of large segments of the American population. Other researchers probed further into the causes of the depression and sought explanation of these causes in "facts." There was an almost complete rejection of a priori theoretical formulations. The shibboleth of the new sociology was fact-finding in the world of reality, and sociologists soon resembled moles digging in the vineyard of the social world.

From the late '30's until World War II, sociologists moved from one extreme of the sociological continuum to the other, from a "social progress" sociology based largely on theorizing and speculation to a naked empiricism which was parsimonious in theory building.

The hard-nosed empiricism has since fared as poorly as the social progress sociology in providing explanations of rapid social change and the impact of such change on existing social institutions. The new sociology is limited and microscopic in its approach, and, as a consequence, ignores grand theories or even middle-range ones which might provide explanations of social conditions and the opportunity for further testing by empirical research. A social problem orientation is rejected here because research for solving a social problem does require some a priori theoretical formulation.

As a result, after World War II, the position of extreme disallowance of social problems as an appropriate concern of the sociologist gave way to a position reflecting growing interest in the etiology, treatment, and resolution of such problems. Health, education, and welfare services became big business, and very complex bureaucratic organizations were established to cope with extensive programs of grants for research and demonstration projects and for outright subsidy to states, communities, and individuals. A search began for supportive theory to provide the framework for fitting together the bits and pieces of empirical data, theory which could provide explanation, and even solutions, for recurrent social ills.

Research and consultancy have become the first order of the day, and projects running the gamut from alcoholism to socialization of the poor and youth development of the deviant are now being undertaken by sociologists in universities and colleges around the country.

THE ROLES OF THE CONSULTANT

In the development of new social policies and the formulation of new programs to enrich or enhance social conditions and to solve critical social problems, the sociologist is often called upon as a consultant, i.e., he becomes a tool for social action.

The term consultant implies that there is something to be sold, that something in the expert's area of specialization aids in the solution of the particular problem. The consultant is engaged for his knowledge in an area with the belief on the part of the employer—in this instance, the government—that the consultant can further the solution of the problem, whether it is overpopulation, the quest for social security, or the treatment of the poverty-ridden family. The consultant role of the sociologist is his most professional one, since he functions in a fiduciary relationship as an expert who places at the disposal of his client his total repertoire of knowledge and skills, as well as the time necessary to diagnose, treat, and solve a given problem.

The consultant role is perhaps the most effective tool the sociologist has to bring about desired social change. One can assume in a consultant relationship that the agency or institution seeking assistance has one or more problems begging for solution and is therefore engaging a person with an apparently high degree of expertise to help solve them. This person's judgments are to be taken seriously since the time involved by all parties to the consultant transaction is quite extensive and costly.

The Back-patting Role

There is a popular quip that agencies usually hire a consultant after he knows definitely what they want to do so that he can evaluate the situation and advise them to do what they have already decided to do anyway. Confirmation of this decision provides the ethos for making the necessary changes in structure, goals, or functions. Similarly, if they are dissatisfied with the consultant's report, they simply bury it and hire another consultant to provide them with the report they wish to have. But it would be a mistake to dismiss the important functions a consultant provides in a "back-patting" role. The nature of the transactions is such that even if a consultant provides support for already determined policies and programs, he nevertheless introduces changes as a consequence of interaction between himself and his client. Out of the crucible of the consultant transaction there often emerges a somewhat different program and policy, although there might be a very close resemblance to the client's initial formulation.

The back-patting role requires the least amount of creative effort, but it may have an important payoff for the consultant in terms of increased recognition and prestige. Selection for this role implies that the client already knows the individual's particular positions and orientations concerning the issue under question. The consultant does not have to "fight" the problem, but can enhance the already derived decision by giving confirmation and indicating how a few of the "loose ends" can be tied up nicely to improve the intended course of action. An illustration here would be the university which has decided to build up a department in order to meet competition for educational preeminence. Administration officials and a few selected faculty members who are given the leadership role in this instance develop a plan and then present it to members of the department, at the same time inviting a sympathetic consultant to function in the back-patting role. Often the exalted stature of the consultant is sufficient to win over those individuals who are questioning the wisdom of the planned changes. In the back-patting role, the client, rather than the consultant, dominates. The back-patting functions of a consultant almost by themselves make the consultant a tool for social action.

The Merlin Role

A still more viable method for introducing social action is the "Merlin" role which the consultant sometimes plays for administrators and for individuals who formulate policy. It is obvious that administrators not only interpret policy but also make policies relevant to certain functions at different levels of their organization. In the Merlin role, the consultant deals directly with a source of authority, and, unlike other members of the organization, has a one-to-one relationship with the fountainhead of authority and power. His major task is to satisfy the needs of his client, the administrator-policy maker, and his analysis and diagnosis of particular problems must fit in with indicated goals and views held by this particular administrator and policy maker. Consensus is not necessary, but articulation of differences, agreements, and objectives is mandatory.

In the Merlin role, one can personally exercise the greatest amount of influence in bringing about social change. The changes may not be radical, as well-entrenched organizational systems do not bend readily to radical changes except under great duress and crisis, but very noticeable and desired changes in forms of policies and programs can be effected if appropriate evidence is presented that these are requisite for the maintenance of the bureaucratic organization over time.

The Merlin role is perhaps the most exciting role available, and it provides the consultant with a rare opportunity to effect changes in active social policy. The consultant has the ear of people in power and his main function is to give advice on a variety of matters. He has a generalized role and is available on call. His effectiveness is measured by the number of successes he has in moving an institution along the path of desired objectives, reducing conflicts resulting from such movement, and generally "keeping the institution out of trouble." This consultant moves from problem to problem and situation to situation, and he is in the enviable position of being unrestricted by the norms of the bureaucratic structure while still having the advantages of the confidante role which characterizes the relationship of the staff or administrative assistant to the administrator.

The Merlin role provides the consultant with the opportunity to introduce new policies and programs. For example, behavioral science projects concerning the functioning of the family received little support for many years. A few years ago, however, a sociologist was asked to develop a research program for a particular government agency, and, because of his interest in family sociology, he was able to formulate a set of policies which, when implemented, provided extensive support for projects concerned with the family as it related to the particular problems covered by the program of this agency. It was also possible for the consultant to influence the selection of core staff and project review members. The methods used can represent a "hard" or "soft" sell, and one should not be shocked by the term "sell"; nothing underhanded is being suggested. If the sociologist cannot or is unwilling to "sell" his ideas, somebody far less knowledgeable may take his place.

The Broker Role

Another aspect of the general consultant role is the "broker" role. This role has two major dimensions: the first is to relate to the institution the concerns, objectives, and interests of individuals who are outside the institutional system, but who wish to be involved with or are affected by the functions of a given institution; and the second dimension is to relate the needs, interests, ideas, and objectives of individual members of different levels of the institutional system to those in leadership positions in the institution. The broker role means harmonizing the interests of individuals within and outside the institution to create greater cohesion and concordance in relation to the structure and functions of members within the institution.

The broker role, then, has a communication function; it is as if one is establishing a harmonious arrangement between a buyer and a seller in the marketplace. Concerning the broker function within an institution, it is obvious that suggestions for programs and changes in social policy coming from a lower level within the institutional bureaucracy can often be viewed negatively as representing the vested interests of a given individual or group. The same suggestions coming from the consultant—i.e., the perceived independent source—can find a more ready acceptance. In the event a similar proposal has already been presented by a lower echelon official, it is likely that the policy maker or administrator will act accordingly, provided the consultant reaffirmed the previously suggested course of action. In effect, the broker cuts across formal lines of authority and brings together component units of the system so that decisions which affect policy and subsequent action can be made quickly.

Government-sponsored health, welfare, and education research and demonstration programs involve huge amounts of money. In the broker role, the consultant attempts to harmonize the real and perceived needs of these programs with the interests, abilities, and concerns of the sociologist who is engaged in related research and demonstration programs. The sociologist-consultant is in the best position to implement the policies of the administration concerned because he knows what these policies and programs are, and, at the same time, he commands a pertinent body of information concerning other sociologists working in the field. While all government agencies have extensive literature on their programs, this means of communication is somehow not as effective in bringing programs and researcher or demonstrator together as is the means employed by the broker consultant.

Another facet of the broker role is bringing into harmony the desires and goals of the lower echelon members of the organization with those of the administrator. The broker consultant has access to all members of an organization, and one of his most important functions is to bring about some consensus concerning goals and practice within the organization. Studies concerned with institutional change indicate that while leaders may wish to change policies and practices, such desires are not generally held by individuals on lower levels of the organization. In this instance, the broker "brings the message" to such individuals, and indicates to them the variety of payoffs that would result from acceptance of new policies and changes in practice. Often members of the second and third levels of an organization may feel there is insufficient innovation or readiness to change administrative policies to meet existing conditions and problems. In this instance, should the broker consultant accept their recommended changes in policies and programs, he can introduce these to the top administrators with or without indicating their source, and he can thereby often "move" the top administrators into acceptance of new policies.

The Shotgun Role

Another component of the consultant role is the "shotgun" function. The shotgun role is a one-time occasion on which the individual is asked to review the situation, most commonly in a speech at an annual meeting or conference. The consultant is supplied with sufficient information about existing problems and institutional arrangements to review, stimulate, and energize the client. The consequences of the shotgun consultant's action are usually unpredictable, and whether he can influence social action in a particular way depends on the nature of the situation; the expectations of his client and of those to be changed; and the readiness, timing, content, and form of his exposition.

The shotgun consultant role is a temporary one, and its subsequent effects and importance are hard to measure. It *may* result in many unintended consequences. Commonly, the client—an educational institution, welfare agency, or government bureau—asks the sociologist to come in to look things over and to give a talk to members of the organization. (Usually it is a one- or two-day affair.) During such "a one-night stand," the consultant can introduce "radical" ideas concerning a policy or a program. This is, in part, what is expected of him; and since the relationship is severed after this appearance, it becomes easier to "blast and let the chips fall where they may." The consultant's pet theory or idea can be presented to a group with the hope that such a forceful presentation will change orientations, attitudes, values, even behavior.

(For example, the exposition by this writer of the existence of an extended kin family network in modern urban society and its implications for decision-making in the functions of other social institutions has been presented to numerous groups throughout the country. While the impact is still indeterminable, there is a growing realization among social welfare agencies that this structure has been ignored to date as a source of support or negation of therapy programs.)

The Arbitrator Role

A fifth type of consultant role which can influence social change is the arbitrator role. The individual is presented with a situation in which there are two or more positions on a given issue. The consultant functions very much like an arbitrator in industrial disputes. In this instance, he does not redirect a course of action; rather, he influences the selection of particular action courses which have already been determined and have become the bases for the dispute which requires the services of the arbitrator-consultant.

The arbitrator role can be a tool for social action, but it is perhaps the least satisfactory of all those presented thus far because it forces a consultant to take sides and consequently gains him some friends while losing him some others. Action by its very nature means alienation of some individuals, but the consultant effecting estrangement wants to be in a position to control the process. In issues requiring arbitration, as the problems have already been stated, the consultant in this important sense does not control the process. One of his best techniques is to effect a compromise so that he is now "loved" by both groups and has essentially thereby taken control of the change process and is effecting action along the lines of his thinking and belief.

Government agencies are constantly facing the problem as to whether they should extend their programs along accustomed lines that seemed to work although not highly effectively, or should pioneer in more experimental programs that would expose them to serious political pressure in the event that they failed. Educational agencies such as universities are constantly debating the question as to whether the focus ought to be on teaching or on research, and sometimes faculties within departments or even within universities are split straight down the middle on such an issue. The arbitrator consultant, in order to effect a meaningful solution by not lining up with one side or the other, must come up with a new plan that mediates the differences. This plan should enable both groups to maintain their basic beliefs, even as they accede that the other group exists and that some experimentation ought to be undertaken in combining the interest of both contenders.

The Self-Generating Role

A sixth type of consultant role is the "self-generating" one. In this situation the sociologist becomes established as a consultant to a variety of groups by virtue of his own action guided by his beliefs and convictions. He becomes active in social and political movements, and before very long he functions in the role of a consultant expert in determining policies, strategies, and appropriate courses of action. This may take the form of "teach-in" demonstrations, letters to the editor, and a variety of activities that characterize social movements intending to bring about changes in institutional arrangements, values, and attitudes. The higher his established position within the university or college system, the "safer" the individual is in undertaking such activities. His status and prestige within the university and the larger academic community of his peers is essentially his "risk capital" which he can use in initiating and promoting social changes he deems necessary and vital for the maintenance of the society.

There may be other types of consultant roles, but the ones I have examined appear to me to be the principal ones. The sociologist today takes on one or all of them, and he is being asked to do so increasingly. A new breed of professional sociologist is developing. He is best characterized as "a knower and a doer." He can stand in his own right as a researcher, scholar, teacher, and theorizer, and, at the same time, feel compelled to function in a wide variety of situations outside of classroom sociology. He is a kind of person who can apply the best theory backed up by empirical research to a variety of problems in a variety of situations. He is truly a generalist when it comes to application. He can take his expert knowledge and apply it in diagnosing and, hopefully, solving a medical, technical, social, economic, political, or other type of problem. He no longer seeks safety in the ivory tower, nor does he agree that the only true path to creative scholarship, research, and teaching comes about from this segregated position. This new breed of sociologist feels, as Robert Lynd stated many years ago, that knowledge is for something and that if he cannot command the use and distribution of knowledge, somebody far less knowledgeable than he will do so. He feels it is now his responsibility and his mandate to help secure desired social action.

PART TWO

PROJECTS AND PROBLEMS

Gloom being traditional on the part of certain prominent demographers, it is a genuine pleasure to read an optimistic account of man's prospects in the struggle to contain the so-called population explosion. Dr. Bernard Berelson's essay has several virtues, not the least of these being his terse and frank account of a well-designed and successfully executed program for the implementation of family planning in Taiwan. Useful for its demonstration of the feasibility of cross-cultural change experiments, the essay challenges a hodgepodge of crippling stereotypes (national as well as foreign) with its finding that "the people needed not so much to be motivated toward family planning as to be informed on how to go about it." In this same spirit of challenge Dr. Berelson concludes by advising we may be going about our applied sociology the wrong way—the right way being clearly and operationally spelled out. Whether you agree or not on either optimism or direction, you will be challenged—and more.

SOCIOLOGY IN ACTION: IN POPULATION AND IN GENERAL

Bernard Berelson

UNDUE POPULATION growth is a major world problem these years. Fortunately, that fact is increasingly being recognized by people in positions to do something about it, country by country. Moreover, a good deal *is* being done so we are beginning to be justified in believing that something *can* be done: that is, that deliberate effort can bring down a birth rate by a substantial amount in a reasonable period of years.

If one experience has contributed as much as any other to this feeling of restrained optimism, it has perhaps been the Taiwan experience of recent years. Especially since 1963, Taiwan has become a prominent example of what can be achieved in this field, and it continues to be one of the two or three leading successes in the world. What was and is done in Taiwan is not only contributing to the easing of the population burden and to the welfare of individual families on that island but is being watched carefully by other countries with similar problems.

With Ronald Freedman and John Takeshita, colleagues from the University of Michigan, I had the privilege of working on this program

15

with our Taiwan friends: Dr. S. C. Hsu, Director of Rural Health of the Joint Commission on Rural Reconstruction; Dr. T. C. Hsu, Commissioner of Health; Dr. J. Y. Peng, then Deputy Director of the Maternal and Child Health Institute; and Dr. L. P. Chow, now Director of the Taiwan Population Studies Center—who collectively gave us a lesson in dedication, industry, and intelligence applied to a professional task. I have space here only to describe a little of what was done, to note the implications for similar action efforts, and then to draw some broader lessons for sociology in action from broader experience.

I

To begin with, compared to other places in the world, Taiwan provides a favorable situation for the implementation of family planning. The island is quite urbanized and industrialized, literacy and popular education are fairly widespread, the standard of living is relatively high, there is a solid network of medical facilities, women are not sharply subordinated, there are few religious or ideological objections to contraception, and the society is well organized with a good transportation and communication system. This combination of fortunate circumstances constitutes an important lesson at the outset: in a difficult task of this kind, start where the job is easier or easiest, not where it is hardest. And in the population field, this goes not only for countries but for regions within them (e.g., cities as against rural areas) and for individual couples within regions (e.g., high parities as against low). That strategy makes for the most economic allocation of scarce resources, and by developing some momentum in the desired direction, it makes an ally of time.

Next we took the problem on "big" and realistically. Up to then, most pilot projects in family planning were on the small side—populations of 10,000 or less, which means not more than 1,500 married couples in the reproductive ages (and by no means all of them "eligible" for family planning)—and the special resources dedicated to the experimental task were typically far beyond those that would be available in a mass effort. Hence, to some degree such studies were artificially inapplicable on the larger stage. In Taiwan we sought to bring family planning to a whole city, Taichung, of 300,000 population, including some 36,000 married women aged 20 to 39. The lesson here is: work on the problem as closely as practicable to its actual character, not on an artificially abstracted version.

Third, we designed an "action experiment" across the entire city—what is, we think, one of the most extensive and elaborate social experiments ever carried out in the natural setting—in order to see how much contraception could be effected at what cost to the program, and supplementarily to see how effective the word-of-mouth support would be once the program had provided the initial stimulus. Accordingly, we allocated the city's 2,400 *lins* or neighborhoods into a design with four "treatments"

—nothing, mailings to high parity and newly married, personal contacts with wives only, personal contacts with both wives and husbands—cross-cutting three "densities." By density we meant the proportion of the *lins* in three equivalent sectors of the city that received personal visits from the field workers—in this case, half of the *lins* in one sector, a third in another, and a fifth in the third. The *lins* receiving home visits were selected at random within each sector and the remaining *lins* were assigned equally to the "nothing" and the "mail" treatments. The idea was to tie the design closely to the administrative concerns that would operate in extending the program to the full population, notably including economic considerations: to what extent were personal contacts by field workers needed and economic; how much would the program be carried by the informal network, once started; would home visits to a third of the target do about as well as to a half?

Fourth, we were careful to get a clear test of the factor(s) considered critical to success or failure. In Taichung, for example, perhaps the leading question was whether the newly-developed intrauterine contraceptive device (IUD) would be acceptable to a large proportion of the target population in competition with other contraceptive methods, in what we came to call a "cafeteria choice." All methods were presented to the potential clients and the IUD was charged for in an amount that is now, two years and two program expansions later, still used in the island-wide program that is under way. The IUD was so popular that the current expansion of the program is virtually limited to that method, which has the great advantage of not requiring sustained motivation, repetitive action, or a continuous supply system.

Fifth, and finally, we built in measurement—measurement meant to contribute directly to policy guidance before and during the study. The basic guideline was a survey undertaken by the Taiwan and Michigan Population Studies Centers and dealing with family planning information, attitudes, and practices—a survey conducted with a good sample of about 2,500 married women aged 20 to 39 in the city. Among other valuable findings—and besides serving as base line for one measurement of "success"—the survey showed that as a group the women wanted to have a moderate number of children; were having more children than they wanted; approved of the idea of family limitation; were trying, though ineffectively, to limit the size of their families; were poorly informed about family planning methods and the physiology of reproduction; were interested in learning and adopting better methods; were aware that infant mortality had declined in the society; and did not feel that family planning conflicted with the traditional Chinese family. Perhaps the most significant finding was that the people needed not so much to be motivated toward family planning as to be informed on how to go about it. Hence the program could be defined and organized as implementation, not persuasion. Importantly, the survey also identified the most likely target group(s) and gave us a reasonable basis for defining "success," in that we were able to identify various "eligible" groups that could serve as the denominators for the numerator of acceptors. A running account of how well the program was doing on a week-to-week basis was provided by records kept by health stations and field workers, on home visits and on acceptances. From them we knew at every point how the program was going, in what sectors and *lins,* among what groups of the population, and at what cost. Indeed, we were able to note a good deal of indirect impact from outside the city itself, particularly for the IUD—upward of a fifth of all acceptors came from beyond the city limits.[1]

So in Taichung, sociology-in-action was involved in a successful experiment to spread family planning. The key points, I would say, were these: The researchers worked directly, closely, and continuously with the administrators responsible for the effort. They offered suggestions on the action side and solicited suggestions on the best way the research could help out on the administrative decisions to be made. The outside advisers kept themselves aware of some broad political issues potentially involved in the program, and did not urge inappropriate actions. The researchers set up their data collection and reporting to be immediately helpful to the administrators. Everyone kept his eye on the problem, regardless of his own special interests (e.g., medical or demographic) or even his personal proclivities. The happy result was threefold: a major breakthrough for family planning in Taiwan, a major model for family planning programs elsewhere in the world, and a major research document (now in preparation at Michigan by Drs. Freedman and Takeshita).

II

The Taichung study, too quickly reviewed here, has turned out to be an influential case in the continuing effort to spread family planning as a matter of public policy. It can also serve as a springboard for some broader observations about sociology in action.

For the past 20 years or so—as university professor, research administrator, and foundation officer—I have been closely involved in putting the behavioral sciences to work, or trying to. Over that period, I have naturally developed some opinions about the matter, and I take this opportunity to set them down.

Not to put too fine a point on the matter, my own view is that the usual rationale for applied sociology is misleading if not mistaken. What is wrong is to think of applied work primarily as a concomitant of basic academic research—to think of applied work as the spill-off from a "basic" study or as a convenient site or subject or fund-raiser for a "basic" inquiry. The result is, more often than not, inappropriate for one or both, or discriminatory against one or the other, or diluted for both. The reason

[1]See Bernard Berelson and Ronald Freedman, "A Study in Fertility Control," *Scientific American,* Vol. 210, No. 5 [May, 1964], pp. 3-11.

is that the basic and the applied are different masters, and it is hard simultaneously to serve both well.

Let me quickly indicate some differences between what seem to me the wrong and the right ways to go about sociology in action—that is, differences that are associated with having an impact on the problem presented, assuming that that is the objective. Obviously, these are matters of degree, but for the sake of brevity—and as what in the trade might be called a "paradigm of ideal types"—I present them here as a simple dichotomy. The following paragraphs may overlap to some extent, but taken together they give the flavor of the distinction I want to stress:

The wrong way to go about sociology in action tends to concentrate on contributing to the theory or the techniques of the discipline. The right way concentrates on contributing to the solution or amelioration of the problem.

The former is ready to work on any problem, since any problem is, at least in principle, equally applicable to theoretical or methodological interest. The latter prefers to work on problems that have important social consequences.

The former insists on sticking with "pure" research. The latter is willing to move into "action" or administration as indicated in order to follow the problem to a satisfying conclusion.

The former seeks generalizations and hopes the present case can be guided thereby (even though the application of the general proposition to his case is often just what the administrator needs help on). The latter is prepared to stick to the individual case and work out from there.

The former tends to go for the "basic processes." The latter goes for what might make a desired difference, however "superficial" it may be.

The former is after the *why*. The latter is after the *how* (assuming that at bottom there's a real difference between them).

The former mainly requires technical judgments. The latter requires, in addition, a sense of what the situation and the personalities will bear, of what the economics will support, of how much change can be introduced and how quickly—in short, mature administrative judgment as well as technical proficiency.

The former is content with small differences, if statistically sound. The latter appreciates that the administrator cannot typically deal with small differences secured through sophisticated analysis of tiny subsamples, so he is looking for the main lines of action: important differences, not just significant ones.

The former is typically after the facts on the assumption that they will point automatically to action. The latter proceeds on the principle that, for action purposes, the researcher should collect no facts unless they speak reasonably directly to administrative decisions, to actionable alternatives usually recognized in advance.

The former aims at publishing a research report, preferably a book (which in major studies will appear, on the average, about five years after the field work is done, if then). The latter is content with a memorandum or a series thereof bringing out the main actionable points quickly.

The former usually reports in the technical language of the discipline. The latter tends to report in the common language since that is where decisions will be stated too.

The one aims at coming to conclusions. The other aims at reaching decisions.

I have deliberately sharpened the case here in order to make the point, as clearly as possible, that there are major differences between what usually passes as "applied sociology" and what could happen if we were more self-conscious about what we are trying to do. For the moment I simply wish to claim that a useful distinction exists—though it is obvious that I think there is a balance here that needs repairing, or at least a neglected opportunity to make sociology in action more effective than it has been.

What this comes down to is a big issue indeed. For what is implicit in these differences is a distinction between an *academic discipline* and a *profession*, and what I am saying is that applied sociology should be modeled more on the latter, not the former. Professions are based on academic disciplines, but they are by no means the same: they deal with individual cases, they are after practical consequences that matter, their first allegiance is to "treatment," they must make decisions despite uncertainty.

If as sociologists we were as objective and severe with ourselves as we are with others, we would have to acknowledge, I think, that a good deal of what passes for applied sociology is less than helpful to the client. We can often provide some "relevant" facts or some "interesting" ideas or some "promising" leads, but how often do we really speak to a client's problem in ways he can implement?

When we do, the contribution is likely not to be what the discipline prizes most, namely, theory (or what currently passes for theory). For example, perhaps the most helpful behavioral scientists on practical problems today are in business, where there is an unambiguous criterion against which the research outcome can be judged. Or, since business is a sphere disapproved of by most sociologists, take perhaps the leading classic of sociology in action, *The American Soldier*. Perhaps the single most consequential contribution from that collection of applied studies was the development of the point system. That was a survey of what the soldiers thought should be taken into account in discharging men from the Army—a piece of research aimed at answering a simple and direct question, with minimal theoretical relevance.

Sociologists are skilled at analyzing how other groups are sometimes caught up in their own social structures, but how about their own? The present arrangements in modern sociology largely run against sociology in action done most helpfully and efficiently: the rewards are given for theoretical or technical virtuosity; the "reference group" consists of sociological colleagues, not practical administrators; "newness" of insight or method or even vocabulary is often valued more than practical results; indeed the justification for doing applied research at all is often tied to the "basic" payoff that will allegedly accrue (the so-called Robin Hood effect of taking the funds from the rich client or foundation interested in the problem and putting them to the use of the poor discipline). The weight of disciplinary opinion, I think, requires one to justify an action study not by its contribution to practical affairs but by its contribution to disciplinary ends—and that is how the final report usually is written.

Has the time come for the emergence of a profession out of the behavioral sciences? My own answer is yes, to a limited degree: limited because we still have few self-conscious and self-respecting practitioners and because the idea needs slow and careful development. In some ways, we are on the road, but only partially so. The several recent ventures at building the behavioral sciences into professional schools of public health, medicine, law, and others is a step in this direction; but even in these areas the behavioral scientist is typically reluctant to take both feet out of his own academic discipline and hence remains caught in trying simultaneously to serve what are sometimes conflicting and usually dissimilar ends.

But what I like to call policy research, in the sense presented here, is certainly coming. If nothing else, the demands of the complex mass society will call forth such applied studies in education, law, health, art and culture, the mass media, urban affairs, crime and delinquency—and, to return to where we started, in population control.

Strategy is a crucial component in projects of directed social change. Its careful employment in a successful effort to rehabilitate a "failing" school and to manage reforms in a large school system is skillfully related below by two education specialists. These men, both close students of relevant sociological work on directed change, demonstrate in their project the inventiveness, flexibility, resiliency, clearness of mission, and willingness to take chances that regularly go into applied work. Their personal record inspires confidence, even as their case provides a useful "lifeline" model for school and school system reform elsewhere. That the writers are not professional sociologists only accents sociology's considerable possibilities; a "plumber's license" in the sense of a formal academic degree is not required to make intelligent use of this social science.

STRATEGIES FOR INITIATING EDUCATIONAL CHANGE IN LARGE BUREAUCRATIC SCHOOL SYSTEMS*

Mario D. Fantini and Gerald Weinstein

ONE OF THE greatest challenges and enigmas facing education today involves the vital need to update the educational establishment. This need is so obvious that to develop a rationale for it would be superfluous. Consequently, we address ourselves here not to the "Why change?" or the "Change to what?" but to the "*HOW*" of initiating change in a large bureaucratic system.

In the case of our recent experience in a medium-sized city containing most problems of large urban areas, one of the local junior high schools we call here the Marris Avenue School was virtually on the brink of becoming a "blackboard jungle." The school system was willing to put aside some of its conventional avenues of attack, and was prone to listen to, and adapt, if necessary, the terms of a solution, even though it might come from outside forces.

*From a paper presented to Public Policy Institute, Teachers College, Columbia University (April, 1963).

DOUBLE TEAMING

Since the two main publics in educational change are the principals and teachers, we sought from the start a strategy that allowed maximum confrontation between the change agents and these two publics. Furthermore, because we were aware that one change agent working alone has a limited sphere of influence, regardless of his position or authority, we deemed it vital that two change agents work on parallel levels to reach common goals. One change agent would develop readiness on the part of the administrator to accept changes he knew were forthcoming from the teachers; the other would develop readiness with teachers to accept organizational changes he knew would occur. Moreover, because of the administrative change agent's visible close association with the instructional change agent, the latter acquired, through implication, authority and power. In this way the double team approach gave the teachers a feeling that anything they developed with the instructional agent would not be lost in the usual bureaucratic red tape. It also provided someone the principal might be more willing to listen to.

This technique supplied something that is completely lacking in most large bureaucracies, a closed-circuit line of communication from the very top levels of the system to the bottom levels. And this direct communication was the main facilitator of rapid-fire change. (There is, however, a serious liability often associated with a closed-circuit system: someone may have to be neglected. In our case, it was the system's subject supervisors. They usually made most of the decisions concerning instructional policy and even recruitment. We took the calculated risk of not involving them in the many ideas that were being developed and, in a sense, went over their heads on all of the major issues. We thus brought about their alienation from the program and criticism for whatever was done without their involvement.)

Contact Strategy with Teachers

The main contact strategies with teachers were effected through Agent B (the sociologist). His role during the first half of the first year was that of listener-sympathizer. In essence, he was something of a confidant and guidance counselor for teachers. Teachers could come to him with their annoyances and dissatisfactions and find a sympathetic ear. When he was asked for specific help, he gave it.

Another technique was to ask the teachers directly: "What materials would you like that you have never been able to get before?" We were thus asking for *their* perceived needs. For dramatic impact suggested materials were acquired with lightning speed. Rarely before had teachers been asked what they wanted. Even if they had been asked, the lumbering wheels of the bureaucracy would have made the process so difficult and lengthy that the element of immediate reinforcement would have been lost and teachers would have deemed the granting of requests virtually impossible. By supplying materials quickly we demonstrated action rather than mere talk. In addition, huge bulletin boards were constructed, painted, and installed within the first two weeks of school. The library and cafeteria were renovated extensively. In other words, a whole atmosphere of motion was generated.

This was reinforced at faculty meetings by Agent A who dramatically articulated the whole scope and relevance of the project, stressing the need for professionalism in the teacher's role. (We have termed this concentrated dose of environment stimulation our "fireworks display.") The agent also emphasized that by the middle of the first year there would be a waiting list of teachers trying to get jobs in the project. (Until this time the project schools had been consistently avoided by teachers.) This waiting list actually materialized due largely to an ad: "Wanted: New Breed of Teacher" sent to all teacher training institutions in New York State. The reverse psychology of the waiting list episode was used again when we suddenly started verbalizing doubt to the teachers about the techniques we had been suggesting. We asked abruptly after several weeks: "Is the nongraded approach really that good?" By doing this, by having them argue for it, we were able to see how well the teachers had internalized these ideas. Once contact had been established, the vehicle of team planning took over, as will be explained.

Contact Strategies with Principals

Since the principal is the manager of *what is,* we successfully broke down some resistance by dealing initially with *his* perceived needs. We asked him what services he had always wanted but had never received. We thus added services that he felt were important, such as an extra secretary, counselor, reading teacher, family worker, etc. All these additive services were in the realm of organizational change which made the principal feel comfortable because he was familiar with them.

Built into this package of additive services was an ingredient that would utilize these services in such a way as to result in structural (behavioral) change, namely, the interaction of the change agents with the added personnel. This interaction altered their roles; in a sense, the added personnel were "our men." The supreme example of this kind of "packaging" involved the role of the instructional change agent (B) himself. He was brought into the system as an "After-School Activities Coordinator and Helping Teacher." These labels posed no problems for the insiders. What if he had been introduced as an instructional change agent? There would have been less immediate contact. Once he was "in," however, his new role and contacts developed.

Status was another need disposition that was considered by the agent in his interaction with the principals. Whenever possible the principals were invited to participate in "status meetings." These were meetings not only with top level school district officails but also with prominent community and university leaders. Principals thus had the feeling of movement in top circles of policy making, and thereby offered less resistance to our change proposals.

Contact Strategies with Central Administration

For our purposes we bisected the central administration along power source lines: the Board of Education and the superintendent.

Achieving a successful initial contact with power sources is so vital that failure at this level cripples further attempts at sustained internal change. As the link between the power sources and the bureaucratic subsystem, the change agent assumes the function of the "lifeline" for the change process. The acquisition of power actually becomes the energy on which change is generated.

With the Board, the strategy was based on its expectations of the new Marris Area Project. By utilizing a carefully planned slide presentation at the first public board meeting, Change Agent A gave a quick, concise picture of the Marris Area Project and projected a dynamism of purpose and direction which prompted several board members to comment enthusiastically about the organization of the presentation. Moreover, having a crowded meeting for this presentation served also to give the board a "bouquet" in that the public response to the presentation won applause. This presentation served to communicate to the members of the board that the project was "off the ground"; their financial investment appeared to be sound; the public seemed to be impressed with the action depicted by the slides; and there was direction to the project. Moreover, the superintendent, present at this event, was able to note the positive reaction of board members to Change Agent A's presentation, something which also strengthened the agent's position with the superintendent.

Contact with the superintendent himself was based on the agent's "action" skill. Capitalizing on a transition between superintendents, the administrative change agent moved quickly to fill a "void" in the school system's top administration. The acting superintendent was encouraged to "lean" on Change Agent A for counsel on various school problems; "make use of my outside perspective" was the administrative change agent's theme. The resulting reliance on Change Agent A by both the board and superintendent provided a direct line to decision making and policy development which became central to the administrative agent's "closed-circuit" connection with the instructional change agent.

Contact Strategy for Community at Large

Three main methods were utilized to attain a strong initial association with the community: publicity, speaking, and initiation of a school volunteer program.

Publicity. Based on the assumption that community expectation was centered on "action" rather than on "talk" we were able to capitalize on the newness of the demonstration project by obtaining news coverage depicting the project's action phases.

Speaking. The administrative change agent assumed a major role in talking with various community groups concerning the nature of the new Marris Area Project. Armed with a slide presentation illustrating a vivid "before and after" picture of Marris Junior High (the school which had the image of a "crime school") contact was made with such groups as Rotary, Zonta, church groups, professional groups, parent groups, etc. Having begun this community speaking tour, word "got out" that the presentation was interesting, and requests for the presentation multiplied.

The above approach coupled with personal conferences with the mayor, account executives, bank presidents, etc., attempted to rally community awareness not only of the problem of cultural deprivation and what the Marris Area Project was doing about it but also of emerging problems, such as dropouts, segregation, teacher turnover.

School Volunteer Program. A significant approach to the community took form with the initiation of a Marris Area Project school volunteer program. The educational rationale for this program was to tap needed skills from lay individuals who could assist teachers and students. The program's responsibility, as outlined by the administrative change agent, was to assume a partnership role with the schools and to develop creative programs within our demonstration schools. Tutoring and clinical programs were initiated in a matter of weeks. Involvement thereby of the wives of community influentials also served to elicit their support. Their understanding soon infiltrated the entire community, and, over time, this program became one of the most successful attempts at keeping the community close to the Marris Area Project. It also kept the board and central office posted with positive communications.

Contact Strategies with Main Publics and Dynamics of Change

It was indicated earlier that the two change agents assume roles in different sectors of the bureaucracy. Diagrammatically this would appear as shown on page 27.

Personnel Problems Encountered

Our strategy for *initially* involving only the most crucial publics for involvement (teachers and principals) had its negative repercussions. This was illustrated by the critical attitudes of the subject supervisors. In addition we faced a similar situation with our own Marris Area Project staff.

Top professional people were hired from different disciplines and told that they would have to undergo an intensive period of aloneness while developing their own roles in a climate of severe confusion. They initially regarded this as "a challenge," and so were taken at their word.

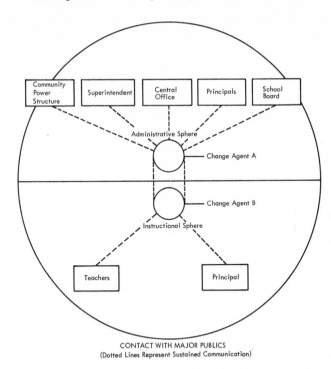

CONTACT WITH MAJOR PUBLICS
(Dotted Lines Represent Sustained Communication)

For the first three months they were completely involved as a staff and our meetings took on the typical flavor of clarifying frames of reference, discussing the multitude of problems, analyzing and dissecting them, etc. We found ourselves entangled in verbalization and inactivity in the face of high expectations for *immediate* action on the part of the community.

Because too many of the staff were not carving out any substantive roles for themselves with a great deal of direction, and because our larger goals were far from being implemented, we had to make a decision for a change of process. We discontinued staff meetings as such, and staff members were thereafter dealt with individually in an attempt to develop some kind of structure with them. The jump from complete group involvement to an incomplete individualized one caused a great deal of resentment on the part of the staff. And yet, this is the direction we have maintained. At this present stage in our work the staff appears more satisfied than earlier since each member now has an area of clearly delineated responsibilities.

Our conclusions about this experience are as follows: we cannot assume that professionals are necessarily new-role-oriented; we should begin with only a very few professionals and, as something structured emerges, bring in more; until that time we should be staffed mainly with graduate assistants who are not as role-restricted.

INITIATING ORGANIZATIONAL AND STRUCTURAL CHANGE

1. **Team Planning (teachers).** Organizationally, and socially, teachers had been occupying self-contained worlds in matters of instruction. Instructional policy was fed from the central administration to individual teachers in the system, but what finally happened in the classroom was a very private matter. Of course the usual kind of shop talk had occurred from time to time in the hallways, lunchroom, and teacher's room, but it was superficial, inconsistent, and usually destructive.

In light of the severity of the educational problems faced by the school, it was imperative that a vehicle be found to accomplish the following:

1. Provide teachers with a *convenient* regular time to work and plan together with qualified assistance from specialists in a variety of disciplines.
2. Provide a way of utilizing the strengths of individual teachers as a common resource to all.
3. Provide in-service training to inexperienced members of the staff and retrain the experienced members in new techniques and approaches.
4. Provide teachers with the opportunity for adapting the school curriculum to the needs and interests of the pupil population.

Change Agents A and B both agreed that to build team planning time into the daily schedule might be the appropriate vehicle. The educational rationale was given by both agents to the principal, who found no objection to their theory. Concern, however, was expressed for the application of the theory—that is, for the technical job of revising schedules so that teachers who had grade and subject matter classes in common could meet every day.

Theoretical consultants usually consider such things as schedule manipulation to be out of their realm. But, as theoretical practitioners, the change agents were responsible for implementation as well as suggestion, and so they began to help the principal actually construct the schedule that would permit the instruction change vehicle to become operational.

Before completion of the schedule, the faculty was assembled and given the educational rationale for team planning as well as a preview of what the specific team planning schedule might look like. Again the rationale was accepted as being logical, clear, and reasonable. Some suggestions and criticisms were offered and accepted concerning the scheduling.

One of the main reasons for the general acceptance was the fact that until this time the faculty had never been involved in any scheduling decisions. In fact they had never been given a chance to preview a schedule in advance of the regular school year. (There was of course the appeal of being released from "teaching time" for team meetings each day which conveyed to many the idea of extra "free" periods.) Thus one organizational change was effected. The problem now was to move toward structural change.

Providing teachers, who up until this time had self-contained orientations to instructional planning, with time to meet together did not necessarily mean they would easily transfer to a cooperative view of planning. A new role was necessary. This was one that for years had been attributed to the principal, but which only rarely became operational: the role of Instructional Leader.

Change Agent B took this role as his major responsibility. It was his task to move the organizational change to structural change. As a discussion leader, he met each day with each team of teachers. He raised questions and offered suggestions which guided the team's thinking about what and how they were going to teach. (Without a discussion leader of his orientation, team meetings could easily have degenerated into the pooling of ignorance.) As a demonstration teacher, he took over the classes in certain areas to illustrate new approaches and techniques for the teachers. As a materials coordinator, he kept in contact with publishers and ordered relevant instructional aids. He planned for demonstrations of the use of these materials and then helped the teachers decide how they could be used most effectively. As a resource person, he kept the team informed of the latest relevant educational developments. He also introduced some of his own instructional ideas and through their use had the team evaluate them (for example, the introduction of a linguistic approach to grammar). As a liaison between the teachers and administration, he kept the administration informed as to how the instructional program was developing and provided a feedback to the principal as to the specific needs of the instructional program. For example, if the teachers wished to experiment with new groupings that required administrative changes, the instructional specialist would try to work this out with the principal. Finally, as a coordinator of the in-service training, he helped to set up in-service workshops and arranged for consultants and other resource people to fill gaps as indicated by the teaching teams.

Thus, in his role as instruction leader, Change Agent B altered the environment by providing leadership which stimulated teachers to search for more meaningful ways of instruction—a search which led to changes in the classroom performance of the teachers.

2. **Team Planning (principals).** As with the teachers, the building principals of the demonstration schools had an isolated orientation. Moreover, they were oriented to the existing process. There was a need to develop an orientation to demonstration and experimentation, including an acceptance of the recommendations which might emerge as a result of the instructional change agents' involvement with teachers.

Accordingly, administrative change agent (A) established weekly meetings with principals. The meetings, rotated by school, paralleled the team planning periods with teachers and became an on-the-job training vehicle for principals. The main purpose here was to develop an awareness of organizational changes necessary to produce structural change. Moreover, if the principals were to see themselves more as "climate setters" rather than as "managers" the entire school atmosphere could become conducive to experimentation and change.

Change Agent A assumed the team leader role and developed the following modus operandi:

He communicated from the outset his understanding of the importance of the principal's role. For example, at one point he would close his remarks by saying, ". . . so important is *your* role that without *you* there could not be a demonstration . . . if one had the best teachers in the world and a poor principal one could not have a good school, but a good principal and mediocre teachers could produce a good school. . . ." Projecting support of the principal also developed a feeling of trust necessary if Change Agent A was to ask them to consider changes. Utilizing his ties with the central office usually helped to accomplish this task. Change Agent A also attempted to soften the impact of the severity of change by appealing to what was educationally sound and by attributing qualities of high professionalism to the principals.

Winning support of the principals through their team meetings was important because the principals were actually spokesmen for the established bureaucracy. As "outsiders" invading the sanctity of the organization we needed to have "insiders" on our side. More importantly, we needed to gain support of certain *key* insiders—those whose words carried weight. One such principal became our strongest link to the formal organization and softened the overall resistance to our efforts.

The team effort had to be reinforced with frequent individual contacts. Operating on the level of personal diplomacy, Change Agent A utilized approaches which took into consideration the need-disposition of the principal described earlier. As illustrated, diagnosing personal needs is vital to virtually all change movements, and cannot be underplayed.

STRATEGIES FOR MAINTAINING PROGRESS

Once progress commences, certain means for its continuance must be secured. To be more specific, the original Marris Area Project was a comparatively small three-year demonstration project. In order to assure demonstration continuity and to expand the scope of the demonstration vehicle, a variety of strategies needed to be employed. Strategy examples identified here are: visibility, proximity, expanding the resource bases, and administrative reorganization. We will deal with these separately.

Visibility should occur on the local level and, if possible, on the national level. Deliberate attempts were made to keep the Marris Area roject visible through local news media and personal slide presentations; these attempts added an aura of prestige and authority to both the demonstrators and the demonstration. The community came to have high expectations of the project. On a national level, participation by the change agents in national conferences produced another kind of authoritative leverage. As the superintendent attended meetings he became aware of the association, on a nationwide basis, of the Marris Area Project with his city. At several board meetings, he spoke of how impressed he had been with the attention given to the reputation of the project. The change agents' contacts with various nationally prominent agencies also reinforced visibility and authority.

The second strategy entailed *proximity*. Assuming a stance of closeness to the power structure enabled the administrative change agent to refuel his own authority continually. Frequent and direct contact with the Board and with the superintendent communicated an important message to the various publics: he (the administrative change agent) was an integral part of the top administration hierarchy. Having gained authority he was in a better position to transmit this authority (again through proximity) to the instructional change agent, who in turn was viewed with respect by the teachers and principals.

Expanding the resource base involved two approaches: the institutional approach, and the approach of parlaying the emerging organizational needs.

All school bureaucracies exhibit forms of crisis: excessive teacher turnover in grey area schools, dropouts, racial imbalance, cultural deprivation, etc. These conditions force the bureaucracy to seek assistance. Moreover, these emerging organizational needs provide opportunities for initiating change. The Marris Area Project was introduced on the wave of an organizational need (cultural deprivation). Having developed a vehicle for meeting this particular organizational need, we were able to expand our original demonstration by assisting the bureaucracy with its other organizational needs (e.g., dropouts, racial imbalance, teacher turnover, etc.). In due course, the Marris Area Project was able to "parlay" the original demonstration into a large-scale five-pronged interrelated demonstration which added time and influence to the internal change mechanism.[1]

The institutional approach, on the other hand, was a direct outgrowth of emerging needs. The Marris Area Project started as a partnership between a university, the public schools of a medium large city, a foundation, and a state department of education. Strengthening these

---

[1] The five-pronged demonstration entailed work with city, state, and federal agencies (such as the National Institute of Mental Health and the President's Committee on Delinquency and Youth Crime) on problems in teacher preparation, dropout rehabilitation, and the schooling of emotionally disturbed children. Acceptance of our proposals by funding agencies created additional revenues, and, by contributing prestige to our undertaking, added fuel to the internal change movement.

ties and forging still others not only strengthened the original demonstration but became the basis for developing other joint efforts (e.g., when an organizational problem such as teacher turnover in some area schools became prominent, the administrative change agent began negotiation with the dean of the school of education for developing a joint research and action proposal on this problem. The College of Education responded favorably to this idea. The result was a foundation grant of $378,000 for the preparation of urban teachers).

Administrative reorganization

As the major demonstration proposals relating to the original project became funded, and as it became clearer to the superintendent and the Board that each proposal was aimed at a real source of concern for them, the rationale for the need of administrative reorganization was achieved.

The administrative change agent took this opportunity to request a change from the original administrative framework which had governed the operation of the Marris Area Project, a change to a larger and sounder framework in which the newly developed projects would be included. The request called for the establishment of an assistant superintendent for special projects who would have system-wide authority and responsibility. We felt the establishment of such authority was necessary for sustained locomotion, for even though the subsystem had been created, there still remained the task of having the ideas developed flow from the subsystem to the large system. This administrative move, if accepted, could provide the needed internal mechanism to accomplish this phase in the change process.

The superintendent accepted the need for reorganization and approved all the conditions except the title of assistant superintendent. Instead, he created a system-wide position, staff director of special projects. The staff director was to be responsible solely to the superintendent.

Having established a firm internal bureaucratic role, the administrative change agent proceeded to identify key personnel he could nominate for roles in the expanded framework. For example, the instructional change agent was positioned differently in order for him to focus more sharply on structural change. His work now was to coordinate the efforts of those personnel in each school whose responsibility it was to influence structural change.

The original Marris Area Project has grown to include eight schools. Our expanding sphere of influence has firmly established the demonstration subsystem as a bureaucratic laboratory for change—at least here in this school system, and, hopefully, it will soon serve as a model in many other cities.

Ｓome programs that seek sociological advice or research prove to be testimonials to the solicitor's steadfast intention from the start to do as he pleases with the sociologist's findings and counsel. A very real danger exists that in "invited" projects the man paying the bills and delegating necessary authorizations will manipulate the results and mock the entire endeavor. Dr. Richard H. Hall warns of this in the essay below, and soberly recounts his own frustrating experience with an educational unit more committed to prejudgments and to the status quo than to research findings and to organizational change. With his warning and example to guide us, we should be able to advance to real organizational reforms— given sincerity and seriousness on the part of project sponsors.

THE APPLIED SOCIOLOGIST AND ORGANIZATIONAL SOCIOLOGY

Richard H. Hall

THE PROBLEMS in applied sociology I want to discuss grow daily in importance as participation in social research attracts more formal organizations.[1] Prime among these problems is the danger that the unwary sociologist may find himself giving unwarranted support to the selective preconceptions of the leaders of the research-sponsoring organization. Especially if the research is solicited, as in the general case of applied research, the process of interpretation and of utilization of the sociologist's findings often appears to be based on (science-disregarding) selective perception. This fact may ultimately place severe—and unsuspected— limitations on the role of the sociologist as a generator of innovations in organizations.

In the case to be described, a colleague and I were asked by a Division

---

[1] The literature in organizational sociology has not reflected the growing amount of applied research. The emphasis continues to be the development of a "pure" science. A number of works in the allied field of industrial sociology come much closer to an action orientation. For example, Miller and Form, *Industrial Sociology* (New York: Harper & Row, 1964) (this book also contains an extensive bibliography); Robert Dubin, *The World of Work* (Englewood Cliffs, N.J.: Prentice-Hall, Inc., 1958); and *Leadership and Productivity* (San Francisco: Chandler Publishing Co., 1965); Rensis Likert, *New Patterns of Management* (New York: McGraw-Hill Book Co., Inc., 1961); and Edward Gross, *Work and Society* (New York: Crowell, 1958).

33

of Student Personnel in a large state university to study it in order to improve its communications and coordination processes. The division had the responsibility for administering the residence hall program, handling problems of student discipline, and helping manage the programs of student activities. As the university itself grew, the size of both the division's organizational structure and its program grew accordingly, if not at an even faster rate. This growth brought about several rather serious problems, the basic problem being, in the eyes of the division's leaders, the alleged fact that personnel on the lower levels, such as residence hall counselors and personnel in student counseling and activities, did not understand or operate by the philosophies guiding the division.

The division leaders, while anxious that their efforts be recognized as effective, were in almost complete agreement that the research should be undertaken and were most anxious to cooperate. At the next level of organization, among subdivision heads, the proposal of research seemed to raise some anxiety. In the first instance, there was simply a concern over their own effectiveness as it might be shown in the research. All of the subdivision heads wanted their own divisions characterized as well-administered, complete with good morale and sound communications. In addition to this anxiety, they also had their own pet ideas concerning appropriate means of improving the division's operations as a whole. They were therefore anxious for our suggestions to support their own preconceptions of appropriate means of improving operations.

For both of these reasons, we were under pressure from the start to provide quick feedback to the organization. Our impressions were sought even before the data were collected or analyzed. This pressure for rapid feedback was further compounded by the fact that the division wanted to implement any changes suggested before the beginning of the next academic year.

The budget under which we operated was one designed for "instant research," meaning that the research instruments had to be quickly and inexpensively devised. In order to get an adequate sample of personnel, we utilized the questionnaire approach rather than the interview technique for the initial data gathering. (Some interviews were, of course, held to determine particular problem areas before the questionnaires were constructed.) The questionnaires we finally employed sought to determine the amount of authority and responsibility which each participant felt he had. Measures of the adequacy of communications, along with perceived efficiency, morale, and autonomy of action were also included. These latter measures were hastily prepared, and there was no opportunity for pretesting or determining if the items involved formed any kind of scale. The separate items had face validity, and were taken as at least crude indicators of the variables under consideration. From the researchers' standpoint, such procedures constituted a distinct departure from commonly accepted research practice, but we proceeded anyway because of extreme time pressures.

Another departure from established procedures was the atheoretical nature of the research. Although we assumed from the literature and our own experience that poor communications would result in low morale and low efficiency, and although we assumed that the latter would be related to a feeling of inadequate authority and responsibility, these were implicit rather than explicit hypotheses.

An interesting aspect of the research was a series of questions which asked the respondents to rate the goals of the division, first in the desired or ideal order, and then in the order in which they actually felt the goals were being implemented by the division. The attempt, here, was twofold. First, we wanted to determine what differences existed between hierarchical levels in the organization in regard to perceptions of the purposes of a division of student personnel. We anticipated lower-ranking personnel would note more practical administrative goals rather than the more lofty goals of student growth and intellectual development. Second, we assumed that any differences revealed by this technique would be a good secondary indicator of problems in the communications system and in the authority structure. The existence of discrepancies on these goal statements was thought to indicate that the leaders of the organization were not getting their own message across to the lower personnel. Also, it might indicate that lower personnel were not given the authority to implement the goals which they themselves thought to be the most important. If they were tied up in administrative details, even a recognition of the ideal goals could not be translated into action.

The mechanics of the research were carried out with little difficulty. Good cooperation was given at all levels. One of the major reasons for this was the fact that the research was in a university setting in which there is an evident commitment to research and a relative absence of fear of questionnaires and interviews. Another reason for the smoothness of the process was the fact that the majority of the personnel were oriented toward improving their own, as well as the division's, performance, and they had some degree of professional orientation. The only group which did not participate as willingly as the others was a group of "middle management" personnel who felt that their own operations might be shown in a bad light. (Such fear on the part of middle management is indicative of their stake in the organization. They are caught in the middle, since any negative findings come most directly to their area of responsibility, while top management is removed from the scene, and lower personnel do not have real responsibility.)

As soon as the data were gathered, the top administrators began formally to ask for feedback so that they could bring about any needed changes. This put the research team in a mild dilemma, since the data analysis properly should have been carried out in its entirety if a total picture was to emerge. But, since we had been asked to do the research for specific reasons, we felt that we should get some information to the organization as quickly as possible. An informal compromise was reached between these conflicting demands, and we hastily fed the data and interpretations back to the organization just as soon as we were reasonably certain of their accuracy and meaning.

A series of meetings was then held with the heads of the various subdivisions. At this point the problem arose of translating the findings into meaningful language and suggestions for improvement. The personnel wanted answers which would tell them what they could do for immediate improvement, while the researchers could only offer a range of suggestions without sure knowledge that any particular course of action was clearly indicated. (This reflected not only the problems of this research, but also the state of knowledge of the field in general.)

The organizational problems reduced to two major issues: First, at least in their own minds, the lower personnel were not given enough authority to carry out what they felt to be their legitimate tasks. They felt that the higher level administrators either by design or by habit were retaining too much authority. On this point, it seemed that the administrators themselves consciously or unconsciously rejected these findings, perhaps because they felt that they were really correct in their approach to delegation of authority or perhaps because of a fear of delegation of their own authority.

The second issue revolved around communications. The lower-level personnel felt they did not receive enough information from the top administrators. In addition, contrary to our expectations, their perceptions of the ideal goals of the division coincided almost exactly with those of the top administrators. However, in operational terms, they felt that the top administrators wanted them simply to be clerks, and to engage in busy work and carry out disciplinary proceedings at a low level. The leaders of the organization had not gotten their own higher goals for personnel through to the lower-level members. In the minds of personnel at all levels, the real purposes of the organization were not being implemented, largely because these purposes were not articulated to the workers. Once presented to them, however, division leaders more readily accepted the problem of communications than they did that of authority.

ATTEMPTS AT REFORM

At this point, the action follow-up phase of the project began. A further series of meetings was held in which both the sociological researchers and the top division administrators participated. These meetings were designed for frank discussion of the research findings and for making suggestions to improve the existing situation. The major finding that lower personnel often did not know the goals of the division was somewhat surprising to the administrators, who had apparently assumed their "message" was getting across. We suggested that a series of division-wide meetings be held at the beginning of the next academic year to acquaint all personnel with the operating goals. We also suggested that meetings within each administrative unit (Residence Hall) be held throughout the year to insure that major operating principles were being maintained.

Our own first suggestion met with some success. Divisional meetings were held, with an emphasis on goals and means of achieving goals. Our second suggestion, however, regarding divisional meetings was not as well implemented. In this case, meetings were held, but under the direction of the "middle manager" in charge of the unit. In some cases, these people were the real cause of the communications and authority problems. These people continued to interpret the goals and the roles of their subordinates as they had in the past. In general, however, the divisional meetings did allow the workers a better insight into what they were to do and why they were to do it.

Another major suggestion of ours dealt more directly with patterns of authority and authority delegation and its relationship to communications. It was evident that the "word" was not getting to some of the lower levels in the organization. The reason for this was that some middle managers were interpreting the purposes of the organization in their own terms. This interpretation left many workers with the feeling that they were simply clerks with no opportunity to exercise their own discretion and to fulfill the purposes of the division. The most obvious solution here entailed replacing the offending managers, but, given their job tenure, loyalty to subordinates, friendships, etc., this was not feasible. Instead, we suggested that the divisional leaders work more closely with the workers, reviewing their work and listening to their complaints, in an attempt to insure that more uniform policies would be followed throughout the division.

This suggestion was not followed insofar as we could determine. The reason may have been the sheer size of the organization and the difficulties in getting to the workers or it may have been the dislike of by-passing long-time fellow workers at the middle-management level. Inertia may also have played a role. In some of the units, the workers remained essentially clerks, more concerned with the proper filling out of forms than with any higher purposes.

In short, the only concrete action taken with respect to our recommendations involved the meetings held with the personnel of the division. While these meetings did have a positive short-term result, we doubt now that any long-lasting changes have occurred. One factor in this has been the division's continued and rapid growth. Divisional meetings have become mass lectures, with little personal contact as a follow-up. Another, and perhaps more important factor is that no changes were made in the organization's authority structure. The same personnel channels are still used for communications. These channels, the middle managers, are in some instances unable or unwilling to interpret the desired directions of the division. Many workers continue to get a distorted view of what they are to do and why they are to do it.

Summary. The most evident problem in the kind of applied research described above revolves around the implementation of the findings. In our situation, despite words to the contrary, the organization primarily wanted verification of its own prior conclusions regarding trouble spots. Where our findings coincided, action was taken. When we pointed to other trouble spots than those originally perceived, the organization tended to ignore them. For whatever reason, action research in this type of setting may prove simply a way of legitimating the preconceptions of organizational leaders.

The resolution of this dilemma requires greater public understanding of the nature of social research, and new appreciation of the utility of social research as a tool for accurately pinpointing the real, as opposed to the preconceived, organizational trouble spots. Organizational leaders especially must look for more than the verification of preconceptions if social research is to demonstrate its ability to analyze accurately a broad range of organizational phenomena. An impressive challenge, though by no means an insurmountable one—as some of us are dedicated to proving.

With increasing frequency nowadays sociologists find themselves drawn into public affairs—regardless of the purpose which first draws them out of the classroom, office, or study. In the case discussed below three sociologists engaged in a conventional community identification project soon found themselves deeply involved in an unconventional public dispute seemingly over school boundaries (but actually going much deeper). The three came to worry whether "bread-and-butter research" could remain free of the biases of its sponsors, and, in due course, came to ponder the significance of variations in the handling of research findings by different levels of decision makers. Their tale, complete even with attacks on their professional integrity, constitutes an intriguing foreshadowing of what kind of action-involvement may lie around the corner for any sociologist—regardless of his decided preference for classroom, office, or study.

SOCIOLOGY AND EDUCATIONAL POLICY

Thomas L. Gillette, C. Dale Johnson, and David Feldman

IN APRIL of 1965, a member of our research team of three sociologists testified before the California State Board of Education on the extent and nature of community identification in the communities encompassed by one of the state's larger suburban high school districts (Grossmont Union High School District). This request was an unanticipated consequence of our team's involvement with a local citizens advisory council in a study of community identification. At the time we three sociologists were, perhaps naïvely, unaware of many of the political and larger public policy implications involved in the meaning of community identification for the problem of school unification. The major reason for the appearance before the State Board was that our sociological findings were critically germane to the problem of elementary school district unification within the Grossmont Union High School District.

In 1962 the California Legislature passed a bill, AB 145, which required massive school district reorganization. The general suburban pattern of the postwar years was one of large districts handling education from the 9th through the 12th grades, within which were smaller autonomous school districts responsible for the lower grades. Each of the districts, the elementary as well as the high school, had its own school administration, elected school board, and separate tax base. Many of these elementary school districts were financially unable to provide the high quality of education which the state of California felt was necessary. To rectify the situation, AB 145 required unification of all educational systems throughout the state. Specifically, the legislation provided for the elimination of separate elementary and high school districts. The existing high school district boundaries were to be the boundaries of the new unified school districts. In the particular case of the Grossmont High School District, there were 11 elementary school districts. Application of the legislative intent to this area would result in a single school district responsible for education from kindergarten through 12th grade. This new district would be called the Grossmont Unified School District.

The legislation did, however, provide that where "exceptional circumstances" existed—and could be proved—deviation from existing high school district boundaries in the creation of the new unified school districts would be permitted. Two kinds of "exceptional circumstances" apparently within legislative intent are geography (natural barriers such as mountains or rivers blocking access between various parts of the district) and strong community identification within separate areas in the existing high school districts which might be destroyed or weakened by unification.

To implement the legislation each county was to establish a county committee on school district reorganization. Typically this was to be a citizens committee charged with presenting a unification proposal to the State Department of Education. The department was required to evaluate the proposal and provide a recommendation to the State Board of Education regarding its acceptance or rejection. The State Board was the final authority.

School unification, potentially at least, promotes controversy and possible conflict in those communities where it is proposed. Some communities fear loss of local autonomy. Many parents feel that unification puts the education of their children increasingly beyond their influence and into the control of remote bureaucratic administrators. And certainly many local school board members and school administrators anticipate loss of their positions. By no means, however, were all opposed to such a social change. Many teachers prefer a unified district which provides a more substantial tax base for school financing and a social-psychological milieu more conducive to exercising professional competence. Similarly, many parents realize the possibilities for enrichment of the educational program in a school district large enough to provide specialized services. Further, the potentially greater economic efficiency of the larger operating unit appeals to many property owners who have experienced the rigors of unending rises in the property taxes which are the major source of school revenue. This latter point is underscored by the $15 per pupil bonus in state aid which is awarded to those districts which achieve prompt unification. In the case of the Grossmont Union High School District, each year of delay in unification costs the taxpayers of the district approximately three-quarters of a million dollars.

Anticipating that antiunification interests would raise the community identification issue, the Citizens Advisory Council of the Grossmont Union High School District engaged the sociologist-researchers (authors of this paper) to assess the level and nature of community identification among the residents of the various suburbs within the district boundaries. Incorporated municipalities and areas bearing distinctive names, it is often tacitly assumed, are "communities" and all that this term implies. That is, each such community is supposed to encompass the major portion of the typical resident's social life and results in his being psychologically identified with it. The major problem of our sociological research, then, was to determine the applicability of this assumption to the separate suburbs within the district.

The prospect of the results of our study being utilized for the partisan ends of the sponsoring agent raised questions relating to scientific objectivity. To put it bluntly, we were concerned whether "bread-and-butter research" could remain free of the biases of its sponsors. Obviously, the public and professional image of the academician-researcher can be negatively evaluated if the research exhibits such biases. With respect to this problem, our experience was a fortunate one. From the time of our earliest contacts with the Citizens Advisory Council it was understood that the sole authority for the design and conduct of the study, as well as for the interpretation and reporting of the results, would lie with the researchers. Most important was the assurance that the council would publicize the study regardless of the findings. At no time during the study did we feel the slightest pressure to introduce a bias in favor of the sponsor. To the extent that our data collection and analysis were biased, the bias was contrary to the interest of the sponsor, that is, community identification was, if anything, overestimated.

The study involved the development and pretesting of a 45-item interview guide, the design of a two-stage cluster sample of the registered voters residing within the most populous areas of the district, the training of 20 interviewers, and the supervised collection of data from 303 respondents. This phase of the research took about ten weeks.

The second phase involved analysis of data and the writing and printing (mimeograph) of the final 85-page report. Hearings by the State Board of Education and the County Committee on School District Reorganization set deadlines for the completion of the work. Tabulation of responses, computations, preparation of 44 tables, the writing of 36 pages of text, proofreading of stencils, and assembly of 200 final copies of the report were compressed into two months of hectic activity (during this time we also met the demands characteristically placed upon full-time faculty members in a state college).

The extent to which the time element loomed as the chief "bugaboo" of the researchers during this phase of the work can be appreciated only when it is understood that all analysis and computation were done without benefit of any of the up-to-date technological paraphernalia most often assumed essential to modern research; i.e., counter-sorters, computers (or even desk calculators!), etc. All sorting was done by hand and the computations were done by slide rule. (Fortunately, one of the authors is a former engineering student.) Altogether, 1,320 percentages based on the handsorts were computed. The two months (more like two years of subjective time) passed and the study was turned over to the sponsors.

Following receipt of the copies of the study, the sponsors requested the presence of one of the researchers at the December, 1964, meeting of the County Committee on School District Reorganization for the purpose of testifying concerning our findings. Copies of the report were distributed to each member of the County Committee. The testimony of our research team, which was a short review of the study and its findings, was met with some hostility on the part of some members of the County Committee who opposed large-scale school district unification. Based on the past action of the committee, the record was clear; the majority were against unification along the lines of the Grossmont Union High School District boundaries. In September, 1964, the committee had submitted a proposal to form four districts within the area. That plan was disapproved at the November, 1964, meeting of the California State Board of Education, approximately one month before the completion of our study. The board denied the proposal on grounds other than "exceptional circumstances." One of the proposed districts would have been below the legal minimum financial capability required for unified districts. While we were prepared to testify concerning the *preliminary* findings of the study, there was no need to do so.

The majority of the County Committee members at both the December meeting, at which one of our team testified, and its subsequent meeting where the study was again a topic for discussion, ignored the findings of the research which indicated clearly that not even a moderate level of community identification existed, much less a high level.

It is recognized by us that this last rather facile statement requires some explication and interpretation. Standardized measures of levels of community identification do not exist. Since communities come into being, grow and prosper, decline and change in other ways, the question of whether or not a given aggregate of people residing in a local area constitutes a community could not be answered with a simple "yes" or "no." Rather, it was necessary to try to determine how many of the essential characteristics of communities the aggregate possessed and in what degree it possessed them. A related problem, and one of great importance in the present study, is that of delineating in a sociologically meaningful sense the boundaries of communities, obviously a matter which cannot be settled by simply noting limits of municipal incorporation.

The simplest and most clear-cut delineations of contemporary communities have been made for rural communities. These studies have typically explored the community identification of farmers living outside of incorporated areas. This has been accomplished by observing patterns of informal acquaintance and social interaction, most frequently used transportation routes to nearby trade centers, location of business establishments where goods and services are secured, and location of churches, schools, and places where recreational needs are met. Even in rural areas, however, identification of the specific community to which a family "belongs" may be problematic, when a family satisfies its needs for (say) groceries, medical care, education, religious services, and sociability in various nearby towns and settlements.

It appeared to us that the problem at hand was to determine whether the residents of the various suburbs included in the Grossmont Union High School District were, in the sociological sense suggested above, members of distinct communal entities to which such labels as El Cajon, La Mesa, and Santee are attached, or whether the total pattern of community relationships in the area must be characterized in other terms. Accordingly we inquired into such matters as place of employment, verbal expression of community identification, location of community services used, memberships in social organizations, knowledge of community leadership, church attendance, informal acquaintance and interaction, and satisfaction of recreational needs. For our purposes, community identification was conceived of in these terms.

Some of the typical findings concerning the above dimensions are: breadwinners were not employed in their own suburbs (more than 80 percent worked elsewhere); approximately half of the respondents could not provide even a rough estimate of the geographical boundaries of their suburb; over one-fourth felt they did not even live in any particular community (when asked the question, "If someone from out of town were to ask where you live, what would you tell him?" approximately one-third named a community other than their own suburb); membership in formal organizations was as likely to be outside of as within suburban boundaries; approximately one-half of *all* shopping for clothes occurred outside the resident's own suburb; more than one-half of the residents used medical facilities located exclusively outside of their own suburb; more than three-fourths of the sample were unable to name two or more community leaders within their own suburbs (we accepted as named community leaders elected officials, school principals, PTA officers, clergymen, Boy Scout leaders, Little League coaches, etc.); and lastly, more than half of the respondents reported that they did not know most of their neighbors, in fact only 17 percent had "best friends" living in the suburb. Visiting and recreational patterns similarly indicated that suburban boundaries were irrelevant for the social life of the residents.

These findings, as well as many, many more, caused us to conclude that the burden of proof of "strong community identification" was upon those who would claim it. An extensive survey of the literature concerning social life in suburban communities revealed that the area which we studied did in some respects approximate the norm of suburban life and social participation, and, in other respects, fell below it.

In spite of these findings, the County Committee voted for a proposed two-district split of the existing high school district. One of their major reasons was "the committee reports substantial community identity in each of the proposed districts," though no substantiating evidence for the claim was cited. The California State Department of Education, in an unanticipated move, approved this proposal.

In April of 1965 one of our team was requested to testify in the state capital before the California State Board of Education regarding the findings of the study. Despite the fact that the State Board characteristically follows the recommendations of the State Department of Education, and despite considerable confidence on the part of many politically astute observers that the proposed two-way split of the Grossmont Union High School District would be approved, the State Board of Education rejected the proposal, concluding that it did not meet the requirement of "exceptional circumstances."

Although we are not really able definitely to ascertain the role our study played in the final decision—other testimony was received by the board—the interest evidenced by members of the board through their questions and comments suggested to us that our study was of significance to them and influenced the decision-making process.

This was an interesting and valuable experience for us in many ways. For example, within the total research process, we learned a great deal about the educational system in our part of California. This included not only knowledge of the formal legal-political structure, but also insight into the political ideologies and interests of various groups across the political spectrum who frequently focus their attention upon educational matters. Illustrative of this was our informal observation that it was the extreme conservatives especially who favored smaller school districts. Interesting also, but hardly valuable, was the experience of having our professional integrity impugned, by implication at least, by some opponents of large-district school unification. (We do not yet, at this writing, completely understand the interests and motivations of the opposing groups.)

Finally, it was personally rewarding to us to experience evidence that sociology has come of age. Our skills as behavioral scientists were needed, recognized, and utilized.

Few occurrences have shaken the academic community as has the recent "Berkeley Affair." In the brief essay below, a sociology teacher relates his various action roles in the controversy, all taken as a leading faculty partisan of the student cause. However one decides to judge the controversy, the account is valuable for underlying the variety of roles available to the action sociologist in a power struggle, especially in a struggle that, like this one, is likely to reappear in various forms throughout the academic community.

SOCIOLOGY IN THE BERKELEY FREE SPEECH MOVEMENT

John C. Leggett, assisted by Gunilla Marton and Joyce Bailey

THE BATTLES waged by a free speech movement against a multiversity[1] offer multiple roles to the sociologist. It is my purpose to discuss the roles I filled as a sociologist in the natural history of a free speech movement. As we shall see, I was able to move serially in and out of several roles, running the gamut from clarifier, through publicist, picket organizer, fund raiser, to research bureaucrat. In my analysis I will not attempt to review or even outline the struggle, but will leave this to other writers.

---

[1] The concept of the multiversity is succeeding the traditional definition of the university. Actually, the multiversity is simply a giant research organization with nominal commitment to quality education. The latter derives in part from size and function of the multiversity. In his *The Uses of the University*, Kerr has observed:

"The University of California last year had operating expenditures from all sources of nearly half a billion dollars, with almost another 100 million for construction; a total employment of over 40,000 people, more than IBM and in a far greater variety of endeavors; operations in over a hundred locations, counting campuses, experiment stations, agricultural and urban extension centers, and projects abroad involving more than fifty countries; nearly 10,000 courses in its catalogues; some form of contact with nearly every industry, nearly every level of government, nearly every person in its region." (pp. 7-8)

Not only size but *function* interests Kerr: "Intellect has also become an instrument of national purpose, a component part of the 'military industrial complex.'" (p. 124)

Of course, some might have moral qualms about such commitment, but "The university has been embraced and led down the garden path by its environmental suitors; it has been so attractive and so accommodating; who could resist it and why would it, in turn, want to resist?" (p. 122)

See his instructive *The Uses of the University* (Cambridge: Harvard University Press, 1963).

THE BERKELEY FREE SPEECH MOVEMENT AND FACULT PARTICIPATION

The Berkeley Free Speech Movement (FSM) believed the universit could become a free community: students plus faculty would co-direc the destiny of the university. The administration would administrate. I would perform service functions.[2] In performing these activities, th administration would stand in a subordinate capacity to both faculty anc students. These two key university groups would elect representative and conduct affairs in a manner consistent with grass-roots democracy (Nevertheless, the orientation of the FSM toward the faculty was hesi tant. It hoped for but did not expect the kind of support later given b this august body to the FSM, support largely possible precisely becaus the FSM was free of esoteric ideology and dogma and hence was no repulsive to most faculty.)

The Preliminary Stage

During the preliminary stage of the FSM's development, the leader faced two major problems: (1) How might they define their conflict witl the university? and (2) How should the Movement answer the charge of communist-domination? To clarify the conflict was difficult, for few had time to ponder the complexities involved. Nonetheless, this intel-lectual exercise provided me with a real opportunity to stress the soci-ological basis for inter-group conflict.

For a variety of reasons, I rejected single-variable explanations of the Berkeley crisis. These interpretations focused on the nasty effects of deep alienation, giant size, student distrust, administration high-handed-ness, faculty and student irresponsibility, the paucity of communication channels, and the like. Rather, my analysis focused on inter-group conflict over concrete issues, and pointed to the analogous experiences of work-men and their Big Business opponents during the 1930's. Much as the struggle then was over the right of workers to organize and to protest their condition as well as the circumstance of others, a "student prole-tariat" of the 1960's—deprived relatively, isolated socially, homogeneous sub-culturally, and organized politically—was struggling now with the Captains of the Multiversity over the rights of students to organize and to carry their fight into the non-university community. I presented these views before a mass meeting of several thousand students. Most agreed with my analysis.

At issue was whether actions of the university should be allowed to undermine the civil rights movement in Northern California. At issue was the administration's right to outlaw on-campus student meetings which eventuated in off-campus civil rights demonstrations and mass

---

[2]See Gene Marine, "No Fair! The Students Strike at California," *The Nation*, Vol. 199 (December 21, 1964), p. 486.

arrests. I went on to stress the historical parallel with the 1930's because I hoped to link the campus conflict with the major struggles of the recent past. I assumed that the creation of a sense of historical continuity among the students would create a mood of rebel legitimacy.

The second problem was how to counter the charge of communist-domination expressed by officers of the university and amplified by the mass media./ The administration refused to recognize the structural sources of discontent, and preferred the plot conception of FSM militance. According to University President Dr. Clark Kerr, the October insurgence stemmed from a "Maoist-Castro" agglomeration, which led the students to surround and capture a police car and to embark upon other rampages. The leadership allegedly consisted of Left Bank participants who plotted to plunge the university into sustained disarray. To answer this widely publicized concept of "Maoist-Castro manipulations," I formulated a counter-concept of "Maoist-Kerr similarity" on questions of bureaucratic subversion of free political advocacy.

In due course, I addressed another mass meeting and elaborated my thesis on the way in which state bureaucracies were aided by their university satellites as the state stifled free speech in many parts of the world. I charged that Francisco Franco, Fidel Castro, Mao Tse-Tung, and Clark Kerr had muzzled free political expressions within their respective universities. All were directly or indirectly involved in thought repression, and all preferred situations where criticism and direct action would be unable to challenge severe restrictions on liberties. My value position was to the point: none of these bureaucrats should have the right to stifle free speech.

The outcome of my attack? The militant left was furious. Many booed and heckled. Similarly, conservative faculty elements were outraged by my placing Franco, Fidel, Mao, and Kerr in the same light. I was not aware of the administration's reaction. Nobody was. However, I did make the assumption that the administration would become aware of my public association of its practices with those used in the totalitarian worlds of Left and Right. It was hoped that this awareness would diminish Kerr's propensity to charge communist dominance of the FSM, if only because he and the administration would thereby expose themselves to criticisms from the democratic left. It could be counted upon to once again charge the administration with practices not unlike those used in Peking and Madrid. Kerr would find such a comparison odious. Consequently, we reasoned he would avoid such charges. Indeed, the administration did cease to red-bait, and Dr. Kerr later admitted that the FSM was a new kind of movement, one clearly something other than just another Red Insurgence.

The Popular Stage

The popular stage was fascinating, since the growth in esteem of the movement helped to precipitate crises which in turn invited my participation as a sociologist in the roles of liaison, propagandist, fund-raiser, and picket-line organizer.

During this period of growth in Berkeley—the "historic moments" of December—the triumvirate of the "prophet" Savio, the "reformer" Weissman, and the "agitator-organizer" Weinberg, commanded widespread support. Issues were discussed at mass meetings and elsewhere. Utopias were constructed on "the free university." Specific problems were developed on university reform. Strategies on student-university conflict were collectively formulated after long and continuous debates, some of which lasted for days. Such brilliance and stamina in student politics had seldom before graced a university campus.

This period of militant euphoria was, nonetheless, a time when one could count upon the administration and its many faculty friends to commit fewer errors and to undercut the FSM. Consequently, I joined others who felt it was necessary to attach the Free Speech Movement publicly to one of the leaders of the Civil Rights Movement, and, through him, to the Movement itself.[3] Such an association, we hoped, would make it clear that an attack on the FSM would be justifiably interpreted by students and many others as an attack on a stubborn section of the Civil Rights Movement. Consequently, I worked day and night for two weeks as a liaison to bring James Farmer (Director of the National Congress of Racial Equality, or CORE, and an old acquaintance of mine) to the Berkeley Campus. Farmer's later appearance and speech convincingly linked the fate of the FSM to the general Civil Rights Movement.

During this period, many of us felt it necessary to add to Farmer's impact among those predisposed to support the FSM. We could not rely upon the mass media to tell the kind of story which might win us sympathy: Most papers (with the exception of the *Berkeley Daily Gazette*) distorted and even omitted the issues involved. One listener-owned, local radio station, however, not only reported the events thoroughly and fairly, but recorded many of them as well. These tapes—120 hours altogether—were edited by them for a long-playing record, one clearly sympathetic to the FSM. Educational packets containing the record and published materials were mailed by us to several hundred influentials located primarily in the Mid-West and the East. In our own unsystematic way, several of us made a special effort to send out the packets to social scientists and editors of liberal and left-wing magazines. The packets not only briefly explained our struggle but sought donations to cover the mailing and record expenses involved. Money was collected in this way, but we have no way now of knowing to what degree we impressed or failed to impress those whom we contacted.

---

[3]Many of the FSM leaders had been involved in civil rights struggles both in the Bay Area and elsewhere prior to the turmoil of the 1964-5 academic year. Savio, for example, had done work with SNCC in Mississippi immediately before returning to Berkeley and involving himself in the FSM.

One thing was clear at the time, however. As a fund-raising device, the propaganda packet flopped: The donations raised failed to match the amount spent for the records. A subsequent effort on my part to supplement this negative balance sheet also came to nought. My appearance as main speaker before a sympathetic Los Angeles synagogue audience failed to average a one dollar donation per audience member, even though my presentation was not rhetorical; the rabbi made the appeal, and the audience consisted largely of parents of the arrestees.

During this same period, I participated in the organization of a student general strike.[4] Shortly after the Sproul Hall arrests began, the students in charge called a general strike that shut down almost all of the university. Along with several students, I was put in charge of organizing a particular picket line. It extended across a truck-car entrance leading to an underground parking complex beneath the student union and cafeteria.

How to handle the police patrolling our line proved difficult. Many officers were hostile towards the student strikers. They seldom engaged in conversation with the picket leaders. However, other police officers sought some way of starting a conversation with the picket line leaders, if only because they seemed unable to continue to receive the hostility of the FSM pickets. Our sensitivity to the ambivalence and needs of the Berkeley police prompted several picket captains to talk to the officers. As a result, the students defeated the intended purpose of the police patrol. Many motorists and truck drivers believed that the police and the picket captains were deliberately blocking the driveway, for these drivers would reach a point near the entrance, slow down, observe, and then drive off. This strategy was used for several hours and proved quite successful.

The Post-Popular Stage[5]

The FSM did not run its natural course. A short time after the general strike the organization began to disintegrate. During this stage, I took the roles of auditor and research bureaucrat.

As auditor, I tried to weigh the FSM's accomplishments, although it was still somewhat too early to do so. Put simply, the FSM had both won and lost. It won for students the right to continue to engage in the Civil Rights Movement. It won in the sense that the dissemination of vital ideas through mass protest continued to characterize the Berkeley scene

---

[4]For a detailed discussion of the latter, see Hal Draper's *Berkeley: The New Student Revolt* (New York: The Grove Press, 1965).

[5]The FSM never reached the institutional stage. Yet, it began to take on some of the characteristics associated with the latter at the very time when it was disintegrating. For an analysis of the characteristics associated with this stage, see Rex Hopper, "The Revolutionary Process: A Frame of Reference for the Study of Revolutionary Movements," found in Ralph Turner and Lewis Killian's *Collective Behavior* (Englewood Cliffs, N.J.: Prentice-Hall, 1957), pp. 317-18.

(as evidenced by the massive peace demonstrations sponsored by the Left and Peace groups during the Spring of 1965).[6] The FSM won also in the sense that it paved the way for its successor, the Free Student Union,[7] and aided the growth of the American Federation of Teachers (AFL-CIO) staff and graduate student locals.[8] The movement won again, in that it stimulated comparable student and faculty movements elsewhere in the United States. The FSM lost, however, in that it did not realize even a fraction of its utopia on university reconstruction. As a specific social movement, the FSM died during the Spring of 1965. Why it did is a complicated problem admirably analyzed elsewhere.

Suffice it to note that during this period of decline, I also used the tools of sociology to help rectify inaccurate notions spread by the community press and repeated by various components of the community's political power structure. Most pertinent in this regard was the denial of use of police violence when Berkeley students were arrested in the university's Sproul Hall. Reports of police use of hands, fists, elbows, clubs, feet, and so forth, were common. Yet the mass media often denied their occurrence. Precisely because these travesties of civil liberties were bypassed or disclaimed, several hundred students and I proceeded to work with the FSM defense lawyers to document police behavior during the arrest. We subsequently put together a 52 page interview schedule and interviewed 699 of the 773 arrestees. We concluded that 148 had been victimized by the police.

We did our social research without a dime of university or foundation help. The gathered information helped not only the defense attorneys, but constitutes the basis for a lengthy manuscript I hope to complete someday on the natural history of an arrest.

SUMMARY

Students and faculty involved in the Berkeley Free Speech Movement worked together as allies with much more sophistication than any of us had expected, partially because not a few of us viewed the world through the lenses of sociology. Of those sociologists who participated, few will forget the utility of our discipline and the fever of the conflict.

---

[6] Demonstrations protesting U. S. involvement in Vietnam were capped by a massive, two day teach-in which attracted approximately 15,000 people to several of the more important speeches. Notable was the list of leading teachers. Isaac Deutscher, Dick Gregory, Paul Krassner, Norman Mailer, I. F. Stone, Norman Thomas, among others, spoke at the teach-in.

[7] The Free Student Union is an organization devoted to developing a union among all undergraduates. The main purpose is to create a group capable of bargaining with the university on undergraduate grievances.

[8] The AFT staff local grew from 25 to 100, while the graduate student local emerged during this period and grew to include approximately 300 dues paying members.

To the surprise of many of us, sociologists can presently be found in a wide range of employments; for example, space agencies, reformatories, centers for the performing arts, manufacturing plants, advertising agencies, summer camps, military bases, and others. Indeed, despite its secular bias, sociology is presently contributing to the more efficient operation of at least one major religious organization—and, to judge from the account below of Dr. Yoshio Fukuyama, it does an effective and significant job. Challenged in this case both by the sparseness of sociological knowledge of organization mergers and by the presence of a potent "hidden agenda," Dr. Fukuyama nevertheless gathered, prepared, and presented data of considerable value to his ministerial employers. His provocative closing thoughts on the field's many action opportunities should remind us of the origins and interests of certain "Sociological Fathers," and should also encourage those sociologist readers among us who would seek in religion meaningful careers of service.

SOCIOLOGY IN ACTION: DECISION MAKING BY A RELIGIOUS BODY

Yoshio Fukuyama

RELIGIOUS GROUPS and their leaders have been both consumers and producers of sociological knowledge since the beginnings of sociology as an academic discipline in the United States. Albion W. Small, organizer of the first department of sociology at the University of Chicago, was an ordained Baptist clergyman. William Graham Sumner, the author of *Folkways*, a classic of American sociological literature, served as an Episcopal rector in New York City before embarking on his illustrious career as a sociologist at Yale University. The first course in sociology offered at Harvard College in the academic year 1891-92 was taught by the Rev. Edward Cummings, pastor of the South Congregational Church of Boston.

Just as clergymen turned to the new science of society in those early years, many sociologists turned their attention to religious institutions. Several of the field studies conducted by sociologists in the early 1900's concerned rural churches, and the founders of the Rural Sociological Society in 1912 included Warren H. Wilson and Edmund deS. Brunner, both rural church directors of denominational home mission boards and major contributors to sociological theory and knowledge.

Since the end of World War I the sociologists' role within the religious group has been increasingly institutionalized. This has been achieved largely through the establishment of departments of research and survey within denominational home missions boards and councils of churches. Thousands of church and community studies have been made by these departments to help local congregations understand the effect of population changes on parish life and to help denominational executives allocate mission funds more effectively. These researchers found in the rapid growth of new residential communities after World War II further occasion to apply the tools of demographic analysis to help the extension boards of denominations locate new churches.

In addition to demographic surveys, sociologists have contributed to the decision making of religious organizations through research, employing a wide range of social scientific methodology. For example, in my role as the research director of a Protestant home missions board, my sociological research has included readership surveys of religious periodicals, role studies of clergymen, experimentation with a new curriculum for our church schools, and studies of the organizational structure of our national boards and agencies. One of my more recent studies explores the attitudes and beliefs of church members regarding civil rights, economic policies, war, peace and the role of the church in society.

In this paper, I would like to describe my role as a sociologist in aiding a newly formed denomination choose a location for its national headquarters. But first, a few words about the setting in which the decision was made.

HISTORICAL BACKGROUND

In the summer of 1957 the United Church of Christ was formed by the union of the Evangelical and Reformed Church and the Congregational Christian Churches of the United States. The two denominations represented prior church unions, the former being the result of the union of the Evangelical Synod of North America and the Reformed Church in the United States in 1934, and the latter uniting the Congregational Churches with the Christian Church in 1931.

This new union brought together the Congregationalists who trace their beginnings to Reformation movements in England, and the Evangelical and Reformed Church which arose from similar movements in Germany and Switzerland. Demographically, the Congregationalists began in New England and moved westward across the North Central states to the Pacific, while congregations of the Evangelical and Reformed Church were most numerous in Pennsylvania and Missouri.

Church unions of this type will no doubt continue in the years ahead. For example, among the more dramatic proposals now before American Protestantism is the possible union of four major Protestant bodies: the Protestant Episcopal Church, the United Presbyterian Church in the U.S.A., the Methodist Church, and the United Church of Christ. Subsequent to union discussions begun in April, 1962, the Disciples of Christ and the Evangelical United Brethren joined in the conversations. Together these six denominations include 21 million church members, or about one-third of the Protestant population of the United States.

Before church union of this magnitude can be consummated, years of discussion take place along theological and historical lines. What are rarely articulated, however, are what have come to be known as "the nontheological factors" which affect church union. The amalgamation of millions of dollars in invested funds owned by the various boards and agencies of the church requires intricate legal work and changes in corporate charters. Wide differences in the socioeconomic status of church members, the geographic distribution of churches, and different styles of life associated with different denominations often pose even greater barriers to unity than differences in theology or polity. A factor which undercuts all major church unions is the necessity of merging the organizational and physical structures of the uniting denominations. It is especially in this area of "nontheological factors" that the sociologist can make significant contributions to current movements for church unity.

One of the first tasks which faced the newly formed United Church of Christ in 1957 was to determine a location for its national headquarters. In consequence of the historical development of the two denominations the Congregational Christian Churches had their national executive headquarters in New York City with secondary headquarters in Boston and Chicago, while the Evangelical and Reformed Church had its national headquarters divided between Philadelphia and St. Louis, representing the two poles out of which that denomination emerged in 1934, with a secondary office in Cleveland. Around each of these headquarters cities there developed groups of churches and church members whose loyalties to the national office were deep and of many years' standing. In addition to these national offices, both denominations were divided into more than 30 state-oriented conferences and synods through which the national staff members worked.

In 1958 the executive council of the new denomination authorized and appointed a committee to make a preliminary study of the factors involved in the selection of a permanent headquarters. This committee, made up of the six top executives of the boards and agencies of the United Church of Christ, was enlarged in 1960 to include 16 additional persons. Most of the new members were ministers and laymen representing the governing boards of the several church agencies and representatives from the six cities in which headquarters were then located. Two of the additions were staff members whose services were requested because of their particular competence as sociologists. As the Research Director of the Board of Home Missions of the Congregational and Christian Churches, one of the major agencies involved in the union, I was one of the two sociologists appointed to the committee. My task was not only to gather the data needed by the committee to arrive at a decision but to help determine the sociological significance of the committee's task.

The original committee of executives first discussed some general problems relating to headquarters location and debated the merits of centralized versus decentralized national offices. One of the more dramatic proposals was to locate the new headquarters near a major jet airport to enable busy church executives and lay committee members to come in and out of the city for meetings with a minimum loss of time. Accordingly, the first meeting of the enlarged Committee on Permanent Headquarters was held at the Cleveland-Hopkins Hotel located next to the Cleveland airport. At this meeting the first major decision favoring a centralized national office was made.

In subsequent meetings, committee members expressed their opinions freely about where the new headquarters might be located. The committee chose to confine the alternatives to the six cities in which offices were then located. The selection of New York City loomed prominently from the outset; hostility to New York City was also clearly evident. For some, New York City represented cultural and social values which were deemed inconsistent with the purposes of the United Church of Christ. The national publicity given to its chronic commuter problem, its subway crimes, rates of delinquency and narcotics addiction, and its sheer bigness elicited expressions of resistance on the part of some members.

Others favored cities where office buildings owned by one of the church agencies could be utilized; still others favored cities which were historically significant to one or the other denomination. One of the recurrent themes was that the "national headquarters ought to be close to the center of our church population."

Another kind of argument stressed the need for staff members to be accessible to interdenominational agencies such as the National Council of Churches(the major cooperative agency for Protestant denominations) since much of the time of staff members was spent in cooperative planning with counterpart leaders of other denominations. Still others spoke of the need to minimize moving costs and to avoid uprooting the families of staff personnel.

SOCIOLOGICAL RESOURCES FOR DECISION MAKING

My first task was to bring together a body of descriptive data concerning the two denominations. The distribution of churches and church members was spotted on maps and comparative membership and financial data were presented. Historical statistics as reported in the yearbooks of the uniting denominations described membership trends, and these in turn were compared with the general growth of religious bodies in the United States as well as with the population in general.

My task was also to help the committee organize its thinking in such a way that objective and functional norms could ultimately be brought to bear on the final decision. To achieve this end, insights from sociological theory were discussed as alternative locations were being debated.

For example, from the viewpoint of organizational theory, the conflicting location proposals were based on different conceptions of the "public" to be served by a headquarters building. Distinctions, I felt, had to be drawn among three levels of "publics" to which a national headquarters might be functionally related. More specifically, the prime function of a headquarters building is to provide housing for the executives and staff of the organization and to provide them with the optimum conveniences to perform their work. In this sense, the "public served" by the headquarters is the executive staff of the national organization. At the second level is the "public in contact," those agencies and organizations through which the national staff carries on its daily work. In the case of church organizations, these include state or regional conferences, national denominational and interdenominational agencies, and other service organizations. The third level is the "public at large," which includes the local churches, its ministers and members, and other institutions to which the national body may have some interest or relationship.[1]

The conflicting proposals for headquarters location may be further understood from the insights of the sociology of knowledge; an understanding of the social context in which a viewpoint is expressed helps us to uncover the real issues which are involved. Staff members are faced with the threat of having to move their families from communities in which they have purchased homes and established roots; trustees of church-owned properties are faced with the economic consequences of

---

[1] For the United Church of Christ, these various "publics" may be briefly described as follows:

Public served: General Synod (chief executive offices); Board for Homeland Ministries; Board for World Ministries; Council for Christian Social Action; Council for Church and Ministry; Council for Lay Life and Work; Office of Communication; Pension Boards; and Stewardship Council.

Public in contact: 44 state-oriented conferences; headquarters of other denominations; National Council of Churches; World Council of Churches; other interdenominational service agencies; national health, education, and welfare agencies; communications media and transportation facilities; and fiscal agencies, etc.

Public at large: 6,800 local congregations; 9,000 ministers; 2,000,000 church members; local health, education, and welfare institutions.

The national office does not normally work directly with local churches but through the state conferences to which the congregations are related. Local church subsidies from the Board for Homeland Ministries, for example, are paid to the state conference to be transmitted to the local congregation. Monies raised for the national church budget are first sent from the local congregation to the state conference and from there to the national treasurer's office.

vacant office space; specific office buildings take on symbolic meanings in the denomination's history; the security of cultural homogeneity is threatened by cultural diversity and conflict; high moving costs have to be offset by a reduction in the support of missionary work overseas. These socially conditioned norms are rarely articulated publicly; they are usually discussed informally in the corridors and unofficially within friendship groups.

A third sort of sociological insight which helped to define the committee's problem came from the field of urban sociology and, particularly, from its description of "urbanism as a way of life." Those who tended to view a major city like New York in purely negative terms needed to be reminded that the city is also a center of political and economic power, the locus of learning, and the gathering place of the cultural elite. While the city has its problems of social disorganization, it also has its great museums and universities; the heterogeneity of its population is as much a source of creative vitality and growth in human understanding as it is of conflict.

Finally, I felt there was a need to help the committee distinguish between the symbolic and the functional aspects of a national church headquarters. To speak of a headquarters being located "close to the center of our church population" is to see the headquarters building as a kind of national shrine to which the faithful are drawn as pilgrims. Such a norm bases its decision on the "public at large" rather than on the "public served" in the sense discussed above.

Furthermore, this notion has its parallel in the "geographic center" of the population of the United States as defined by the U.S. Bureau of the Census. It is not only a highly abstract concept, but it has no significant consequence for the manner in which we organize our political or economic life as a nation. What, after all, would be the functional advantage of locating our nation's capital in the middle of a cornfield in southern Illinois, or the headquarters of the United Church of Christ on Lake Erie?

SELECTION OF CRITERIA

The committee decided early in the process that the criteria for the decision about location should be determined before any further data were gathered. The various criteria expressed, or implied, during the preceding discussions were listed and thoroughly debated. In order to set priorities, each criterion was given a numerical weight, ranging from one for the least significant (though necessary) to ten for those considered to be absolutely essential. The following criteria were finally adopted, together with the numerical index signifying their relative order of priority:

1. Access to offices of other denominations and interchurch agencies. (10)
2. Concentration of United Church of Christ membership. (5)

3. Population center of the United Church of Christ. (5)
4. Transportation. (10)
5. Communication. (10)
6. Clerical personnel. (3)
7. Staff housing. (3)
8. Rental and construction costs. (3)
9. Fiscal facilities. (4)
10. Cost of living. (3)

These criteria and their respective weights made clear the presuppositions under which the committee decided to carry out its assignment.[2] The "public served" by the headquarters location was clearly the executive offices of the denomination, and the "public in contact" was the national offices of other denominations, cooperative and service agencies, and state conferences rather than the pastors of local churches or their members. The high priorities placed on transportation and communication pointed to the optimum convenience for national executives and their need to travel to the various sections of the country rather than to the convenience of local pastors or church members and their need to visit the national headquarters. The relatively low order of priority assigned to economic factors such as clerical or housing costs indicated that the needs of the denomination's program were to be served first by their decision.

Once the criteria were adopted and the priorities established, we were ready to gather our data on the six cities for the ten criteria under consideration and to rank each city according to how it fulfilled the requirements of each criterion. The most authoritative sources of information were used: the *Yearbook of American Churches* published annually by the National Council of Churches and the official statistics of the United Church of Christ were sources of religious data; the U.S. Bureau of Labor Statistics and the U.S. Bureau of the Census provided economic and demographic data.

The ranking of the six cities in terms of their accessibility to transportation facilities was made on the basis of domestic flights listed for each city in the most current issue of the *Official Airlines Guide*. (An informal survey determined that except for very short trips, church officials used airlines almost exclusively for their travel.) The accessibility of commu-

---

[2] In further describing my role on the Committee on Permanent Headquarters I would state a viewpoint I share about the place of value judgments in sociological inquiry. I do not believe it is possible to achieve a value-free social science. Values insinuate themselves on all levels of sociological inquiry from the selection of the problem to the interpretation we give to our data. The fact that we choose to study housing or race relations or the recruitment of seminarians implies our value commitments as sociologists and as individuals. The selection of criteria for decision making by the committee made explicit the value orientation which was to surround our data gathering and its interpretation. As a member of the committee I participated in making these value judgments. As a sociologist, however, my task was to gather and interpret the data without the distorting effects of my subjective judgment or the imputation of additional criteria.

nications media was determined by referring to the *Directory of Newspapers and Periodicals* published annually by N. W. Ayer and Sons, the most comprehensive and authoritative listing available. Inquiries addressed to chambers of commerce in the six cities and to denominations which had recently built headquarters buildings elicited further data for the committee. Extensive inquiries about available space were made with the management of the Interchurch Center in New York City, one of the specific locations being considered.

Some of the major findings of this survey are described below.

1. An analysis of the principal headquarters locations of the 33 denominations affiliated with the National Council of Churches revealed that 11 of them had their primary headquarters in New York City, 5 in Philadelphia, and 2 in Chicago.

In its listing of 24 "national cooperative organizations" most frequently contacted by denominational officials, the *Yearbook of American Churches* listed the primary headquarters of 12 of them in New York City. The remaining 12 were located in ten different cities.

2. *Yearbook* data revealed that the concentration of the United Church of Christ membership was partly the function of the size of the city. Boston, Chicago, and New York contained the greatest number of churches and church members, St. Louis and Cleveland the least.

3. While the population center of the church membership was not computed, the spot maps showed that the membership of the denomination was concentrated in the Northeast and North Central regions. This data was presented schematically among the geographic divisions of the United States.

PACIFIC 7%	MOUNTAIN 2%	WEST NORTH CENTRAL 12%	EAST NORTH CENTRAL 30%	NEW ENGLAND 21%
				NORTH ATLANTIC 18%
		SOUTH CENTRAL 2%		SOUTH ATLANTIC & PUERTO RICO 6%

4. According to the *Official Airlines Guide*, the three airports serving New York City accounted for substantially more flights in and out than any of the other cities under consideration. These airports accounted for:

> 5 times as many flights as St. Louis
> 4 times as many flights as Cleveland
> 3½ times as many flights as Philadelphia
> 2½ times as many flights as Boston
> 1½ times as many flights as Chicago.

Flight availability was clearly a function of the size of the city.

5. The primary offices of the three major network radio and television broadcasters (ABC, CBS, and NBC) were all located in New York City.

Of the 161 newspaper feature, picture, and news syndicates in the United States listed in the *Directory of Newspapers and Periodicals,* content analysis revealed that 73; or 45 percent of the total, were located in New York City. Only seven were located in Chicago, two each in Boston, Cleveland, and Philadelphia, and one in St. Louis.

These and other findings were used to compute an index based on the ranking given each city for the ten criteria resulting in the following relative scores: New York 248; Chicago 192; Philadelphia 186; Boston 144; Cleveland 106; and St. Louis 78. The conclusion drawn from our data as they related to the evaluative criteria established by the committee clearly pointed to New York City as the optimum location for the head-quarters of the new United Church of Christ.

The final report to the Third General Synod in 1961 contained a significant change, however, one which departed from both the criteria adopted by the committee and the results of the sociologists' findings. The report recommended New York City as the location of the administrative offices of the United Church of Christ and suggested the authorization of a continuing committee to work out the details of the "precise location, design and proposed financing for headquarters." It went on to conclude that "the weight of its studies so far points in the direction of a location in the (sic) Philadelphia-New York metropolitan area." While according to the criteria adopted and the data presented Philadelphia ranked third behind Chicago, Philadelphia *was* the location of an office building owned by one of the uniting denominations, a factor which finally superseded attempts to reach a decision in accordance with purely normative or functional terms.

CONCLUSION

While the effort to achieve a decision by the application of functional and objective norms was not completely successful, the Committee on Permanent Headquarters did distinguish with some success its evaluative and fact-finding roles. In the latter role, we tried to present the facts needed by the committee in an orderly manner, relying on what we considered to be the most authoritative sources of data. Throughout the various stages of the committee's work, we fulfilled in some measure a teaching function, as we drew on our understanding of sociological theory ranging from urban sociology to theories of bureaucratic organization.

The final recommendation made by the committee (i.e., to include Philadelphia) points to the persistence with which unspecified values sometimes intrude on sociological inquiry, distorting the final outcome of research. This experience suggests the need for continued research into the dynamics of decision making by corporate groups, particularly the manner in which the "hidden agenda" of participants impinges on the course of the group's deliberations.

Other areas for action-oriented research which come to mind include the following:

1. Studies of the organizational structure of denominations, describing the ways in which power and authority are distributed, would make significant contributions to future church unions. An excellent example of this type of research is Paul Harrison's *Authority and Power in the Free Church Tradition* (Princeton, N. J.: Princeton University Press, 1959), a social case study of the American Baptist Convention.

2. Sociologists have turned to theories of professions to study the roles of clergymen and religious educators, but systematic research about the role of denominational executives is less common. Part of the difficulty faced by our attempt to locate our national headquarters (as well as to reorganize the denomination) was due to our lack of knowledge about the functional role of the denominational leader.

3. Since the publication of H. Richard Niebuhr's *Social Sources of Denominationalism* in 1929, it has been axiomatic among sociologists of religion that differences in socioeconomic status were significantly related to the proliferation of American Protestantism into numerous denominational groups. Some see in current movements toward church unity in the United States indicators of the lessening effects of social class on religious affiliation. The current climate of cooperation among denominations suggests that new studies of denominational social class differences might give more clarity and direction to future union negotiations.

Religion in American society will continue to provide sociologists with new frontiers for research. The employment of trained sociologists by religious organizations will continue to increase as religious institutions, like other social institutions, continue to grow in size and complexity.

There are no guarantees of success in anything—including a well-intentioned project in applied sociology manned by well-intentioned, able, and intelligent men. Indeed, as demonstrated several times elsewhere in this volume by contributors Hall, Fukuyama, Schwartz, and others, the obstacles to success are considerable—and, as made especially clear below, the situation worsens when the target group is unfamiliar with sociology, when the sponsor of sociology's use lacks status and power, and when the sponsor fails (or is unable) to make clear its expectations from sociology. Dr. Herbert Bynder's frank and unsparing account of two frustrating years as a medical sociologist is not a tale of failure, for there is much of value that he points up from his experience. Success in the introduction of applied sociology to completely new situations turns in large part on our demonstrated ability to truly learn and grow from his painfully acquired insights.

SOCIOLOGY IN A HOSPITAL: A CASE STUDY IN FRUSTRATION

Herbert Bynder

DURING the past decade, medicine has become an important area of sociological interest. Various problems, including the doctor-patient relationship, the processes of medical education, and the hospital as a social institution have been studied. While some of the social scientists involved have been primarily interested in the elaboration and testing of concepts and methods, others have been more concerned with applying their sociological knowledge to the problems of the practitioners in the health field. Some of the more significant studies, e.g., *The Mental Hospital*, by Stanton and Schwartz,[1] have managed to do both.

The hospital is a particularly important setting for sociologists with both interests, for over the past few decades it has become the major institutional context for the provision of medical care. Almost everyone, at one time or another, will enter a hospital and become a participant in a social system very different from that to which he is accustomed. In the hospital the patient will come into contact with many different profes-

---

[1] Alfred H. Stanton and Morris S. Schwartz, *The Mental Hospital* (New York: Basic Books, Inc., 1954).

sional and technical personnel who will provide him with a varied range of services. The universality of the hospital experience and its significance in the struggle against disease and disability can provide many opportunities both for sociological investigation and for the application of sociological knowledge to many of the problems which emerge in this organization.

Because of my professional interest in medical sociology as a substantive area of inquiry as well as a subject useful in an applied setting, I was encouraged by my associates to seek a position in a hospital. When an opportunity to work as a social researcher in the social service department of a large general hospital became available, I accepted the position with great expectations.

A Research Program: Transformation of Original Goals

My employment was the result of a decision by the hospital's social service department to establish a three-year experimental research program. I was to help establish research projects in conjunction with the administration and the staff of the department. Research was to be developed in the following areas:

1. Administrative programs, e.g., analysis of case loads,
2. The social components in disease, e.g., diabetes, cardiac disease, alcoholism, and schizophrenia; and
3. Evaluation of the efficacy of social services.

The research program thus planned for the social service department was to focus on problems of primary concern to the social worker, and not those of interest to the hospital in general.

Nevertheless, at the end of two years with the hospital, the bulk of my efforts and time had been directed *not* to the areas which supposedly justified this social service research program but rather to areas of administrative medicine and medical care. At the end of this two-year period, detailed (but still incomplete) drafts had been prepared for three very large project proposals *outside* the basic area of social service concern as expressed in the projected goals for the research program. These projects were:

1. A study of the efficacy of organized home-care programs. Its aim was to determine whether homebound patients brought to a day care center at the hospital for their medical, social, and rehabilitation care would regain their health more quickly and make quicker strides toward rehabilitation than patients treated in a traditionally organized home-care program.
2. A project to study hemophiliacs. The aims of this project were to determine the physical status of hemophiliacs and the type of medical care they had been receiving; the impact of this condition on their social functioning; and to identify the treatment and service needs of these patients.

3. A project to test the relative advantages of a hospital-based sheltered workshop in preparing for rehabilitation individuals who believed themselves too sick to work and consequently were unemployed for extended periods of time.

This is not to say that research aimed at the original program goals was completely abandoned. The major study proposals mentioned above did have an important social service component. In addition, an attempt was made to define an area of social service interest in a large study of handicapped children being carried out by two other departments. Finally, because I wished to carry out some research while preparing the larger project proposals, I conducted a small pilot study on the usefulness of medical charts as an indicator of social need, which did fit in more closely with the goals of the originally proposed research program.

Overall, however, the major part of my time during my two years with the hospital was spent in preparation of the above-mentioned project proposals as well as other proposals, which, while they did contain an important social service component, were primarily in the area of medical care and administrative medicine.

Why was there a transformation of the original goals of the research program? Why was the department of social service willing to commit itself to medical care projects, any one of which would have directed all the energies and resources of the department in research to an area *not* of primary social service interest? Why did the department of social service propose a research program in social service and then proceed to direct its energies to nonsocial-service research?

In my opinion, there were two major factors which influenced the final direction of the actual research program. These factors were the concern for commitment in this action setting and the relative lack of power and prestige of the social service department in the hospital.

Commitment in an Action Setting

While social scientists are committed to discover and to understand, often without primary concern for the consequences of this knowledge, social workers, as well as other action-oriented professionals, are explicitly committed to the use of knowledge to help people. As a result, action-oriented persons are basically concerned with "relevant research," i.e., research directed toward current problems, and research whose consequences can be anticipated. Social scientists who use an action setting to study problems of personal concern and/or are curious to discover "unanticipated consequences of social action"[2] are often unwelcome, especially when the research runs counter to many values action-oriented persons cherish and to assumptions under which they operate.

---

[2] Robert K. Merton, *Social Theory and Social Structure* (New York: The Free Press of Glencoe, Inc., 1957), p. 61.

The relative security of an action profession, which is a product of its acceptance by society and the prestige which it enjoys, will undoubtedly influence the extent to which it will encourage and utilize scientific research. Medicine, the most secure of the helping professions, has incorporated research into its educational program and its clinical resources. Social work, on the other hand, has not made social science research an important aspect of its educational program, nor has it incorporated research within its practice area. One of the reasons for this, I believe, is that social work demands commitment to its values and goals before it will accept the social scientist. In practical terms, the "concern for commitment" often leads to massive interference in the research function, and, as a consequence, actually lessens rather than enhances the value of the social scientist to the social agency.

The need for commitment was explained to me many times. At my very first job interview, the hospital's reluctance to hire a nonsocial worker was frankly stated. The social service department felt it could be sure of the values of the social worker-researcher, but not of the social scientist. I was questioned about my attitudes toward helping people in general, and toward social work in particular. In response, I explained my vital interest in the programs and problems of social work and medicine, as well as my desire to become involved in action programs. While I was not equipped to participate directly in such programs, I hoped to contribute to their development and implementation through my role as a social researcher.

As a social scientist, however, I was *also* committed to the values of scientific investigation. Indeed, it was as a social scientist that I expected to make my major contribution to an action program. At the time I did not perceive the potentialities of a clash between these two commitments. In retrospect, it seems that the administrators of the social service department who were hiring me were probably more aware than I of a potential clash between social science and social work, for many of their comments indicated a belief that only a social worker-researcher would place a commitment to social work above all else: only a social agency employing this type of person could be assured of "desirable" research, anticipated findings, and consequences nonthreatening to the agency.

I was, of course, hired because a social worker-researcher simply could not be found. While I was not the "typical" social scientist, my commitment was not completely to be trusted. Research directed within areas of primary concern to the department was therefore not advisable, at least not until I had demonstrated the proper commitment.

The Power and Prestige of the Social Service Department

One of the major latent functions which a researcher served for the department of social service was to enhance its power and prestige vis-à-vis other hospital departments. Since the social service department was one of the few professional departments without a strong tradition of research, the very presence of a researcher, regardless of what he did, added somewhat to the department's prestige. In addition, by concentrating its research efforts in the interdisciplinary area of administrative medicine and medical care studies, the social service department opened up the potentiality of equal participation, i.e., principal investigatorship, with traditional departments in a hospital research program.

Under normal circumstances the social service department's participation in research was limited to supplying an occasional social worker to collect any required social data. The department was not recognized as an equal participant in this research and, of course, usually had little voice in related policy decisions. However, when the social service department became the only one with an employee trained in social and administrative program research, it claimed acceptance as an equal partner in research endeavors, and eventually hoped to earn a reputation as a department which participated in one of the most prestigious types of work of the teaching hospital.

Whether my presence actually brought the department equality or enhanced prestige is, in fact, doubtful. Perhaps, if the first project proposals had been funded and had therefore achieved an early and very significant measure of success, the position of the department might have been enhanced and its ability to claim equality respected. However, the three projects were not funded during the period of my employment, and thus the social service department was not accorded the equal partnership it so deeply desired.

Further Complications in a New Role

There is more to my tale of discovery and disappointment than failure in original research designs; the problems of a "pioneer" sociologist in a bureaucratic setting range farther and deeper. Three such problems particularly merit discussion: role conflict, problem choice, and differential perspectives.

1. **Role Expectations and Social Control.** While some research activity had previously been carried out in the department, the social service unit had never worked with a person devoted to full-time research. Lacking an appropriate role model for me, I was expected to fit the role model of the agency social worker. In consequence, conflicts between expectations of a social worker's behavior and that of a social scientist, especially in the area of social control, became a constant and an increasingly serious source of dispute between myself and the administration of the department.

Supervision, the control mechanism characteristic of subordinate-superior relationships in a social work agency, was made applicable to me as well. The department sought to have strict control over what I was doing and the way I was spending my time. In very subtle but distinct ways, a relationship emerged in which I was supposed to report on my activities of the previous week in a manner not equivalent to the explanations and justifications given a professional colleague in the social sciences—outside of social work, that is. Before long, I discovered that not only was I subordinated to an administrative superior in administrative matters, but, more crucially, in research matters as well. This professional subordination was particularly unreasonable because my "superior" was not a professional colleague. While he contributed significantly to the development of many of the proposals, he had no special training as a social scientist or as a social researcher. Yet, I was subordinated to his control on matters of professional judgment. Even if exercised by a colleague, this type of control would be an unstable factor in any professional relationship.[3] It was particularly unstable when exercised by one not specifically competent in the area of research.

Accountability of place and time was the most disturbing control. Along with the social work staff, I had to sign in at a reception desk and indicate the time of my arrival. Whenever I left my office, I had to indicate my destination. While these procedures were justified for social workers on the grounds that emergencies required hospital knowledge of one's whereabouts, there was no justification for this location control of a researcher. (I was never called for emergency duty!)

The attempt to control my time extended to the request that I keep a statistical count of my activities. All social workers kept monthly statistics on the number of client interviews, as well as the number of contacts they had with physicians, nurses and other agencies. These monthly statistics were said to have value in rationalizing the distribution of work loads and in planning for new facilities and staff. While the social worker had a set of categories in which to put her statistics, it was not possible to keep statistical count of research activities and the request for this information was soon dropped.

When one's time, however, must be accounted for so completely, there tends to be a transferring of one's concern from the nature and quality of work to what one is doing at every hour of the day (the quantity of work). Because time, rather than product, becomes the measure of control, there is a tendency to become engaged in "make-work," i.e., activities whose prime purpose is to fill time. Since the weekly meeting with my supervisor was the occasion for demonstrating 40 hours of production for 40 hours of work, I gradually found myself more concerned

[3]Goss points out, in her study of the relations among doctors in a hospital, that, while a physician would respect the authority of a superior physician in administrative matters, he would not do so in matters of professional judgment. In this area, a superior could influence a subordinate only through the mechanism of advice, which the subordinate could always legitimately refuse to accept. See Mary E. Goss, "Influence and Authority Among Physicians in an Out-Patient Clinic," *American Sociological Review*, Vol. 26 (1961), pp. 39-50.

about showing tangible increments in my work than in being primarily concerned about the quality of the increments thus produced.

This was a difficult problem to handle, for there is no way to measure whether a piece of creative work *should* have taken 4 hours, 40 hours or 400 hours of work. The problem was compounded because one engaged in research is also supposed to think, and it is difficult in an action setting to account for time spent thinking. While no one ever told me to think on my own time, it would not have been an unlikely comment, for social workers who entered my office would leave with puzzled looks when they found me "just sitting there." Thinking is not a tangible use of time, and, therefore, could not be accepted in an agency which measured work in terms of clients interviewed, physicians contacted, meetings attended, and pages written.

2. **The Decision to Study a Problem.** An additional source of difficulty for me in this action setting centered around the question of who was to make the decisions about which problems to study. The social service department reserved this right; that is, control over the direction of research was to rest with the social work staff and not with the social scientist.

In my opinion, there were two factors which influenced this policy decision. The first factor concerns the relevance of a study to the agency's needs, which was discussed earlier.

While it is legitimate for an agency to suggest broad areas of concern, it is questionable whether the agency hiring a research specialist should control the specific nature of a study, and, as I discovered later, its methodology, as well as the very framework of its findings. While social workers were the experts in the substantive areas under consideration, there is no reason to believe that they would necessarily be aware of the most significant problems or even of how to ask the significant questions. Because of their involvement in day-to-day activities, it is possible social workers were not seeing the really significant problems. As a nonsocial worker I might have served a useful function by identifying problems from a different perspective.

The administration of the social service department would not accept this, and, I believe, the reasons stemmed, in part, from the second factor which motivated their need to control decisions about problems to study. This factor had to do with professional security.

The social work profession has not yet achieved full acceptance in our society. In a setting in which the social worker is the only or dominant professional, social workers can count on full acceptance by their colleagues. In a setting such as a hospital, on the other hand, the social worker is less likely to be accepted and his usefulness is frequently questioned. Many physicians do not understand the function of social workers nor do they know how to use them; a significant number even question whether social work has a legitimate function in a medical setting.

Social workers are quite aware of the attitudes of medical people toward them; as a result, they are defensive about their role and insecure about their lack of full partnership in the hospital world. It is therefore impor tant that social work demonstrate its usefulness in the hospital setting

One of the major functions of establishing research in the hospital' social service department, I now believe, was to begin to determine and to delineate those areas of knowledge and practice which were unique or at least of primary significance to social work within the hospita setting. Since one of the core aspects of professional status lies in the ac quisition of a body of abstract knowledge sufficiently different from tha utilized by other fields,[4] exhibiting this knowledge would enable socia work to claim recognition as a legitimate profession and thus enhance its security within the hospital setting. It was probably further assumed that if social workers controlled the direction of my studies, my work would more likely lead to the delineation of this body of knowledge than would occur if a nonsocial worker controlled these decisions.

3. Differential Perspectives: The Clinician and the Researcher. In discussions with the directors of a proposed project to establish a day-and-night psychiatric treatment facility, I was told by these clinicians that they could not see the need for a social researcher, since most physi cians had clinical and/or laboratory research experience. This medica type of research experience, I argued, was not sufficient for every type of program research. The social researcher, I explained, was uniquely trained to focus on the role relationships between people (e.g., psychia trist and patient); between people and organizations (e.g., patients and the Day and Night Center); and between organizations themselves (e.g. the Day and Night Center and the hospital). These could be important areas of concern in evaluating the impact of any treatment program.

In the opinion of most clinicians, if the social researcher had a role to play, it was as a technician rather than as an equal participant in the total endeavor. The social researcher was someone to carry out the clin ician's instructions, translating ideas into a researchable form or analyz ing data required by the clinicians. He was not seen as a person with a professional competence which enabled him, even more than the clin ical directors of the project, to engage in and carry out a particular research function. (This viewpoint may have had its roots in the fact that physicians in hospitals work with nonphysicians in a superior capac ity, or, more specifically, because as a social researcher, I was part of a department whose subordination to the medical staff was very clear.)

The different goals of the clinician and the researcher also may ac count for the subordinate role assigned to the latter. Clinicians are pri marily interested in enriching the treatment program of the hospital. Re-

[4]William J. Goode, "Encroachment, Charlatanism and the Emerging Profession: Psychology, Sociology and Medicine," *American Sociological Review,* Vol. 25 (1960), pp. 902-14.

search and evaluation were not seen as being of importance to the ultimate goal of providing better care. Although project-granting agencies demanded research and evaluation, there was reluctance among the hospital's clinicians to give prominence to the research function.

Final Comments: The Role of the Social Scientist in an Action Setting. My experiences in this hospital can indeed be considered a case study in frustration. I was under tight administrative control, my ability to make professional judgments was seriously restricted, and I found a basic lack of respect for research and evaluation. The result was a serious interference in the research function with its ultimate consequence a failure to develop an ongoing program of either social service *or* administrative medicine and medical care research.

In one sense, I contributed to this interference, for I not only accepted the primacy of treatment over research goals, but, in addition, felt so deeply committed to the basic aims of this action agency that at times it overrode my commitment to social research. It was only at the point of serious interference that the realization of my conflicting commitments was unavoidable. The social scientist whose role is not clearly defined, as was true in my case, is frequently placed in a position of role conflict. He wavers between fulfilling his expectations of what the role of social scientist should be and those of the action role defined for him by the agency. In the face of conflicting expectations of one's behavior the dilemma is often resolved in favor of meeting those expectations which are more likely to be sanctioned.[5] Since those who wielded effective sanctions in the hospital were the same ones who defined my role in action terms, I tended to resolve the role conflict in ways detrimental to my role as a social scientist.

Even though my own experience was a frustrating one, I still believe that the sociologist can make important contributions to the success of action programs. If research and evaluation, however, are to make significant contributions, the research role must be respected and the social scientist acknowledged as an equal participant in all stages of a project's development. To have creative value in an action setting, the social scientist must be free of unnecessary bureaucratic control; he must be allowed the freedom to make judgments within his area of competence and to participate in the identification and investigation of problems which he sees as significant. Even as an agency can demand that a researcher be committed to the basic values underlying action, the agency, in turn, should be prepared to respect the researcher's commitments to his role as a social scientist.

While it may be difficult for those in administrative positions to allow

---

[5]Two interesting studies which illustrate this pattern of role conflict resolution are: Roger W. Little, "The 'Sick Soldier' and the Medical Ward Officer," *Human Organization*, Vol. 15 (1956), pp. 22-24, and Waldo W. Burchard, "Role Conflicts of Military Chaplains," *American Sociological Review*, Vol. 19 (1954), pp. 528-35.

the social scientist this freedom, his usefulness increases under these conditions. If research and evaluation are serious concerns of those engaged in action programs (and this seriousness is not to be taken for granted), the trained sociological researcher, not immersed in day-to-day program activities, and able to view problems in a hopefully new and refreshing way, may yet provide a unique and invaluable dimension of understanding.

It might be thought that the least likely setting for a successful project in applied sociology would be a mental hospital, given its presumed exclusive concern with psychotherapy, social psychiatry, clinical psychology, and psychiatric social work—in short, with the patient's history and present psychodynamics. A case to the contrary is offered below by Dr. Morris S. Schwartz, who demonstrates with his essay that the patient's social context plays a crucial role in his action decisions, even in decisions made by psychotic individuals with a long history of repetitive pathological behavior. Probing with sociological skills the patient-staff relations, the intrastaff ideological conflicts, and the processes of staff decision making, Dr. Schwartz analyzes the relationship of directed change in these items to the initially desperate behavior, and later dramatic recovery, of an institutionalized psychotic patient. In so doing Dr. Schwartz underlines the larger, vital point that we have only begun to uncover problems amenable to sociological aid, and ought now to consider "nothing human foreign to us."

THE USES OF SOCIOLOGY IN THE MENTAL HOSPITAL*

Morris S. Schwartz

I SHOULD like to describe to you one way sociological and social psychological analysis and conceptualization can be used to contribute to achieving the goals of an organization. Specifically, I shall present a series of concrete events and analytic steps that culminated in the interruption and termination of a patient's disturbed and disturbing behavior on a mental hospital ward. My purpose is twofold: (1) to formulate a mode of procedure for applied sociology, and (2) to show how an understanding of the relation between the individual and his immediate social context can be used to facilitate changes in individual behavior.

The institutional context within which the project[1] took place was a small, psychoanalytically oriented hospital, a full description of which

*This paper was presented at the American Sociological Association meetings in Washington, D.C., August, 1962. It is reprinted here with permission of the author and *Social Problems*, from the issue of Winter, 1963.

[1]This project was supported in part by a grant (M.H.-0682201) from the National Institute of Mental Health.

is given in *The Mental Hospital*.[2] The project I shall describe was organized in order to develop further the findings presented in that volume. My formal role as investigator was to analyze social process on the disturbed ward, to identify social patterns that produced or maintained illness, and to work closely with the staff in planning and executing changes. The regular ward participants consisted of fourteen patients, a physician who was administrative head of the ward, one charge nurse, two to four staff nurses and aides, and one to three student nurses on the day shift, with approximately one less staff member on the evening shift. There was, in addition to myself as investigator, a nurse-observer who was working in the dual capacity of ward nurse and research assistant on my project.

Out of a year's intensive participant observation, I shall select for analysis here a set of events that were strikingly dramatic while they persisted and were also instructive to me as an applied sociologist. These events concerned a 43-year-old female patient's extreme indecision; that is, her inability to make up her mind about the most elementary matters. It was a situation in which she continuously hesitated and asked for orders and directions on issues we ordinarily resolve automatically, not considering them worthy of our focused attention or pausing to confront them as problems. In order to make clear the nature of her disturbance, let me present a brief description of the patient's course during the first five weeks of her stay on the ward.

When the patient came to the ward from another part of the hospital, she was confused and hallucinated. The first two days after her arrival, her eating and sleeping were no great problem. But on the third day she began to show marked fluctuations in these processes. During the next week (the first week), her disturbance in eating and sleeping and her desperation and confusion increased markedly. During the second and third weeks her desperation manifested itself in overt hallucinated behavior, in continuous obsessive repetiton of other people's words, in clinging to personnel both physically and verbally, and in frequent panic states in which she screamed and cried wildly. Concomitant with and as part of her disturbed state, the patient was almost totally unable to make any decision on any matter that affected her current behavior. She couldn't make up her mind whether she should chew food or swallow it once it was in her mouth, or whether she should move from one part of the room to another.

A nurse describes the behavior of the patient (Miss Bates) in the following way:

. . . she was extremely disturbed, crying, standing in the hall, praying to the lights, tears streaming down her face, not eating and not sleeping. There was

---

[2]A. H. Stanton and M. S. Schwartz, *The Mental Hospital* (New York: Basic Books, Inc., 1954).

a constant demand on somebody all the time. "Can I do this? Can I do that? How should I do it? Which toilet should I use? Should I flush it before?" It was just like she was waiting for people to say "Breathe in, breathe out."

The patient speaks about herself as follows:

I don't know if I'm doing right or wrong by staying in my room or going out. I don't know am I a man or a woman? I'm so confused, I haven't slept for nights. I don't know positively, if I should go over the threshold or not.

The patient stated specifically that she hesitated to eat because she was afraid she was eating people and that the messages she heard told her that food represented certain people on the ward. She asked personnel to feed her because the messages told her not to eat by her own efforts. The patient expressed herself in the following manner:

Should I eat or shouldn't I eat? Is it all right for me to put the food in my mouth? Should I chew it? Should I swallow it or shouldn't I? Am I eating people? It is right for me to take that [some food] in my mouth? What will happen to me if I do? What should I do with the food tray or tray food?

During the two weeks the behavior persisted and flourished, a great deal of affect was aroused in the ward staff and much of their time was spent talking about Miss Bates and trying to to cope with the problems she presented. During the weeks that followed this period of greatest disturbance (the fourth and fifth) the patient gradually improved in her eating, sleeping, and ability to make decisions for herself so that five weeks after her admission to the ward she was noticeably less disturbed, manifested little indecision, and was much more realistic and coherent in her behavior.

With this brief sketch as background I shall try to explain the emergence and continuation of the patient's indecision during the first three weeks of her stay on the ward and I shall try to account for its cessation at the end of the next two weeks. My focus will be primarily on ward social processes—on the way they stimulated and evoked this patient's indecision at that particular time and in that peculiar way. I shall, in addition, be concerned with the way changes in ward processes resulted in a radical alteration in the patient's mode of participation.

In taking social processes on the ward as the point of reference, I am deliberately excluding a psychodynamic interpretation of Miss Bates' indecision; that is, I shall not view her inability to make up her mind as a function of her personal history or her present psychodynamics. This is not to say that an understanding of her psychic or emotional life is neither relevant nor important. It is; for the very patterns of indecision with which we are here concerned had been a continuing problem for her and a central part of her personality and pathology for a long time. Where I do take personality and psychodynamic factors into account, I shall handle them only in a peripheral way. I focus on social process because I assume that human beings, even psychotic persons with a long history of repetitive pathological behavior, have alternative courses of action open to them, and that the social context plays a crucial role in determining which alternative is pursued.

I

During her first week on the ward, Miss Bates' behavior quickly became troublesome and burdensome to the staff and puzzling and challenging to the investigator. She was identified as the major problem on the ward by personnel, and I saw her as representing a research problem of considerable importance. As her behavior persisted and clearly formed patterns began to emerge, I conceived my immediate task to be the formulation of a hypothesis that might account for the patient's modes of participation in sociological or social psychological terms. I asked myself: If I view Miss Bates' indecision as a sick mode of participation (sick from the point of view of being self-destructive as well as highly unacceptable to others), what specific aspects of the social environment are eliciting or maintaining this behavior?

When one turned attention away from the patient, and this was hard to do because of her desperate state, and looked carefully at the staff, some significant things came into view. From the beginning the patient's requests, demands, and entreaties to have decisions made for her were met by evasion or rebuff. The essence of the staff response was, "You'll have to make up your own mind." During the first week a consensus crystallized among the ward staff that they would not tell the patient what to do, but require her to make her own decisions. The following illustrates the staff's handling of the patient:

When a nurse came into Miss Bates' room the patient said to her, "Shall I stay in my room or come out on the hall?" The nurse replied, "You'll have to figure that out for yourself." The patient immediately became more disturbed, desperate, and cried, "Help me. I need help!"

A nurse went in with Miss Bates' tray. The patient asked her, "Shall I eat or shan't I? Am I doing wrong in eating?" The nurse replied, "You'll have to make up your own mind." The patient becomes more agitated and says, "Please help me, I'm afraid." The nurse makes no move to help the patient but tries to leave. The patient clings to her becoming more panicky. "I don't know if I should eat the food trays." The nurse stays with the patient a while, still not helping her with the food.

The mode of response that became patterned filtered down from the supervising nurse to the charge nurse to the ward personnel. The nurses in authority urged personnel not to accede to the patient's request to be told what to do. This form of action was derived from, was supported and sanctioned by, institutional ideology. Since the hospital was psychoanalytically oriented, the psychotherapeutic hour and the therapist's mode of participation in it served as a model for ward personnel behavior. The supervisor and the charge nurse concluded that the best way to proceed was to pattern their responses after the psychotherapist's responses to the patient. Since he asked the patient to arrive at her own decisions, they assumed that a similar course of action would be appropriate for nursing personnel. Nursing personnel also felt that they were supported in their approach to the patient by the patient's therapist. They concluded this from a note that the therapist had sent them when they asked him for guidance. The note was promptly lost but was publicly interpreted as a request on the part of the therapist for them to treat the patient the same way she was being treated by him. Interestingly enough, when I asked the therapist about his instructions to the ward staff, he indicated that the note only described his way of handling the patient and did not ask the ward personnel to emulate him. He had asked instead that they treat the patient in a way that "made them feel most comfortable."

Another set of factors that played an important role in fixing the pattern of response was the personnel's need for security and definiteness in a situation that made them anxious, uncertain, and helpless. Thus, they were quick to lean on the authority of the therapist and nursing supervisor and to use them as a guide for their actions. In addition, the mode of response itself served to protect them to some degree from a patient who made them feel desperate and inadequate. The formula of asking the patient to "make up her own mind" permitted them to keep some distance from Miss Bates and to retain some impersonality in their relationship to her. To handle the situation in any other way would mean becoming "involved" with her in the web the patient was constantly weaving and pulling personnel into.

On the basis of these observations and interpretations I hypothesized that the patient's indecisive mode of participation was a function of a social field in which the staff was consistently rejecting the patient by refusing to give her instructions, directions, or guidelines for her behavior. The patient experienced the staff's response as a rejection not only of her requests, but also of her as a person. Since Miss Bates' demand for guidance revolved around such vital matters as eating, breathing, and sleeping, she experienced their refusal to tell her what to do as "no one cares if I live or die" (a statement the patient made during her upset state). Confronted with this total rejection she fell back on her old defense, indecision, communicating that she wasn't sure if she should live or die.

During the second and third weeks the staff continued their "analytic" approach and the patient's condition worsened. She was in an upset state at all hours of the day and during a good part of each hour. She ate hardly anything, slept very little and, although personnel were very much concerned about her, they tended to avoid her whenever they could. They could not, however, avoid her very much since she was continuously after them and since her desperate plight required their attention.

At the beginning of the third week, Miss Smith, the nurse-observer, returned to the ward from a vacation. She had been absent the two previous weeks and had not participated in the collective decision on how to handle the patient. Quite spontaneously, and without first discussing it with me she immediately took issue with the commonly practiced modes of response to Miss Bates. She told the patient what to do, and helped her do it, especially in such critical areas as eating. Her approach is illustrated by the following:

The patient had been eating scarcely anything for the past few days. Miss Smith took the tray of food in to the patient. The latter said: "Where am I eating?" Nurse: "You're sitting on the chair. So I'll put the tray on the bed. You can eat here." Patient: "Should I eat or shouldn't I eat?" Nurse: "Yes, you should eat. Start with your chicken."

The patient is hesitant and undecided. The nurse picks up some chicken on a fork and puts it in the patient's mouth. The patient gets her mouth full of food and then asks what to do with it. The nurse tells her to swallow it and the patient does. The patient becomes distressed about eating the potatoes and peas. She says the potatoes represent a man and the peas a woman and she doesn't think she should eat them.

She asks the nurse: "Should I let the food be people or should I let it be food?" The nurse replies, "While you are on the ward, you should let it be food. In your analytic hour you can let it be people." The nurse helps the patient eat by feeding her. The feeding process goes on for about two hours during which time the patient has eaten two-thirds of her meal, and has taken a few bits of food on her own volition.

Not only did the nurse-observer perform in the above manner, but she tried, with my private support, to get other nursing personnel to change their approach to the patient.

During the third week, as a result of Miss Smith's impact on the ward, a reorganization took place among the ward staff. There were now two chief protagonists advocating diametrically opposite points of view and practices to be undertaken with the patient. Each of the protagonists had one or two followers but the majority of the staff was undecided and vacillating, shifting from one approach to the other, pulled at one time in one and at another time in the opposite direction. The difference of opinion between the two protagonists was vigorous and continuous and the patient remained disturbed and indecisive.

Since both of these protagonists (the evening charge nurse and the nurse-observer) were senior nurses on the ward, the other nursing personnel would alternate in their approach depending upon who was in charge of the shift or on the shift at any particular time. Thus, one day or on one shift a staff member might be following "the analytic approach" and the same staff member on another shift on another day vould follow the "practical approach." Similarly, on any particular shift, different staff members might be doing diametrically opposed things with the patient. Some of the personnel were persuaded by both protagonists and others were given contradictory orders on how to handle the patient. Because of this conflict and contradiction in approach and the pulling in different directions, nursing personnel became confused and undecided.

A nurse, typical of the undecided majority, responded to my question, "What do you feel is the best way to handle Miss Bates?" with the following:

I don't know. *I really haven't made up my mind yet.* I think there are situations which arise with her where we have to say, "This is what you do." I can't quite go along with telling her every move . . . at one time she was so undecided that it would have involved telling her practically everything. *I'm not too sure* what I think about this.

The person who advocated the "analytic approach" to the patient, when asked why this approach would benefit the patient provided the following rationale:

Since this is the way the patient is handled in the therapeutic hour, it should be the way the nurses treat her—the therapist doesn't make her decisions and we're going to follow what the therapist does.

If you give in to some of her requests she will suck you in to making more and more decisions for her, until you'll be deciding every little gesture. She'll get you so confused and wound up you won't know what's happened, and soon she'll suck you in to making every little decision for her.

Telling her what to do is giving her directions and this is what she has had all her life, and this is the reason she can't make any decisions for herself now. We'll just perpetuate this by deciding for her. She wants to be ordered around and is trying to get us to do this.

During the controversy, Miss Smith pointed out to some of her antagonists that telling the patient what to do and helping her to do it seemed to reduce the patient's anxiety and helped her panic and desperation subside markedly. By contrast, being noncommittal brought about greater disturbance on the patient's part. These personnel agreed that the observations were valid, but maintained their position with the following statements:

Even if the patient's anxiety is reduced in these situations, you're only buying temporary short-range comfort at the expense of the patient emerging in her own right. We shouldn't ever turn away from things that cause distress. She is going to have to do things on her own.

We need to get underneath this defense. We should question her in order to make her aware of why she has to be certain of every detail in the environment. If you deal with her on a realistic level she may function better, but she may turn out to be a robot.

The arguments advanced for taking the "practical" approach to the patient were the following:

When you tell a patient to make up her own mind, especially around such important issues as eating, you're in effect saying "I don't care what you really do, whether you eat or not."

The patient is asking: "Can I depend on you to help me?" If she found some one she could depend on, that is, if she were sure of some one, then she wouldn't be so indecisive and she wouldn't have to keep on asking.

You put the patient in an impossible situation when people on the ward also maintain a high level of anxiety for a patient, as does her therapist, then the patient has absolutely no out.

At the end of the third week the social field appeared to be split into three parts: a few personnel practiced the "analytic approach," a few engaged in the "practical approach" and the majority were undecided. At this point in time I formulated a second hypothesis. The patient's indecisive and desperate behavior was reinforced and maintained by a set of patterned processes which included:

1) *Subjectively felt indecision* on the part of many persons about the best course to follow in interacting with the patient;

2) *Hesitation* and *indecisive action* on the part of nursing personnel when they dealt with the patient;

3) *A split and uncertain social field* in which vacillation between the two polarized approaches to the patient was the dominant theme.

Thus, I hypothesized that undecided individuals in a field dominated by indecision and contradiction served to continue the patient's indecision; that the patient's response pattern was a function of this ward organization and process; and that, in turn, the patient's indecision served to perpetuate disagreement, contradiction, and indecision among the staff.

In this situation, personnel were caught in the same self-defeating, circular process as the patient; the separate actions of the patient and staff members joined together to form a stabilized integration. The patient desperately tried to obtain some support and security from the environment, yet most of her actions tended to make personnel act in ways that were not security-giving. Similarly, personnel wanted very much to help the patient over her disturbance, yet their indecisive or rejecting actions tended to keep her upset and unhelped.

With this hypothesis as an explanation for the continuation of the patient's behavior, I began to concern myself with intervention. I asked: "How can I intervene in this circular process and change the equilibrium that has been established?"

In view of the two hypotheses I formulated, i.e., that at the earlier point the patient's indecision was a function of a consistently rejecting field and that her later indecision was related to a split, indecisive field, it seemed to me that intervention would have to be oriented toward eliminating the rejecting processes and instituting consistent, definite, and supportive ones. With this in mind I took a clear public position siding with Miss Smith and urged the staff to deal with Miss Bates in a "practical" way.

II

The series of steps I describe as constituting the intervention sound more orderly and organized than was their actual occurrence.

My first step at the end of the third week was to bring my observations to our research group. This group had been formed at the beginning of the project to deal with just such problem situations. It consisted of the investigator as the group leader, the administrative physician of the ward, a psychotherapist who was treating a patient on the ward, the charge nurse of the day shift (actually the senior nurse on the ward), and the nurse-observer. I related my observations to them, told them what my hypothesis was, and suggested that we think about how we might foster a consistent approach to the patient that supported her, one which was patterned after Miss Smith's way of handling the patient. The nurse-observer was quite forceful in backing this suggestion. The others were originally more or less neutral but after much discussion an agreement was reached to try and influence the ward staff to follow the "practical" approach. Thus the initial step was to reach the decision makers, to influence them on the basis of the evidence presented, and to get their agreement to try and follow the course that had been formulated. The agreement was only a tentative one on the part of the charge nurse and the administrator. They said they were willing to try it to see how it worked.

The second step was to convey our thinking to the ward staff. This was done at a series of ward conferences during which the charge nurse, the administrator, and myself, as well as the nurse-observer, spoke on behalf of a consistent "practical" approach. At the end of these meetings a tentative agreement was reached to "try it."

The third step consisted of the nurse-observer, the charge nurse, and the administrator using their authority and influence with ward personnel as they performed their roles on the ward. They were asked and urged to "tell the patient what to do," and to make decisions for her where necessary. An encounter of Miss Smith's with the patient was held up as an example of how the patient might progress if she were handled in this way. In this situation the patient asked Miss Smith to feed her. After Miss Smith spoon-fed her once, the patient took the spoon out of the nurse's hand and fed herself. Significant here was the "follow-through" on the tentative agreement.

The last step in the intervention procedure was a fairly generalized attempt on the part of nursing personnel to deal with the patient in a "practical" way. Although they weren't fully convinced that handling the patient in the manner suggested would work, they went along because persons in authority wanted them to and in order to "see what would happen." In instance after instance personnel reported success when they tried the "practical" approach with the patient. She became less desperate and so did they. Situations were resolved quickly and easily, and the patient showed no apparent regression because she was being told what to do. As a matter of fact, she could do more for herself once personnel initiated some action to help her do what she couldn't immediately do for herself. The initial successes reinforced their belief in the value of the approach and so they continued to use it and in turn the patient continued to improve. Thus, what was critical in this last stage was the validation of the usefulness of the approach to both the patient and the staff. By the end of the fifth week Miss Bates was eating in the dining room and her overt indecision had disappeared as a problem to herself and to ward personnel as had her desperate, clinging, panic states. This is not to say that there was a personality transformation so that she was now a decisive person. Rather, decisions around elementary matters such as eating, sleeping, and moving were now being made automatically without doubt and hesitation. On the other hand, there was conviction among some of us that the resolution of this problem played a significant role in her subsequent improvement and departure from the hospital.

I felt that this dramatic shift in patient behavior was attributable to the change in her immediate social field and supported the hypotheses that I had advanced. I set about trying to confirm or disconfirm my convictions on this score. The following events reinforced my belief in the validity of the hypothesis:

1. *The patient's statement.* Sometime after the situation had been resolved, I talked with the patient about it and asked her what she felt had helped her. She said, quite convincingly, that Miss Smith's helping her to eat had contributed considerably to her ability to overcome her inability to eat. She felt that nobody had really cared for her when they would not tell her what to do and that they indicated their concern and care when they finally helped her to do what was necessary.

2. *Proximity in time.* The patient's pattern of indecisiveness was eliminated in about a week after the intervention was crystallized and carried out.

3. *Repeated small-scale interventions.* During the course of the third week it became obvious to me that when the patient was fed and helped to perform, her indecisiveness and desperation diminished; and, when she was not, it increased.

4. *Repetition of the situation.* Some six months later when new personnel came on the ward, they started Miss Bates with the "analytic approach." During this time the patient again became indecisive and overtly disturbed. We intervened by telling these personnel about our

previous experience and by asking them to use the "practical approach." They did, and the indecision disappeared.

5. *Lack of change in therapeutic hours.* When the patient's therapist was asked about her therapeutic hours, he indicated that the patient was having a difficult time communicating with him and that nothing of significance had happened in the therapy that might account for a change in the patient.

6. *Consensus on intervention.* There was consensus among personnel that the intervention was a significant variable in altering the patient's behavior.

It might be useful to summarize the sequence of events described above:

1. A patient's pattern of behavior was identified as disturbing and undesirable.

2. The multiple processes that characterize the patient's social field were carefully observed and analyzed.

3. Interlocking and successive types of patterned social processes were hypothesized to be significant in eliciting, continuing or reinforcing the patient's behavior.

4. A mode of intervention was projected on the basis of the analysis and hypotheses.

5. Mechanisms for instituting the projected changes were developed.

6. The investigator used his influence with the ward authorities to ensure the carrying out of the intervention.

7. The processes and consequences of intervention were observed.

8. Data were gathered subsequent to the intervention on the basis of which it was concluded that the formulated hypotheses were supported.

What can be said in a general way about this kind of action research as a mode of sociological endeavor? It seems to me that the chances are good that combining action and research will lead to fruitful consequences. Action can lead to new insights, understandings, and hypotheses about human behavior. For in initiating action on the basis of one's analyses one might uncover phenomena previously unrevealed and see connections heretofore not seen. In addition, action can provide support or lack of support for our hypotheses. For in committing oneself to a course of action on the basis of formulated hypotheses we have the opportunity to verify, if only in a rough way, the relevance and accuracy of our interpretations. In turn, research might inform the action one undertakes and hopefully increase the probability of success.

Finally, for those of us who feel it is important for the sociologist to confront and deal with the values woven into the social phenomena we study, action research permits us to make a direct contribution to organizational goals and social ends we value.

Group dynamics is a promising educational technique currently earning considerable use in various mental health efforts; e.g., family and individual therapy, marriage counseling, delinquent reform, and mental hospital work. A major variant with a large sociological component, "sensitivity training," is especially popular in industrial training programs. It is discussed below in terms of a novel and exciting effort to emphasize the personality's constructive or "self-actualizing" processes as contrasted with its pathologic or growth-resistive processes. The authors, Dr. Robert Tannenbaum and Dr. J. F. T. Bugental, a sociologist and a psychologist, report a "feeling of progress" in their pioneering effort to make reasonably healthy individuals develop their potentialities still further. Their work is in itself a healthy antidote to our too narrow preoccupation as action sociologists with status quo-oriented reforms. It is time, for example, that we go beyond our conventional expectations of mental health to systematically explore new and untapped possibilities in our personal growth.

SENSITIVITY TRAINING AND BEING MOTIVATION*

J. F. T. Bugental and Robert Tannenbaum

"SENSITIVITY training" is a name often applied to programs in which personal experience in a group is used to aid individuals in becoming more aware of themselves and of the manner in which they affect others and in turn are affected by others. Such programs are conducted in a variety of settings, most notably at the National Training Laboratories[1] at Bethel, Maine; the Western Training Laboratory at Lake Arrowhead, California; and in various other regional and organizational laboratories. At the University of California, Los Angeles, the Twenty-Third Workshop on Sensitivity Training[2] was conducted in the fall of 1962 under

---

*The essay is reprinted with permission of the authors and the *Journal of Humanistic Psychology*, from the issue of Spring, 1963.

[1] National Training Laboratory in Group Development. *Explorations in Human Relations Training: An Assessment of Experience, 1947-1953.* (Washington, D.C.: National Education Association, 1953).

[2] A. Macleod, "Sensitivity Training for Managers," *Empire*, April, 1959, pp. 2, 12 ff.

the auspices of the Institute of Industrial Relations and Graduate School of Business Administration.

Typically a sensitivity-training group consists of fourteen to sixteen participants and one or two staff members (called "trainers"). In the UCLA format, the groups begin with a weekend residential program held at some place where a degree of isolation from everyday concerns and distractions is possible. Subsequently the groups meet weekly for nine late afternoon and evening sessions, including dinner. About half to two-thirds of the way through these nine weeks, a Saturday session of some six hours is scheduled. In all, the groups will thus have about 50 hours of scheduled meeting time, with another 30 or more hours of informal association at meals, coffee breaks, etc.

The participants consist chiefly of mature people in managerial, community, and professional fields. They come to the program after hearing of it from former trainees or from public announcement, or they are encouraged to attend by their employers. A proportion receive some or complete financial support from their employers.

Although trainer philosophies, procedures, and styles are varied, in general certain commonalities are identifiable.[3,4] Usually the trainer refuses to act as a traditional teacher or group leader, implicitly—and often explicitly—conveying to the group that it will have major responsibility in determining the nature and direction of its own activity. Early in a group's life, trainers try to focus participants' attention on and clarify the process—as opposed to the content—aspects of the group's activities. They may call the group's attention to power struggles among the participants, to rivalries of subgroupings, to blocks and aids to free and open communication. Trainers often watch for opportunities to point out common human experiences to reduce feelings of isolation and difference, to demonstrate handicapping and false standards (e.g., "a real man doesn't feel or show tender emotions"). By making an observation or providing personal feedback to an individual, they help him see aspects of himself of which he is typically unaware. On occasion they may aid a participant who has difficulty being heard or understood, support another who is being made too uncomfortable, or display to the group some persistent theme implicit but unrecognized in the group's discussions. They may propose procedures or tasks which they feel may aid the group in what it is trying to do: e.g., role playing, using a questionnaire or sociometric, having one subgroup observe another and then share its observations and impressions with the observed subgroup. Often the trainers use a brief period before a meeting or occasions during a group session to present conceptual material (a "lecturette") based

---

[3]H. A. Shepard and W. G. Bennis, "A Theory of Training by Group Methods," *Human Relations,* Vol. 9 (1956), pp. 403-14.

[4]I. R. Weschler, R. Tannenbaum, and J. H. Zenger, "Yardsticks for Human Relations Training," *Adult Education Monographs,* No. 2, 1957.

upon and growing out of preceding group experiences. Trainers generally feel that for greatest learning impact, experience should precede the attempt to give it cognitive form.

The group's activity generally moves toward the expression of individuals' perceptions of each other, the revealing and sharing of personal concerns and emotional conflicts, the recognition of commonalities of experience, and the discovery of numerous common difficulties in relating with those encountered in "outside" life.

For some participants (particularly in the early stages of training) the experience is disappointing and frustrating, as they fail to secure the authoritative guidance and "answers" which they seek. A majority, however, find enough stimulation to cause them to persist with varying degrees of involvement and even of enthusiasm. A goodly number seem to value the relative genuineness of relating which develops and which they find contrasts with their usual daily experiences. They increasingly experiment with and begin to find satisfaction in being more open with appropriate expressions of feelings (both positive and negative) in their relations with others, both inside and outside the group. Thus, they report that they are beginning to venture somewhat more in the direction of authenticity in their lives, though the extent to which this generalizes and persists is not known. For a smaller number the sensitivity-training experience seems to have a therapeuticlike outcome, evidenced by definite change in their lives involving greater personal effectiveness, deeper satisfaction, or reduced personal tensions.

The question is frequently asked: How does sensitivity-training differ from group psychotherapy? Suffice it to say here that there is certainly much overlap between the two, but that there are some significant differences also.[5,6] In most instances, sensitivity-training does not inquire into historic roots of behavioral patterns, into the socially taboo areas such as sexuality, or into the realm of the truly unconscious impulses and defenses. It focuses only on matters which can reasonably be dealt with in the relatively brief available time. It is centered much more in the conscious and preconscious and seeks the gains more readily available from insight and corrective emotional or behavioral experiences rather than attempting a genuine "working-through" therapy. In a word, its aim is more re-educative than reconstructive.

Sometimes sensitivity training has been regarded as conformity training. *Time* magazine,[7] in a rather shallow coverage of the program, certainly gave this impression. Actually responsible sensitivity training,

[5]J. F. T. Bugental, "Five Paradigms for Group Psychotherapy," *Psychological Reports*, Vol. 10 (1962), pp. 607-10.

[6]I. R. Weschler, F. Masserik, and R. Tannenbaum, "The Self in Process: A Sensitivity Training Emphasis," in I. R. Weschler and E. H. Schein (eds.), *Issues in Training: Selected Readings, Series Five* (Washington, D.C.: National Training Laboratories, 1962).

[7]"The Blood Bath Cure," *Time*, Dec. 22, 1961, p. 48.

whether conducted at UCLA or at one of the training laboratories across the country, is almost the antithesis of conformity training. The attempt is made to teach the valuing of individual differences, to help the participants learn to use conflict constructively, to develop an appreciation for differing answers to the same question, and to encourage a tolerance for ambiguity and the fundamental unresolvedness of most of the problems which modern man confronts in his interpersonal living. The varied training patterns followed by most of the people conducting sensitivity training militate against a common mold being impressed on each participant.

A SECOND PROGRAM

From the first, participants in sensitivity training have asked for additional related experiences. A variety of formal and informal programs have been attempted to meet the need. A modest but consistent proportion of trainees are known to have entered individual or group therapy of one kind or another. Some groups have been formed on the participants' initiative to carry on after the end of the regular program. Several "advanced" or "continuing" programs have been conducted at the training laboratories. In general, these different programs have tried to continue from the basic model of the original program, with some relatively minor variations.

In the fall of 1961, in a series of joint staff meetings between the U.C.L.A. Human Relations Research Group[8] and the staff of Psychological Service Associates, an effort was made to design a program which would place primary emphasis on the constructive or "self-actuating" processes in the personality as contrasted with the more pathologic or growth-resistive. In general, the orientation parallels the difference Maslow makes between D- (or Deficiency-) motivation and B- (or Being-) motivation.[9] Said differently, much of the typical sensitivity-training program and most of psychotherapy have been concerned with exposing and (hopefully) overcoming those forces within individuals which limit their abilities to realize upon their potentialities fully. The notion upon which plans for a new "continuing sensitivity training" were developed was that it might be possible to aid people already reasonably healthy in their functioning to develop their potentialities more directly. An analogy might clarify this point: It is as though we had traditionally focused our efforts in helping sprinters to run by demonstrating to them how bulky clothing, poor starting posture, and bad breathing habits have slowed them. Now we proposed to concentrate on helping them

---

[8]Institute of Industrial Relations and Graduate School of Business Administration, University of California, Los Angeles.

[9]A. H. Maslow, "Deficiency Motivation and Growth Motivation," in *Toward a Psychology of Being* (Princeton, N.J.: Van Nostrand, 1962).

build stronger leg muscles, gain more spring in their starts, and achieve a better pacing of their energy expenditure. As the analogy should make evident, there was no implication that one approach was superior to the other, only that each deserved attention, and thus far one had tended to outweigh the other.

By late winter of 1962 the joint discussions had progressed to the point where we felt we wanted to try some of our ideas in practice. Accordingly, a group was recruited and the two present writers were designated to serve as its trainers.

A general announcement of the program was sent to participants who had completed sensitivity training at the Western Training Laboratory in recent years, and about 30 applications were received. Selection from these was made in terms of the following statement:

Participant selection. — While ideally the program should seek participants free of psychopathology, this is admittedly unrealistic. Instead, it is desirable to screen candidates to rule out grosser evidences of emotional and social disturbance and then to examine the extent to which each approximates the ideal in the following ways:

1. Functional excellence in
   a. vocation
   b. marriage
   c. friendship relations
2. An observing and curious ego manifesting a desire for further self-exploration and greater self-actualization.
3. Adequate tolerance for psychic stress, e.g., from
   a. ambiguity
   b. intrapsychic conflict
   c. interpersonal conflict
   d. uncertainty and risk
4. Motivation for group interaction.

A group of 12 was chosen, chiefly on the basis of assessments provided by their former trainers, modified by an effort to get heterogeneity related to sex, variety of backgrounds and professions, etc. The group consisted of ten men and two women, with an average age of 44 years. They averaged a little more than 17 years of education, i.e., near the master's level. Eight were married, four widowed or divorced. Four had had psychotherapy, but only one of these had had an intensive experience. Occupationally they were in the professional and managerial ranks, with about an equal number in each.

Some funds for research were available to the Human Relations Research Group, and so Drs. William Broen and Irving Weschler, of U.C.L.A., laid out a program of pre- and post-testing and arranged for observations of all sessions of the group by two graduate students in clinical psychology, Keith A. Druley and Ira A. Nathanson, of the same university.

The schedule for the program was basically the same as that described above for beginning groups. Early in the life of the group, each participant was given a mimeographed statement which read as follows:

HORIZONS LIMITED AND UNLIMITED

Our perspective for Continuing Sensitivity Training is that of gaining an expanded range of possibilities for each of us. It is our conviction that each of us gets embedded in presuppositions about the way each of us is and about the way the world is and that these presuppositions — which may or may not be accurate — serve to delimit our views of what is possible. It has seemed to us, therefore, that a very fundamental mission Continuing Sensitivity Training can perform is to help us develop awareness of and skill in the ways in which we can:

a) discover the presuppositions about our outer and inner worlds within which we tend to limit our operations,

b) test those presuppositions to see whether they are indeed intrinsic, necessary, and reality-founded,

c) evaluate those which are not intrinsic to determine whether they serve us usefully or not, and

d) try out setting aside those limitations which we find to be neither intrinsic nor useful; i.e., operate in new and freer ways.

A second part of our (the trainers') perspective for Continuing Sensitivity Training grows out of the manner in which you have been selected for this group: insofar as possible, each of you is deemed to be a person of reasonable maturity, personal and social effectiveness, and possessed of some degree of creativeness. (It is recognized that each of us — group members and trainers alike — is far from the ultimate or even the optimum in each of these ways. Nevertheless, it is reasonably certain that each of us has these qualities in some measure — no matter how much we may each recognize the ways in which we do not manifest them.)

From the composition of our group, then, grows the second hypothesis about how we may best serve each other. This takes the following form: We are of the opinion that the pooled motivations and the combined creativities of all of us can best be consulted to guide us in the sorts of activities we want to undertake at any particular point in the life of our group. We, the trainers, do not feel that we have the wisdom or the experience to predetermine what sort of procedure will best serve the group on the third or eleventh or any other particular session.

This is not to say that we have no ideas about activities in which we might usefully engage. We do. But we invite — more, we recognize the implicit necessity of — the group to take a mature role in determining its own life. To this end, we have brought together in these materials a number of thoughts we have developed about this program — about the kinds of goals or end-products it may hopefully achieve for each of us, about the types of conditions which might facilitate our attainment of the goals, and about some of the forms of group activity which might be used by us to achieve our goals.

In setting these forth in this manner, we must recognize a reality: the group (including the trainers) is responsible for itself, each of us must exercise his personal and joint responsibility if any degree of "self-actualization" is to be achieved. Further, we are approaching a relatively uncharted frontier about which we as yet know little. Thus, we will inevitably extend this list as we exercise our ingenuity in finding further and more effective ways to make the total Continuing Sensitivity Training experience a productive one for each of us.

What has been said so far tends to be cast in terms of overcoming limitations. This effort is certainly worthwhile and one thing we hope this experience can facilitate. However, a third part of our perspective as trainers has to do with our belief that much may be gained from developing the positive, the creative, the "growth edge-ful" in its own right. (Let us hasten to make explicit that we mean neither Coué-ism nor Pollyanna-ism.) To the extent that we can be skillful in recognizng that which is positive, enriching, and meaningful in ourselves and our experiences and to the extent that we can be effective in nurturing and expanding such processes, we are convinced that we shall be forwarding the purposes for which we are all in Continuing Sensitivity Training.

SOME OF OUR HOPES

We hope that this joint venture will help each of us make personal progress along at least the following paths:

— Experiencing personal outcomes in ways we have previously assumed to be unattainable for ourselves.

— Experiencing our relatedness to all men as personally enriching and as potentially enhancing to them and to us.

— Experiencing our individual uniqueness with its potential for personal satisfaction and creativity, and recognizing (but seeking not to be limited by) the fear of being different.

— Being able to distinguish between the realistic limits (both within ourselves and without) on our own functioning and growth and those which are unrealistic (neurotic), and to be able to free ourselves from the latter.

— Being able to recognize and to utilize an increased number of alternatives as we face the omnipresent necessity to make choices.

— Gaining respect for the use of feelings and moods, fantasy and speculation, tenderness and concern, sharing.

SOME POSSIBLE FACILITATING CONDITIONS

We believe that the attitudes which we each bring to the group will be fundamental in determining the degree to which we are able to make of the group an effective tool for our purposes. Some of the attitudes which we feel will be most helpful include:

— Seeking an ever-increasing awareness of one's own feelings at each moment.

— Accepting as fully as possible and assuming responsibility for personal feelings of which we are aware.

— Sharing with the group as much of what we are aware of as may be possible at any point, and constantly striving to increase the degree to which we can so share.

— Being willing constantly to consider and experiment with the feasibility of alternative ideas and methods in order to move toward new possibilities and new experience.

— Being willing to live dangerously — facing the personal risks of satisfaction, success, and adequacy as well as of embarrassment, exposure, and failure.

— Accepting and valuing — for ourselves and others — the realities of being human.

— Being willing to accept our own difficulties in fully being everything implied by the above.

SOME POSSIBLE METHODS OR PROCEDURES

We present the following ideas only as "starters." The range of possibilities available to us is extensive, and many of the most productive ones probably yet remain to be created.

— Using the basic sensitivity training group for the purpose of sharing and exploring, but with an emphasis on the goals of this advanced program.

— Focusing on our hopes and aspirations, and on the means for their realization.

— Making force-field analyses; i.e., examining the facilitating and constraining forces related to possible new behaviors.

— Sharing the existing creative products of our personal lives — paintings, writings, films, designs, pottery, theories, artistry, wood or metal work, sewing and knitting, etc.

— Engaging in spontaneous creative or expressive activity — producing a play, writing poetry, singing, composing a melody, producing a product, painting, conducting an orchestra, etc.

— Confronting existential moments — birth, fear, stress, elation, death, helplessness, success, exhaustion, etc. (arranging for visits or activities to make this possible).

— Utilizing a visiting resource person; e.g., a specialist in dance therapy or an artist.

— Maintaining diaries to capture and preserve our developing experiences and insights.

— Utilizing questionnaires or other instruments to collect relevant data and to provide feedback.

— Utilizing a "what if . . ." technique; i.e., making the assumption that certain usual constraints on one's behavior are not present and experiencing what it might be like if one were able to avoid such constraints.

— Experiencing and conducting experiments in extrasensory perception.

FINDINGS FROM TRIAL PROGRAM

Our experiences in the program cannot be detailed here. Instead we will report some of our tentative learnings about such an enterprise and briefly indicate some next steps. First, we will examine some disappointments:

1. We were much too ambitious in our conceptualization of the program. Although beginnings were made toward our goals, their attainment still remained very distant at the program's conclusion.

2. Our hope to select a group freer than usual of deterrents of psychic disturbance was vain. The group was a fairly typical selection of 12 functional, reasonably socially effective people who nevertheless were beset by a clear range of emotional interferences with their functioning.

3. We, as trainers, were severely handicapped in attempting to give primary emphasis to positive forces in the participants' personalities by our own unresolved neurotic components and by our years of training and experiences which have been largely in the frame of reference of psychopathology and dealing with deficiency motivations. Time and again we found ourselves most active in the familiar ways of pointing to interferences and distortions and least effective in facilitating growth, venturing, and creativity.

4. The participants, as faithful products of their culture and personal histories, seemed more ready to recognize and deal with that which was negative and pathologic within themselves and were unsure and self-conscious about the positive and creative.[10]

On the more encouraging side, several observations may be made:

1. The participants showed a real readiness to adopt a more open approach and thus to experiment with group activities in a way that beginning sensitivity-training groups frequently resist. Moreover, they reported some carry-over of this attitude to their "outside" lives.

2. Some individuals in the group felt they had experienced major insights or changes of outlook which they thought would have profound effects on their lives. For example, one wrote:

For me, the sessions have been the most frightening, frustrating, soul searching, exhilarating, rewarding experiences of my life. I just cannot adequately express my feelings about this. I sincerely believe that these past few weeks have altered the future course of my life. My past efforts in the field of human relations have been directed toward becoming more effective in my relations with other people. While this is a worthy goal, I failed to

---

[10]One may be drawn to speculate how pervasive in all phases of our individual and group living is a whole outlook arising from our centuries of preoccupation with contending with deficiency problems.

realize that I must first learn to get along with myself. I doubt that I will ever be 100% successful in this but I have made a good start.

3. The possibility of using more active participation around projects or procedures was demonstrated as useful but requiring more planning and effective guidance in some instances than we gave to it.

4. One observation, in accord with many made in other settings, was that the relations among pairs of individuals in the group were of especial potency. Similarly, the opportunity for one part of the group to watch another part at work on a problem was frequently highly productive.[11,12]

FOLLOW-UP SESSION

Approximately nine months after the completion of the program, a reunion meeting was held. Ten of the twelve participants returned and told of their experiences in the interim. The most frequent reports were:

1. The experience was remembered with a kind of nostalgia and warmth. Several were very explicit in saying how much they missed having the opportunities for such open communication and genuine acceptance.

2. The most frequently mentioned gain from the program was an increased willingness to experiment in living, to take a chance (interpersonally), to attempt some things which previously one had hesitated about doing because of fears of not being adequate. Some examples offered included making new friendships, expressing opinions in discussions, trying a creative project.

3. Closely linked with the willingness to live more experimentally was a report by several of decreased fears of failure or being different and of performing more spontaneously.

4. About half of the group expressed a feeling of pronounced need for some program which would provide "booster shots" or spaced reinforcements for efforts toward the values implicit in the program. In one way and another it was made clear that to live more in terms of "being motivation" is difficult in our culture and that the participants felt their gains slipping away and old patterns reasserting themselves.

SUMMARY

Sensitivity training is a social vehicle for helping individuals increase

---

[11] J. V. Clark, "Authentic Interaction and Personal Growth in Sensitivity Training Groups," *Journal of Humanistic Psychology*, Vol. 3, No. 1 (Spring, 1963).

[12] R. Tannenbaum and J. F. T. Bugental, "Dyads, Clans, and Tribe: A New Design for Sensitivity Training," *NTL Human Relations Training News* (in press).

their effectiveness in self-fulfillment and in relating to others. Participants in the experience generally find that the more authentic communication, the chance to exchange candid "feedback" with others, and the working out of meaningful relationships are valuable experiences. An effort to develop a program to carry these values further, particularly through emphasizing "being motivation" has been described. The first pilot group carried through this second program seemed to value the experience, but the trainers did not feel that the program was as successful as it can be with further experimentation and refinement. The experience has encouraged a continuation of the joint staff program mentioned above and additional experimental programs in the fall, 1962, and spring, 1963, semesters. Overall, we share a feeling of making progress on a tremendously important and challenging frontier.

■■

Unanticipated consequence" is a classic sociological concept—a favorite of the middle-range theorists. The essay below offers a provocative example of just such a phenomenon—or the unanticipated strengthening of local Midwestern communities in the wake of new federal legislation tying the communities still closer to the government exchequer (and seemingly closer to the various nongovernment organizations that make a business of helping grant-seekers satisfy federal "red-tape" requirements). If the small town is to survive as a proud and autonomous enterprise in a mass society, it will require the kind of effort reported here by Dr. Otto G. Hoiberg, a Nebraskan sociologist. Note especially in evaluating his work the striking similarities that exist between it and the "War on Poverty's" urban effort to "involve the poor" (described later in this volume); in both cases applied sociology is in the forefront. The significance of this rural-based kind of work is very great: as Dr. Hoiberg suggests, "There is nothing more vital to the survival of democratic institutions than the democratic decision-making process, even where this relates to small issues in the small town."

■■

SELF-HELP PLANNING IN SMALL COMMUNITIES

Otto G. Hoiberg

IS IT FEASIBLE and worth the effort for a small community to use the self-help approach in developing a "master plan" under appropriate professional guidance? If so, does a state university have a responsibility to provide such guidance? These questions came abruptly to the fore in Nebraska during 1964 as one small town after the other obtained approval for senior citizens' low-rent housing projects under the Housing and Home Finance Agency (HHFA) program.

In return for federal financial assistance on a project of this type, the HHFA required the local community to draw up an approved workable program for Community Improvement, including a comprehensive plan for guiding future development. Routine procedure was for the local community to retain the services of a firm of professional planning consultants to prepare the comprehensive plan, with federal "701" support for two-thirds of the cost involved. But even the one-third payable by the local community appeared burdensome to a number of smaller towns, and they began to look around for a solution.

It was at this juncture that the problem came to the attention of our Community Development staff in the University of Nebraska's Extension Division. David K. Peterson, a recent graduate in architecture, and a new member of our staff in the University Extension Division, offered a suggestion that these small communities might be able to do their own planning work if we could guide them with a professionally competent hand. We considered it worthy of major effort, and the HHFA gave us an affirmative nod to experiment with municipalities below 1,000 population. We felt that our two-man architect-sociologist team was well adapted to the task at hand, and work was begun without delay on two fronts. In the office we undertook the preparation of a manual for self-help community planning; and in various small towns throughout the state we begun our field work with planning commissions that had requested assistance. Our services were gratis as a phase of the University Extension Division's 16-year-old program of community development, but we required a written statement from the village board in each case whereby it agreed to provide its local planning commission with $300 per year for the planning period to cover mapping, drafting, printing, and other essential costs.

The first obstacle appeared in the form of rumblings from private enterprise where eyebrows were raised at this seeming entry of the university into the "planning business." The need for clarification of this issue became urgent when a private planning firm, having just quoted a price for a comprehensive plan to a certain small community, was informed by the village board that "We're going to hold this over awhile until we see what the university will do it for."

Without delay, we invited the principal private planning consultants operating in Nebraska to attend a session for a discussion of university policy. In the ensuing dialogue we made it clear that the university was not "in business." Our was essentially a program of adult education whereby small communities were enabled to engage in certain self-help planning activites under appropriate educational guidance. This policy orientation was also communicated to small towns throughout the state to forestall any further thoughts of the University Extension Division as an agency which "would come out and do our planning for us."

A few months after the field work was launched, Dave Peterson resigned to accept private employment. He was replaced by Dr. George T. C. Peng, an architect-planner with an ideal background for the task at hand. At this writing, Dr. Peng and I have worked together for about five months. Active self-help comprehensive planning programs are under way in six small towns. The various units of our self-help manual are being completed in time for use by the local planning commissions as needed.

Generally speaking, it is estimated that a two-year period will be required for the development of a comprehensive plan by a small community. In the execution of this program, the local planning commission assumes responsibility for all "leg work" involved in the gathering of essential data; it finances all operations requiring outlay; it conducts discussions and hearings that are essential to the clarification of issues and policy formulation; and it makes all decisions, subject, of course, to ultimate formal approval by the village board (council) under which it serves.

From the university's side, the overall direction of the self-help planning program rests in the hands of our professionally trained planner, Dr. Peng. The design of the entire program is his, and he has established the procedures to be followed. One of his most important tasks is that of helping the planning commission to gain a vision of what their community might become by the year 1980 or 2000 and to show how the facts now being gathered and the planning being done relate to the attainment of this goal.

In this context my role as sociologist is varied and in certain respects must be played by ear. The principal subject areas in which I have been able to contribute are the following:

1. *Basic Sociological Orientation.* While most small towns were relatively independent entities a generation or more ago, they are today becoming integral parts of larger configurations of communities, depending increasingly upon more populous adjoining trade centers for goods and services. Full recognition and understanding of this growing involvement in expanding social systems is essential to effective planning for the future of the small town. A case in point is an attractive village which has lost population steadily during the past 30 years due to the decline in surrounding farm population but which may experience a reversal of this trend as a nearby growing city yields commuter families which prefer the small-town atmosphere.

2. *Socioeconomic Trends.* People in small towns have a fairly good understanding, in a general way, of the trends that are having an impact upon community and family life. To plan intelligently for the future, however, they need more specific and detailed information on many long-term changes including the following: the increasing size of farms and the drop in farm population; mechanization of agriculture; out-migration of youth; school district reorganization; the changing role of government; increasing mobility; shifting age composition; and urbanization of tastes and standards in rural areas.

3. *The Process of Social Change.* The typical planning commission is engaged in a continuing effort to promote, guide, or adjust to social change. To this end they need to understand more fully the processes by which it occurs. What are the factors encouraging change, on the one hand, and inhibiting it, on the other? How, for example, is a new high-

way likely to influence community life, and how should a plan for the community's future take this into account?

4. *Principles of Sound Community Development.* Before embarking upon its comprehensive planning program, one of our six small towns was engaged in a community development program which was, in effect, a one-man show. The dominant figure in this situation had taken an almost possessive pride in doing virtually all of the work and in making decisions for the group while the others went passively along. Involvement of the planning commission as a whole, to say nothing of the community, in the gathering of data and the performance of other essential tasks was lacking. The lesson of cooperative teamwork toward attainment of common goals had to be tactfully taught here to broaden their entire base of operations and to make the decision-making process more democratic. This educational task concerning the principles of sound community development must be performed, in some measure, in all communities and can run the whole gamut of concept, philosophy, organization, procedure, interpersonal relationships, and evaluation.

5. *Group Dynamics.* Situations frequently arise where the sociologist can encourage more effective work in a planning commission by offering helpful suggestions on procedure. Physical arrangements occasionally require attention, as in one situation where several timid or self-conscious members sat at some distance from the table and failed to respond to the chairman's invitation to move closer. In this case I jokingly made reference to "moving the mountain to Mohammed"; and we then picked up the table and moved it and ourselves over to them, thus improving the seating arrangement and breaking the ice at the same time. Other obstacles to effective functioning of the group have included the following: lack of communication among members due to timidity or dominance of certain persons; failure of some to comprehend fully what was being said; and diffuse discussion requiring summarization of points made. With his knowledge of small group dynamics and role theory, a social scientist can do much toward helping a planning commission to conduct more productive meetings.

6. *Survey Procedures.* A small-town planning commission ordinarily needs substantial assistance in relation to methodology and research tools such as questionnaires to be used in gathering sociological data as a foundation for planning. This need extends also to the processing and analysis of data, graphical presentation when necessary, and interpretation of findings.

7. *Resources.* An ever-present responsibility of the university "expert" is to help local citizens increase their awareness of the many resources that are available to them: federal, state, and local; public and private. Such resources would include publications of all kinds, audio-

visual aids, financial assistance, and a wide variety of professional services related directly or indirectly to their planning program.

8. *Leadership.* In the average rural community, the recognized leaders are often used to the point of misuse, and public responsibilities need to be more broadly distributed. Suggestions are always needed whereby latent leadership potentials can be identified and activated. This does not imply a sacrifice in quality of personnel. The success or failure of a planning program depends in large measure upon the type of people serving on the planning commission, and this fact must be clearly understood by the local authorities who appoint them.

9. *Social Cleavages.* In planning desirable changes for the future, a planning commission must be aware of social strata, group cleavages, and power structure within the community. It must have a reasonably adequate understanding of how these relate to social progress and the realization of maximum potentials. The relevance of one facet of this broad sociological phenomenon was brought home to the town members of a planning commission that was discussing the Nebraska statute which gives villages authority to plan and zone an area extending one-half mile beyond their corporate limits. A farmer who was present stated in unmistakable language that he "would take a dim view of the town's planning commission trying to tell me what I can use my land for" in this peripheral zone.

In general, the extension sociologist has responsibility for sensing the developmental pattern of the community and its value system. What is important to the people who live there? What has been accomplished along community lines in years past and how were the results achieved? What are the current positive and negative factors relevant to further progress? With this "feel" of the community in mind, the sociologist draws upon his knowledge of social theory and the findings of pertinent empirical research and translates these into the vernacular for use by the people in their planning and decision-making operations.

A self-help program in comprehensive community planning does not function without complications. In one community, for example, there was a basically faulty orientation to be overcome. The planning commission seemed to feel that its work should be done only to meet a federal requirement, a sort of tit-for-tat arrangement whereby the community agreed to develop a comprehensive plan in return for federal aid in obtaining low-rent housing for the elderly. This attitude, of course, defeats the whole purpose of a comprehensive plan. In the first place, it leads to efforts to "beat the game" by doing everything according to minimal standards; and second, upon completion of the plan, the community is likely to regard it as a dead letter because they had never really intended to use it anyway. Where this attitude has been in evidence, we have made an extra effort to show the planning commission that their planning program can stand on its own merits and that its potential bene-fits to the community extend far beyond the housing project concerned.

A second hazard lies in the temptation revealed by some planning commission members to seek involvement of their university consultants in the decision-making process. We are, of course, involved but only as resource persons. If we were to go beyond the latter role, the decisions probably would (and should) ultimately be rejected by the community as "the work of outsiders"; but, even more important, we would be guilty of making decisions for them, thereby weakening rather than strength-ening the foundation of democratic action in the local community. There is nothing more vital to the survival of democratic institutions than the democratic decision-making process, even where this relates to small issues in the small town.

A further complicating factor in a self-help planning process lies in the ebb and flow of enthusiasm for the work to be done. For the most part, we have found among planning commission members a sustained, aggressive determination which leads to steady progress, but in certain instances there has been too much reliance upon "the spirit" to move them.

In addition, the effective functioning of planning commissions has at times been impaired by poor attendance at local meetings due to the difficulty of finding open dates for such meetings. A certain inviolable routine or group loyalty seems inherent in bowling and other team rec-reational activities, for example, making absence to attend community meetings of any kind unthinkable. (I might add that this is hardly peculiar to the small town.)

Inadequate communication between related community organizations has occasionally also been a problem. It is widely believed that every-body knows everything about everybody else in the small town, but this is certainly an overstatement. Contacts may be personal and frequent, but this does not necessarily mean that essential information flows. In one instance there was virtually no effective communication between the local housing authority and the planning commission, and this situ-ation was aggravated by confusion as to the relative roles of these two agencies, both of which were involved in the federal low-rent housing program. Generally speaking, the planning commission should maintain liaison with all local organizations that are actively interested in com-munity affairs.

Despite problems and complications such as those described briefly above, the self-help comprehensive planning program is progressing favorably and on schedule. The planning commissions are viewing their tasks in proper perspective, and their approach is characterized generally by enthusiasm, determination, common sense, and a positive interest in the future of their respective communities. Although a comprehensive plan developed in this manner by a small town may be somewhat less pol-ished than one that could have been produced by a firm of professional planning consultants, the plan is *theirs* in a very unique sense. As one local resident put it: "This is a lot of work, but we're sure learning something about our community!"

In conclusion, let me propose a short prayer for the extension sociologist: "Lead me not into temptation . . . to manipulate people for quick results at the expense of educating for community development."

The community research and guidance work of Dr. Ritchie P. Lowry is unusual in several respects: He attributes a significant role in its origin to his own students, a group sufficiently serious in their interest to join him as associates in the ensuing field project. He frankly recalls stumbling upon the problem (a "hidden" slum) and inviting himself to undertake remedial action. He explores quite delicate questions of strategy in research scope and findings. He calmly reports the necessity of working as long as six years in one community to secure desired results; and he anticipates likely criticism of the decision made by the Lowrys (husband and wife) to play active mediating roles in several controversial community issues. With considerable success Dr. Lowry challenges the truthfulness (and usefulness) of the so-called social science search for abstract truth and amoral reality; with considerable novelty and boldness he claims instead that their "very ability to play moral and political roles provides social researchers with a device and a strength that other scientists do not possess." Evaluate the work of the Lowrys against this claim—particularly their welcomed refinement of Merton's classic distinction between Locals and Cosmopolitans—then judge for yourself whether or not it holds up.

INFLUENCING LEADERSHIP IN COMMUNITY STUDIES:
MORAL AND POLITICAL ROLES OF THE SOCIAL SCIENTIST

Ritchie P. Lowry

SOCIOLOGY, and, for that matter, most of social research, is a moral and political science. It is moral in the sense that the primary datum is man—the moral animal—and, in dealing with and studying man, the social scientist cannot avoid moral judgments. At every step in his research the scientist must make judgments of value. Furthermore, sociology is political insofar as it is oriented to action. The potential applied aspects of sociological knowledge demand that researchers constantly take into account the possible perceptions and inclinations of the users of the knowledge.

Certainly, to an extent, other "sciences" share these characteristics.

Fields like medicine, genetics, and psychiatry have long recognized the unique marginal role of the practitioner as lying somewhere between the abstract, unbiased, and unemotionally rational scientist and the deeply empathic, morally concerned critic, consultant, and interviewer. Interestingly enough, only recently have sociologists become overtly and publicly aware of their dual role in modern society as scientist and social consultant.

What I am implying is that for the modern sociologist the idealized fiction of the scientist as a value-free seeker of abstract truth and amoral reality will simply not work. First, many have questioned whether this fiction has even been true for any social or physical science.[1] This very volume of Dr. Shostak's is a testament to those doubts. Second, the social scientist's universe of analysis does not consist of value-free and amoral beings. Human beings simply do not rigidly follow the laws of chance and probability as if free of a world of beliefs, ideas, and biases. Third, the social researcher himself is a part of the very universe that he analyzes, and his act of analysis intimately influences the environment, including the outcome of his analysis. This listing of the dimensions and context of social research which make the sociologist's "scientific" role somewhat unique could be extended at great length. However, it is not my purpose in this short essay to cover all aspects of this problem, something which has been done extensively and perceptively by previous writers.

What I would like to do is concentrate upon, and give several examples of, two aspects of the moral and political role of sociologists which have not received great special attention. First, despite general unawareness of the fact, nowhere is this role more evident than in the field of community studies. Even the most scientific study of a community, once reported, becomes a public criticism of contemporary community life. Moral judgments are at the very least implicit about the role of the community in the context of a larger set of social and cultural values and beliefs. Therefore, the community researcher must and does constantly address the major value problems of our society. Second, and most important, techniques for accomplishing both applied and methodological research aims can be developed and employed for scientific studies of community life, which, by taking into account moral and political problems, provide information not otherwise attainable. In other words, by adhering too strictly to the idealized role of the scientist a community researcher may severely limit his ability to perform that very

---

[1]This question has been discussed at length, of course, in the following kinds of publications: Alvin W. Gouldner, "Anti-Minotaur: The Myth of a Value-Free Sociology," in Irving Louis Horowitz (ed.), *The New Sociology* (New York: Oxford University Press, 1964), pp. 196-217; George A. Lundberg, *Can Science Save Us?* (New York: Longmans, Green and Co., 1959); C. Wright Mills, *The Sociological Imagination* (New York: Oxford University Press, 1959); T. C. Schelling, "Strategic Analysis and Social Problems," *Social Problems*, Vol. 12 (Spring, 1965), pp. 367-79.

role. This is a function of both the nature of the social universe which is being studied and the researcher's relationship to that universe. Thus the latent consequences of acting effectively as a pure scientist may be an attenuation and weakening of the scientific role.

Let me examine these points in more detail and illustrate what I mean by drawing from a recently completed community study of mine. This five-to-six year analysis of a rapidly changing small community was concerned with leadership problems at the grass roots in contemporary America.[2] As a part of this general focus, I was concerned not only with describing and depicting leadership interaction and structure but also with influencing the community's leaders to bring about a more effective response to an increasing number of daily problems and challenges. My role, then, was clearly moral and political in addition to being scientific.

THE MORAL ROLE IN COMMUNITY STUDIES

Early in the research it became necessary for me to take into account the relationship between my scientific role and my moral role. Part of my study concerned itself with an analysis of local social problems and the impact these problems had upon community leadership—that is, the extent to which community leaders were aware of crucial problems and responded adequately. It was apparent without seaching analysis that many problems were of such a sensitive and unpleasant nature that community leaders not only did not respond, but acted as though the condition or situation did not exist.

In Micro City such a problem involved the existence of a small, but extremely poor Negro slum. It lay just outside the city limits and bordered upstream on a major creek running through the heart of the town. During the winter months the water in the creek frequently undermined the banks causing open privies to tumble into the creek. As a consequence, several years before Micro City had been designated as a "potential typhus" area by state public health officials. In spite of this, the newcomer to town had long been proudly told "our city has no slum, no race tensions, or any of the other typical urban problems."

One day, I discovered the Negro slum almost by accident. Upon moving to Micro City I purchased an older home and, with my family, set about remodeling it. While taking debris to the city dump, I came upon the slum unexpectedly (it bordered both sides of the highway for about three or four blocks). The majority of the residents were obviously nonwhite and appeared predominantly Negro. When I later told a group of my students at the state college of the experience, I was immediately pressed by some of the students to do a study of the area. Of such random experiences is social research made!

---

[2]Ritchie P. Lowry, *Who's Running This Town?* (New York: Harper & Row, 1965).

The Micro City Study Group which I later helped to form consisted of ten students and myself. Our immediate purpose was to do a study of the Negro slum area I had stumbled upon and to present these findings to community leaders to show that our "fair city" did, indeed, have many typical urban problems. However, we were also especially anxious to execute and produce the study in such a way that it would put maximum pressure on Micro City's leaders to take effective action. This, at first, seemed to constitute a problem, since we were disclosing an unpleasant situation which openly contradicted many of the sacred myths of community residents. In addition, we fully anticipated the terms "slum" and "race" would elicit negative responses from many.

As a result, we decided upon two special research tactics—decisions which were at the outset more moral than they were scientific in nature. First, we formulated and used as working hypotheses a set of stereotyped explanations of why people live in slums (e.g., only Negroes and other minorities are involved; those people are all transients; they can't afford any better; they are basically no good). The idea here was to strike a happy balance between a fairly rigid and unemotional adherence to the scientific method and to develop a final report which could openly address all the rationalizations and excuses we fully expected to receive.

We then carefully inspected the slum area and surrounding region by foot and automobile. All residents were nonwhite; every home could be classified as a "shack"; open privies and outside faucets were the only apparent facilities available. Surrounding this four block "core" area was another region about two to three blocks in depth, and obviously in transition. Here the residents were largely white; shacks and some rather expensive homes existed side by side; land use and condition varied enormously. We knew there would be much support for our study in this second area as the property of the residents was obviously being adversely affected by the neighboring slum.

We knew also that to include this larger area in our sample of households would bias our results. We would lower the percentage of nonwhites in slum and nonslum housing; we would raise the income level and estimated value of property; we would probably raise the percentage of homeowners and nontransients. Nevertheless, the decision was made on both scientific and moral goals to include the second region. Scientifically, we could represent the findings as a study of a slum and the surrounding zone in transition (relating this to theories by Burgess and others.)[3] More importantly, our initial hypotheses would not, then, tend to support the popular stereotypes. By including, for example, only the Negro slum we would have no white slum dwellers in our sample. It would be an easy matter for community leaders and citizens to explain away the findings. It would also be an easy matter for the Micro City

---

[3] See Chauncy D. Harris and Edward L. Ullman, "The Nature of Cities," *Annals of the American Academy of Political and Social Science,* Vol. 242 (November 1945), p. 12.

boosters to continue to ignore the major problem, which certainly was having a detrimental effect on many residents, regardless of race, home-ownership, length of residence, etc.

When the study was completed our study group was able to show not only Negroes were involved; many Negro and white residents of slum shacks could afford better in terms of income; many residents in the area of transition who were white had a very substantial income and yet were adversely affected by the slum; and many residents of the two areas were not merely transients (farm laborers, migrants stopping for a short while, etc.). These findings received wide attention in Micro City and in the nearby urban press. The conscience of the community was directed toward the problem and shortly thereafter a one-and-a-half mil-lion dollar 100-unit low-rent housing project was initiated to replace slum dwellings in five separate areas of the city. It is doubtful the same results could have been achieved had we been content merely to study the well-defined Negro slum using a rigid application of the scientific method in terms of framing hypotheses and selecting our study area. Yet, within the larger area studied, we were able to apply the standards of scientific research by selecting our households for interviews on a ran-dom probability basis, by testing specific hypotheses relating to slum residence, and by presenting community leaders with definitive vital sta-tistics upon which they could formulate effective policy (for example, showing that residents of the area could afford somewhat higher rents for adequate low-rent housing units).

THE POLITICAL ROLE

The illustration of the political role of the community researcher which I will use involves our influencing community leaders to respond in par-ticular ways during the course of our research. This strategy was em-ployed toward the end of the six-year study to test in the field certain theories I have long had about types of interaction between groups of leaders.

As a guiding framework for analyzing Micro City's leadership struc-ture, Robert Merton's classic distinction between Local and Cosmo-politan leaders was employed from the outset of the study. Data were collected on such descriptive variables as years of residence in the com-munity, city and region of birth, age, occupation, and memberships and positions held in community, regional, and national organizations. In addition, through observation of community leaders responding to local problems and issues (a freeway dispute, right-wing charges of subversive activities, a civil defense evacuation exercise dispute, etc.), and by use of extensive interviews with a selected sample of 78 key leaders, infor-mation was collected on attitudes toward community problems and gen-eral sociopolitical ideology. These data were initially collated by using Merton's dichotomous types.

In doing this, we discovered that many leaders did not adequately lend themselves to such a simplistic categorization.[4] Some displayed local attitudes and beliefs (generally conservative in social and political orientation) even while exhibiting cosmopolitan behavior in terms of group memberships. The reverse was also true. Furthermore, a sizable number of leaders seemed to overlap the two categories (in terms of group membership, for example), falling somewhere between Merton's types (in terms of age or length of residence in Micro City) and acting quite differently in specific situations of community crisis than either typical Locals or Cosmopolitans. It was apparent that a new conceptualization was needed, and, as a result, I devised the concept of "mediating leaders."

Mediators were so termed because they were polymorphic, possessing overlapping memberships and informal relationships in both local and cosmopolitan groups. In contrast to both Locals and Cosmopolitans they came from a diversity of occupational fields, all of which, however, provided them with a common orientation—an interest in larger social processes and their implications for the local community. Through key mediating leaders extreme and opposing ideology groups in Micro City could confront one another directly and intimately. Without the channel of the mediating leaders, interaction between leadership groups became personalized, hostile, and negative, resulting in alienation of interest groups throughout the community. Mediators also provided effective leadership for the formation and maintenance of a multitude of mediating groups. These groups were absolutely necessary to the sustaining of a daily democratic political context, where community attention was vigorously focused upon current problems and a variety of opinions could be adequately expressed.

Though this theory of the dynamics of effective grass-roots democracy in Micro City was obtained through logical analysis of empirical data on community leaders, the concepts of mediating leaders and mediating leadership still needed to be verified by observation of specific situations of community interaction. It would, of course, have been possible to wait for the next community crisis in the hopes of observing such leadership patterns. However, this procedure was discarded for several reasons. First, there was no guarantee that the next community crisis would be soon forthcoming, and, whereas researchers have waited for disasters in order to study collective behavior in a "laboratory" setting, such waits can entail long delays in the completion of the project. Second, and much more important, there was no guarantee that effective mediating leadership would be evident in the next community crisis. As a matter of fact, previous observation of community issues disclosed that ineffective, alienated, and hostile leadership patterns were the typical response in Micro City.

---

[4]See Lowry's "Mediating Leadership and Community Interaction," in Alvin W. Gouldner and S. M. Miller (eds.), *Applied Sociology: Opportunities and Problems* (New York: The Free Press of Glencoe, Inc., 1965), pp. 226-36.

For these reasons, my wife and I decided to play active mediating roles in the next several community issues that arose, and, in this manner, to observe (1) whether or not the theory of mediating leadership was valid and (2) the responses of other community groups to such a role. Two such issues were a dispute over maintenance of a childrens' playground in downtown Micro City and an attempt to revitalize a previously inactive Micro City Community Council. In the first issue my wife mediated between Locals who wished to preserve the playground and a downtown business group that wanted to change the property's use and financial support. In the second issue, I mediated between a group of Micro City's state college professors who wanted the Community Council to play a controversial and professional role in community issues and the Micro City service organization members who favored a more perfunctory and noncontroversial role for the council.

The information that my wife and I obtained from our successes and failures was invaluable in refining our notions of the origin, dynamics, and consequences of mediating leadership. We brought back personal and intimate human information that could not have been obtained by traditional techniques of observation. At the same time, we both played practical political roles in the community's daily life. Such "observer participation" also allowed us to obtain information free of the formal restrictions of confidence and anonymity involved in typical interview techniques.

Naturally, the major academic charge that can be made in using such a technique is one of bias (personalized interpretation of events) and deliberate manipulation of the situation. To be sure, we both favored specific outcomes in each issue, and our preferences no doubt made impersonal analysis more difficult. My wife found herself more in sympathy with the arguments of the Locals; I found myself favoring the position of the college professors.

Yet it is the argument of this paper that the overscientific conception of impartiality and complete objectivity is a fiction in community studies. First, human beings are able to play multiple roles simultaneously. My wife and I were being activists and observers at the same time. Second, observing our own actions in these situations was technically no different than observing the actions of someone else. Others playing the same role would also have had personal preferences for specific outcomes of the events. Finally, it should be recalled that I had originally decided to do the Micro City study precisely because I felt major value problems were involved—basically, the issue of ineffective, weak, and negative leadership in grass-roots America.

From the start, then, my interests in our Micro City study were moral and political. To abdicate moral and political roles while doing research would be simply to deny myself information and a depth of understanding crucial to the findings. In other words, to understand fully the concept of mediating leadership I felt one must take and play, as well as observe the role. As a matter of fact, this very ability to play moral and political roles provides social researchers with a device and a strength that other scientists do not possess.

There is evidence today of a healthy official interest in a new balance between municipal physical and social planning. While physical planners continue to dominate most American urban renewal programs, increasing attention is being paid to the sociological and social-psychological dimensions of city planning. It is seldom easy, however, to redress a serious imbalance, as is made plain in the following account of an unsuccessful effort to "sell" the leaders of a disaster-struck city on an intelligent new master plan. Fortunately, much can be learned from the Anchorage "failure," much of use in either disaster work (pre-and postdisaster maneuvers) or in city planning. Mr. Jerome R. Saroff's discussion of "government by technicians," along with his insights into the strategic role of the local influentials, can profitably serve those who would have sociology play a larger and more successful role in disaster studies and in urban social planning.

SOCIOLOGY IN THE RECONSTRUCTION OF ANCHORAGE, ALASKA: A MISSING FACTOR

Jerome R. Saroff

A DECADE ago the term "sociology of disaster" would have left many sociologists unclear as to precisely what it implied. Today, it is a recognized and growing area of sociology deserving serious attention. This essay deals with a specific case study of disaster—Anchorage, Alaska—viewed through the prism of a city planner (with a sociological background) actually involved in postdisaster planning.

Repeated natural disasters, often striking at specific areas with predictable frequency, have stimulated disaster research. In the United States alone, the incidence of destruction in the tornado belt or flooding in the great river valley basins, with their aftermath of physical damage and human suffering and dislocation, has generated a significant demand for disaster research. The federal government, of course, has a substantial interest in disaster research as it increasingly stands the bill for disaster reconstruction and wants some assurance that the money and effort it expends will not be wasted.

The sociology of disaster is still in the stage of development where the collection of information is its major concern, and much of existing disaster literature is essentially descriptive rather than analytic. Nevertheless, even present-day disaster studies can have great practical significance, for communities can learn how to cope better with a disaster on the basis of other communities' reactions, and their success (or failure). Having a description of what to expect if a disaster strikes *can* help a community preplan, anticipate, and mitigate some of the effects.

Government by Technician

Before proceeding to analyze my personal experience as a city planner in a postdisaster situation, I would like to offer one stage-setting example of the kind of disaster occurrence sociologists can forecast.

The literature of disaster is replete with accounts of the "convergence syndrome" in the wake of disaster. This is the tendency of loved ones, charitable organizations, government aid, and the mass media to impose themselves on an area after a disaster with emergency aid, personnel, messages, etc. One class of "convergers" worthy of particular attention consists of engineers, planners, sanitarians, and an assortment of personnel preoccupied with immediate rehabilitation of essential facilities and elimination of major physical hazards.

What makes this category of rescue workers especially unique is that they stay not merely through the immediate post-trauma period but often for weeks and even months. Perhaps because of the unusual physical damage caused by the quake, the weakening of what were literally the underpinnings of the Anchorage downtown, and the need to construct engineering works of a size previously unknown to eliminate soil instability, this phenomenon became exceedingly clear. It was the ascent of the technician-professional to the point where he became almost coequal to the local officials and influentials in the decision-making process. Particularly in the several months after the disaster there was a shift in power—not perceived as such in Anchorage itself, but real nonetheless—a shift in power over to these technicians, both local and (in particular) imported. Such a shift is predictable from previous disaster studies by sociologists, and, as such, should be considered in every community's master plan of adaptation to disaster.

Rehabilitating Anchorage: A Case Study

To turn now to a more personal account, I propose here to analyze the outcome of an attempt by my associates and me to win approval of a new master plan for a disaster-struck city—and to demonstrate through this unhappy experience of ours the considerable limits that remain on social action even when to be forewarned means to be forearmed.

The Political Setting

To understand most of the problems created by the disaster in Anchorage, we must first grasp the political and sociological milieu which existed before the March 27 earthquake.

Anchorage has a council-manager form of government which theoretically vests all administrative and managerial responsibility in a professionally trained government administrator, the city manager. Municipal elections are nonpartisan, political organizations do not effectively operate on the local level, and councilmen are amateurs in government who run as individuals. The council is basically a body of equals with a mayor as only first among equals. Before the earthquake the City Council and the city manager were attempting to run a tidy "housekeeping" operation. Emphasis in government was on efficiency in operation, and even before the quake it was apparent that council had great difficulty in arriving at basic policy decisions if there was even the slightest controversy about them.

Group Interaction in the Political Scene

There is a basic phenomenon which has long existed in Anchorage: this is a conscious and divisive awareness of two separate groups in the population. The first is comprised of "insiders," long-term Alaskans. Much of the administrative and political elite and the business community are part of this group. The second group is comprised of "Cheechakos," or "outsiders," and it takes in the military population, the transients, and the Alaskans of under five years' residency. This second group, which comprises about three-quarters of the population, nevertheless has had little voice in the operation of the city, due basically to its transiency. Unlike most other transient populations the Alaskan outsiders do not have the illusion they may become permanent, and they are uninterested in the local government. Nowhere else perhaps is the classical concept of in-group and out-group more applicable.

An awareness of the community's division and the resultant existence of these two groups is crucial to an understanding of the problems growing out of the earthquake. Anchorage old-timers have always been skeptical of advice from outside professionals. Pride in their role as pioneers has often led them to reject suggestions of others who allegedly "don't know Alaska" and "haven't first-hand knowledge of our problem." On this basis, technical advice on economic, agricultural, or physical development has been frequently rejected by all levels of Anchorage government. Significantly, the group of newer citizens, or "outsiders," has never been interested, cohesive, or vocal enough to counteract this situation.

At the time of the March 27, Good Friday earthquake in 1964, Anchorage was Alaska's largest city and actually the only cluster of population worthy of such a designation. It had exploded from 10,000 people in 1950 to 50,000 in 1964. Massive growth (and prosperity) brought many changes to the city of Anchorage which had existed before the boom. But one thing did not change: those groups and individuals who were settled in Anchorage before such growth remained there. The insiders ruled Anchorage when it was a city of 10,000, and the insiders continued to do so when the figure was 50,000.

Reconstruction

Anchorage was hit hard by the quake, although much less so, relative to its size and resources, than some Alaskan communities. Aside from the loss of many homes and businesses as a result of earth slides in two different locations, the major damage was to streets, sewers, and water lines.

The significant characteristic of the emergency phase of Anchorage's rehabilitation was that it was almost reflexive. In most cases the job to be done defined itself. Repair of broken water lines or of a damaged power generator, etc., did not require major policy decisions and hardly even major internal decisions; in effect, an alternative did not exist. It was not debatable.

For example, the actual direction and work of rehabilitation in Anchorage was largely carried out by technicians of the Public Works Department, Municipal Light and Power, and Municipal Telephone Department. In less than an hour after the 1964 Good Friday quake had devastated half the city, men had reported for work, and engineers and other technicians were going about the actual business of rehabilitation: repair of broken water and gas mains, bulldozing of roads, emergency generation of power and heat. Forty-eight hours after the quake, power was restored to most of the city; within three to four days most areas had gas heat. These activities did *not* take place at the direction of the elected representatives, and only indirectly at the behest of the city manager. Anchorage had government by technician. Council sat almost every night, but only to ratify, only to dispose.

The second phase, however, that of reconstruction, was not a self-executing operation, as there existed real alternative paths of action.

It was apparent to geologists and planners that the quake had done much more than create great surface damage. The earthquake demonstrated that the city's central business district was perched on the edge of a potential earth slide area. The stability of the soil in the downtown was dependent on experiences of minor earthquakes only. Major quakes could create hazardous earth slides; and Alaska is located in one of the zones of highest seismic activity in the world.

Public safety demanded at least a partial shift of the business district from its prequake location. From the standpoint of physical and social planning, the quake appeared to create such a discontinuity with the past that it seemed possible to look at the downtown afresh. It seemed to those of us in the City Planning Department that circumstances had made possible creation of a radically different downtown, a more efficient, beautiful, and functional downtown. Our premise was that the *status quo* had been greatly altered, a fluid situation now existed, and this circumstance could be exploited if someone (us) presented an imaginative and well-conceived course of action: a downtown master plan.

This brought us to a general and basic problem which concerns all practicing community planners: how does one arrive at a sound and acceptable master plan? In the normal course of master planning, we seek to ascertain and formulate community goals on which to base future and, hopefully, improved development. Generally, this nearly always involves contact, discussion, and agreement with political leaders as well as with panels of "influentials" (downtown property owners, etc.). These citizens help us, albeit in self-serving ways, to translate some more general goals into operational specifics. This process of goal formulation and eventual consensus almost always receives extensive coverage by the news media, an additional shaping process.

The foregoing plan is one carried out with varying degrees of sophistication, intensity, and, one might add, with varying degrees of success. Regarding the latter, observers have extensive documentation of the low rate of effectuation of master plans. Even when acutely aware of the need for support of the political power structure, various interest groups, and the general citizenry, community planners nevertheless seem unable to achieve substantial realization of their plans.

In Anchorage, the situation was even more complicated than usual. The need for a downtown master plan was urgent. Within weeks after the quake, preliminary engineering-geologic information indicated that reoccupancy of the prequake business district was undesirable if not downright hazardous, as the district was vulnerable to future sliding. But already there were businessmen anxious to rebuild in the hazard zones.

There was actually no time for those of us involved in the process to seek out a group of influentials with which to trade views. Even though, as social scientists, we may have realized the power-political considerations, we were, as city employees, too busy with the technical aspects of the new plan to do much else. Thus, the combination of the lack of adequate interaction between the planners and the power structure during the planning process, the radical change proposed, and the feverish desire of Anchorage to rebuild without delay really sentenced the plan to limbo from the very beginning.

Three months after the quake the downtown master plan was produced. It was presented to the City Council and they were momentarily enthusiastic (as we later found out). Then, purported influentials (bankers, leading businessmen, downtown property owners, the Chamber of Commerce, etc.) were shown the plan, scale model and all. Its economic, functional, traffic, esthetic, and sociological advantages were glowingly elaborated. The reception, however, was highly variable even though one of the authors of the plan was a leading local architect with entree into allegedly influential circles. The net result of the presentation of the plan was that it was simply ignored—not fought, or assailed, or cursed, but simply ignored.

The interesting question that remains is "why?"

As a sociologist I have concluded that we simply failed to evaluate the sociological situation accurately, and the earthquake, rather than loosening the *status quo,* actually made it seem all the more desirable: anything that promised still more change in the wake of the quake was doomed. (Experience with other disaster communities indicates that the desire to rebuild as before, in locations of known hazard, is not uncommon. The mechanisms underlying this phenomenon are well worth studying.)

Future Pathways

Obviously, much more sociological work needs to be done before setbacks such as the one our team of planners experienced can be avoided.

Previous sociological and social-psychological studies of disaster situations, some conducted under sponsorship of the National Academy of Sciences[1] and others under the Disaster Research Center at Ohio State, offer some reliable information on which to base expectations of how a population will react to a disaster as well as how immediate rehabilitation will take place and who will help carry it out. In this respect past sociological research is helpful, as a descriptive tool.

This information, however, is generally unknown to responsible officials conducting rehabilitation and reconversion efforts.[2] (It is a com-

---

[1]The Disaster Research Center at Ohio States does attempt to get personnel to the disaster scene as soon as possible. They use interviews, supplemented by some direct observation. But their focus is somewhat different and not as long term as I believe desirable. See National Academy of Sciences, National Research Council Series: Fred C. Hill and Harry V. Kincaid, *Social Aspects of Wartime Evacuation of American Cities · with Particular Emphasis on Long-Term Housing and Re-employment,* Disaster Study No. 4; Moore, Bates, *et al., Before the Wind—A Study of the Response to Hurricane Carla,* No. 1095; and Bates, Fogleman, *et al., The Social and Psychological Consequences of a National Disaster,* No. 1081.

[2]Panic and looting, for example, were expected after the Anchorage quake. Accordingly, National Guardsmen were called in to help patrol the areas that were considered vulnerable. But this manpower could have been more beneficially disposed elsewhere for the emergency repair and rescue work, as past disaster studies show that panic is rare and looting is similarly uncommon. Thus, even when relevant information was available it was not used, because Anchorage authorities were not aware that it existed; because those with such knowledge did not present it appropriately (or perhaps even knew to whom to present it); and because those in command were too busy to sit down and read about disaster behavior (or seriously to ponder the significance of a new master plan).

mentary on the irregular dissemination and rare application of social scientific knowledge that sociologists and psychologists available in the Anchorage area were not specifically called upon for information and assistance. To my knowledge, it might be added, these professionals did not present themselves and offer such information.)

This too common situation raises some rather serious questions about the role of the sociologist or sociologically oriented city planner. *If* applied sociology is to be a field in "action," rather than "inaction," it is necessary to *preplan* models for the relief of disasters to the extent that pertinent sociological and psychological information can be disseminated in a manner at least as effective as that now used in providing field sanitation facilities. This necessitates a degree of active involvement by sociologists in pertinent governmental activities that so far has not generally characterized the disaster-studies area of sociology. It implies active membership in pertinent organizations, participation outside the academic community, and willingness to become involved in local government at least as resource persons, and, at best, as unpaid consultants in the affairs of the community.

If sociology is to become a sociology in action and a guide for action, we need systematic participant observation studies of pre- and post-disaster communities in operation, of internal operations of government departments, of the relative weight of political versus technical advice in given situations (such as the need for a master plan), and so forth. The list is virtually endless. The problem is difficult, and the need is very great. But what I am asking for also has a disturbing ethical aspect: Why do we need to know about the power structure in disaster situations? The answer must be blunt: To manipulate events and actors and to assure outcomes based on technical considerations *or* on certain philosophical or political or partisan grounds. This type of question is beginning to be asked about opinion polling, and should be asked—and answered—about the uses we would make of our community disaster studies.

───

As important as it is to have a guiding theoretical framework when undertaking an applied project, it is even more important to be resilient enough to revise it to accommodate the challenge contained in the immediate feedback (unique to applied projects). This process and several others related to a desirable synthesis of clinical and research issues are reviewed in the essay below by Dr. William H. Key. His account deals especially with intervention strategies developed and later altered in mid-project, interdisciplinary strategies that "meet the test of scientific respectability without violating the demand for clinical and ethical respectability."

───

CONTROLLED INTERVENTION—THE HELPING PROFESSIONS AND DIRECTED SOCIAL CHANGE*

William H. Key

TO BE ABLE to test intervention (helping) theories realistically, new ways to control the intervention have to be devised. For example, to talk realistically about the impact of urban renewal, one has to know its impact on those who were helped as well as on those who were hurt. Making constructive suggestions about how to ease the pain of forced relocation requires the establishment of a helping program within which both the timing of the proposed intervention and the content of the intervention are controlled, and the effect of the intervention is assessed.

The opportunities for such prevention research are increasing as the tempo of change and the centrality of control increase. Urban renewal, public housing, and the antipoverty program are only three of many recent opportunities to develop programs of controlled intervention. You can undoubtedly think of other settings in which this kind of *action-research* is possible. It requires patience, research skill, and appreciation for learning on the part of practitioners and a willingness to have your helping efforts looked at intensively.

---

*Delivered at the 1965 annual meeting of the American Orthopsychiatric Association, and used here in abridged form with the permission of the author and the Association.

I would like to turn to a description of two experiments which are being carried out in Topeka, experiments based on the philosophy outlined above—that *the maximum amount can be learned about social and personal dynamics only by attempting to change specific situations.*

The first opportunity to experiment, using this philosophy, came when I was retained as a consultant on relocation by the Topeka Urban Renewal Agency and charged with the responsibility of utilizing social science principles to develop a relocation program. My charge was not only to help people find other houses but also to develop a program which would make maximum use of this opportunity to help. The Urban Renewal Administration and the local agency gave me, within the limits of financial resources and legislation, a free hand in developing a relocation program which was consistent with what we knew about social stress and forced relocation. In addition, we were given the freedom to call upon a wide variety of professionals for advice in how to help. The theory guiding our intervention efforts was a variation of the "crisis theory," most fully developed in the works of Caplan and Lindeman. A few aspects of this theory relevant to the program are recapitulated below.

An individual faces a crisis when something interferes with his usual modes of adjustment. His usual problem-solving mechanisms (including avoidance) do not work or the problem is such that it cannot be avoided. The outcome will be determined by choices which are made partly actively and partly by chance. Caplan views crisis as a transition period, with an opportunity for personality growth, but with the danger of increased vulnerability to mental disorders during and after the crisis. The intervention process begins with the identification of a crisis: for example, the birth of a premature baby, the birth of a baby with a congenital abnormality, the diagnosis of tuberculosis among family members, etc. In these cases, a psychiatric first-aid squad can approach the individual or family to offer assistance in the adjustment to the crisis.

In urban renewal project, all of the families were facing crisis: i.e., the necessity of moving. They were approached by a relocator who intervened by offering some direct assistance to the family and by offering to mobilize the existing resources of the community to supplement the direct help provided. The relocators went beyond the crisis theory developed by Caplan, as we intended to use the crisis situation as an avenue of contact between the worker and the client. This emphasis on the relationship of the relocation worker to the family was an attempt to integrate portions of the theories of "milieu therapy" or "therapeutic community" into the relocation program. We tried to use the relationship, once established, to discuss problems in the lives of household members, whether directly related to moving or not. Thus, the crisis situation was viewed as an opportunity to assist the individual and families in a more satisfactory organization of their lives, since problems of relocation were recognized as not isolated from the individual's whole life. Thus, it became what has been called a program of "guided mobility."

The counseling staff consisted of subprofessionals selected, supervised, and trained by professional personnel. We had planned to have available a set of highly trained professionals—psychologists, psychiatrists, social workers—who would intervene with a selected sample of the people by supplementing the efforts of the subprofessionals. We failed to secure support for that aspect of the project and were thus unable to utilize the highly trained and better-established professionals. This, however, proved to be the springboard to a larger study. The relocation program finally developed sought not only to find alternate housing but also to help with any reality problem faced by the people involved by giving direct service or information and by providing a stable relationship during the transitional period. No outline or list of services was established, since the service to be provided in addition to money to help with moving expenses consisted of providing whatever the interviewer thought the family or individual householder needed, based on his knowledge of the family.

The primary task of the relocation worker was to become acquainted with the household, to assess its strengths and weaknesses, to identify its problems, and to assist its members in utilizing the available resources necessary to solve the problems they saw. The relocation worker (generally a woman) was encouraged to become as intimately acquainted with the families as was possible within the limitations of responsibility for the satisfactory relocation of 200 households over a period of four years. She was "aggressive" in the sense that she did not wait for someone to come to her with a problem. She approached the family and as soon as she knew enough about it to anticipate the problems it might face, she started to deal with the members through whatever activity seemed appropriate. This might include providing transportation to buy groceries, stopping to visit someone who was lonely, helping a housewife clean up a filthy house and learn housekeeping patterns, interceding with an unscrupulous real estate agent to protect a family's cash investment, helping people open bank accounts, organizing group training sessions for people about to move into public housing, and so forth. Inevitably, of course, the workers found households where some or all of the members needed help with psychiatric problems which the workers were not equipped to give. In such cases, since we did not have a psychiatric team, the worker's role was to act as a referral agent. At the same time, I met regularly with the Urban Renewal Agency board and other staff as a consultant, attempting in areas other than the relocation division to influence agency policies towards the goal of enhancing the post-relocation adjustment of the family. This, then, was the theory guiding the actions of the agency in this specific instance of directed social change, but it lacked one precious ingredient—a research design and related procedures—to make it a complete program.

Our first step in the establishment of the research design was to designate those aspects of the lives of the people displaced that we anticipated would be affected. A recordkeeping system was established so that accurate base-line data would be available, and process notes were kept so that we could describe the linkages between the condition prior to the forced moved, the intervention, and the condition subsequent to the forced move.

A simple follow-up of our displaced persons could never tell us anything definitive. We needed a comparison group. Fortunately for research purposes, the federal Interstate Highway Program decreed that an interstate highway would come through Topeka bisecting the urban renewal area, and the timing was such that the displacement of people from the highway area would occur at the same time as the displacement from the urban renewal area. Thus, we had two populations subjected to the same stress—forced relocation—one being helped and one receiving no form of intervention. We thus had our comparison group.

What we lacked was a control group which was similar to the urban renewal and highway populations but which was not forced to move. We found this group when we interviewed households in an area adjacent to the urban renewal area and the highway area who did not have to move. Thus, we had a theory, an active program, and a research design which had the possibility of telling us something about the impact of a directed social change, as well as evaluating the effectiveness of a program of planned counseling.

RESULTS

As we worked, we became less and less satisfied with crisis theory as a model. True, it gave a focal point to the original discussion, but whether or not an event represents a crisis is dependent upon what W. I. Thomas many years ago labeled the "definition of the situation." We were pre-judging the situation. Thus, for many people in the urban renewal area, moving was a way of life. It posed no threat or crisis and their attitudes and techniques were well suited to dealing with moving, even though they might have serious problems with, for example, work adjustment. The transition for the relocation worker from being a helper for problems of moving to being a helper for general problems was often not made. We felt that in part this was due to the identification which resulted from association with the Urban Renewal Agency. The family perceived the relocation workers as a resource for help with moving but the "helping contract" into which they entered left the rest of their lives untouched. (It seems that this is the fate of many specialized agencies, most notably public welfare agencies.)

Since we were dealing with the lower class, we frequently met the familiar "multiproblem family" whose entire life situation constituted a "chronic crisis," though nowhere was there the brief episode with identifiable beginning and ending points which we could label a "crisis."

Rather, crisis seemed to be a way of life for the family or individuals. Firm patterns of adjustment had been solidified by apathy, excluding any motivation to change. Or, the prospect of change was so limited that help secured from a specialized agency for a particular problem left untouched the limited capacity of the family to cope with the larger problems it faced.

My colleagues and I, at the Menninger Foundation, were dissatisfied with what we perceived as the limitations of crisis theory, the constraints of operating a helping program under the aegis of an Urban Renewal Agency, and our inability to utilize fully trained and experienced professionals.

We compared our experiences and insights gained from the urban renewal study with the reports of other investigators, particularly with that group of studies which focused on the urban lower class. Our experience agreed with the many reports which documented the evidence of higher pathology in the lower class, the relative inaccessibility of help, and the almost complete failure of the helping professions to break the cycle of poverty, lack of motivation, ignorance, and emotional disorder. The Midtown Manhattan studies had been carried out so thoroughly and so brilliantly by Srole, Langer, *et al.* that the facts of the case were clear. But what were the dynamics? What needed to be done? How could we reach, understand, and ultimately help this "hardcore group"?

We had been impressed during our urban renewal research with the apparent receptiveness of most of the area residents talking to people who *came to them* and were willing to listen to their problems. We began to get some insight into one of the consequences of twentieth century social change which had made a good many of these people superfluous. It seemed that frequently the most difficult cases were rejected by the agencies established to offer help, or these agencies dealt with them in a fashion which contributed to the continuance of a dependency status. What we thought was needed was to perceive cultural deprivation and emotional disorder as disabling and to adopt as a model the stance used so successfully in vocational rehabilitation where the client is seen as a whole person in a social situation: A model was sought in which the individual's or family's limitations are described, their resources are assessed, and a program developed to move the family toward some goals mutually established by the helper and the helped.

With these tentative commitments in mind, we wanted to build on our experience gained in the urban renewal study, but we wanted to avoid its limitations. Since, in our society, so much depends on how the family is related to our economic institutions, we chose work adjustment as our primary variable and the topic around which we focused our initial discussions with our families. We were attempting to answer two questions: (1) what factors in an individual's personality and social environment interfere with or facilitate adequate work adjustment; and (2) in those families where there are problems, what kind of intervention is needed to improve the work adjustment? Thus we had minimal theory to impede our efforts and we were free to focus on methods of helping. This does not mean that our clinical workers abandoned their clinical theories—they still had their disciplined intelligence to bring to bear on problems. It did mean that we turned the usual clinical situation upside down. Let me briefly describe our study.

We sent two-member clinical teams, usually consisting of a man and a woman drawn from the mental health disciplines, into the community to knock on doors at preselected addresses (we had five such teams). When they received a response they usually began by introducing themselves, "We are doing a study of work and work adjustment in Topeka—could we talk to you about your work experience?" In approximately 80 percent of the cases they were invited in to talk. They attempted to involve the whole family, but most often talked to the wife. Though they initially sought information about work, the conversation often broadened into the familiar topics of life, birth, death, patterns and problems of interaction, and the quest for status and self-respect.

The team members returned to our field office without discussing the case and independently dictated a process recording of the interview. They then went through a "debriefing" session in which they were interviewed by a research assistant using a structured interview schedule. The team members also filled out a number of scales developed by our research director to describe the family and the individuals within the family. They continued these fact-finding visits until they were satisfied that they understood the family and the situation. They discussed the case with a supervising psychiatrist and decided if there were sufficient problems to warrant intervention.

If this consensus rating indicated a problem family, they turned to our research director, Dr. James B. Taylor, who told them whether or not this family had been assigned to the experimental or to the control section of our working sample. If it was a control case they did nothing. If it was an experimental case, an intervention program would be developed. The team would return to the family and continue the process of developing what we have come to call the "therapeutic contract," granting the team permission to intervene in the lives of a family. We have tentatively labeled our efforts "broad spectrum" because the intervention may range through all the familiar helping techniques. No rigid program is developed to apply to all families or individuals. The intervention is tailored to the needs of the family. No family is ever labeled hopeless or "not a good candidate for intervention." We are committed to working with all of them.

During all of these visits, our research team would monitor the activities of our clinicians and their interaction with the family. We would also try to describe and understand the sociocultural context within which the family lives, the history of the community, the lines of communication within it, the interactional pattern in the neighborhood with special reference to the place of the particular family in such pattern, and the nature and programs of various institutions—for example, the school, the church, the neighborhood bar.

After the intervention efforts have been terminated we are planning an evaluation of both our experimental and control samples, to see what differences there are as a consequence of the intervention. The evaluation will be carried out in three ways: (1) One of our teams which has worked in the project from the beginning will "cross over" to some cases the team has not seen. Our clinical people are careful to refrain from discussing their cases with other teams. (2) An independent "uncontaminated assessment" team will be given a period of training in the instruments of evaluation, and will evaluate hopefully all, but certainly a randomly selected sample of both experimental and control cases. And (3) we will carry out a program of monitoring of contacts with the caretaking agencies of the community.

It is too early in the life of the project to talk about the outcomes of our helping efforts, but we do know that the method works. Our clinical workers were, at first, worried and frightened about their radical departure from conventional practice, whether they would be rejected, and the obvious ethical questions. All of their questions, at least in their original form, vanished when they actually went into the field, and our clinicians are now comfortable in their new role. There are still disappointments when the research design imposes more structure than our clinical workers think is desirable, e.g., when they see a family with many problems which they think they could help, a family that falls into the control group (which they are forbidden to help). Personally, my greatest satisfaction has come in developing a situation where research and clinical work is functionally integrated, where clinicians are concerned about research issues and researchers are sensitive to clinical issues and neither demands sacrifices in the *quality* of the other.

Our concerns have shifted now to the problem of how we can effectively intervene. The situation is so much more complex when we get out of the office and into the home and the community that we have a new set of questions in both the areas of helping methodology and research methodology. How do we appear to our clients? How can we objectively describe the reciprocity of helper and helped? Can any intervention program that focuses on the shortcomings of an individual or family (e.g., the poverty program) and omits a consideration of the social milieu ever succeed? How do we offer help without assaulting the self-esteem of those to whom it is offered? How can we use existing sociological descriptions of social class in developing the intervention process? How can we explicate and overcome the resistances which the middle class have to the impoverished? Does a society *functionally need* a lower class so that some of us can practice "one-upmanship"?

To summarize, we are trying to understand the psychology of the poverty-stricken, and attempting a program of controlled intervention into their lives. This intervention aims to improve their ability to cope with their life situation. We will try to utilize this intervention experience to confirm whether or not the lower socioeconomic classes really suffer more emotional disorders than the middle class and why existing modes of treatment have been unsuccessful with them. Ultimately, we hope to develop a rational basis for changes in the existing patterns of services.

In this paper I have tried to argue that social changes in the United States are with increasing frequency being centrally controlled and directed and that in an increasing percentage of the programs clinicians and social scientists are being asked not only how those programs can best be achieved but also about the goals of the programs. The imperfect state of our knowledge and our relative unfamiliarity with community action means that in most cases our response will be imperfect and our fear of failure will encourage some of us to remain in the security of our professions, our offices, and our institutions. From another point of view, however, these societal trends offer us an opportunity to test our theories of human behavior by permitting us to control the content and timing of our intervention. I have described two such attempts at controlled intervention which we feel meet the test of scientific respectability without violating the demand for clinical and ethical respectability.

This does not mean that there are not risks or that we have not been troubled by technical, clinical, and ethical questions. However, if we are to be involved (as I think we must) in the management of planned social changes, it is incumbent upon us to develop a set of principles and an expertise in the application of those principles which are fruitful in a community setting. To develop these principles, we need to experiment in our communities, which constitute an important laboratory for the social sciences. To carry out successful experiments we must control our interventions more scientifically than at present. We will not be faithful to our intellectual and moral commitments if we fail to utilize fully such opportunities.

In possibly no other section of the country are applied sociologists as urgently needed—or as precariously positioned—as in the nation's uneasy southland. Damned bitterly by many Southern whites at the time of the 1954 Supreme Court decision on public schools (a decision widely misrepresented as a "sociological" one), the area's sociologists have come under great pressure ever since to support all sides in the ongoing struggle. The essay below constitutes, in the first instance, a field report from a man who has been there—indeed, who remains there on the job. Dr. J. Kenneth Morland's examples of area problems provide a vivid approximation of the quality of life in a land under siege, a land seeking in many different ways to achieve a new identity and purpose. His essay also provides an intriguing account of the support one peace-loving man has known from his sociological training as he has sought to help conciliate Southern race disputes. A more trying trial of the discipline's usefulness is hard to imagine; a more useful endeavor hard to know.

RACE RELATIONS ACTIVITIES OF SOCIOLOGISTS

J. Kenneth Morland

THE FAR-REACHING changes now taking place in race relations in the South involve sociologists both in basic research and in the practical application of their knowledge. The South provides a realistic setting for testing hypotheses about such items as the social correlates of attitudes toward desegregation, the Negro leadership in the protest movement, the roles of religious leaders in desegregation, and the relation of demographic factors and pro-integration activity. In the area of practical application, sociologists are serving as expert witnesses in desegregation cases, as directors of surveys for intergroup organizations, and as consultants for governmental and other agencies seeking to bring about change in race relations. In addition, various sociologists are active participants in partisan race relations organizations.

Along with a number of other Southern sociologists, I have been involved in each of these aspects of race relations. My sociological research has been primarily in the area of race awareness of young children,[1] relating such awareness to the variables of race, age, social class, and extent of segregation. My applied work has been with organizations committed to furthering racial desegregation. I have appeared as a court witness for the NAACP in one of the five cases on which the U. S. Supreme Court developed its 1954 school desegregation decision. I have conducted surveys for the NAACP, the Southern Regional Council, the Potomac Institute, and the Virginia Advisory Committee to the Civil Rights Commission.[2] And I have served as a consultant for the Southern Regional Council, the Community Relations Service of the U. S. Department of Commerce, and the Equal Opportunities Program of the U. S. Office of Education.[3] In addition, I have spoken at a number of conferences designed to increase equal treatment of races, conferences sponsored by such governmental agencies as the President's Committee on Equal Employment Opportunity, and the Department of Health, Education, and Welfare.

Sociology and Practical Problems: an Illustration

Although sociology does not primarily train one for practical application, it does offer theoretical knowledge and methodological skills useful for working in social situations like race relations. Several such contributions can be pointed out in any of the practical tasks I have undertaken, for example, in my current part-time work as a conciliator for the federal government's Community Relations Service.

---

[1]Publications include: "Racial Recognition by Nursery School Children in Lynchburg, Virginia," *Social Forces,* Vol. 37 (December, 1958), pp. 132-37; "Racial Acceptance and Preference of Nursery School Children in a Southern City," *Merrill-Palmer Quarterly,* Vol. 8 (1962), pp. 271-80; "Racial Self-Identification: a Study of Nursery School Children," *American Catholic Sociological Review,* Vol. 24 (1963), pp. 231-42; "The Development of Racial Bias in Young Children," *Theory into Practice,* Vol. II (1963), pp. 120-27. Unpublished papers include: "Race Awareness in Northern and Southern Children," read at the American Orthopsychiatric Association meetings in New York, March, 1965; "Regional and Racial Variation in the Perception of Race," read at the Southern Sociological Society meetings in Atlanta, April, 1965.

[2]For the NAACP: a report on a student strike over desegregation in White Sulphur Springs, W. Va., in 1955. For the SRC: effects of lunch-counter sit-ins in Texas ("Lunch-Counter Desegregation in Corpus Christi, Galveston, and San Antonio, Texas," Special Reports of the SRC, Atlanta, 1960); school desegregation ("Southern Schools: Token Desegregation and Beyond," New York and Atlanta, 1963). For the Potomac Institute: opinions of Southern educators about desegregation ("School Desegregation—Help Needed?" Washington, D. C., 1962); opinions of Southern school personnel about educational problems occasioned by desegregation, in March of 1965. For the Virginia Advisory Committee: the closing of public schools in Prince Edward County, Virginia.

[3]For the SRC: conferences with state organizations on civil rights, and an evaluation of a remedial educational program in several Negro colleges. For the CRS: field visits as a conciliator to three communities in 1964-65. For the USOE Equal Opportunities Program: an evaluator of proposals offered under Title IV of the Civil Rights Act of 1964.

The Community Relations Service (CRS) was established as a part of the U. S. Department of Commerce under Title X of the Civil Rights Act of 1964. One reason for its establishment was the government's desire to help to bring about voluntary local compliance with federal directives calling for the elimination of racial discrimination. The CRS tries to help a community work out its own peaceful and amicable settlement of disputes, hopefully without the necessity of lawsuits or force. CRS may offer its service either at the request of persons in the community, or by its own initiative.

In each of my conciliator assignments, the CRS offered its services on the basis of community requests. One such request complained about the harrassment of Negro pupils in a newly integrated high school. Fear was expressed by the Negroes that they were being deliberately driven back to their segregated schools and that some form of violence might break out. Another request asked that CRS try to do something about the exclusion of Negroes from places of public accommodation and from job opportunities with the local government. A third had to do with fears that protests against alleged racial discrimination in voter registration would lead to severe community disruption.

The Task of the CRS Conciliator.   There are no hard and fast guidelines for the conciliator to follow when seeking to settle a dispute, and what is done varies with the particular situation; however, a few broad generalizations can be made about the task.

The first step is to find out as much as possible about the nature of the dispute and about the community in which it is taking place. Some of this can be given in the CRS briefing, but often the difficulties in communities arise quickly and the situation requires immediate attention so that there is limited time for the service to accumulate detailed information. The conciliator has to find out a great deal on his own.

Initial contact is usually made with those who have requested help from the CRS. Then the officials of the town are met (provided they have not already been met as the ones making the request), and are informed by the conciliator of his presence and purpose. Following these first contacts, a series of interviews is held with persons on each side of the dispute and with influential citizens who are not directly involved. It is essential from the beginning that the conciliator find out as much as possible about the way those most concerned feel about what is happening. A conciliator makes every effort to gain the confidence of both sides; this is encouraged by the assurance of confidentiality, an assurance supported by the requirements of Title X of the Civil Rights Act. (This assurance has proved highly beneficial in that it has considerably increased the candidness of respondents.)

After the various points of view have been ascertained, the next objective is to interpret each side to the other. Often in such disputes there is a lack of genuine communication, and a person from outside whose purpose it is to bring about conciliation can help to bridge gaps of mis-understanding. Of course, the basic task is not simply to conciliate but to move those in disagreement toward the elimination of racially discrim-inatory practices. In this the conciliator has no power except that of per-suasion, although those in authority can be reminded that if a commu-nity disagreement cannot be settled locally, there are possibilities of con-tinued disruptions and of a solution forced from the outside.

Sometimes conciliation can be arranged without bringing those in dis-pute directly together, but more frequently face-to-face meetings are needed. The conciliator himself might moderate such a meeting, one in which full and open discussion is encouraged and steps toward a settle-ment begun. Sometimes those in power in the community do not know how seriously minority members view the situation, and face-to-face en-counters can help to clarify misunderstandings. But just as often the dis-agreement is known, and it goes so deep on both sides that a solution is not easily or readily effected.

Sociological Aids in Conciliation.   I have found sociological knowl-edge helpful in each step of the processes of conciliation outlined above. Such knowledge has tended to rest in the background of my thought and action, rather than being explicit or taking the form of a set of rules to follow. This background has affected my approach and outlook as a conciliator rather than provided specific techniques of procedure. (In citing, mostly in retrospect, what specific knowledge has been helpful, I will speak of residual knowledge blended from a number of sources, and will make no attempt to document sociological generalizations with specific references.)

1. *Definition of the Situation.*   The most important contribution a con-ciliator can make is to enable each side to understand the viewpoint of the other. This is not so much a matter of what the objective facts are as what each side thinks the facts are, and how each side interprets what it sees. In the communities where I worked this turned out to be primarily a problem of getting whites to realize how Negroes saw the dispute, al-though the reverse was sometimes also necessary.

The importance of clarifying how each side was viewing the dispute was demonstrated to me in a situation where Negroes were seeking lib-eralization of voter registration requirements and were protesting what they considered racially discriminatory practices in registration proce-dures. (Their calculations suggested at the present rate it would take over 40 years for local Negro adults then living to be processed for registra-tion.) Negroes in this community felt desperate, they were demonstrat-ing, and they were allowing their school-age children to demonstrate dur-ing school hours.

Local white leaders, on the other hand, said that the area Negroes were not really interested in registering to vote. The usual arguments were given: They claimed that "outside agitators" were stirring up local Negroes and "using" them to further goals of their national organizations. They claimed that special arrangements for speeding up registration had been made, but that the Negroes did not take advantage of these arrangements until the "outsiders" arrived. Furthermore, they strongly deplored the permitting of Negro children to miss school to demonstrate, as they claimed it was inexcusable to damage the educational future of these children.

2. *Relative Deprivation.* The concept of "relative deprivation" has proved helpful in interpreting reactions. In the voter registration issue whites did manage to liberalize voter requirements but they then could not understand why Negroes continued to complain about the procedure. They failed to recognize that in a nearby large city a much faster process of registration had been instituted, so that, relative to those in the larger city, local Negroes still had greater restrictions.

3. *The Relation of Discrimination to Prejudice.* In studies of the social system, sociologists have found its practice of socially sanctioned discrimination an important factor in developing racial prejudice. In other words, it is more accurate to say that discrimination leads to prejudice rather than the other way around. Sociological research has shown repeatedly that a necessary condition for altering racial prejudice is the prevention of discrimination. Thus, in the communities where I encountered the notion that attitudes and feelings had to be changed before any other changes could be effective, I knew this was incorrect. Without arguing the point, I could speak about the elimination of discrimination with the assurance that this was a necessary step in changing feelings.

4. *Scientific Knowledge of Race.* The system of racial discrimination is supported, in part, by unscientific notions about race. These notions are bound up in the doctrine of racism, a belief in racial superiority, and the importance of race, per se, in the identification, evaluation, and placing of a person. Although the belief in their own racial superiority, or, more accurately, belief in Negro inferiority, is not something Southern whites are blatant about, I found it very helpful to be well informed about scientific knowledge of race.

5. *Directed Social Change.* The last of the insights from sociology I will mention are two related to the directing of social change, the fundamental task of the conciliator.

Sociological research suggested to me that both the introduction of, and the willingness to accept, change were related to the amount of dissatisfaction with the existing system. This dissatisfaction in race relations, expressed through protests and demonstrations, was a necessary condition for change. Conciliation then, as I practiced it, did not mean merely eliminating tension. Rather, it involved the constructive use of the tension in the situation to move the community toward equality of treatment.

Second, I found that an appeal to the value themes which sociologists told me were generally shared by Americans proved constructive. White leaders in each of the communities where I worked responded favorably to the notion that better jobs would increase motivation and educational achievement for Negroes. They also agreed that higher educational attainments and higher standards of living throughout the community would increase the likelihood of attracting industry.

Conclusion

Sociology, as I understand it, does not have as its basic job the training of persons for the solution of immediate, practical problems. Rather, its task is the solution through scientific methodology of theoretical problems relating to the structure and function of human groups. Its goal is the development of sound knowledge about the process whereby human groups hold together, vary, change, and affect the behavior of persons who belong to them. Yet, in providing sound knowledge about human groups, sociology can give us valuable help in solving delicate and potentially explosive problems of human relations. In my opinion this knowledge should precede and undergird whatever techniques are used to solve practical problems if these techniques are to be successful.

Most of the emphasis in this paper has been on the contributions of sociology to the solving of practical problems. This, however, is not a one-way contribution. The discipline of sociology can benefit from practical application as well. Consultation and applied research can act as means of pragmatic testing of theory and techniques of measurement, for they can give an opportunity to see how sociological generalizations apply in a practical situation. Perhaps Evans-Prichard's belief that fundamental and practical problems cannot be investigated at the same time is correct.[4] Nevertheless, applied social science can come forth with hypotheses for testing and with suggestions for new data-collection techniques.

A warning from sociologists such as Alfred McClung Lee[5] is applicable here, namely that sociologists should guard against rigidity and professionalization. New insights are constantly required to further the discipline, and they can come from any direction. Engaging in the application of sociology and in citizen activities can loosen rigidity and provide stimulation—as long as the role requirement of each activity is kept clearly in mind, and as long as it is remembered that effectiveness in applied sociology and in citizen activity is dependent upon the development of a sound theory of human groups.

---

[4]Referred to by Lisa R. Peattie, "Interventionism and Applied Science in Anthropology," *Human Organization*, Vol. 17 (Spring, 1958), p. 6.

[5]From his presentation in "The Responsibilities of Social Scientists," at the annual meeting of the Society for the Study of Social Problems, 1961.

Certain combinations of events can so complicate an applied project as to lift it considerably out of the category of "typical." Such is the case analyzed below, one which had the sociologist, Dr. Lewis M. Killian, in the very difficult position of doing government-sponsored action research on school desegregation for a beleaguered Florida attorney general. This potentially explosive research was made the more difficult by the harsh pressure of eager newsmen, the necessity to take delicate political considerations into account, the requirement that the sociologist play a public relations role, and the misgivings the sociologist had about the use lawyers and politicians would ultimately make of his work. Despite all this, Dr. Killian does not hesitate to conclude the problems and risks were worth it: the new audience of decision makers gained for social science knowledge, and the education that followed for the public in race relations combine to endorse his effort, and to encourage others of us in the taking of similar "calculated risks."

THE SOCIAL SCIENTIST'S ROLE IN THE PREPARATION OF THE FLORIDA DESEGREGATION BRIEF*

Lewis M. Killian

ONE OF THE significant features of the 1954 desegregation cases was the extensive, even though indirect, involvement of social scientists in both the arguments and the decisions. Social science work had been cited previously in cases involving racial segregation, but never before had it played so important and influential a part. In the further hearings of the cases, at least two of the briefs, that of the NAACP and the *amicus curiae* brief of the Attorney General of Florida, relied heavily upon social science findings for their arguments. Once again the problem of the role conflicts that the social scientist encounters when he enters the field of applied research presented itself for analysis.

This problem is of particular interest when it involves the collaboration

---

*Reprinted here with the permission of the author and *Social Problems*, from the issue of April, 1956.

of social scientists with legal authorities rather than with administrators. The *ad hoc* team of the lawyer and the social scientist constitutes a structure of roles which the occupants themselves usually try to keep clearly separated. The lawyer is first and foremost the advocate; the social scientist constantly guards against becoming an advocate. It seems evident that much of the desegregation process will transpire in the arena of the law, as it already has. If social scientists are not to remain aloof from this process as it develops, they must risk encountering such role conflicts and must examine realistically the implications for them as both scientists and citizens. The participation of the writer in the preparation of the Florida brief provides material for a case study of collaboration between social scientist and government official.

HOW THE BRIEF WAS PREPARED

The prime mover and the leader in the group that collaborated in preparing the Florida brief was the state Attorney General. It was he who decided that his state should file a brief and that this brief should be based upon a scientific study of the problems of desegregation. In his hands rested the final decision as to what should go into the brief as a legal document.

The Florida Attorney General felt that the answers to the questions asked by the Supreme Court could be found only in the types of data social scientists were accustomed to collecting. Therefore, he organized a biracial committee of 18 people to plan and conduct such research. The committee included social scientists, educational administrators, personnel from the state's Department of Education, and lawyers from the Attorney General's office. This committee was asked to recommend the kind of research which would produce the best answers to the Court's questions IV and V, concerning the pace and manner in which the decision was to be executed. It was also entrusted with the responsibilities of selecting personnel to carry out the research, analyzing the findings, and presenting conclusions to the Attorney General for his consideration in writing the brief.

The committee decided that the most feasible and meaningful research would be a study of the opinions and attitudes of officials and prestige leaders at the local level whose responsibility it would be to implement whatever decision the Court handed down. It was felt that this group of subjects would include both opinion leaders and people who would be acquainted with the problems which desegregation would create for local communities. Briefly, the research findings seemed to support the argument of the Attorney General, made before the Court, that a program of gradual integration under the supervision of lower courts should be ordered.

The writer occupied the key role in the Research Supervisory Committee, as coordinator of research. He designed the research, with the broad, general advice and direction of the entire committee. He carried it out, with the assistance of a paid staff, and wrote the final research report. The research was designed and completed before the writing of the legal portion of the brief, the argument, was begun. The coordinator's research report and conclusions were reviewed and approved by the entire Research Supervisory Committee before they were presented to the Attorney General as the official findings of the group, but the major part of the interaction during the entire process took place between the Attorney General and the coordinator of research.

THE ROLE OF THE ATTORNEY GENERAL

The Attorney General himself was confronted with a definite role conflict. In his capacity as Attorney General, he is the chief legal officer of the state. He pleads the case of the state when it is in court, much the same as any counsel does for his client. As an elected official, however, he has another role—that of the politician, responsive to the will of his constituency. While the layman may think of the lawyer's and the politician's roles as being almost identical, there was a definite conflict here.

The shrewd lawyer desires to present the best plea for his client that he can, even though sometimes this plea may be "guilty." As an effective legal advisor, he is not completely responsive to the wishes and hopes of his client—he is an adviser, not just a mouthpiece. The wise lawyer knows also that a good case rests on sound, unimpeachable evidence. Hence it was very much to the interest of the Attorney General, as a lawyer, to obtain honest, independent findings and advice from his social science advisers.

The politician, "good" or "bad," usually wants to keep his job. If a "good" politician, he may wish to keep it not simply for the sake of personal gains but so that a "worse" politician will not dispossess him. An elected attorney general must, in deciding how to plead a case, reach conclusions that will be acceptable to his constituency and state them in a language which will not furnish ammunition to his political enemies.

The Attorney General of Florida was certainly caught in the conflict between the lawyer's and the politician's roles, but he did not seek to escape from it. In the South it seems to be a widespread assumption that the politically safe course at this time was to ignore or defy the Supreme Court. When the Attorney General accepted the Court's premise that the propositions stated in IV A and IV B were the only available alternatives —i.e., that segregation be abolished either "forthwith" or gradually—he closed this door. The possibility remained that the research findings might show a "forthwith" decision to be the evident answer to the Court's question. Were this to be the case, the only choices would be to relinquish the role of politician or simply not present a brief. That he might follow the latter course remained a real possibility until the research was completed and the data analyzed.

THE ROLE OF THE SOCIAL SCIENTIST

The sociologist finds himself in strange company when he works with lawyers, providing them with data which he knows will be used—or not used—in support of a legal argument. The most obvious problem for him as a social scientist is that which presents itself in any applied, "bought" research. He knows that his conclusions are to be evaluated in terms of political expediency and of a policy over which he has little or no control. He will always ask himself—but will never know—to what extent his research is subtly colored by his knowledge of what conclusions would best serve the consumer.

Yet the social scientist should not assume that in conducting applied research, direct attempts will always be made to dictate his conclusions. As has been pointed out, the capable counsel or administrator recognizes that it is in his best interest to get independent, objective findings. There are other pressures on the social scientist, however, which are direct and obvious.

The nature of these pressures makes very clear the meaning of the term "independent research." One of these pressures was that of having to design and execute research in the glare of publicity. Any significant social science research has some news interest, but the scientist usually has control over what information will be released to the press and when it will be released. Often, indeed, he has to arouse the press's interest in order to get the publicity which he may desire. But when a sociologist studies such a controversial issue as desegregation, and does it under governmental auspices, he does not have to look for newspapermen. Public policy, as well as the insistence of the press, requires that all operations be open to public scrutiny. At every step of the research the coordinator had to ask the question, "What if the newspapers get hold of this?" This can be an annoying handicap to such operations as formulating instruments and pretesting them. Even when the instruments reached final form, there remained the danger that the subjects on whom they were to be used might be forewarned that they would be subjects, an eventuality hardly guaranteed to produce spontaneous responses. The possibility that subjects would be "contaminated" before they could be interviewed was increased by the desire of the press to publish the instruments themselves. At the very conclusion of the research the committee was hampered by the presence of newspapermen at the meeting in which it discussed the coordinator's conclusions, to decide whether the data supported them. It would have provided a juicy item for the newspapers had the committee itself begun to wrangle over the significance of the findings.

The presence of publicity is intensified by the fact that in this sort of research the social scientist is perforce a public relations man. This is not to say that good public relations are not always important in research with human subjects. In this case, however, the coordinator was public relations man not only for himself, as social scientist, but for the Attorney General as a politician. In planning his research he was dealing with laymen who knew neither the theory nor the methods of social science. The political official is, in turn, highly sensitive to the expectations of a public of laymen. For the subjects, too, had a dual role: they were subjects, but they were also voters and political leaders. If offended by the technique of an interviewer or the content of a question, they might not only refuse to cooperate but might also retaliate politically. This circumstance inevitably influenced the type of questions that could be asked, the wording of the question, and the language of the conclusions.

Selection of subjects was affected, too, as to both number and identity. For instance, questionnaires were sent to more people than the requirements of social science would demand, for sheer numbers of subjects impress the lay public. Even then, some groups in the state were offended because they were not polled. The need for a research project of such large dimensions brought pressure of another sort upon the research workers. The scope of the study could not be tailored strictly in terms of the time available for efficient research. The scope had to be determined on the basis of good public relations, and the time found to do it on this scale with a minimum of error.

ADVANTAGES TO THE SOCIAL SCIENTIST OF STATE-SPONSORED RESEARCH

Myrdal has dissuaded us of the belief in the possibility of a sterile objectivity in social science research. Yet the social scientist still prefers to do independent research, designed and executed only in terms of the best principles of scientific methodology. Obviously when he engages in applied research for a political agency, he sacrifices some of this independence and thereby runs the risk of reducing even further his already imperfect objectivity. Perhaps the wise course is to remain "simon-pure," staying clear of such applied, sponsored research. No doubt there will be many situations where this is the only ethical course to follow. But to follow this course in every case would mean that the sociologist, particularly in the South, would completely forego an opportunity to have some influence on governmental policy on such an issue as desegregation.

There is no doubt that, in terms of his occupational ethos, the sociologist is expected to take a position in opposition to "gradualism" if that means simply delay or evasion. Even if he adopts a "gradualist" position, he still risks the charge of suffering from the conservative bias of the Southern culture. On the other hand, even gradualism is considered radical by many Southern politicians; hence, sociologists in the South have rarely had the opportunity to set foot inside state capitols—unless they were under investigation! It may be argued that when the doors are opened to him, the social scientist should be prepared to take a calculated risk by working with government officials. The Florida experience seems to show two reasons why taking such a risk may be justified.

The first of these is that government officials do not always want simply to "use" the social scientist. As has been indicated, it may be to the best interest of the client to give a scientist as much independence as possible. More important, in cooperating with government officials, the academician gets an opportunity to bring social science theory and findings to bear on policy at the top level. He can never be sure that these theories will be accepted or how they will be used, but he does gain an audience.

It represents a marked advance in the South when social scientists are regarded as competent in the field of race relations, when they come to be viewed as "experts" rather than "agitators." One of the most important by-products of the legal fight against school segregation will be the education of the public in race relations. Operating under the auspices of duly elected government officials, sociologists may get an even larger audience. Not as a sociologist or as a college professor, but as consultant to the Attorney General, the writer has had countless opportunities in recent months to address a wide variety of audiences. In the role of consultant to a state official, as well as in the role of the objective social scientist, he has been precluded from advocating any particular course of action with reference to school desegregation. Yet as an objective, scientific "expert," he has been able to present a broad range of social science findings in race relations to a greatly extended audience.

I have included the unusual essay below as much for the lesson contained in its very being as for the considerable merit contained in its lessons. That is, I seek with this piece especially to underline the desire (and felt need) of activists to better communicate with one another. Illustrated here is a too rare method of improving communications, namely, the Sunday Morning Informal Discussion Group. Often a pleasant relief from the artificial formality and real banality of too many paper-reading sessions at sociological meetings (and the meetings of other social sciences as well), the Sunday gatherings may constitute the last refuge of meaningful academic communication. Consider, for example, the provocative material contained in this taped transcript of a high-quality discussion of civil rights and applied sociology: new insights are offered into crisis research, "manufactured" news, the strategic nature of nondramatic events, and a few of the real problems one runs into in trying to give advice to the civil rights movement. I hope the essay's example will combine with the opportunity for audience participation to bring you to such a Sunday morning gathering—particularly to one concerned with applied sociology.

THE SOCIOLOGIST-ACTIVIST IN THE CIVIL RIGHTS MOVEMENT

Martin Oppenheimer, with the collaboration of
Jonathan Freedman, Kurt Lang, and Jerome Kirk

IN 1917, LENIN broke off working on *State and Revolution*, explaining that it was more pleasant and useful to go through the experience of revolution than to write about it.

This role conflict has been a persistent one for sociologists, though for many years prior to 1960 it appeared to lie dormant. With the outbreak of the "sit-ins" in February of that year, however, the problem once again became acute. There had been little activity in the field of social movements in this country since the 1930s; the sit-ins and subsequent events were welcomed by that handful of sociologists interested in the study of movements. But even more important, college support for the sit-ins rejuvenated campus political life in general, propelling students as well as faculty into direct participation in the civil rights "revolution."

135

There had always been sociologists interested in "race relations." The social scientists' statement in the Appendix to the Appellants' Briefs in *Brown* vs. *Board of Education* (1954) is a well-known example of such interest as applied in action. But prior to 1960, few social scientists were involved in the civil rights movement as such. The sit-ins helped to develop techniques (nonviolent direct action, mainly) in which average citizens could be useful, and so social scientists found themselves involved as citizens.

On the one hand, there were the sociologists of race relations, somewhat committed to action insofar as their research led to specific recommendations, and, on the other hand, there were the new sociologist-citizens. But between them there was a gap; few sociologists were applying their know-how specifically to problems of the movement.

Within the last five years a relatively small group of social scientists (historians such as Staughton Lynd, Howard Zinn, and August Meier; psychiatrists such as Robert Coles; and a few sociologists from the more traditional "race relations" field) have become involved in the movement, not only as citizens, but also as scientists, bringing with them their special know-how. Those of us involved have not limited ourselves to demonstrating and picketing, nor have we been content with research divorced from the immediate problems of the movement. We have gone further, to act as consultants to the movement, negotiators and interpreters for it, teachers and trainers within it, and we have in other ways applied our specialties to its day-to-day problems. Hence the term "sociologist-activist."

In a short time an informal fraternity of social scientists, crossing disciplinary lines, began to exchange ideas, information, and articles. At this point some of us sensed a need for something further. We sought ways to bring the traditional race relations researchers more closely into contact with the problems of the movement. We wanted to make those of our colleagues who were involved as citizens aware that they had a wider responsibility in terms of their professions; and finally, we felt we needed to communicate on a formal level among ourselves, because very few of us were actually in contact—we wanted to talk about mutual problems.

The initial effort, aimed at all three audiences, took the form of a panel discussion at the meetings of the Eastern Sociological Society in New York City on April 11, 1965. The remarks of three sociologists which follow this introduction are excerpted from a tape recording made of the initial presentations. This writer organized and chaired the panel.

Excerpts from the tape.

FREEDMAN: There are two projects I'm involved in that are interesting in terms of this panel. One is what we call at Brandeis the Crisis Research Team, a group of students from Brandeis now being augmented by students at Boston University, who go and observe demonstrations, among other kinds of crowd activities.

The other kind of research is a program which could perhaps be called "action sociology," for lack of a better term. I'm living in a new community in one of the Negro areas of Boston, housing that has been "urban renewed." I am a resident there, and I am also something of an expert, and I'm used as such. I also am doing some research on the side. Whether all these things are compatible, I'm not sure. At any rate, one planned part of this research is to share with the community the benefits of what I can learn as a sociologist, that is, give direct feedback into the community as the community develops, or as the neighborhood develops into a community.

The Crisis Research Team program is an attempt to train a group of sociologists to be the strategic air command of sociology, if you will pardon my war metaphor, a group of people who would be available at a moment's notice to cover events around the country of sociological interest. It seems to me that there is too much of a delay between the time something like Selma happens, and the time sociologists get to write about it. Everett C. Hughes talked about this in his presidential address at the A.S.A. a few years ago. We are not involved, at this point, in such a full-scale operation, partially due to a lack of financing. This is a very marginal extracurricular program.

There is also the matter of training. It is my feeling that before you send people into situations like this they should be very well trained. And so, at this point, a lot of our work involves various kinds of training sessions such as studying a group or covering a meeting to look for different kinds of things, we are trying here to increase the perceptual sensitivity of the observers whom we are going to use in this program. This is done in part by looking at nonverbal aspects of communication of one kind or another.

The sorts of things that we have done as far as the civil rights movement goes are in terms of covering demonstrations of various kinds. We had a team covering the opening day of the World's Fair in New York in 1964. We had people who would be at different CORE headquarters, and other people who felt that they wanted to stall-in. We do not really determine too much what role our people are to take. They pretty much decide this for themselves. In a way, we try to train autonomous field workers, people who, given certain cues within a situation, can decide what roles to take, what sort of behavior to affect.

We divided the fair into quadrants, and had observers in each quadrant. Luckily, we had an observer covering every major demonstration that took place outside and inside the fair during the day. The team consisted of ten observers. We do not take notes much in the field. Afterward we write up our field notes, or tape record them. We then have a group discussion of what took place.

After the fair experience we all became very fascinated with a serendipidous finding, namely, that in a great many cases there were events being created for the press and other media and the media were also creating events. This relates to the Lang study of the MacArthur Day parade in Chicago, where they found that the size of the crowd was being systematically overestimated by the news media. This led us to try to come up with a range of what we first called pseudoevents, and later came to call nonevents. These included a reporter from *Time* magazine, for example, taking a girl out of the picket line and placing her on a lamp post apparently exhorting the people, then taking a picture of her which appeared in *Time*.

There was what we saw as a continual press conference, a continual event for the press, in which the national civil rights leaders, who were not directing the activities at the fair, had continuous press coverage from the time they entered the fair until they left. For example, an hour elapsed from the time when the police told them to move until the time the police carried them away, so that they could continually talk to the press. And when they were carried away there were pressmen on all sides. Maybe a hundred pressmen were taking pictures and watching the scene, yet all the pictures in the newspapers give the impression of one pressman there and no one else. So we came into another kind of an event distortion. A paper on this, "Reports and Realities," was read at the Montreal meetings of the Society for the Study of Social Problems. . . .

A proposal I would like to see come out of this is for a group to cover events of this kind, and then have built into the group some way of getting reports out very quickly, perhaps as an antidote to the press report. The culture has changed so much in terms of the report of the event becoming much more important than the event itself. Perhaps if there were an antidote to press distortions, either in a journal, maybe called a Journal of Real Reporting, or as a series of news releases that could come quickly after an event, this might be an effective way to have demonstrations covered accurately, at least.

LANG: The situation I've been studying is a relatively unimportant one. It's a worm's eye view on the civil rights movement from the local neighborhood. We've had a few little arrests; we've had garbage bags left in front of doors of neighbors; sociologist-activists have even been thrown out of meetings, etc. What we tried to do is study developing controversy in a local New York area—the issue being one of pairing of two schools—from two sides.

This leads me to a closely related point, and I'm a little dismayed by it, though I may share some of the guilt. That is the emphasis on a study of demonstrations as dramatic events. I think it's very important in our research to gather the kind of data that are likely to be corrections of what may be distortions or perspectivistic bias. It's not always deliberate, but I do think that social scientists have something to contribute to this emphasis on dramatic events.

I'm worried a little about this: Social scientists should not serve *only* as journalists. And I am a little dismayed by the fact that in focusing our research the standards that we apply in deciding what is important to be observed may be a little too similar to the standards that are being used by the press. This is not to say that this is not something that should be done, but there is a euphoria in being a part and parcel of a major event. I know I had that feeling of satisfaction when 33 of us were part of the MacArthur Day event. It's very genuine. It is a good way to do research. But I would be very leery about being carried away by this because you can become one-sided. You can ignore something that is equally important as a corrective.

In other words, I'm not only concerned about what is selected during a particular event. I am concerned about the fact that a movement such as the civil rights movement, which is operating on so many levels —on a level of demonstrations, on a neighborly relations level, on a national level—is likely to be reported only in terms of the dramatic event. Social scientists ought to devise methods of reporting the *nondramatic* because that's what we need in order to understand events when they really become open.

There is one final point to make. I have found in my own observer role, in studying a movement in the manner that I suggest it should be studied, that one encounters the same problems as in studying an organization. A movement, like an organization, has its secrets. It is not always desirable for these secrets to be uncovered. This too can create dilemmas, and I think that from the viewpoint of the sociologist-activist, there may be some real problems and role conflicts between the two sides of the hyphen. I'm not saying they cannot be resolved, but I'm saying that at least they ought to be faced. And I certainly have had the experience, especially when I have tried to study both sides, of becoming a target for the hostility of both.

KIRK: What we're all talking about here are the kinds of roles that a sociologist—qua sociologist—can play in the civil rights movement. The important question is whether there's a role which utilizes the sociologist's technical skills more than just carrying a sign, but which involves more direct commitments than a genuinely neutral scientific observer is able to have. I think we do have important and nontrivial things to say about organization and mass influence, political processes, and probably about the tactics of social change in general, as well as specifically sociological insights, skills, and possibly research methods. These can be of great pragmatic use to the movement, particularly in the area of strategic planning.

But intellectuals of any profession, and particularly white intellectuals, run into some real problems trying to give advice to the civil rights movement, even as occasional consultants. A consultant in a civil rights movement is in a very different position from a consultant in a commercial organization. A business firm that wants advice is specifically in the market for advice from an outsider. And the consultant in a business firm is given great deference even when his advice is ignored. But the civil rights movement is different because, in the movement, status is largely allocated on the basis of demonstrated commitment, loyalty, and possibly courage. The outsider is automatically at the bottom of the heap.

Now this can be pretty frustrating and it can also undermine the recommendation which the outsider is giving. I think one of the worst consequences of this is that the consultant to the civil rights movement very frequently feels himself under pressure to move along the continuum from a staff role to line, from being an outsider to being an insider, from being an adviser to being a leader. There are certainly very obvious problems in an outsider trying to insinuate himself into the leadership of this movement. . . .

(The chairman then pointed to several areas in which some differences of opinion seemed to have developed, particularly the traditional problem of role conflict in terms of "the two sides of the sociologist-activist hyphen," and also the difficulties facing the activist contemplating working with the government, in terms of the political problem of "cooptation" of activists into the governmental and welfare structures. The floor was then opened to further discussion.)

―――

Too rare is a frank and straightforward discussion of what a sociologist can gain as a sociologist from his (or her) participation in action programs. Little attention and less credence has been paid the (persisting, if "underground") notion that a sociologist might uniquely sharpen his professional skills through programmatic involvement in public affairs. The following essay seeks to redress this imbalance; the many professional rewards made possible by the appointment of the writer to a township civil rights commission are clearly illustrated and analyzed. Above all, the rich character of Dr. Rhoda L. Goldstein's insights into the civil rights struggle provides the greatest support for her thesis—it is plain that her involvement in action sociology has brought her a deep, personal knowledge of her major interest.

―――

THE PARTICIPANT AS OBSERVER: SOCIOLOGICAL GAINS FROM PUBLIC ROLES*

Rhoda L. Goldstein

I WOULD like to discuss the neglected subject of how community participation contributes to the sociologist's knowledge and insight.[1] As one who, for a period of several years, has taken an active citizen's role in intergroup relations and, subsequently, a minor political role, I would like to point out some positive advantages to the sociologist that accrue from such experience.

A brief review of the "setting"—the community observed—will be followed by examination of each of these gains.

―――――――――――――――

*Reprinted in abridged form by permission of the author and *Phylon*, from the issue of Fall, 1964, where it was entitled "The Participant as Observer."

[1]Most notable of the social action sociologists in my memory is the late Louis Wirth. Professor Wirth retained popularity as a speaker despite his obvious delight in "give 'em hell" speeches to community organizations. He was long active as head of the American Council on Race Relations and the Committee on Education, Training and Research in Race Relations of the University of Chicago. Students who profited in seminar and lecture halls from Professor Wirth's immense scholarship seemed to regret the fact that his involvement in real life left him less to pass on of more tangible works.

The community observed is a fast-growing New Jersey township of 20,000 persons. While still largely rural, the town has been having difficulty resisting the invasion of housing developers. To those with long residence in the township, more families mean more schools and higher taxes. And, indeed, the school system always seems to be behind in its expansion program. Efforts to attract industry as a tax source have increased in momentum but are not succeeding too well. When I became a resident in the town in 1957, the old township council had just been replaced by the council-manager form of government, and "nonpartisan" elections became the rule. The Democratic Party split into an old-line conservative group and a liberal wing. The latter attracted newer residents, intellectuals, and garden apartment residents. The Republican Party split, much less publicly, into liberal and conservative factions.

A racially integrated garden-apartment type of cooperative had been slipped in, in 1957, but most Negroes, constituting about 10 percent of the total population, lived in an area of high Negro concentration. This area formed part of the same voting district as the co-op, a factor of political significance. Quite a few Negroes had shared in appointments to the various unpaid commissions and agencies of the township government.

Partly because of professional qualifications and partly because of past activities in civil rights, I was appointed to a township civil rights commission, subsequently becoming its chairman. Two major issues were fought during my tenure of office—the proposed site for a public housing project and a *de facto* school segregation case. A political coup by the minority party put me out of office, after which I worked more directly with nongovernmental groups.

Participation in this community in a civil rights role made possible the gains which will be analyzed now.

1. *An increased awareness of the need for a social science framework rather than a narrowly sociological one in the study of community action:* The sociologist finds he needs other types of social science knowledge in order to function effectively in a community role. By combining sociology and political science approaches, for example, one is able to note the sociopolitical manipulation of the values of the community. "Keeping taxes down" is an undisputed value and the most acceptable public argument against change. Politicians in the township supported Housing Authority members in the contention that to locate a public housing project elsewhere than in the Negro district would cost too much. School desegregation was opposed on the grounds that it would add to the school budget. On the other hand, legal expenses in defending the position of the Board of Education against a segregation suit are voted without a murmur, though they may amount to more than the cost of desegregation. When state or federal money is available for projects which are unpopular locally, the economic argument is more difficult to use. Here figures are kept vague and rumors used to exaggerate costs. The sociolo-

gist's sensitivity about values permits him to question the oversimplification of the public economics argument.

2. *An inside view of the day-by-day dynamics of a social movement:* What are some of the aspects of a social movement that the activist observes? Such things as decision making, problems of leadership, public *vs.* private attitudes, internecine warfare, interorganizational conflict, communication problems, and the effects on an organization of the status characteristics of its members are some of the elements that come under his purview.

By being part of a social movement, with access to the decision-making bodies, one can observe the faltering, the mistakes, the failures to act, the accidents, the conflicts, the afterthoughts as well as the actual visible decisions. The informal organization is seen in much of the fullness of its operation—the telephone relationships, interaction at meetings, criticism of fellow members and of other organizations. One becomes acutely aware of alternative paths of action that might have been chosen had circumstances varied slightly. The role of the individual leader becomes clearer, interpersonal links between organizations become known.

The process of self-assessment by leaders is highly instructive, as one gets to share in the self-doubts and self-criticisms of public figures. One recognizes the problems of the leader as he projects the public image he desires and reconciles his own personal feelings with it. The voluntary acts of the political leader—"the everyday acts of political will," described by Professor Norton E. Long[2]—are very much apparent. Acts of leadership which emerge in a clear-cut pattern when history is written are seen at the moment as sometimes painful and faltering choices of alternatives.

An example which I observed involved a decision that had to be made by a Negro civil rights leader, Mr. "Thomas." The appointment of an old-style Negro spokesman, Mr. "Cole," to a state civil rights agency had just been announced in the press. Mr. "Thomas" painstakingly weighed the desirability of publicly opposing this appointment. However, once his decision to do so had been made he spoke out in the most vigorous terms, accepting the public role of leader of the opposition. A wave of other consequences followed his act of political will.

Another aspect of social movements known in depth to the participant is the organizational conflict that takes place. The public school *de facto* segregation case in my town involved joint action by a number of organizations which had been traditionally hostile toward one another. Those Negro and civil rights organizations which were relatively inactive experienced little friction. The two very active organizations, however, were involved in continuous conflict. Although these organizations were of local origin, their conflicts provided a microcosm of similar ones taking place on a larger scale in the civil rights movement.

---

[2] "The Political Act as an Act of Will," *American Journal of Sociology*, Vol. LXIX (July, 1963), pp. 1-6.

One of the local organizations, the Association of Parents, was interracial, almost all female, middle class, and purportedly educational rather than political. It operated through numerous general meetings and much voting, requiring frequent ratification of actions of the executive board by the general membership. Leaders frequently met before or after larger meetings to settle problems. Most of the women were not in the labor force, or were only partially employed, and they used many daytime hours for informal visiting, rehashing, planning, and analyzing the virtues and defects of fellow leaders.

The Community Association, whose officers had almost complete power to act in the name of the organization, was smaller and consisted mainly of men of working-class or trade union background long accustomed to the political process. The key officers of both groups freely expressed lack of trust for each other.

The differences in status characteristics of their memberships served to exaggerate the distrust between the two groups, a distrust that similarly characterizes joint efforts of civil rights groups in many cities. (At the same time that these local organizations were questioning each other's militancy and wisdom, headlines demonstrated a similar type of conflict between two Brooklyn, New York, groups which had engaged in joint mass action.) Disagreements developed over the question of whether to continue demonstrations in order to prove militancy or to discontinue them as unwise. When was compromise to be considered "selling out"? When was militancy required and when was it an action that helped one's foes? The local organizations could no more see eye to eye on these questions than civil rights organizations elsewhere. The need for unified action in the face of differing assessments led to much hostility. As in many complex situations, there was a tendency to blame individual leaders and personality clashes for the disagreements.

After the first joint action of the Association of Parents and the Community Association resulted in agreement by the leaders that they would no longer work together, a cooling-off period ensued. Because I was not a member of either group at the time, I was utilized as a go-between to negotiate a renewed working relationship when the time came for another public effort. My sociologist's assessment that the same state of disharmony would inevitably result was disregarded, as the leadership of both groups reluctantly concluded that they must hold another joint rally. At the conclusion of this second rally the leaders were again firmly convinced that they could not work together. However, as on the national scene, the urgent sense of necessity arises to overcome personal distastes and predilections in the face of renewed crises, and, more important, the will to ignore these distastes reoccurs.

3. *Perception of the functional relationships between civil rights activities at various levels—local, state, and national:* The civil rights movement now involves activities at all political levels—local, state, national, and

various subdivisions of these. It involves purely local organizations and those which have other affiliations. Included are organizations which focus on specific problem areas and others which include a wide range of concerns. The mutual influence and dependence of their activities upon each other is complex. Here are some fairly obvious examples.

The conflict among Negro leaders regarding the extent of militancy necessary to achieve one's ends, previously described, may be expected to characterize any social movement as it gains momentum. As the movement encompasses more people and more organizations, it is bound to involve differences in opinion. There is much consensus on ends and much divergence on means and priorities. This is true both nationally and locally. To the extent that similar needs are generating the movement for rights throughout the country, local organizational development tends to parallel that on the national level and to mirror disagreements. The contagion of ideas and actions is also apparent.

The national movement is functional to local civil rights organizations in many ways. To name a few: it provides unifying goals and symbols, improves the climate for local demands, and may be used as a means of measuring the commitment of local leaders.

National goals are more readily agreed upon than local tactics, and provide a basis for unity among warring local groups. At the same time that an uneasy alliance of national organizations was formed in order to carry through the March on Washington, so an uneasy alliance developed to manage a local rally. Focus on national issues, and especially on the march, brought organizations together at a common rallying point.

Mass demonstrations may help provide a favorable climate for demands in localities other than the ones in which the demonstrations take place. A group of civil right leaders, assessing the success of the picketing of public construction in a nearby city, agreed that no very substantial results had been achieved. However, the group felt that the picketing had served latent functions locally; it had made contractors more sensitive to renewed hiring demands.[3]

An individual's position with regard to national issues may help to define his role in the local community. Mr. "Cole," the new state appointee, was the only well-known Negro in the area who publicly made negative statements about the March on Washington. When his appointment was criticized, he suggested that Mr. "Thomas'" organization was radical, citing its support of the March on Washington in corroboration. This statement was used as further damning evidence of Mr. "Cole's" backwardness. His new employer, while unwilling to admit many of the allegations made

---

[3]Believers in mass action tend to feel that fear, discomfort, and threat of economic loss will sensitize communities to their demands. It is more often the white "liberal" who fears a hardening of resistance as the result of mass action. A number of case studies in various communities might provide more concrete data on the functions and dysfunctions of mass action.

about Mr. "Cole," admitted this evidence as relevant. Thus national and local issues are joined.

4. *An increased sensitivity to the limitations of public documents such as newspaper reports and official statements:* Involvement in local activity provides revealing insights into the meaning of publicity, public relations, and the mass media. One learns the circumstances under which news is created, and the way in which facts are manipulated to produce a newsworthy story. The reading of reports of meetings at which one has been present provides the opportunity for comparison between what one has seen and the facts, fictions, and emphases shown by the press. One also may determine the effectiveness of efforts to gain coverage by examining what is published.

Active participation permits daily comparisons between public and private statements of individuals and organizations. A public official, running for reelection, denied in print that he had ever been involved in the picketing of Woolworth stores in the area, and his friends (with whom he had picketed) maintained a discreet silence. A spokesman for the Association of Parents reported to the press that there would be no school sit-ins for the present. The paper headlined this, "Sit-In Threat Lifted," thereby getting the publicity chairman into trouble with her organization, and her organization into trouble with the Community Association.

5. *An understanding of the community achieved by the opportunity to observe its life from many status vantage points:* As participant in many roles in community life, the careful observer can make an on-the-spot community study. Being a parent, a Parent-Teacher Association member, an election worker, a neighbor, a supposed expert on civil rights, a sociologist, and other things gives various statuses, each of which provides a different view of community affairs and of various publics. The connecting links between different groups become known. As commission chairman, I read local newspapers avidly, keeping track of leaders, organizations, local politics, and local economics. Having children in school who reported reactions and conversations of schoolmates and teachers added another dimension. For example, when a number of parents engaged in picketing the Board of Education, the children reported how teachers had handled the attention drawn by this occurrence. (Rumors *can* be traced back to their sources, upon occasion.[4])

---

[4]A case of distortion worthy of any rumor clinic is the following: Percentages of Negro pupils in one school could be made to vary, depending on the inclusion or exclusion in the count of the two classes of educable retarded children who came to the school by bus. The Association of Parents excluded the educables in their count, and reported that 85 percent of the pupils were Negro. The Board of Education included the educables in their count and reported that 76 percent of the pupils in the school were Negro. Thus, the classes with students of below average mental capacity had proportionately fewer Negroes than other classes in the school. A school teacher in the system, commenting to a neighbor, explained the difference in percentages by saying that the Association of Parents had included educables in their count, thereby finding a higher proportion of Negroes. How consciously was this switch made, and in what stage of communication did it occur?

6. *The acquisition of first-hand teaching material:* The vividness of examples from one's own experience added to the fund of materials required by the sociologist as teacher must at least be mentioned. His understanding of the complexities of subject matter related to his community activities tends to be greater than that obtained from secondary sources. When necessary, he can develop special techniques to minimize the effects of his own biases. His experience may provide him with arguments opposed to his own views, one technique being to play the role of someone he knows to have opposed his views. In acting such a role before the class, the instructor forces himself as well as the student to think and argue.

The adequacy of such concepts as social role, social movement, and community power structure becomes much more apparent as these concepts are tested against the dynamics of real situations.

This paper has discussed advantages that accrue to the sociologist when he takes an active part in community life. The activist in a social movement, if he is deeply involved, is bound to have problems and disappointments, be involved in controversies, and have his personal life affected. The sociologist may expect all of this, but he is in the fortunate position of gaining considerable professional rewards out of each of these experiences.

In the majority of cases the applied sociologist is invited by a sponsor to pursue a project defined, underwritten, and later managed by the sponsor (Dr. Hare's work with the Peace Corps, described elsewhere in this volume, is a good example). In the situation described below, however, alcoholism expert Dr. David J. Pittman illustrates the intriguing instance of a sociologist pointing up a problem, rallying cosponsorship for a remedial project, helping to raise the necessary funds, and remaining on to influence the ideology and management of the project. That all of this is compatible with attention both to significant research concerns and the legitimate role prescriptions of the social scientist is made quite clear, as is also the price one may have to pay in uncertainties about financial support, staff rivalries, and ideological clashes.

THE OPEN DOOR: SOCIOLOGY IN AN ALCOHOLISM TREATMENT FACILITY*

David J. Pittman, Ph.D.

BACKGROUND

THIS ESSAY is concerned with the role I played as a sociologist in the development, planning, and operation of a special-treatment facility for alcoholics in a university-affiliated, municipal psychiatric hospital in St. Louis, Missouri. It is a study in social change focusing upon planned intervention in the community's care of alcoholics.

The story begins in the fall of 1958, when I added to my role as a sociology professor a three-fourths-time appointment as a sociologist with the Department of Psychiatry at Washington University. My appointment to the medical school faculty was the first such appointment of a sociologist, although several sociologists were supported within the department by research projects with outside financial support. My instructions at the time from the chairman of psychiatry were quite open-ended, namely, "develop a research program in a significant social psychiatric area." My decision to focus on alcoholism stemmed in large part from my ten years

* Supported (in part) by a mental health project grant (MH-657) from the National Institute of Mental Health, United States Public Health Service.

of research in Rochester, New York, concerning the chronic drunk offender,[1] and the fact that I had recently signed a contract to coedit a book in the area of drinking patterns.[2]

The Alcoholic at Bliss in 1958

For some years the university-affiliated Malcolm Bliss Hospital, an admitting and short-term acute psychiatric treatment institution, had accepted approximately 800 alcoholics yearly. Specializing in the care of seriously disturbed mentally ill persons, the hospital had neither a regular alcoholism treatment unit nor any special treatment program for the alcoholic; therefore, for the most part, only a 24-48 hour drying-out service was offered. Alcoholics could not stay longer unless another psychiatric diagnosis was appended.

In this situation, the hospital director and I came to believe that Bliss needed a special in-patient treatment facility on a separate ward for alcoholic patients. Our impression was that the general hospitals in the community were unsympathetic to the dilemma of the alcoholic.[3] Furthermore, significant numbers of hospitals refused to admit patients with a primary diagnosis of alcoholism, and others (including Bliss) required the alcoholic be hospitalized in the psychiatric unit. No other hospital in the area except Bliss showed an interest in the creation of a treatment program for the indigent alcoholic. Our plan was to develop a special treatment facility for alcoholics with social and medical therapies geared to their particular problems.

Grass Roots and Public Relations

Neither the St. Louis City Hospital Division, of which Bliss was a part, nor Washington University had available funds to create a special treatment facility (a situation possibly related to a low priority assigned the treatment needs of alcoholics). We, however, did have an unused hydrotherapy ward on the Bliss Ground South floor which could be converted to an alcoholism unit. As this ward, however, was located directly above the steam pipe lines, it would be usable only if air-conditioned. This

---

[1]The results of this study were published in David J. Pittman and C. Wayne Gordon, *Revolving Door: A Study of the Chronic Police Case Inebriate* (New Brunswick, N. J.: Rutgers Center of Alcohol Studies, 1958).

[2]David J. Pittman and Charles R. Snyder (eds.), *Society, Culture, and Drinking Patterns* (New York: John Wiley & Sons, Inc., 1962).

[3]These impressions of the ineffectiveness of traditional health and welfare service to cope with the problem of alcoholism later were documented in an intensive field study in St. Louis. See David J. Pittman and Muriel W. Sterne, *Alcoholism: Community Agency Attitudes and Their Impact on Treatment Services* (U. S. Dept. of Health, Education, and Welfare, Public Health Service Publication No. 1273) (Washington, D.C.: U.S. Government Printing Office, 1965); and Muriel W. Sterne and David J. Pittman, "The Concept of Motivation: A Source of Institutional and Professional Blockage in the Treatment of Alcoholics," *Quarterly Journal of Studies on Alcohol*, Vol. 26, March, 1965.

added considerably to the projected costs and created strains immediately with the rest of the hospital staff who were in nonairconditioned space.[4]

The obtaining of funds to create a public facility for alcoholics loomed from the start as a formidable obstacle. Previously, in 1955, a local St. Louis group composed of physicians and other citizens had attempted to raise money to begin a local council on alcoholism. Their efforts brought forth only $400 in contributions, and their movement collapsed. After this abortive effort a local public relations executive advised the group to wait until there was an event of consequence that "would trigger interest in the plight of the alcoholic in St. Louis."

In the fall of 1958, the event occurred. An alcoholic veteran of World War II, who had been hospitalized previously in Bliss, committed suicide while his wife was on the telephone attempting to secure help for him. This alcoholic refused to return to a facility where he would be hospitalized among mental patients.[5] A local reporter, Marguerite Shepard of the *Globe-Democrat,* by her stories about this tragic occurrence, the military funeral for him, and subsequent articles,[6] brought into community awareness the lack of adequate public treatment facilities.

Thus, in late 1958, the ingredients for a community attempt to create a public facility were present in three forms: (1) the tragic event of an alcoholic's suicide; (2) intensive coverage of the alcoholism problem by the mass media; (3) leadership in the presence of Dr. Ulett, Bliss director, myself, and others. Our immediate goal was to create "an alcoholism center" by converting unused space at Bliss into a 30-bed treatment facility. The first projected cost was $64,000 for the remodeling. The cost for additional treatment personnel had been promised by the City of St. Louis.

Dr. Ulett, the Bliss director, and I attended scores of meetings with ministers, Alcoholics Anonymous members, physicians, and church auxiliaries, and appeared on numerous radio and television shows to explain our treatment center and the necessity for public support. We also re-

---

[4]Bliss Hospital, like many public facilities serving the indigent in American society, was constructed and provided with the barest amenities. It has always been necessary to solicit private organizations for such furnishings as draperies, record players, television sets, rugs, etc.

[5]This point always has been difficult for some professionals to understand—particularly those who view alcoholism as the symptom of an underlying psychiatric disorder. As a sociologist, the crucial point is the person's perception of his condition. Rightly or wrongly, most alcoholics view their disorder in terms of drinking, not emotional problems. They do not view themselves as being mentally ill and resent being placed in mental institutions.

[6]The St. Louis *Globe-Democrat,* especially M. Shepard, had extensive coverage of the alcoholism problem; for example, my appointment to the Washington University faculty was the subject of a feature story in October, 1958, as was also Marty Mann's visit to St. Louis in November, 1958. Information articles on alcoholism and on efforts to create a public facility for alcoholics were fairly common.

cruited a number of citizens who volunteered to solicit industry for funds. To help in this drive, we prepared a small brochure entitled, "Alcoholism Center for the St. Louis Community—Here's Why We Need It and Here's How We Can Get it."

In due course, the community's characteristic lethargy was broken.[7] A pledge of $5,000 was obtained in February, 1958, from the McDonnell Aircraft Corporation, the largest employer in the state, and our effort became respectable—and successful. In May, 1959, our drive assumed an organized form through the appointment by Mayor Raymond Tucker of an effective Citizens' Committee to raise funds for the treatment center.[8]

This particular experience focused my awareness upon the fact that social innovations in society's handling, processing, and care for particular problem groups rarely come from the traditional institutional structures, whether they be private agencies or state governmental departments. For example, the mental health movement is especially indebted to the mental patients Dorthea Dix and Clifford Beers; changing concepts of the alcoholic as being a legitimate group for social concern largely date back to the pioneers in Alcoholics Anonymous; and currently, innovations in the care of the narcotics addict are being spearheaded by Synanon. As a sociologist I was aware that our effort would face resistance from traditional caretaking agencies; I was more surprised to discover desire for change in the care of alcoholics was deeply rooted in significant community power groups. More specifically, while Alcoholics Anonymous per se is not a powerful organization in any community, some of its individual members do occupy positions of high prestige and power. This fact worked to our advantage in that several "recovered" alcoholics joined our effort and were able to help secure the cooperation of the business and political elite in the community.

In summary, our success was directly related to our having mobilized at the grass-roots level a climate which was favorable to change; but, more importantly, elements of the power structure of the community supported our goals.

---

[7] Even in 1965, Missouri remained one of the few states without a viable state program on alcoholism and St. Louis the only major city without a voluntary agency active in this field. Previous abortive attempts to form a St. Louis Council on Alcoholism are reported in David J. Pittman and Muriel W. Sterne, *The Carousel: Hospitals, Social Agencies, and the Alcoholic,* report presented to the Missouri Division of Health, 1962.

[8] Our original estimate of a total cost of $64,000 proved too low as we also needed funds for equipping the unit. The final cost estimate was projected as being $90,000, one-half of which we planned to secure by matching funds under the Hill-Burton Hospital Construction Act. Thus, our final fund drive total was $45,000. By the fall of 1959, pledges from around 100 business and industrial firms and labor unions for over $40,000 had been received; further pledges from over 200 individuals swelled the total to $46,153. A Hill-Burton grant of $47,500 was awarded to Bliss for the alcoholism center's construction. Thus, over $93,000 was available for constructing and equipping the alcoholism unit.

Planning the Treatment Facility

After the appointment of the mayor's fund-raising Citizens' Committee in May, 1959, I was confident that an alcoholism facility would be obtained. Therefore, in conjunction with Dr. Ulett, I began planning the program for the facility. Our planning divided into two parts: (1) community, and (2) hospital aspects.

Community Planning. I felt our hospital unit would operate more effectively if we possessed systematic knowledge about existing community attitudes and resources in the area of alcoholism. To this end, funds were secured from the Missouri Division of Health to complete a sociological survey[9] of the extent and location of the alcoholism problem in Metropolitan St. Louis, the existing community services and resources for handling the problem, and the attitudes of community agency personnel toward alcoholism as a disease, its treatability, and the alcoholic patient or client's role performance. Such information promised to give us not only an indication of the scope of the problem and the character of related attitudes, but also a base line against which to measure changes in the community after an alcoholism program was instituted. (Briefly stated,[10] the survey uncovered a substantial alcoholism problem in the metropolitan area, with approximately 56,000 persons, or 6 percent of the population 20 years of age and over, estimated to be alcoholic. The survey also found hospitals and agencies were not anxious to render services to alcoholics.)

It was from this study of the community that the decision was made to gear the new Alcoholism Treatment and Research Center (A.T.R.C.) toward a demonstration mental health project model eligible for support by the United States Public Health Service.[11] Thus, the community study focused our attention on planning a facility that would emphasize in-

---

[9]This study was supported by funds available under the National Mental Health Act to the Missouri Division of Health (H. M. Hardwicke, M.D., Acting Director), from July 1, 1959-July 30, 1962, and completed by support (in part) from a mental health project grant (MH-657) from the National Institute of Mental Health, United States Public Health Service.

[10]The findings of this survey are reported in detail elsewhere. The report presented to the Missouri Division of Health is Pittman and Sterne, *The Carousel, op.cit.* An abridged version is published as Pittman and Sterne, *Alcoholism, op.cit.* Other findings are published in the following articles: M. W. Sterne, D. J. Pittman, Thomas Coe, "Teen-agers, Drinking, and the Law: A Study of Arrest Trends for Alcohol-Related Offenses," *Crime and Delinquency,* 11:78-85, 1965; M. W. Sterne, D. J. Pittman, T. Coe, "The Value to Missouri of Uniform and Centralized Crime Reporting," *Missouri Police Journal,* Autumn, 1963, pp. 15-17; M. W. Sterne and D. J. Pittman, "The Concept of Motivation," *op. cit.*

[11]This application, entitled "Alcoholism Treatment and Referral Demonstration Project" (MH-657), was awarded for an original period of three years (Dec. 1, 1961-Nov. 30, 1964) and was extended for two more years (Dec. 1, 1964-Nov. 30, 1966) by the United States Public Health Service. The principal investigator for both periods was D. J. Pittman. Thus, funds were awarded for the demonstration project before the actual opening of the unit to patients.

patient treatment and systematic referral of alcoholics to appropriate agencies.

Planning the Hospital Unit. In constructing and planning the A.T.R.C. an attempt was made to incorporate basic sociological principles concerning group and organizational structures into the physical design and treatment program.

Briefly stated, the A.T.R.C. is a 30-bed unit within a 228-bed hospital for acute psychiatric cases. It is a separate ward and contains only those patients whose primary diagnosis at admission is alcoholism. The unit has its own dining room, lounging area, snack bar, reading room, and group therapy room (known as the community room). Auxiliary resources of occupational therapy, recreational therapy, and volunteer programs centering in other sections of the hospital are also available to the patients.

The offices of the professional personnel—social workers, physicians, and nurses—are located within the unit. This reduces the social and physical distance between the staff and patients, allows intensive observation of patient behavior, and creates a favorable physical climate for the development of a community of alcoholics and nonalcoholics. As we believed there was no reason for isolating the acute cases involving delirium tremens, alcoholic hallucinosis, and related complications, we made provision for two single-treatment rooms on the unit. Our assumption was that acute cases would respond to treatment better if they were surrounded by ambulatory patients and received intensive nursing care. Thus, the community of patients could help the sicker among them.[12]

This air-conditioned and attractively decorated facility, complete with beds for 24 men, 4 women, and 2 acute patients of either sex in single-treatment rooms, is furnished in a casual, comfortable fashion. Our major effort was to remove the ward as far as possible from the "drunk tank," so typical of American municipal hospitals.

Friction at the "Bliss-Hilton"

Since the fund drive had been successful, the nursing staff was designated by Dr. Ulett to choose the beds, bedside tables, chairs, lamps, and so forth, for the facility. Mostly selected were modernistic hospital furnishings, which stood in bold relief to the shabby institutional furniture in the rest of the hospital. The new equipment, coupled with air-conditioned facilities, led that part of the hospital not connected with the A.T.R.C. to refer to it as the "Bliss-Hilton" even before it received patients.

Hostility to both alcoholics and the unit took many different forms. One "organically oriented" psychiatrist, on observing the glass windows on the nursing station, stated: "They [the glass windows] will only last a week. Some drunk will break them." One laboratory technician, when

---

[12]This assumption appears to have been justified in that the length of stay in the acute treatment room has averaged 1.7 days; it is common to find these same patients in group meetings on the third day after admission.

viewing the three-foot lamps unsecured on two tables in the TV room, remarked, "You'd better bolt them down before the patients are admitted." At this time most of the friction remained under control because of the charismatic leadership exercised by Dr. Ulett.

Open Doors

The treatment context was outlined in great detail in the demonstration application before the facility opened. As a sociologist I strongly influenced our choice of the treatment model of a therapeutic community with its emphasis upon group living, group psychotherapy, and patient responsibility.[13] An account of the A.T.R.C. during its early months when I served as Program Director follows:

The Alcoholism Centre, run on an open-ward basis, is modelled along the lines of a therapeutic community. Thus, the staff functions on a team basis, interacts frequently and permissively with the patients, encouraging, but not requiring them to participate fully in the programme, and discusses the alcoholic's programme with him or her according to the patient's desires.

Furthermore, the staff emphasises the creation of patient groups for therapeutic purposes. An unstructured group therapy session is led three times a week by the psychiatrist, internist, or social worker. Furthermore, there are four small intensive therapy groups conducted by social workers and psychiatrists. On the three alternate week days, structured therapeutic sessions are held for the imparting of information materials on alcoholism and personality development. Group meetings are held three evenings a week, two of them conducted by Alcoholics Anonymous personnel, and the third, a group therapy session which patients and their families may attend. All patients are urged to return to the Centre for weekly group therapy sessions, held in conjunction with the current group of in-patients.

The staff has encouraged the development of a patient self-government system which mobilises patient responsibility for helping more acutely ill patients and for light housekeeping tasks. The purpose of this system is to engender patient responsibility for their behaviour which we hope will continue after discharge. To encourage self-government, an opportunity has been provided for weekly patient meetings from which the staff are excluded.

These in- and out-patient groups are organised not only for their inherent therapeutic properties but for the establishment of non-drinking groups in the hospital which will extend beyond the patient's stay and act as a partial deterrent to community drinking groups.[14]

---

[13]I also am deeply indebted to other professionals who shared the milieu therapy approach and helped to establish this program at Bliss, namely, our first psychiatric residents, Ronald Catanzaro, M.D., Edwin Wolfgram, M.D., and Donald Seidel, M.D.; the chief psychiatric social worker for the project, Laura Root, M.S.W., and an exchange social worker from the Netherlands, Johanna Bilsen; the total nursing staff of Malcolm Bliss, especially Vonceal Poiner, R.N., and Jeanne Baker, R.N.; the psychiatric aids; the custodial staff; the patients; and my fellow sociologists, particularly Muriel Sterne, M.A.

[14]David J. Pittman, "The Role of Sociology in the Planning and Operation of Alcoholism Programmes," *British Journal of Addiction*, 59:35-39, 1963.

Organizational Problems

The history of the A.T.R.C has been marked by four problems in social organization relevant to sociological work in a medical setting.

First, shortly before our unit opened the superintendent and medical director (Dr. Ulett) resigned to become director of the Division of Mental Diseases of Missouri. Unlike her predecessor, the new hospital director had minimal identification with the alcoholism unit. Succession in leadership often brings about increasing bureaucratization; this proved the case at Bliss.[15] Staff members of A.T.R.C were expected to adhere rigidly to all rules and regulations in the *Hospital Manual of Procedure,* to "clear" all communications with the outside through the director's office, and to have all policy decisions involving the unit approved by the Bliss Hospital policy committee.

Second, a major cleavage associated with bureaucratization developed around the treatment ideology which guided the A.T.R.C., for our philosophy contrasted with that employed in other sections of the hospital. Our unit was developed and operated as an open-door facility, emphasizing the therapeutic community approach and employing the concept of a mental health treatment team. This was a radical departure in treatment ideology for Bliss personnel who reflected an organic and psychopharmacological approach—one which I term "organic pessimism" in contrast to the "environmental optimism" of the therapeutic community.

The schism in attitudes toward treatment was symbolized in locked and open doors. All wards in Bliss prior to the opening of the A.T.R.C. were locked,[16] and there was much concern about allowing our unit to be unlocked. When the hospital policy committee approved the unlocked doors, one psychiatrist stated, "Why don't we try it locked for a couple of months and see how it works." The anxiety around unlocked doors was so great that on the first night after opening, one psychiatric resident who was having difficulty with an agitated patient locked the door for a couple of hours. The next day the resident was reprimanded, and this never occurred again. The "open door" became a symbol around which we in the A.T.R.C. integrated ourselves. We explained to patients in their group meetings that this procedure was being evaluated, and it was up to them whether the door would stay open. In the first six months no patients from the A.T.R.C. "eloped" (left without permission), although several patients "eloped" from the locked wards. Furthermore, the patients named their ward newspaper *The Open Door.*

A third problem reflected basic dilemmas in the role definitions assigned to treatment personnel. The more traditional definitions of treatment in medicine and psychiatry see it as being exercised by the well-trained physician involving basically medical techniques and utilizing in subordinate positions nurses, attendants, social workers, and psycholo-

---

[15]Alvin W. Gouldner, *Patterns of Industrial Bureaucracy* (New York: The Free Press of Glencoe, Inc., 1954).

[16]At this writing in 1965, all wards are locked except for the A.T.R.C.

gists. Milieu therapy defines treatment in the broadest context of the total environment of the patient. Thus, the physical facility, the personnel, whether the charwoman or the psychiatrist, the patients themselves, and the patients' relatives are all ingredients in the treatment process. Furthermore, the principles of environmental therapy place great emphasis upon an equalitarian ethos in the treatment team. This approach, by its very nature, is threatening to some hospital personnel, particularly those with an upward mobility syndrome.

Finally, a problem in social organization relevant to the sociologist turns on the fact that his role in a treatment context is a problematic one at best. Since this hospital had had no previous sociologists and since I succeeded in being differentiated early in the planning from the social workers and the psychologists, it was difficult for the medical personnel to assign me a position in the status hierarchy. It was known that I performed research; this was positively evaluated, as this hospital was connected with a university medical center. But my sociological role in relation to the organization of treatment services in the A.T.R.C. was never really accepted. Occasionally, psychiatric residents would report to me the concern of certain psychiatric supervisors that "Dr. ———— says that you're going to run the alcoholism unit when it opens." It must be stated that at no time was it expected that I would assume charge of the total A.T.R.C. operation; I, however, was to be the chief of the demonstration project grant.[17] These incidents, however, highlight the concern that some medical personnel expressed about their prerogatives in reference to the treatment function.[18]

Conclusions: Hospital and Community Innovations

The question of whether our planned intervention in the community's care of the alcoholic succeeded in a strictly scientific sense is still being measured. In our minds, however, there is no question of our success in instituting basic sociological principles in the treatment process of this hospital. The 30-bed therapeutic community for alcoholics at Bliss still operates on this model with the doors open; for all practical purposes the program remains as originally created.

The greatest success of our intervention has come in the area of changing the treatment methods and attitudes of community agencies and hospitals that deal with the alcoholic. Only one example will be mentioned: In late 1963, key police personnel visited the A.T.R.C. and held many informal conferences with our staff members. In early 1964, the St. Louis

---

[17]In 1963 my role in the A.T.R.C. had to be reduced to a 10 percent time endeavor when I accepted the directorship of the university's Social Science Institute; in 1964 the institute assumed full responsibility for the research demonstration project, and the A.T.R.C. now remains a major field site.

[18]These problems are not unique in my case. The question of the differentiation of administrative responsibilities in a hospital between hospital administrators (non-physicians) and the medical staff is fraught with difficulty in many situations.

Metropolitan Police Department made it mandatory for all individuals "picked up" from the streets of St. Louis to be taken to the emergency rooms of the two city hospitals for physical examination. This means that routine physical evaluation is provided all alcoholics processed by the police; if these individuals are in need of medical care, they are hospitalized instead of being jailed. This is one of the few American cities in which this innovation in the handling of the public intoxication case has occurred. Hopefully, this breakthrough will be followed by the abandonment of the current primitive process of jailing public problem drinkers; if so, it will be in no small measure the consequence of the efforts of applied sociologists.

In our standard discussions of action projects we often lose sight of a number of ancillary matters that can be crucial in a project's performance. The essay below, written by a three-man interdisciplinary team of professionals in charge of a pioneer, ongoing venture at rehabilitation and relocation (the Philadelphia Skid Row Project), frankly explores the relation of such matters to changes in the project's research design and implementation. The essay ranges over the costs and benefits of an action-research synthesis, the project's popular reputation, the use of indigenous workers (ex-skid row men), the use of a multidiscipline approach, the fact of much media publicity, the support of key community influentials, and the presence of dependency-fostering agencies. One leaves the essay properly impressed with the complexity (and frequent success) of project management in the real world.

THE PHILADELPHIA SKID ROW PROJECT:
AN ACTION-RESEARCH PROGRAM

Leonard Blumberg, Irving Shandler, Thomas E. Shipley, Jr.

THE DIAGNOSTIC and Relocation Center of Philadelphia is an agency created to develop ways to relocate homeless men from skid row at minimal danger to the health and safety of the larger Philadelphia community. Affiliated with Temple University through its Center for Community Studies, the center has developed a pilot project under a demonstration grant from the Housing and Home Finance Agency. The present essay discusses some activities of the center that may be of special interest to students of sociology. The discussion is organized in terms of five sociologically relevent categories: the *ideology* of the center's program, the *development of an image* of the center by the skid row men, the *role-related relationships* found at the core of the center's organization, the ways in which *social power* is manifested, and the significance of *power phenomena* for the center.

This plan of presentation is chosen to anticipate the discussion of the center's ideology, because from the very beginning the orientation of the center has been interdisciplinary. That is, it was our own explicit

158

intention to create a team approach in which the sociologist might contribute his skills and knowledge, but no area was carved out for his special attention and the center is not the sociologist's project any more than it belongs to other members of the interdisciplinary team.[1]

Ideology

The center was established by persons with a strong conviction that social welfare programs and social-action programs should include a research component. This would include (A) "pure research to make a contribution to man's knowledge, and (B) administrative research to assess the effectiveness of the program. In this way the social welfare (action) agency would contribute to the growing edge of knowledge, as well as to applications of that knowledge.

This particular ideology has received a mixed reception among the various publics on which the center's projects have relied. The officials of the Housing and Home Finance Agency have shown a lively interest in a research design and implementation that would contribute to the evaluation of the effectiveness of the demonstration grant, but little interest in research per se. Furthermore, from time to time we still find it necessary to continue to argue the importance of combined action-research with those action-oriented persons who say: "We have enough research—we know what needs to be done—what we need is action!" We have heard this comment from various social welfare agency officials, from some university officials, and even from some of our own staff.

On the other hand we have also found some university officials who have argued that it is inappropriate for a university or a university-affiliated agency to engage in any social action—that it should be restricted to research and scholarly publication. The ideological problem has also been evidenced in the withdrawal of contributions of service and money by a health agency because there was fear that the agency board would find the specific project inappropriate—apparently alcoholism is a health problem for some purposes, but not for others, especially when there is a research component in the project. We have found no ready solution for the desire to exclude research and concen-

---

[1] Of course the sociologist did bring his training and ideas with him and they became a part of the thinking of the other members of the multidisciplinary team. This included the importance of sampling procedure in order to permit generalization to the larger population of skid row; the value of comparison with the working men living in the "normal" community in order to put the skid row men in proper perspective; the function of skid row as a service area for homeless and indigent men of the entire Philadelphia region, providing them with cheap lodging, cheap food, and work; the significance of the skid row way of life as different in some ways from, but strongly reminiscent of, the way of life of the general unskilled working class, and the importance of downward class mobility into skid row for achieving that social alienation that sociologists have, since Durkheim, called anomie. However, our attention is directed to some of our most important problems and what happened to the project as a result.

trate on action, or to exclude action and concentrate on research, except to continue to collect necessary data insofar as possible and to seek to demonstrate the possibility of implementing the ideology successfully.

A second major ideological consideration deals more specifically with the field of social work. The approach of the center can be called "aggressive casework," (i.e., the staff seeks out the client and tries to motivate him to come into the center). Within the center the staff seeks to help the skid row man to find ways of rehabilitation and to accept housing relocation in non-skid row areas.

Committed as they are to the full practice of social work skills with their clients, social workers have found it next to impossible to live up to certain experimental plans developed before the project got under way. Thus, our initial plan called for one sample of skid row men to be interviewed and referred to another agency for service, while another sample of skid row men would be interviewed and given considerable attention and also be relocated by the staff. Each sample was to be chosen randomly. The research design broke down because the social work staff found it next to impossible to withhold their skills from one population and give it to the other. The arbitrariness of the randomizing procedure alone would have created a considerable problem of rapport with all the men because the staff would have been unable to give a satisfactory explanation for the arbitrariness in treatment of the men. Furthermore, the randomization procedure would fly in the face of efforts to motivate men to come into the center, since many would receive nothing. (Men out on the street would quickly know, for there is a very adequate grapevine on skid row.)

It became necessary to drop this research plan and substitute a set of procedures aimed at the description of the men at various stages of progress through the center's program in demographic categories (such as age, education, marital status), attitudinal categories (such as skid row identification, class identification, and anomie), and behavioral categories (such as drinking behavior, employment history, and medical characteristics). The net effect was that a research plan with some elegance was drastically simplified although we were able to retain a general predictive orientation.

It should be stressed that we do not regard this outcome as a function of the intransigence of the social work staff. Rather, the initial research plan was drawn up without adequate appreciation of what the practical problems would be. The research team learned that the world does not stand still for science and that it is far easier to set up a well-defined research proposal than to implement it. The service-oriented staff learned the basic value of research and gradually came around to a deeper commitment to the research plan as time went by. If research must be "in at the very beginning" in order to get satisfactory research results, then the action staff must also be "in at the beginning" in order to incorporate satisfactory action procedures and to engender acceptance of the intrusions of research into social work procedures.

Image

The center's demonstration grant had developed from a successful census taken in Philadelphia's skid row in 1959–60. In that census, white-coated medical school juniors and seniors, addressed as "doctor," had been able to interview approximately 80 percent of the skid row men. When the interviewing began on the demonstration grant out of the center, the interviewing staff largely consisted of middle-class members of the staff. We quickly found that a more effective job of establishing rapport could be done by using some ex-skid row men who were involved in an Alcoholics Anonymous program which was the responsibility of one of the staff. In the first six months we found that these ex-skid row men on our staff made an important contribution toward the establishment of a favorable image of the center on the part of the men who still lived on skid row. Our ex-skid row staff men spoke the language of the "Row." They were known as having recently lived on the Row. They knew the problems of alcoholism and so they "understood" the men on the Row, and men on the Row perceived that they understood. Finally, the ex-skid row men knew their way around the area in a way that none of the rest of us possibly could.

An example was the extremely effective job of communication done during the Christmas holidays of 1963 when 31 men died of methyl alcohol poisoning from drinking industrial canned heat. The ex-skid row men mimeographed a circular and distributed it widely on the Row. When the center's ex-skid row men said "don't drink that squeeze, there's a bad batch on the Row," they were heard and listened to! In recognition of this, the center's staff has included a number of ex-skid row men in such capacities as administrative assistant to the director, interviewer, messenger, and cook. These men are an integral part of the staff.

This has had its price, however. During the early period of our relationship, the ex-skid row men were still strongly identified with the Row, which facilitated their rapport with the men. It meant, however, that they tended to view the center as fair game for exploitation; they were inclined to "con" us. A consequence was that we got more volunteers walking into the center than we had planned for. Looked at in perspective, we see this as something of a trade-off. The image and the rapport contributed by the ex-skid row men may have given us better data from those who gave data, but it was at the cost of considerable deviation from the random sample design we had originally planned.

Role-related relationships

The center's staff is a mixture of professionals and nonprofessionals. The professional approach is multidisciplinary—social casework, social group work, internal medicine, psychiatry, podiatry, public health, osteopathic medicine, clinical psychology, social psychology, and sociology are all represented. There are residual interprofessional tensions, but these are largely focused on the "artificiality" introduced into professional activities by the researchers, rather than on differences in professional ideologies. These tensions are moderated by a relatively high congeniality between the staff. The tensions are further moderated by a commitment by all persons, whatever their professional role, to the ideology of action-research, so that differences that crop up are regarded as minor irritations to be discussed and reconciled and resolved rather than as grist for the mill of conflict.

The interprofessional tensions are further moderated by the center's focus on a problem population rather than on a single frame of reference or theoretical position. The staff is committed therefore to work toward solutions to problems of the skid row man and it recognizes that all the professionals can make a contribution because of their complementary skills. Different disciplines, as such, just get in the way.

At the same time, we have noted that professional ideologies have created minor problems for some of the staff outside the center. To cite just two examples: we wondered whether our osteopathic physician would be permitted to visit some of our skid row men in a local hospital, but he was quietly given a staff appointment after some friendly negotiation; and some of our social work staff felt that they would be perceived by their professional peers as professionally offbeat, but in fact they were met with interest and cooperation. (As the center serves a population welfare agencies normally do not reach, the staff did not compete with, and the center was possibly not perceived as threatening, other agencies.)

Finally, we think that the selection of a social worker with considerable sociological training as the director of the center has made an important contribution to the moderation of professional role-related tensions. We can develop a *post hoc* explanation of this—the social worker is the focal point of the relationship that the skid row man has with the center —but the fact is that there was a strong element of chance matters turned out this way.

Power Structure

Power considerations have been important in the affairs of the Diagnostic and Relocation Center's program. First, and probably most important, is the influence of the Greater Philadelphia Movement in the establishment of the program and in its continuing support. The Redevelopment Authority of the City of Philadelphia already had plans to redevelop the area to the north of Independence Hall. The Greater Philadelphia Movement, a local civic organization of 35 top leaders in commerce, banking, and industry gave impetus to these redevelopment plans as a matter of civic pride. The Greater Philadelphia

Movement served as prime contractor for the skid row census and is now the prime contractor for the center's demonstration grant project. When it became necessary to create a nonprofit corporation to receive certain grants, the skid row subcommittee of the Greater Philadelphia Movement were the principal incorporators. The law firm of one of the Greater Philadelphia Movement (G.P.M.) members is the law firm for the Diagnostic Relocation Center. The director of the center has at all times had the ear of the executive director of G.P.M. and the G.P.M. skid row committee.

While the active support of the power structure, through G.P.M., has been of immeasurable help, the center has also had excellent support from the mass media. From the very beginning of the project the mass media saw the center and its program as good copy. Full cooperation was extended to the representatives of the press, radio, and television. The only request made by the center was that there be recognition of the special audience on skid row. In almost every situation, this request has been honored and each article or TV show (there have been four 30-minute and one 60-minute presentations) has been favorably received by the general community, and specifically by the skid row men.

Another dimension of power bears more directly on the day-to-day work of the center. It has become quite clear to us that the skid row landlord can make or break any research sample that is planned for skid row. For example, from the very beginning it was difficult to get into certain skid row hotels to interview men picked for our sample. In one hotel it was virtually impossible. The hotel owners correctly saw that every man persuaded to leave their hotel and be relocated was money out of their pockets. Legally, the project rested solely upon voluntary cooperation and, while we tried to develop ways of using pressure through the city's Department of Licenses and Inspections, we were not very successful. Various types of strategems were used to get around landlord opposition, the most effective of which was for the interviewer to go to the hotel when the hotel operator was not present. On the other hand, one landlord was able to arrange for advance acquisition of his properties (whether the fact that his brother was a member of the legislature had anything to do with it we cannot say) and he was extremely cooperative.

The power of the skid row landlords was significant in yet another way. Many men received disability checks, old-age insurance checks, and retirement checks. These checks were delivered to the hotel where the men were domiciled. The man would endorse the check over to the landlord, who would credit him for rent until the next check arrived, and then take out any money he may have advanced, returning the balance to the man. There was a reasonable probability that the man would then go out and get drunk and be jackrolled while drunk. Not infrequently he did not even have time to get drunk, but was mugged shortly after leaving the hotel. He then had to borrow from his landlord until his next check came in. Thus, a system of dependency was established which made it extremely difficult for the man to move from skid row. Where would he get the credit that he needed to survive until the next check? Who would take an interest in him outside of skid row? Thus, the fact that the interest on skid row might be exploitative was irrelevant.

We have tried to solve this problem through development of closer relationships with the Department of Public Welfare (a city agency) and the Department of Public Assistance (a state-county agency), and we are convinced it is possible to break the debt dependency relationship although we have not always been able to persuade the men of this.

Power is manifested in yet another way through formal governmental authority. The agencies of the city and G.P.M. are concerned that another skid row not develop elsewhere in the city. This is a major concern of the Redevelopment Authority and it is a responsibility of the Department of Licenses and Inspections. Skid row represents a locale in which homeless men congregate for cheap lodging and food. Under the present housing code it is neither financially feasible nor legally possible to open up new skid row hotels after the present ones are demolished. Thus, one major source of housing will be eliminated.

The other major source of cheap housing is the missions. While the center has maintained good relationships with the missions, it is no secret that the missions are viewed as an element of skid row life that fosters dependency in the men. They are not an effective force in helping men to leave the Row. It is our feeling that if the missions, as currently operated, relocate and provide housing on the same basis as they now do, they will draw skid row-type men to them and contribute to the formation of a new skid row area. From time to time meetings have been held to interpret our program to skid row landlords and to clergymen who have an interest in the missions (under the Council of Churches). The plans of some of the missions are still very much up in the air. It seems probable that one with the least adequate sleeping accommodations will probably go out of business at the time of redevelopment.

But the problem of prevention goes still deeper, for, to the best of our knowledge, we must identify "incipient skid rows" and try to get city officials and others to secure a reversal of trends. We believe we have identified at least one such area, and there is inconclusive evidence that trends in the neighborhood have in fact halted, as the neighborhood is being absorbed relatively rapidly into a Negro and Puerto Rican housing market more profitable than a skid row housing market. In addition, a series of inspections for code violations by the Department of Licenses and Inspections, inspections intended to measure the tendency toward skid row development, may have had a boomerang effect; i.e., the residents and businessmen in the area may have begun to rehabilitate under the impetus of the code inspections. Thus, our assessment procedures have a tendency to interfere with the outcome of the "natural experiment."

Conclusion

Multidisciplinary approaches *can* be successful if participants focus attention on the problem at hand rather than on the ideology of their own disciplines. There will be persistent and realistic problems with respect to action-research projects. We cannot maintain that action and research necessarily foster the commonweal. It seems to us, however, that action without research is a treadmill and that research without action neglects important human values.

What kinds of events in a delinquency prevention planning project lead a once enthusiastic sociologist to conclude that there was "much frustration and little gratification" in such a project? How much can be learned of a transferable, preventive nature from a full and sobering account of project life in the real world? These and related questions are addressed by the essay below, an account of the recent involvement of Dr. Michael Schwartz in an ill-fated precursor project to our current "War on Poverty." His story is rich in insights into such strategic, if underdiscussed items as project leadership, interagency relations, and community acceptance.

THE SOCIOLOGIST IN AN UNSUCCESSFUL DELINQUENCY PREVENTION PLANNING PROJECT

Michael Schwartz

A FEW YEARS ago, the late president John F. Kennedy formed the President's Committee on Juvenile Delinquency and Youth Crime, a group that sought to encourage local communities to plan and implement antidelinquency programs. Seventeen cities eventually received planning grants, with the clear understanding that only about half were to receive further financial aid in support of their project's action phase. Only one planning grant was made directly to a mayor; the others were made to existing or newly formed nonprofit youth agencies or to coalitions of agencies, both public and private. Under study in this paper is the unique situation wherein the planning grant was made directly to our city's mayor and where the planning project failed to materialize into action—or success.

In all of the nation's delinquency-control planning projects the most essential goal was proposed action aimed at alterations of existing social structure. There was sufficient evidence to indicate that the overwhelming majority of delinquents were not psychotic, neurotic, or feebleminded. Thoughts of saturating high-delinquency areas with therapists were discarded from the start, and the general emphasis was not on personality shifts but on social structural modifications. This attitude was firmly

166

set by members of the President's Committee, and few quarreled with it.

The implications of planning in order to alter the social structure are enormous, and it is not important to this paper to review all of those details here. The most essential point is this: the function of local planning committees was to create a new social system out of the bits and pieces of older ones. Most projects took as their tasks: (1) the innovation of programs for youth and their parents; (2) coordination of the activities of the various agencies dealing with the same population; and (3) changing the ways in which services are "delivered" to people. Some examples of these three activities may clarify the point:

First, certain programs for youth had never been tried before in our community. The establishment of "halfway houses" for juvenile offenders or nursery schools for the "culturally deprived" child are examples of innovations in programming for youth that were considered.

Second, as elsewhere, the local web of social service agencies was very complex. One agency might deal exclusively with a mother, another with her sons, a third with an alcoholic father, while a fourth attempted to interest the parents in the local school. Frequently enough, each agency was unaware of the activities of other agencies with respect to the same family. Some agencies jealously guarded their records to such a degree that sharing privileged information, even with other agencies, was out of the question. Coordination, then, of the various public and private social agencies had the potential for vastly increasing the effectiveness and decreasing the costs of services to agency clients.

Third, changing the nature of delivery systems of social services was considered a critical issue. For example, an unknown number of local people refrained from taking advantage of the facilities of local employment service offices. The reasons were varied, but clearly some feared the endless filling out of forms (which, of course, requires one to be able to read and write); others simply lacked the skills for behaving effectively in bureaucratic settings. Storefront branches of employment offices, run on an informal basis with clerks to fill out the forms, were thought by some planners capable of delivering a service to a segment of the eligible population never before reached.

The aims of the project were simple enough but there were innumerable factors that quickly caused them to become very complex.[1] Major issues were agency autonomy, agency control, and the proper allocation of available funds. Drawing social service agencies together for purposes of central recordkeeping, training, and information initially seemed like a good idea—except that the fear of loss of autonomy was an easily predictable one. Dealing with bureaucratic-type personalities was also a predictable problem as were problems associated with motivating

---

[1] For an excellent description of research problems in action programs of this sort see Walter B. Miller, "The Impact of a 'Total Community' Delinquency Control Project," *Social Problems,* Vol. 10 (Fall, 1962), pp. 168-91.

certain heads of institutions to sponsor pilot programs of innovative designs. While these problems were foreseen, the failure of the planning project clearly indicates that they were not well handled.

The task was large, but it was not impossible. There was resistance of the bureaucratic variety, but resistance came from other sources as well. When the planning grant was made, there was both overt and covert hostility in the city. Open criticism came from some mass-media sources which argued that the city had been involved in a number of planning programs in the past but little action had ever come from them. They argued that the money was about to be wasted again, that we knew what to do (i.e., get more police action) and we ought to get on with it. Covertly, middle-class whites argued that we were about to spend more tax dollars on the Negroes and that it would not help, while some Negroes resented the city's apparently saying that juvenile crime was only a Negro problem. Furthermore, while the planning committee was established and appointed by the mayor, the City Council had to approve expenditures. At this time the mayor was confronted by a relatively unfriendly council, representing yet another source of resistance.

Local business and industry engaged in what might best be termed "passive resistance." Representatives of these institutions did not offer aid, even though the question of jobs and job training for youth was of major importance to the project. A brief anecdote may serve to illustrate this point: In my capacity as a project consultant, I was visited by two representatives of an advertising agency who handled a large auto manufacturing account. They wanted to know how their client could best help in the program. I believe at that moment I had approximately 20 different ideas and offered them all with some enthusiasm: job training, after-school jobs, work-study programs, visits to the schools to tell the kids about the facts of economic life and the skills they will need, and so on. "Well, we were thinking more in terms of something like a soap-box derby." I believe that I spent several hours trying to describe what the real needs were and trying to convince them there was a long-run payoff for the company (altruism was clearly a futile appeal). But for the most part my suggestions fell on deaf ears.

Interestingly, a very major source of support for the program came from religious institutions. Since the formal church atmospheres seemed to have little appeal to either lower class Negroes or whites, the churches had already been involved in trying to establish storefront Protestant churches. They had also been working on informal church-sponsored recreation programs and coffee shops, and were trying to find employment for some youths. While the ministers provided great support for project morale, their power to influence key decision makers in government, business, or social agencies was very limited.

One final note on early resistance to the project: Without elaborating or belaboring the issue, it is obvious that in any delinquency prevention program, the public schools will be very heavily involved. Some criminologists, like Cohen and others, view the school as the key institution in terms both of its meaning for lower-class life and its possible role as the source of more problems for children than it solves. The planning program necessarily had to deal with the schools, which were not controlled by city government officials. But the time was inauspicious. Two teacher factions were waging war over unionizing the teachers; both were pressing serious demands on the school board. A referendum to increase property taxes for school support had just been defeated; and the superintendent had just put the first, third, fifth and seventh grades in all schools on half-day shifts. Approaching him with issues of expanding certain services, initiating new programs, and changing to nongraded primary schools proved futile. If ever a single situation contributed to the demise of a project, this was it. It placed such structural constraints on the planners that they, in effect, had to plan *around* what was perhaps the single most important institution in the community. The superintendent of schools refused any and all commitment to the project from its very beginning. That fact in itself was enough to doom the project, but there were other factors which made modification of the school situation impossible.

The point of all of this discussion is to indicate two things. First, there existed serious structural constraints on the success of the project in the community before the planning program ever began. Second, my attention as a sociologist had been almost totally diverted from these constraints and was focused almost entirely upon the scope of the delinquency problem and its etiology. Though most of these constraints were not immediately apparent to me, within a month or two they became clear. They seemed, however, important problems for the planning committee to handle, and it was my assumption that this was precisely what the committee was to do. But the external constraints were not overcome, and there are several important reasons for this.

It is necessary to emphasize again that the planning was carried out by a mayor's committee. That fact was important for two reasons. First, the mayor was permitted under this arrangement to make all appointments to the committee without the consent of the city council. And second, the members of the committee were not to be civil-service employees, since their positions were viewed as temporary ones. That is, everyone who was to serve on the committee would be on leave of absence from some other position, such as a university professorship. The first issue is most critical, but the second point is of some concern also, because a hostile city council was now free to harrass the mayor by harrassing his committee.

The council had no control over the appointments, but it did control the committee's funds. It pressed hard to place the committee on civil-service status and consumed an enormous amount of the committee's time in council hearings and in civil-service commission investigations. One reason for attempting to place committee members on civil-service status may well have been an attempt to cut salaries, which were higher than those of members of the council in several cases. When this attempt failed, the council exercised its right to control the allocation of funds earmarked for the committee's use. If we wanted to shift some money from one planning project account to another, it had to be approved; there were several battles on that score.

That all of this occurred was no secret to administrators of social agencies who were beginning to believe that the committee was being "emasculated," or, at least, was becoming a political football. This belief did not relieve their feeling that the committee threatened their autonomy, but rather reinforced the feeling. The private agencies were now less likely to become involved with the committee if involvement meant similar political entanglements and a reduction in freedom of operation. The political nature of the situation made the situation with the community service agencies much more difficult than it had been originally.

The mayor's plan was to appoint an executive director who would make other committee appointments with the mayor's approval. The selection of the director was a key issue in determining the success or failure of the project. It was not enough that the director be knowledgeable with regard to the city and its problems, he also needed to be respected by social agency heads, school personnel, law enforcement officials and the like. He had to be free as well from local political ties to prevent city council members from involving him in irrelevant disputes.

Even with 20-20 hindsight, I cannot be sure of the reasons for the mayor's final selection of his director, since I was not appointed to the committee until nearly a year later. But it had been widely rumored that the appointment was clearly political in nature. The man finally selected as director was a probation officer; some social agency personnel believed he had worked hard in the mayor's campaign for election and assumed that the mayor was now simply repaying him. At the same time an office manager and a "community organization coordinator" were appointed. The latter was a political hanger-on, and his appointment reinforced the community-wide notion that the directorship itself was now a political position.

These appointments were ill-advised for several reasons. They provided the hostile council members with a new weapon; they antagonized—even infuriated—local social agencies; they were unacceptable to the few community leaders in the local area where action was to have been directed. From this point forward, whatever support the project had developed was lost. There was city-wide consensus that it was a political boondoggle—but the appointments stood. The director tried to hire other staff members: a research coordinator, a program coordinator, an agency service analyst, and a person to serve as a liaison officer with the schools.

In nearly a year he failed to fill even one of these positions. Locally, the community had been so broadly antagonized by the appointments that no one would accept a position, and a broader national search proved ineffective also, largely because the positions were only temporary ones. Consequently, on a two-year planning grant, the first year was lost. This was, then, a massive self-fulfilling prophecy. Local people believed the project doomed to failure; they withheld needed support; the project failed.

At about this point, the President's Committee intervened, it being clear to them that little was being done. Local persons concerned about the situation informed them of it and they made every effort possible to alter it. The situation was taking place, after all, during an election year in a politically important city, one with a liberal mayor but which had supported a Republican governor.

After a considerable amount of cajoling, coercion, and persuasion, it was announced that the present director of the project would become the administrative director and that an executive director would be hired. The mayor backed away from his appointment, and asked a search committee to locate a new director. The man chosen appeared a good choice. The new director had no political ties; he was a professor of education, well respected in his field; he knew many local agency heads, at least casually; and while the first director was white, the new one was a Negro. He did not live in the city, but took a leave from the university and moved to town.

The new director seemed equal to the task. Resistance was higher than it had been in the past, but some of the personal hostility toward the directorship had abated. There was still a wait-and-see attitude everywhere. The new director immediately began to locate and appoint personnel. His program coordinator came from the Urban League and it was generally agreed that he was an excellent man; I agreed to leave the sociology department of the university for a year and became research coordinator; the juvenile court statistician was hired; an unexpectedly fine public school principal joined the staff as liaison with the schools. In addition, a female social worker joined the staff and a second woman with an M.A. in sociology was hired as a sort of Jack-of-all-trades. All of these appointments took place within 30 days of the new director's taking office, but it was another month or two before all staff members were on the job. What had been a two-year planning project was now left with about nine months. That meant working seven days a week and evenings. We believed that we were beginning to move and we knew that our progress was being observed carefully.

My job as a research coordinator was clear. It involved locating a "target area" of the city—an area with the highest rates of delinquency, adult crime, welfare cases, unemployment, etc. These data were readily available and a block of contiguous census tracts was defined as the target area. The next step was to assess the variety and extent of social services available to people in that area, to determine the manner in which those services were delivered, and to estimate the degree to which people were not being served and the reasons for that lack.

This task proved nearly impossible. In the first place, agency data were either inadequate or were not made available to us. Second, the social worker who was to aid me in this work at one point simply refused to do so, claiming that she was a casework specialist and found the leg-work of such data gathering to be demeaning. Her orientation to psycho-analytic casework caused her to oppose practically every bit of research and planning to be done. Five months later, she was fired.

The "target area" research task was never adequately completed. Aside from internal conflict and unavailability of data, time was short, and a research staff of one man seemed to be ludicrous. The best I could do was analyze the vast complexity of the network of interrelated agencies, indicating, for example, the fact that clients often had to travel long distances by bus to reach agencies which then sent them back across town to other agencies. Even from such a simple analysis, some reasonably fruitful ideas for programs did emerge.[2] Nevertheless, this bit of work was extraordinarily frustrating. The most difficult problem was the obvious lack of access to data protected by the agencies. No amount of pleading with the project director was sufficient to get him to intervene. I assumed, at that point, that he was willing to sacrifice the adequacy of the research in order to preserve the good will of the agencies for later negotiations with them over new programs. But since those programs would depend heavily on research, his attitude seemed self-defeating.

Three more research tasks of major concern were undertaken. First, I decided extended interviews with adolescents in the target area were necessary to plan programs to meet the self-perceived needs of the adolescents. The research went very well, and the interview data were transcribed, coded, and analyzed in about five months time. The interviews provided some first-rate insights into the problems that adolescents perceived and gave us some clues to the kinds of programming most needed and most likely to succeed.[3] In a second way, this was very

[2]For example, we were able to propose a central service agency for the target area. That was to have been one building with at least one representative from every relevant agency located in it. It was to have included facilities for central record-keeping, training of new personnel, and most important, it was to be open 24 hours a day, 7 days a week. It was designed to untangle the web of services, make data on families immediately available to concerned agencies, and to make access to service more open.

[3]These data have been published: Michael Schwartz and George Henderson, "The Culture of Unemployment: Some Notes on Negro Children," in Arthur B. Shostak and William Gomberg (eds.), *Blue Collar World* (Englewood Cliffs, N.J.: Prentice-Hall, Inc., 1964), pp. 459-68; Michael Schwartz and William Burkhart, "Self Concept In Casework With Adaptive Delinquents," *Social Work*, July, 1964, pp. 86–90; Michael Schwartz, "Some Collected Notes on Negro Youth From the Low Socio-Economic Class," *Interracial Review*, February, 1965, pp. 38–46.

satisfying work. While our main research concern was with providing interview-based data useful for programming, I was additionally able to examine some of Cohen's propositions[4] on working-class delinquency, and some of Miller's as well.[5] While this may seem to be a trivial point, one of my major problems was my transition from academic preoccupation with theoretical and methodological issues to an atmosphere of practical, applied research demanded on schedule. Importantly, there was little conflict between research and planning personnel on this project, but that is not always the case. This bit of research experience was gratifying.

The third study that was conducted was also most rewarding. The goal here was to determine differences in family structure, mobility, and employment patterns between the Negroes and the Southern white migrants in the target area. Our purpose was to determine the extent to which different patterns of social organization and subcultural phenomena might require different program approaches. We learned, for example, that the position of the southern whites in the labor market seemed to be a fair equivalent to that of the Negroes. We also found evidence that the southern whites were underrepresented on welfare and relief rolls and that Negroes were overrepresented. We located two important and related pieces of data: First, the southern whites returned to the South when they were "broke" as often or more often than when they had money, and second, they often developed patterns of exchanging interfamilial economic aid when some were unemployed. These factors kept them off the relief rolls and supported the impression that the southern whites maintained an ethic of independence and did not easily become urbanized. These were most important observations for our planning.

Armed with such data, members of our committee met with several social agency heads. And here, I think, came one of the greatest frustrations of the entire experience. I argued that our observations indicated that delivering services to Southern whites in the same manner as to Negroes would likely prove unsuccessful, or, if "successful," could mean increasing the dependency of the people served where such dependency had not previously existed. There is the possibility that the presentation of our data was not very tactful. But I had resolved to make my point as strongly and as logically as possible. I concluded by asking the agencies to consider alternatives to their usual approaches; I wanted the agencies to become part of the planning process and to develop some commitment to the project on their own. Their response was unimpressive. Follòw-up phone calls usually produced no results, and we began to find fewer and fewer people in their offices. I was sure that the response to the

---

[4]Albert K. Cohen, *Delinquent Boys: the Culture of the Gang*, (New York: The Free Press of Glencoe, Inc., 1956).

[5]Walter B. Miller, "Lower Class Culture as a Generating Milieu of Gang Delinquency," *Journal of Social Issues* 14: April, 1959.

data was hostile and that I had finished the job of thoroughly alienating the agencies.

Much later, after the program had collapsed, some agency people explained to me that they had found the data significant, especially since the data backed up many of their own hunches. They had not been responding to the data in a hostile way at all, but to something quite different. For nearly 18 months the agencies had been fairly well ignored as a source of planning ideas. Their interpretation of the meeting was that we were in a bind and could not understand an issue that was a social work problem because we were not social workers. Now it was their turn to let us "sweat a bit." At this point the new project director should have mollified the agencies and persuaded them to participate, and he did not.

Any social psychologist would agree that the determining of a man's motives is at best a difficult business. But my impressions of the situation are clear. The director gave an average of three or four public speeches a week, and he had moved to a very high-status area of the city. His prestige in the middle-class Negro community was soaring and he seemed to enjoy it. The building and maintaining of that prestige consumed much of his time and ours, at a period when time was the one fixed variable in the situation. Negotiating with agencies also required much time and energy, but the planning project received less and less of the director's time each week. While he possessed the requisite skills for negotiation, he apparently perceived his position as that of a figurehead occupying an honorific position with few obligations attached. He seemed to think of himself as the "company Negro" on display; the innumerable invitations to speaking and social engagements reinforced that self-percept. Agency heads began to think of him in this way also, and he was consequently eliminated from the negotiation process. This combination of his definition of his role and his delight with newly acquired status helped lead to the ultimate collapse of the project.

Only two of us were left to carry out the crucial negotiations: the research coordinator and the program coordinator. As negotiators, we were both most unsatisfactory substitutes for the director: neither was a social worker, neither was over 30, and neither was widely known in the community. Moreover, both of us were clearly defined by the agencies as staff people, well down on the status hierarchy. Nevertheless, the two of us had to carry on the negotiations, and this was added to our already enormous work loads.

The more we attempted to carry on the negotiation process the worse became our relations with other agencies. Heads of agencies did not expect to be asked to discuss such critical issues with people in lower administrative positions, and they began to withdraw all support. Recognizing that it was futile to continue in this way, we halted our efforts in this respect very quickly, and the end of the road had been reached.

Only a rapid shift in the behavior of the director could have salvaged the project and we were quite unable to bring it about. It is clear that the members of the President's committee were aware of these problems and, while they made efforts to alter the situation, the extent to which they felt able to intervene again in local affairs was restricted and the time was too short.

In any case, by this time the planning period was ending. Committee members were going through the motions of completing reports and compiling them in book form. As research coordinator I went through the motions of designing evaluation research projects for programs of action which clearly would never come into being. It became an intellectual challenge, but there was always a feeling of futility about that work. And somehow, sociologist or not, I kept hoping for an accident to occur—some unexpected, low-probability event that would get us to the action stage. It did not occur. Our staff flew to Washington for a review of our work. It was all very polite—and the project was finished.

There remains the real frustration of having seen the outcome in advance and having been powerless to alter it. I would like to believe that I had not defined the situation as a failure in advance and then aided in causing that failure to occur. I believe that the structural and social-psychological constraints on success were so strong that little could have happened to alter the events. The frustration is increased because I could have resigned when the realities became apparent but I elected to stay on, since leaving might have damaged the project still further. And the feeling of defeat is only strengthened by the fact that there are about 80,000 children and adolescents who are, after all, the victims of such a failure. Their lives might not have been made easier by the proposed action programs, but there would have been at least some chance for them.

It should be clear to most observers of the human scene that the death of such programs only rarely is accorded a full-fledged funeral. In this case, to permit public awareness of the defeat would have been gross political stupidity, and a most convenient "out" was at hand. City government was getting some planning under way for an antipoverty program. The newspapers carried a story indicating that the delinquency prevention planning program was to be absorbed by the antipoverty program. Many of the programs planned by our committee were most suitable for inclusion in a "war on poverty" program. But while the delinquency prevention program was dead, the community never understood what had happened. The project appeared to be involved in bureaucratic reorganization at the point at which it disappeared from public view.

Much of the above description is, in my judgment, accurate. Some may wish to argue with my interpretation of the events, and I must point out that to some extent I have written from limited information.

But, in any case, it is a view of the scene from the position of one of the actors. The work of the planning committee may yet pay off in unexpected ways. Personally I found much frustration and little gratification. It was always a case of knowing what needed to be done and being continually unable to do it. Other projects in other cities failed also; some for similar reasons, some for different ones. The sociologist's task in reviewing these situations is to point out the causes of failure and suggest possible directions for their elimination. In some cases he will be able to act in terms of his observations, in other cases he will not. Regardless, the task needs to be done.

- -

B lank spots or gaps in the coverage of sociology's various specialties—
family, race, criminology, and others—are many in number, significant
in character, and seldom the target of remedial attention. The spotlight
in this paper turns on a major (representative) gap in the specialty of
criminology, a gap made all the less excusable by the pioneering applied
research of the "spotlighter," Dr. Donald J. Newman. Irreverent and biting
in his comments on textbooks and current research targets, Dr. Newman
reports on a five-year large-scale project in criminal justice administration potentially able to close some of the gap—if only more sociologists
were to avail themselves of the project's many products. Concluding with
a terse inventory of attention-deserving applied problems, Dr. Newman
raises a significant general question: how far, how really far, can any of
sociology's various specialties go without more adequate attention to
their action-oriented gaps?

- -

SOCIOLOGISTS AND THE ADMINISTRATION OF
CRIMINAL JUSTICE

Donald J. Newman

THE AMERICAN BAR FOUNDATION SURVEY

SOME FEW years ago, at the urging of the late Supreme Court Justice
Robert Jackson, the American Bar Foundation (ABF), a research wing
of the American Bar Association, undertook a comprehensive survey of
the administration of criminal justice in the United States.[1] Financed by

---

[1] See Arthur H. Sherry, *The Administration of Criminal Justice in the United States,
Plan for a Survey* (Chicago: American Bar Foundation Pamphlet, 1955). Arthur
Sherry, Professor of Law at the University of California, was the overall project
director. The first chairman of the Advisory Committee was Justice Robert H. Jackson, who was largely instrumental in getting the project under way and to whom
the volumes resulting from the analysis are dedicated.

The study began, on paper, in 1953. Field research teams were sent into Detroit,
Milwaukee, Wichita, and other cities in Michigan, Wisconsin, and Kansas during 1956
and 1957. Some 3 million words in "field reports" and 1,000 "exhibits" were collected
and summarized in a seven-volume, mimeographed *Pilot Project Report* in 1958. Since
that time, full-scale analysis and final write-up have been under way.

a grant from the Ford Foundation, a committee was appointed, a director of both the field and analysis phases was named, and various consultants were employed to plan the study.[2] In one sense the study was intended to update the crime surveys of the late twenties and thirties which were still being cited as authoritative a quarter of a century later. In another sense, however, the ABF study was designed to go beyond these earlier surveys and provide a more detailed and sophisticated analysis of important issues and problems in the whole criminal justice system from the early stages administered by police agencies through the parole process.

The ABF project was clearly an operational study, an analysis of law in action, based upon detailed observation of police, prosecutors, courts, and correctional agencies. It was not designed to provide statistical data on the frequency of arrests, convictions, or other such determinations; it was not a *counting* study but was rather an observation and analysis of the range and types of decisions made by various agencies, and their relationship to each other and to the formal requirements of law. In short it was a *verstehen* study, an attempt to ask what goes on in the administrative process and to understand its significance.

My own role in the study as a sociologist was limited to the analysis phase. At the time I joined the staff the data had been collected (in 1956 and 1957) by field teams in various communities in Michigan, Kansas, and Wisconsin, the three states selected for what at the time was considered a "pilot" project.[3] The data were largely written observations of police contacts with suspects, of prosecutor's functions in charging, of court procedures in both adjudication and sentencing, and also material related to certain correctional processes, mostly parole. There were also recorded interviews with police, prosecutors, defense counsel, judges,

---

[2]The cost of the project was met by a series of grants, eventually totaling $520,000, from the Ford Foundation. Frank J. Remington, Professor of Law at the University of Wisconsin, was named operational director of the study and is currently editor of the resulting books. I think it accurate to say that everyone connected with the project recognizes the tremendous contributions of Frank Remington to both execution and analysis of this survey. Frank worked longer and harder and thought more deeply about the issues involved than any other single participant. In a very real sense, he shaped the study and guided it through its many complexities of method and conceptualization for a period of almost 12 years.

[3]The original plan was to study criminal justice operations in every state. Three states, Michigan, Kansas, and Wisconsin, were selected for "pilot" work to test research teams, to discover what types of problems might arise in this type of research, and to point up significant preliminary issues. The three states were not selected randomly but were chosen because they had some significant differences in legal structure; they had a good rural-urban balance and yet they did not present the overwhelming size and complexity of such states as New York or California.

It soon became apparent that this pilot study was more involved and complex than anyone had anticipated and the idea of applying the same type of survey to all other states was abandoned. The pilot study itself, from field work to analysis, took nearly ten years.

and correctional personnel. In all, this large collection of field reports presented a really formidable task of unscrambling and analyzing.

The chief analytical function for the social scientist was conceptualization (the ordering of the data so that major issues at each step in the criminal justice process would be highlighted and the relationship between these issues would become apparent). This was not the traditional task of quantitatively testing research hypotheses. There were no specific hypotheses in the usual sense; the study had proceeded on a broad mandate to observe and record all decision-making activities in the daily operations of the system. There were neither explicit theories nor strong points of view to be tested. The director of the project was expected to bring order out of this chaotic mass of observations.

Consultants, while many times helpful, provided divergent and sometimes conflicting advice. In the police field, for example, some saw the major issue to be problems of police management (such as the question of whether patrol cars are more efficient if manned by one rather than two officers). Others argued for the analysis of the discretion in decision making of police, prosecutor, court, and correctional agency. Still others talked of the propriety of police practices (e.g., the use of dogs on patrol or the use of wiretapping). Some consultants (sociologists in particular) urged a role analysis approach; others saw the proper position to be one of merely describing practice, the "law in action" against the rule of "law in the books."

It was decided, and I think wisely, to organize the data around the critical steps in the process: investigation of crime, arrest, in-custody interrogation, charging, conviction (by plea of guilty) or acquittal, sentencing, and release from custody. Data were to be used to illustrate current practices at each of these stages, but the major task was to put the information into narrative form in such a way that it would point up critical problems at each stage and also demonstrate the interrelationship of decisions made at one point in the process to decisions made both earlier and later. This was not an easy job; the analysis phase of the project has gone on for about eight years, and it is still not finished.

Only the first of five proposed books based on the data has appeared,[4] but the second is in press,[5] and the others will follow shortly.[6] However, the impact of the study has already been great. There has been a good deal of prepublication interest in, and almost continual use of, some

[4]Wayne R. LaFave, *Arrest: The Decision to Take a Suspect into Custody* (Boston: Little, Brown and Co., 1965).

[5]Donald J. Newman, *Conviction: The Determination of Guilt or Innocence Without Trial* (Boston: Little, Brown and Co., scheduled March, 1966).

[6]The volumes in preparation are: Donald M. McIntyre, Jr., Lawrence P. Tiffany, and Daniel L. Rotenberg, *Detection of Crime: Search and Seizure, Stopping and Questioning, Entrapment;* Frank W. Miller, *Prosecution: The Decision as to the Charge;* Robert O. Dawson and Harry V. Ball, *Sentencing: Length of Incarceration, Probation and Parole.* All will be published by Little, Brown and Co.

part of the data. Approximately 20 articles based on this study have been published.[7] Various conferences and seminars built around this analysis have been held.[8] There is clearly a resurgence of interest in criminal justice administration which is in many ways attributable to this project.

Predominant professional guidance and participation in the project was by lawyers; after all, it was a Bar Foundation project. Police administrators, correctional personnel, political scientists, and social workers were all involved, either directly in the field or the analysis phases or as consultants. Five sociologists were direct participants in the project.[9] Other

---

[7]Abernathy, "Police Discretion and Equal Protection," 14, *S.C.L.Q.*, 472 (1962); Allen, "Federalism and the Fourth Amendment: A Requiem for Wolf," in Kurland, *The Supreme Court Review* (1961); Barrett, "Police Practices and the Law—from Arrest to Release or Charge," Vol. 50, *Calif. L. Rev.*, p. 11 (1962); Goldstein, H., "Full Enforcement vs. Police Discretion Not to Invoke the Criminal Process," May 22, 1963 (paper presented at the National Institute of Police and Community Relations, Michigan State University), "Police Discretion: The Ideal Versus the Real," 23, *Public Administration Rev.*, 140 (1963); Goldstein, J., "Police Discretion Not to Invoke the Criminal Process: Low-Visibility Decisions in the Administration of Justice," 69, *Yale Law Journal*, 543 (1960); Kadish, "The Advocate and the Expert —Counsel in the Peno-Correctional Process," 45 *Minn. L. Rev.* 803 (1961), "Legal Norm and Discretion in the Police and Sentencing Processes," 75, *Harvard Law Review*, 904 (1962); LaFave, "Detention for Investigation by the Police: An Analysis of Current Practices, 1962, *Wash. U.L.Q.*, 331, "The Police and Nonenforcement of the Law—Part I," 1962, *Wis. L. Rev.*, 104, "The Police and Nonenforcement of the Law—Part II," 1962, *Wis. L. Rev.*, 179; LaFave and Remington, "Controlling the Police: The Judge's Role in Making and Reviewing Law Enforcement Decisions," 63, *Mich. L. Rev.*, 987 (1965); Miller and Dawson, "Non-Use of the Preliminary Examination: A Study of Current Practices," 1964, *Wis. L. Rev.*, 252; Miller and Remington, "Procedures Before Trial," 339, *Annals*, 111 (1962); Miller and Tiffany, "Prosecutor Dominance of the Warrant Decision: A Study of Current Practices," 1964, *Wash. U.L.Q.*, 1; Newman, "The Effect of Accommodations in Justice Administration on Criminal Statistics," 46, *Sociology & Social Research*, 144 (1962); in Gouldner & Miller (eds.), *Applied Sociology: Opportunities and Problems*, (1965); chap. 12; Ohlin and Remington, "Sentencing Structure: Its Effect upon Systems for the Administration of Criminal Justice," 23, *Law & Contemp. Prob.*, 495 (1958); Remington, "Criminal Justice Research," 51, *J. Crim. L., C. & P.S.*, 7 (1960), "The Law Relating to "On the Street" Detention, Questioning and Frisking of Suspected Persons and Police Arrest Privileges in General," 51, *J. Crim. L., C. & P.S.*, 386 1960, "Social Change, the Law and the Common Good," in *Papers Presented at the Tenth Annual National Institute on Police and Community Relations* (1964); Remington and Rosenblum, "The Criminal Law and the Legislative Process," 1960, *U. Ill. L.F.*, 481; Robinson, "A Proposed Study of Chicago Police Department Arrest Procedures to Determine the Proper Use of Summons and Notice to Appear," 45, *Chicago Bar Record*, 434 (1964); Rotenberg, "The Police Detection Practice of Encouragement," 49, *Va. L. Rev.*, 871 (1963). A brief description of the survey may also be found in Radzinowicz, *In Search of Criminology*, pp. 132–34 (1962).

[8]Three summer seminars focused around the Bar Foundation material have been held at the University of Wisconsin. Two were sponsored by the Ford Foundation, one in 1958 and the other in 1963, and in 1960 a seminar was underwritten by the Social Science Research Council. With the exception of the 1963 seminar, which was designed to acquaint "young criminal law professors" with the operational dimensions of the criminal justice system, the seminar participants were from various disciplines including law, sociology, social work, psychology, and political science.

[9]These were Lloyd E. Ohlin, Donnell M. Pappenfort, James D. Turner, Harry V. Ball, and myself.

sociologists were peripherally connected, and some are now becoming aware of the project and are interested in its results.

In general, however, this project could hardly be called a sociologists' enterprise. By and large the issues dealt with here have not been given a high priority in sociological circles, even among those sociologists who define themselves as criminologists. This seems strange, for sociology, more than any other discipline, has assumed a major responsibility for the study of crime and criminal behavior in our society. Partly by design and partly by default, the high priests of criminology, in the best tradition of Comte, are sociologists. One would think that research into police operations, into the functions of prosecutors and courts, into the flow of the whole complex system of justice administration would be of paramount sociological concern. Sociologists have indeed a traditional interest in system and process. There is considerable sociological work done in the study of bureaucracy, of large-scale organization, of professionalization, and of role, power, and authority. Yet, while no one is quicker than a sociologist to analyze a factory, a mental hospital, or an army, the systematic study of the criminal justice process has been left a world apart, almost totally neglected, and not commonly within the ken of even the most devoted criminologist. Why has this been? and further, why should it be?

CRIMINOLOGY AND CRIMINAL JUSTICE ADMINISTRATION

The nature of sociological interest in crime, while purportedly very encompassing, actually has been highly selective, touching only narrow aspects of this whole problem.

A typical textbook in criminology begins by flaying the pioneer criminologist Lombroso, and the phrenologists (long dead horses in any case); it ends with a pitch for white-collar crime just to show 1) that crime is pretty much what you define it, 2) that criminal conduct crosses class lines, and 3) that some older, single-factor postulates about criminals, such as feeblemindedness, do not apply to bankers and business leaders who violate their positions of trust.

There has been a traditional interest by criminologists in building their own theories of crime causation and in demolishing the theories of others. Whatever the merits of such theorizing, this limited type of exercise makes up the predominant sociological thrust in this whole field. The emphasis is on explanation of criminal conduct; upon the motives and mechanics of criminal careers. Much less attention has been paid to what might broadly be termed *crime control* or to the way our social order organizes to deal with ongoing crime and the detection, detention, processing, and treatment of criminals.

This is not to say that this segment of criminology has been totally ignored, only that it has received less attention. Textbooks in criminology are traditionally divided into two parts: theory and control; the latter is usually referred to as "corrections" or "criminal justice." This is the "practical" part of criminology, considered less prestigeful than theory, but, with few exceptions,[10] included to give a well-rounded assessment of the crime problem, a reluctant bow to the fact that prisons *do* exist, that cities *do* have police, and that courts daily confront thousands of criminal cases.

An interesting thing occurs between the beginning and the end of most criminology texts. The first half, the theory part, is conceptually organized and is full of references to the meaning and significance of research. The latter half, the control part, is, however, ordinarily largely historical-descriptive, intended, presumably, to be informative rather than evaluative. Conceptualization of the kind necessary for theory building or process analyzing is usually absent altogether. This section may contain a chapter on police and another on criminal justice (describing, as if for the first time, such a term as "arraignment," and pointing out that prosecutors, judges, and lawyers all have "roles" in criminal justice). This is followed by a few chapters on prisons, probation, and other aspects of correctional administration. There is also usually a chapter making the point that the death penalty does not really deter crime, inevitably noting with some satisfaction that pickpockets congregated at public hangings of pocket pickers in Europe. There is no serious attempt either to systematically describe or to evaluate the process of criminal justice administration in criminology texts or, for that matter, in sociological works of any kind.[11]

Where there has been sociological focus on the criminal justice system it has been primarily segmental (see, for example, the chapters on police in *any* criminology text). By and large data are old, of questionable value, and lead nowhere. The dominant theme seems to be gross police misconduct—the third degree and corruption—with virtually no recognition or assessment of police and policing as critical, ongoing parts of current criminal justice administration. Sociological contribution to this problem has been limited; even worse than this, evaluation of the police has been, and remains, essentially naïve. The contribution of sociological knowledge or evaluation to the other parts of the criminal justice system, up

---

[10]See, for example, George B. Vold, *Theoretical Criminology* (New York: Oxford University Press, 1958).

[11]In part, I think, this is because sociologists typically do not survey law reviews and other law journal sources in building bibliographies. While there are limited exceptions—for example, Herbert Bloch and Gilbert Geis, *Man, Crime and Society* (New York: Random House, Inc., 1962)—most recent texts in criminology contain no references to law review articles or to significant, recent case law, changes in court rules, or proposed model legislation in discussing any part of criminal justice administration. A great many articles based on the Bar Foundation study have appeared in law journals but apparently these have simply been overlooked by sociological text writers.

to and including sentencing, has been, if anything, even more limited. It is almost as if the court processes did not exist at all and, except for imputed shabby treatment of Negroes and other minority group members, were totally unworthy of sociological interest.

The contribution to corrections, and here I must admit some exceptions,[12] has likewise been somewhat unsystematic, largely episodic, and rather fragmentary. There are really only two major areas in this field where sociologists have shown any sustained interest: one is parole prediction,[13] and the other concerns analysis of the prison community and the process of "prisonization."[14]

Parole prediction is interesting, but is commonly set in no context other than its own. There has been no systematic study of parole in relation to other aspects of the criminal justice system, no sustained focus on decision making here in relation to sentencing, or revocation, or the impact of parole on police practices, or myriad other things that one would suspect would interest sociologists very much.[15]

Like parole prediction, the study and classification of inmates by proponents of the "rat-fink" school is an interesting exercise, and it is certainly more enjoyable reading than multiple regression tables, but its contribution is essentially anthropological. It is fascinating as a description of tribal rites, but it is an extremely limited contribution to the analysis of criminal justice administration.

ON THE ABSENCE OF RESEARCH

I suspect criminologists have largely avoided more systematic involvement with the criminal justice system for two different reasons: (1) To begin with, criminological prestige is traditionally related to theories of *crime causation*. By and large, the sociologist has defined his criminological task as a social-psychological one. The primary focus has been on the study of criminal behavior with a dual objective of accounting, first of all, for the existence of crime in our society and, secondly, for the selection of criminal careers only by certain persons within the society. The goal is etiological theory building; the best criminologist is consid-

[12]For example, Paul W. Tappan, *Crime, Justice and Correction* (New York: McGraw-Hill Book Co., Inc., 1960); Donald R. Cressey, *The Prison: Studies in Institutional Organization and Change* (New York: Holt, Rinehart and Winston, Inc., 1961); and Daniel Glaser, *The Effectiveness of a Prison and Parole System* (Indianapolis: Bobbs-Merrill, 1964).

[13]The literature on parole prediction is extensive. See, for example, Lloyd E. Ohlin, *Selection for Parole* (New York: Russell Sage Foundation, 1951).

[14]See, for example, Gresham M. Sykes, *The Society of Captives* (Princeton, N.J.: Princeton University Press, 1958); Richard A. Cloward *et al.*, *Theoretical Studies in the Social Organization of the Prison* (Social Science Research Council, 1960).

[15]A notable exception but very definitely a product of the Bar Foundation study is Lloyd E. Ohlin and Frank J. Remington, "Sentencing Structure: Its Effect upon Systems for the Administration of Criminal Justice," 23, *Law and Contemporary Problems*, 495 (1958).

ered to be the one whose research leads in this direction. In rejecting the theories of Lombroso, most criminologists nevertheless accepted his postulate that the basic question is the cause of crime. Given lesser consideration was the question of the causal process of imprisonment which was also implicit in the work of Lombroso. This is basically a question that calls for operational, rather than social-psychological, analysis.

Second, the analysis of criminal justice administration requires knowledge and skills other than sociological. The sociologist who finds himself at all interested in criminal justice administration finds himself in a world he never made. He has no responsibilities here; he is neither police officer nor judge nor even correctional administrator. Other professions and disciplines claim substantive expertise; other professions are involved in running the system. The sociologist is not only an outsider physically, but he generally feels uncomfortable with what he conceives to be a basic lack of knowledge: unfamiliarity with the language, traditions, objectives, and problems of the lawyer, the judge, the police officer, and the warden.

Two things generally occur: in many cases the sociologist backs off entirely; in others he attacks a peripheral problem. How can he really study the process of arrest, for example, without familiarizing himself with the complexities of law relating to arrest? How can he analyze parole revocation without extensive knowledge of correctional programs and policies? When faced with esoteric legal terms and processes, the sociologist abandons thoughts of operational analysis. He can and does turn to counting the number of delinquents who come from poor homes as a more comfortable and a more traditional sociological enterprise. If he persists in his operational interest, he tends to concentrate on those aspects of the problem more amenable to his skills (i.e., parole prediction, or such areas of gross breakdown in law enforcement as police brutality or corruption in the correctional process); it does not require sophisticated legal knowledge to assess the third degree or the bribery of a parole board member as improper.

Sustained, sophisticated involvement with the overall criminal justice process, a study of decision making in the routine operations of this system, has not really caught on in sociological circles.

THE POTENTIAL OF SOCIOLOGICAL CONTRIBUTION TO CRIMINAL JUSTICE RESEARCH

In my own opinion, sociologists can, and should, turn their attention to the criminal justice system for at least two reasons: (1) Issues in the operation of this system are perfectly consistent with much of traditional sociological inquiry. The administration of criminal justice involves a complex process of decision making and the operational implementation of policy and authority comparable to similar processes in any large-scale organization. This should not be solely of criminological concern: the process of arrest, charging, conviction, sentencing, and treatment of offenders comprises an elaborate system of decisions, of interrelationships among bureaucratic structures, and of roles, status, and power of much more general sociological interest.

(2) Issues in criminal justice administration are important in their own right and deserve professional attention. Systematic research and analysis of the way crime is defined, the way persons suspected of crime are processed, and the way convicted offenders are treated in our society is, to say the least, a worthy enterprise.

Sociology has been criticized for researching trivia, for stressing methodology and ignoring content, for emphasizing rigor to the detriment of relevance. In my opinion, much of this criticism is justified. It is time, in criminology and in other sociological pursuits, to give some priority to relevance. Cumulative studies pointing to the "reality" of white-collar crime are no longer really necessary. Prison community studies have sufficiently demonstrated their worth and their techniques. I feel that it is important now for the sociologist to attack questions raised by the relationship of legislature, court, and administrative agency in the ongoing operation of a very important system for the control of deviant conduct. Etiological analysis should by no means be abandoned, but it is necessary that analysis of administrative operations be fully and systematically pursued.

AREAS FOR ATTENTION

Without trying to make an exhaustive list, I would think sociologists would be interested in some alternative types of analysis of the criminal justice system: attention, for example, might be turned to—

The consequence of multiple objectives on operational procedures. The question here is how a complex system, made up of diverse agencies and processes, responds to demands that it solve crimes, protect individual liberties, deter lawbreaking and rehabilitate offenders all at the same time. Perhaps this question is too broad, but the idea is essentially to analyze the reality of achieving the multiple *purposes* of criminal justice activities.

System-maintenance accommodations in criminal justice administration. All complex administrative systems must pay attention to the balance and flow of daily business. They must get the job done and maintain some form of stability, and yet be flexible enough to absorb change. The criminal justice system, involved in the daily processing of thousands of cases, is no exception. Each step in the process is related to the next, so, for example, the frequency and types of arrests ultimately determine prison populations and programs. The question here is how the system balances itself, how it gets things done, without too great disruption of administrative efficiency. (The Bar Foundation study demonstrated some of these accommodations; my own analysis of the guilty plea process is another case in point.)

Communication patterns in the criminal justice system. Appellate courts regularly decide cases which have, in theory at least, great significance for operational procedures in criminal justice administration. An interesting question is whether these opinions are communicated to the agencies and translated into practice and if they are, how this is done. This is communication in a linear direction from court to agency; another question is the extent to which agency operational problems and practices are communicated to courts for their consideration in deciding cases affecting procedure.

The effectiveness of administrative practices. There is ample evidence that police, prosecutors, courts and correctional agencies pursue certain policies and practices in anticipation of specific results. The question is whether these practices really do achieve the desired results or whether, put sociologically, they result in unanticipated consequences. Does it make any difference in terms of recidivism that certain offenders are held in prison for five years while others, guilty of similar offenses, are released in two? Does a sustained police effort to search persons in "high incidence" areas for weapons actually result in fewer knifings?

Agency discretion in criminal justice administration. This was an important focus of the ABF study and, in my opinion, is worthy of further and more intensive analysis. In general, this approach views the system as a series of interlocking, discretionary choices—police discretion not to arrest certain suspects but to arrest others, the prosecutor's discretion whether to prosecute and what charge to bring, discretion of the trial judge to reduce charges or to acquit certain defendants, judicial sentencing discretion, and institutional, parole, and revocation discretion. The analysis of criteria used in exercising discretion and the consequences for the agency and the system of the exercise of discretion are obviously important problems, and are eminently appropriate for sociological concern. These, and any number of other problems and approaches to problems are, it seems to me, relevant to sociological inquiry.

RESEARCH ISSUES

Based on my experience in the American Bar Foundation study, I feel that sociologists *can* contribute to the study of the criminal justice system and *can*, at the same time, benefit from it.

Such studies will in all probability be interdisciplinary. Lawyers, social workers, police administrators, political scientists, psychologists, and perhaps other professionals all have an interest in this type of research. In my opinion this type of interdisciplinary commitment is healthy. I think there is little doubt that joint efforts are apt to be better conceived, more meaningful in the long run, than an isolated approach by any single discipline.

Reluctance to conduct research on that which is essentially a sociological process—because other professions have an operational interest in it—gives too much credit to the "difference-between-professions" myth. Criminal justice research is operational; while lawyers and sociologists indeed acquire different substantive knowledge, their concerns in researching criminal justice in operation are remarkably similar. I am certain that whatever professional differences exist at the beginning of any project will dissipate as common problems are examined and various approaches planned.

If the sociologist is to contribute to this type of effort, it *will* require familiarity with the overall criminal justice system and with current significant issues in it. This does not mean that the sociologist must study law or acquire a substantive knowledge of correctional administration or any other discipline. Certainly the sociologist does not have to go through West Point to study the Army or take graduate work in commerce to study the factory.

Finally, there is a rather common assumption on the part of other professional persons, unfortunately shared by many sociologists, that the major contribution of the sociologist to such analysis is methodological. The sociologist, presumably, can provide the research tools for answering questions put by others. While there is no doubt that the competent sociologist can contribute to methodology, I feel that he can make an even more valuable contribution to the conceptualization of the research, to the framing of significant questions, to the planning as well as to the design.

SUMMARY

I think that sociology is missing an opportunity if it does not soon turn more sustained and action-oriented attention to the criminal justice process. I feel particularly that criminology, as a specialty of sociologists, cannot develop much further without such an interest.

A key piece of legislation won in 1965 by the architects of the Great Society substantially revises and liberalizes the terms of the 1952 McCarran-Walter Immigration Act. The history of federal legislation in this matter is also the history of sociological involvement, uneven and divided to be sure, but continuous nevertheless, and often significant. Dr. Richard Robbins, a first-hand participant in the last full "go-around" (1952), recounts both records—federal and sociological—paying special attention to the uses (and abuses) made of sociological testimony and reasoning. In so doing he introduces the intriguing specialty of "applied political sociology," and explores three roles available here for the action-oriented sociologist. The numbers of such sociologists should grow, he concludes, for we can, none of us, remain indifferent to the lawmaker's shaping of immigration policies—or any other policies for that matter.

SOCIOLOGY AND CONGRESSIONAL LAWMAKING: IMMIGRATION—A CASE STUDY

Richard Robbins

Of the Making of Laws

OF THE making of laws there is no end. The process goes on in countless city halls and in fifty statehouses. The most far-reaching decisions take place, however, in Washington where the President proposes, Congress disposes, and the Supreme Court interprets constitutionally. It is naive to imagine that this emphasis results from a dark conspiracy on the part of "big government." Rather, "Washington" is everywhere and omnipresent principally because neither private associations nor state governments nor municipal agencies have been fully able to meet our needs and protect our rights. Obligations defaulted in one sector of society result in power accumulated in another. The Great Depression of the thirties demonstrated the incapacity of private capitalism to heal itself unaided and led to the New Deal's patchwork reforms. Today, under welfare capitalism, we take for granted Washington's basic role in stimulating employment and productivity. Abroad, the global demands of World War II, followed by the revival of Europe and revolutionary developments in Asia and Africa, have thrust upon President and Congress undreamed-of responsibilities in the perennial task of balancing national interests and international commitments.

Thus, as a result of history and necessity, the Congress finds itself at the vital center of issues once left to the private sector or reserved to local and state governments. If decentralism could achieve Paul Goodman's "restoration of community" at the local level, if reapportionment could restore vitality to archaic state legislatures, our system of political pluralism would be the beneficiary. Still, these would be changes only in degree. A healthier federalism would further balance, but in no sense undo, the dominant position of Washington.

This granted, we may turn to congressional law-making as one expression of welfare state and postindustrial society. Congress is chosen rather than the presidency or a major regulatory agency because, for all the criticism of a "House out of order" and an encrusted "Senate Establishment." Congress remains a broad-based national body, roughly responsive to the electorate and reasonably representative of our multigroup, diversified society.[1] It is, for better or for worse, characteristically American. It contains Neanderthals, conservatives, moderates, liberals, militant liberals, loners—and somehow brings them all into working, if creaking, coalition. It rewards the timorous and the time-servers, chiefly through the seniority principle which provides undistinguished Congressmen, continuously returned from safe districts, with strategic chairmanships of committees. Yet for the able Congressman the committee process can be an ever-changing educational experience.

I do not suggest that invoking a "happy pluralism" explains Congress or refutes the familiar criticisms that Congree fails to truly debate, trivializes what it does debate, and misuses its investigative power. I do hold against the sweeping conclusion that, as a result of these obvious deficiencies, congressmen have become little more than parochial political traders, trapped, as C. Wright Mills observed "in the semi-organ-

---

[1]There is a rapidly growing body of literature, by social scientists and by congressmen themselves, on the structural defects of Congress which leave the House and Senate unequal to the great challenges of the twentieth century. Most of the critics argue for urgent and needed reforms within the present framework of congressional and party government. On the social science side see, for example, James McGregor Burns, *The Deadlock of Democracy* (Englewood Cliffs, N.J.: Prentice-Hall, Inc., 1963), and David Truman (ed.), *The Congress and America's Future* (Englewood Cliffs, N.J.: Prentice-Hall, Inc, 1965). On the congressional side the most astute critiques are those by Senator Joseph Clark, *The Senate Establishment* (New York: Hill & Wang, 1963), and Representative Richard Bolling, *House Out of Order* (New York: E. P. Dutton & Co., Inc., 1965). The influential journalist William White is the chief proponent of the counterthesis that the Senate is the fount of measured wisdom and sensible, moderate liberalism.

ized stalemate of the middle levels of power."[2] Such a verdict seems premature and, possibly unjust. By no means has Congress been reduced to dividing the money for rivers and harbors or making minor adjustments in policies of the President and the Pentagon. Eventually the Senate and the House come to grips; sooner or later they do legislate.

Action Sociology and Congressional Law Making

Conventionally, the professional study of Congress is part of the discipline of political science or government. At an early age, the American encounters, in the guise of high school "civics," the congressional legislative process—considerably tidied up and idealized. Little stick figures place bills in hoppers; the bills travel along dotted lines to committee; return to the floor for passage; travel on to conference for adjustment of different versions; terminate in presidential signature. Thus are we taught "how a bill becomes law."

Later, political science teaches us a much more sophisticated and realistic understanding. We learn of the loose fit between parties and congressional blocs, of lobbying and "pressure groups," of the tangle of checks and balances among the three federal branches, of the complex role of "the fourth branch," the departments and agencies.

But even at this advanced level, the organizational approach suffers from too restrictive a mandate. Hence, in recent years many political scientists have been disposed to "move out" from their core field, the structure of government, to a consideration of that societal group life which gives government its shape and direction.[3] They have been concerned with the social origins of senators, with group life and role playing within a congressional committee, and with the broader issues of voting behavior and party affiliation as they are affected by such sociological factors as class position, ethnic identification, family socialization, and regional subcultures. Here they have met many sociologists interested in the political process insofar as class position, ethnic identification, family socialization, and regional subcultures have a bearing not only on voting behavior or party affiliation but on the activity of senators and congressional committees as well.

---

[2] C. Wright Mills, *The Power Elite* (New York: Oxford University Press, 1956), Chap. 11.

[3] The seminal work which made of group life and political life a seamless whole and which was "rediscovered" by political scientists after being well known to sociologists for decades is Arthur F. Bentley's *The Process of Government*, first published in 1908 by the University of Chicago Press. The most systematic sociopolitical attempt to apply Bentley's work to contemporary government is David B. Truman's *The Governmental Process* (New York: Alfred A. Knopf, Inc., 1953). Bentley himself went on to a position far beyond conventional "group interest" analysis and entered into a fruitful, working relationship with John Dewey on the philosophy of "transaction."

This convergent interest has lately made possible a political sociology in general, and a sociology of the legislative process in particular. For present purposes we may define "political sociology" as an interdisciplinary field, drawing upon political science, sociology, and social psychology. It is concerned with the allocation of power among group interests, whether within the special realm of government itself or in the general social structure where a relationship exists between the political and social systems. Applied to congressional lawmaking, political sociology seeks to trace the development of specific policies, in successive stages, from deep-lying groups in the social system on up to the "narrower" group activity and power within Congress itself—the conventional organizational approach of "how a bill becomes a law."[4]

On any given issue, such as national health insurance or federal aid to education, the sociologist takes up seriatim: the state of national public opinion on the issue as measured by the polls; the more revealing differences expressed in regional patterns and urban-rural contrasts within regions; the further definition of the issue in terms of class and ethnic divisions; the incorporation of the issue into the activity of formal interest groups and organizations; and finally, the resolution of the issues in the congressional arena. Case studies of particular laws can "pick up" this sequence at different stages, depending on the field of interest of the investigator.

In tracing a given congressional law the political sociologist or political scientist is basically analytic and diagnostic. His is not an active role in decision-making itself; he is not usually practicing "action sociology." The term "action sociology" invites a variety of definitions among sociologists, but in general it may be agreed that, first, the sponsoring private or governmental agency *has already formulated a policy* and, second, the reliable knowledge which the sociologist provides to the agency *will contribute to making the policy more effective.* (To be sure, a sponsoring agency such as the Peace Corps or the Urban League anticipates criticism as well as constructive suggestions; both are implied in the "effectiveness" mandate.)

Congressional law-making, however, presents a different picture to the sociologist moving on from the analytic-diagnostic role to the action role. Policy has not been formulated; it is still in the making. And far from working to provide reliable knowledge which will advance a program's goals effectively, the sociologist finds himself in the middle of an argument, with various groups "for" and "against" the program's goals and the means for carrying them out. Since the action problem here is

---

[4]There are literally hundreds of such studies by political scientists, but many are confined to a "late" organizational stage in the sequence. One of the best of the more comprehensive types, and a model of the case study method, is Stephen K. Bailey's *Congress Makes a Law* (New York: Columbia University Press, 1950).

thus more difficult than in going to work for a planning commission or a health department, we need to explore briefly three role options available to the action sociologist concerned with congress.

First, it is possible to become directly engaged in the congress by becoming a congressman-sociologist oneself. However, few social scientists are inclined to travel this hazardous, expensive, and time consuming road. And those so inclined are more likely to be economists, like Senator Paul Douglas, or political scientists, like Senator Mike Mansfield. (I know of only one prominent sociologist, Arnold Rose, who has been a state legislator in recent years. One prominent senator once taught sociology en route to the Senate. That is the record. However it is intriguing to imagine, say, David Riesman in the Senate or Robert Merton in the House.[5] As a rule, social scientists gain access to power and policy indirectly by serving candidates in a research-advisory capacity and then taking up positions as specialists in a wide range of Congressional committees and administrative agencies.

The second role, familiar and modal, is that of the professional expert who proffers testimony "for" or "against" during the time in which congressional legislation is taking shape. A well-known instance concerns sociology itself, the effort by social scientists to persuade Congress to add the behavioral sciences to the research mandate of the National Science Foundation. The most celebrated recent example involved the Supreme Court rather than the Congress. The Court was preparing to hold racial segregation in the public schools unconstitutional in 1954. A group of social scientists filed a supporting brief based on the professional opinion that racial segregation had harmful effects on the development of Negro children. The Court was not, however, "Practicing sociology instead of law." The brief was auxiliary to a determination squarely on the basis of the Fourteenth Amendment.

In principle, the congressional committee hearing is the decisive arena for matching professional roles. Sociologists, among others, are called upon to provide balanced views along the full spectrum of opinion on a given issue, to the end of sound legislation. In practice however, the committee hearing is all too often a ritual drama of adversaries, with "equal time" given to specialists and lobbyists alike. Congressmen get their work done before and after the televised proceedings. The public tends not to be aware that frequently, if the measure be valuable knowledge, the least publicized hearing is the most valuable and vice versa.

---

[5]Donald R. Mathews, a political scientist, has sociologists in his debt for his perceptive studies of the social origins of congressmen. See, for example, his *United States Senators and Their World* (New York: Random House, Inc., [Vintage Books], 1964). The idea of the "typical" senator is a useful fiction and Mathews, properly qualifying, defines him as a "late middle-aged or elderly, white, Protestant, native-born man with rural or small town and upper-middle-class origins, a college-educated lawyer, and a 'joiner.'" (p. 44).

Nevertheless, the public hearing, with its mixture of witnesses, professional and partisan, is an artifact of the democratic process and a useful means for disseminating sociological research to a lay audience. As we shall see, it has worked that way with regard to "national origins."

The third and broadest role conjoins the status of social scientist and citizen. The social scientist, as an *individual* member of a concerned community of interest, calls upon the President or on the Congress to "do something" about Viet Nam or racial injustice. All this constitutes conventional protest-role action. But just beyond lies a thorny ethical issue. Suppose a professional sociological association "speaks out" *as a group* on a controversy before the Congress? Are the research functions of the association and the second type of action role of its members thereby compromised? It is hard to say. The Society for the Study of Social Problems called upon Congress to pass the Civil Rights Act of 1964 without its individual members assuming that their individual research on race relations had been cast into doubt. Just so, the physical scientists associated with *The Bulletin of the Atomic Scientists* appealed to the Congress to ratify the Kennedy administration's proposal to ban the testing of atomic bombs without its individual members assuming that their laboratory research had been called into question. All the same, there are many social scientists who share views such as the above but who fear the consequences to a professional association's scholarly standing if its membership's "lines up" on issues like a pressure group.[6]

Without arguing for any priorities among these roles which supply the action emphasis in applied political sociology, we may now consider a single piece of legislation, the McCarran-Walter Immigration and Nationality Act of 1952. In such a case study we see the political sociologist coming to grips with the legislative process in terms of both the analytic role and the three types of action role.

Immigration Law: Analytic Political Sociology

American immigration is a vast and complex subject of interest to sociologists concerned with the assimilation cycle, with "melting pot"

---

[6]Here is a recent case in point. At its Montreal meeting in 1964 the American Sociological Association's business meeting section passed a resolution deploring political attacks on the Mobilization for Youth program in New York City and urging that the program be judged on professional standards. Agreeing with the point of view, Robert Bierstedt questioned, nonetheless, "whether we want, as a scientific society, to pass *any* resolutions on matters of public policy," and argued that sociologists maintain their traditional role of active involvement *as individual citizens*. Replying, Herbert J. Gans did not see a deep contradiction between taking a political stand in the A.S.A. and maintaining a scientific posture. "Objectivity requires only that we do not do research and be politically active *on the same topic at the same time.*" These quotations are from "The A.S.A. and Public Policy," *American Sociological Review*, February, 1965.

and "ethnic pluralism."[7] Here we attend, however, not to immigration in general but to its interplay with congressional lines of policy.

The Immigration Act, passed in 1952 over a veto by President Truman, continues a tradition of restrictionism which dates from the period following World War I. After the great post-1900 surge of immigration into our expanding urban-industrial society, the American people began to doubt the wisdom of open-door massive immigration. They turned toward restrictionism, and some of them turned toward nativism, that simplistic doctrine which charges to "foreigners, Catholics, and Jews" responsibility for social disruptions which are, in fact, inevitable consequences of the transition from frontier society to the society of the city and the factory.

Previously, in 1882 sectional group interests had succeeded in persuading Congress to exclude Chinese and to bar them from citizenship. The 40 large volumes of the Joint Commission on Immigration, presented to Congress in 1911, gave a kind of social research sanction to further restrictionism in the making. The first quota law, passed in 1921, concentrated on quantitative limitation; total quota immigration was fixed at some 350,000. Then came the basic Immigration Act of 1924, passed overwhelmingly in both House and Senate. It broadened the exclusion and ineligibility-to-citizenship provision to include all Asians. It tightened deportation and naturalization procedures.

The Act's key provision—which was not implemented until 1929—was the famous "national origins" formula. Working with a reduced total European quota of 154,000, proportions were worked out for each country based upon an elaborate statistical measure of the representation of each nationality in the total population over time. This technique, intended in the words of the reporting House committee to prevent a situation where "the balance of racial preponderance must in turn pass to those elements of the population who reproduce more rapidly on a lower standard of living than those possessing other ideals," produced a ratio of "old" to "new" immigration of about six to one. The restriction issue had been settled in favor of the restrictionists.

Additional provisions opening immigration on a nonquota basis to peoples of the Western Hemisphere, which raised the annual total to some 300,000, did not counterbalance in any real sense the policy of restriction against the "new" Europeans. The Great Depression and World War II, following hard upon the economic crisis, provided a more legitimate basis for continuing the policy. And the postwar admission of nearly 400,000 refugees and displaced persons was achieved principally outside the quota system, as part of the U.S.'s international commitment to an "emergency situation."

---

[7]See on the general assimilation problem an excellent work by Milton Gordon, *Assimilation in American Life* (New York: Oxford University Press, 1964).

The McCarran-Walter Act of 1952, operative until the passage of the new Immigration Act of 1965, retained the national origins formula and the restrictionist approach to deportation, naturalization, and visa procedure. Racialist exclusion of Asians was eliminated, as was their ineligibility to citizenship, but some special discriminatory quota provisions against Asians were still retained. As before, a significant proportion of the "old" European quota visas went unused while many "new" Europeans continued to wait for years because their country's quota had been heavily oversubscribed. Over the years the Truman, Eisenhower, Kennedy and Johnson administrations made successively stronger efforts to revise the McCarran-Walter Act. President Kennedy, grandson of immigrants himself and author of the widely read booklet criticizing the national origins system, *A Nation of Immigrants,* judged congressional restrictionist sentiment too powerful to accomplish anything more than an annual transfer of unused visas, to be distributed according to a set of functional priorities. Even this the late President did not live to see.

It remained for President Johnson, for reasons to be discussed below, to initiate and to sign the Immigration Act of 1965. This Act eliminates the national origins system (effective in 1968) and replaces it with an annual quota outside the Western Hemisphere of 170,000, with no single country receiving more than 20,000. It institutes for the first time an annual quoto of 120,000 for the Western Hemphere, but sets no limit for individual countries (a not very meaningful provision since the basic controls affect *individual* Latin Americans in terms of job assurances and health and welfare standards). It liberalizes the exemption provisions for parents, spouses, and children of U.S. citizens, and it expands the first preferences within quotas for refugees, members of separated families, and those with special occupational skills. In general, it allows a prudent increase in immigration to take place after the three-year transition period. The Act's most important and immediate result is to allow potential immigrants from "new" countries to move to the United States during the next three years on unblocked transferred visas without having to wait interminably, as in the past, for available visa numbers.

With his flair for the dramatic, the President chose to sign the law underneath the Statue of Liberty, guarding the harbor through which millions of immigrants passed in the nineteenth and early twentieth centuries: "The days of unlimited immigration are over. But those who come will come because of what they are—not because of the land from which they sprung. . . . Today, with my signature this (national origins) system is abolished."

How does the political sociologist, pursuing the *analytic* role, undertake to trace this history, culminating in the Act of 1952? He follows the sequence already suggested: from underlying value systems, to patterns of public opinion, to the interplay of group interests focused on the Congress, to the Congress itself. The two general contending forces are restrictionism and antirestrictionism, the first organized around retention of the present policy, including national origins, the second organized around a goal of moderate increase in overall immigration, together with either reform of, or eventually elimination of national origins. Around these two positions the group interests move.

In 1952 the value outlook and general public opinion were, on the whole, restrictionist. But, as already indicated, the issue was no longer as salient; a majority of a national sample, polled in 1955, were unfamiliar with the 1952 act. Since hostility to immigration was present, but latent and diffuse, the antirestrictionist groups were able to exploit this advantage and they achieved the passage of the two postwar displaced persons acts. They could not touch national origins, however.

Much more significant in 1952 was the differential response to the law in the social-geographic regions of the country. Roughly, restrictionism had its maximum strength in the South, antirestrictionism in the Northeast. The South and sections of the West were more rural, more agrarian, more homogeneous with respect to religion and ethnicity. The congressional representation tended to reflect, approximately, this insular pattern. In some contrast the congressional districts in the Northeast and certain densely populated areas of the Great Lakes states epitomized the urban, industrial, more heterogenous society, with its concentration of "new" immigrant stock, Catholics, and Jews. The antirestrictionist forces were invariably led by congressmen, from "old" as well as "new ethnic background, with these constituencies. The same tendencies were repeated in the ethnic blocs loosely assembled around the two-party system. Northern, urban Democrats and a cluster of Republicans from comparable constituencies represented antirestrictionism; Southern, conservative Democrats and a scattering of Republicans from rural and small-town constituencies in the West formed the core of the restrictionist coalition.

Of course, socioeconomic classes and ethnic blocs cannot in fact be parceled out so neatly in terms of general political orientation, much less in terms of a single law. But beneath the fluidity and the change these relationships persisted through the fifties. Within Congress they emerged in roughly the same balance: restrictionism supported by conservative southern Democrats and conservative midwest Republicans; antirestrictionism supported by liberal and ethic-religious Democrats, together with a sprinkling of liberal Republicans, nearly all of whom were from the Northeast. I take the terms "liberal" and "conservative" in the conventional contemporary sense, yet with respect to the McCarran-Walter Act as an expression of liberalism one caution is in order. Antirestrictionism has been part of the liberal outlook for many years, but a considerable number of the Democratic party regulars from ethnic and Catholic constituencies in Northeastern cities, while voting within the liberal bloc, were doing so mechanically in a special matter involving "their" people and their constituencies. In general liberalism they showed little interest.

Setting aside this qualification, let us bring together the analytic elements just discussed in the final congressional test: the floor vote. In the following compilation on the successful vote to override President Truman's veto of what he termed a "discriminatory" law, a "yes" vote to override represents restrictionism, a "no" vote anti-restrictionism.

Party Wings:	House				Senate			
	Republican		Democrat		Republican		Democrat	
	Yes	No	Yes	No	Yes	No	Yes	No
	157	13	3	2	32	4	3	1
Conservative: N. & W.	6	0	67	0	2	0	16	0
Conservative: South	5	9	13	84	0	5	1	13
Liberal: N. & W.	0	0	29	5	0	0	6	6
Total:	168	22	112	91	34	9	26	20

Thus the results in 1952. Thirteen years later the powerful coalition of restrictionist conservative southern Democrats and midwest Republicans had given way considerably before change and time. The Civil Rights Act of 1964 and the Immigration Act of 1965 were introduced, and became law.

Immigration Law: Action Political Sociology

Months and months of committee hearings and congressional debate preceded final passage of the 1952 McCarran-Walter Act.[8] The question that can be raised for this paper is: *To what extent did "action sociologists" contribute, if at all, to this process?*

On the whole, those sociologists and anthropologists who had worked in the ethnic-racial field or had concerned themselves with acculturation theory were strongly opposed to the national origins formula. Their opposition stemmed directly from their recognition that the assimilation of immigrants was a product of culture and was not the result of a set of assertedly inborn traits which "old" immigrants possessed and "new" immigrants did not.

---

[8]The full study is contained in Richard Robbins, "*The Immigration Act of 1952: A Case Study in Political Sociology*" (Urbana, Ill.: Unpublished doctoral Ph.D. dissertation, University of Illinois, 1958). The full record may be consulted in *Revision of Immigration and Naturalization Laws* (Joint Hearings of the Subcommittee of the Committee on the Judiciary, 82d Cong., 1st Sess.). (Washington, D.C.: U.S. Government Printing Office, 1951). Also, *The Immigration and Naturalization Systems of the United States* (Committee on the Judiciary, Senate Report No. 1515, 81st Cong., 2d Sess.) (Washington, D.C.: U.S. Government Printing Office, 1950).

In the twenties, when the basic immigration legislation was under review in the Congress, many sociologists still held to pseudobiological explanations of both Negro–Caucasian and native–immigrant differences; the congressional immigration committees drew upon this sociological work to sustain the thesis that "homogeneity" of the national population was being weakened by new types of immigrants who were "unassimilable." By 1951–52 a few social science specialists could still be recruited by the restrictionist forces in support of such a position. But among those in the behavioral sciences who were at all interested in the legislative issue, the overwhelming majority were favorably disposed toward the antirestrictionist group by virtue of their professional commitment to a cultural, rather than an asserted racial explanation of the assimilation cycle.

In particular, what disturbed social scientists in 1951 even more than the national origins formula was the provision of the existing 1924 law which excluded Asians as a racial group and barred them from citizenship. (A decade before, in 1943, the Congress had terminated Chinese exclusion. The then-pending McCarran-Walter Act of 1952 ended racial exclusion generally—a victory for the cultural point of view—but new rules were added which, in effect, continued to apply criteria of ancestry rather than residence to certain types of Asians seeking admission as immigrants.)

The major professional contribution of social scientists lay in making available to the leaders of the antirestrictionist forces in Congress (primarily Senators Herbert Lehman and Hubert Humphrey, and Representative Emanuel Celler) the great mass of material which had accumulated on the dubious rationale of the national origins principle.[9] Included also were other sets of propositions—for example, that moderate increases in immigration did *not* have a harmful effect on domestic employment, or that the admission of refugees in the thirties and displaced persons in the postwar forties *had* contributed materially to the social and economic welfare of the country. This was the extent of the first, or advisory, role.

A group of prominent sociologists and anthropologists, among them Maurice Davie and Margaret Mead, took up the second role, that of extending the professional point of view into the public arena. They testified at the McCarran-Walter hearings, qua professional experts, that the national origins system reflected an outmoded sociology. Finally, a number of other social scientists adopted the third role: active, partisan

---

[9]A very useful compilation in this respect, and available to the congressional antirestrictionist forces, was Willaim S. Bernard, *et al.*, *American Immigration Policy: a Reappraisal* (New York: Harper & Bros., 1950). Typical of the treatment in social problems, textbooks, providing "equal time" to both sides, is the section on immigration policy in William Petersen and David Matza (eds.), *Social Controversy* (Belmont, Calif.: Wadsworth, 1963).

protest to the Congress, qua private citizens, urging repeal of "this discriminatory law." As already noted, however, here too the action roles were of a limited and auxiliary kind. In 1952 the antirestrictionist and liberal groups had to contend with a somewhat hostile but largely indifferent public opinion outside the Congress. They had to contend with a skilled and strategically placed restrictionist conservative bloc inside the Congress. However soundly the "action sociologists" and other social scientists played their parts in the legislative process, whether as background research specialists, as expert professional witnesses, or as impassioned partisans of immigration reform, the results were bound to be the same because the antirestrictionists could not summon up sufficient support to sustain President Truman's veto. To say this is not to minimize the sociologists' role in congressional lawmaking; it is only to say that in a particular case, whatever the merit of their position from the point of view of social science research, they should not expect the Congress always to react accordingly. Other cases, other results. For example, there seems little doubt the economists of the academy have successfully persuaded the Kennedy and Johnson administrations to translate new Keynesian approaches to deficit financing and tax reduction from theory to practice. And Congress has acquiesced.

How, then, *do* we account for congressional reversal on immigration policy between 1952 and 1965? In the first place, although the action sociologists have now won in the specific sense that the Congress has acquiesced in their contention that the archaic and unsound national origins principle should be replaced, the basic dimensions of the immigration problem remain roughly what they were. The congressional concession to social science does not change the fact that even under the quota limitations annual non-Western Hemisphere immigration has been running in any case at roughly 300,000 rather than the prescribed 154,000 owing to the many provisions for dependents and other special cases. Now, while the total may eventually rise to roughly 400,000 annually there is consensus among both antirestrictionists and restrictionists that in urban industrial societies such as ours, where the economy is "filled up" save for highly specialized needs, immigration can play only a modest part is assessing the total population profile. The difference between 300,000 and 400,000 is not likely to be remarked in a population rounding 195,000,000. Knowing this, the restrictionists could afford to be magnanimous.

In the second place, as noted above, the immigration question which once agitated the entire nation no longer does so. Given time and the assimilation of three generations immigration has receded as a sociological issue. Civil rights and the Negro revolution at home, the crises of the less developed nations abroad, these are the questions of moment about which sociologists, in their research, expert, and citizen roles, now have something important to say to congressional committees.

Finally, we should attend to recent short-run changes, in the context of a political sociology, affecting both the Congress and the presidency. Among the conservative Southern Democrats, consistently the strongest supporters of the national origins system, we have been witnessing the decline of those hard-core traditionalists whose outlook always included a linked definition of Eastern Europeans as "unassimilable" and Negroes as "inferior." The newer type of younger Southern legislator is disposed to yield gracefully, for a variety of reasons, to currents of inevitable social change expressed in such matters as elimination of the poll tax or reform of immigration policy. Additionally, in 1964 a considerable number of the Republicans from more insular and conservative districts, who formed another bulwark against change in immigration law, went down to unexpected defeat in the disaster of the Barry Goldwater candidacy. In this there was a nice irony. Rep. William Miller, the vice-presidential candidate, had tried, unsuccessfully, to make something of the immigration issue in the larger industrial cities, warning darkly of "floods of immigrants" who could jeopardize American jobs. In fact, in presenting President Johnson with so great an electoral margin, the Goldwater-Miller ticket probably did more to bring about the end of the McCarran-Walter Act than all the professional testimony of the sociologists combined. Needless to say, President Johnson skillfully exploited an advantage not available to President Kennedy. On October 10, 1965, he signed the new law.

In 1952, sociologists, seeking a more open and flexible immigration policy, had to accept a law which, while eliminating the unsound principle of racial exclusion, continued the unsound principle of admission based on national origins of a favored type of ethnic population. In 1965 sociologists presented the same critique along the same lines, this time to be rewarded with the elimination of the national origins formula, a prize beyond the hoped-for reform of transferring unused quota visas. If, in both instances, the action roles were secondary to the conflict of group interests in the congressional arena, they represented a contribution just the same. For sociologists have a professional obligation to point to ways in which national policy appears to contradict what we profess to know about social and cultural processes, whether the issue concerns drug addiction, poverty, race relations, or immigration. This obligation they exercised, in different ways, with regard to the national origins controversy. This obligation to play the research and professional expert roles, the first and second role options, they will continue to exercise in the legislative process as new controversies arise. To that degree they affect decision making where, in Walton Hamilton's phrase, the Congress giveth and the Congress taketh away.

In social research, to be able to "take" the role of another is good; to temporarily be another is even better. Rare, however, is the criminologist who has "served time"; the industrial sociologist who has "met a payroll"; the labor sociologist who has "hit the bricks," and so on. Dr. Arnold Rose is the only sociologist commonly known to have served as a state legislator; his experience well illustrates both the contribution made and that received by the sociologist who dares venture beyond the "Tower's walls." His essay, rich in the analysis of role, leadership, expertise, and lawmaking, goes on to challenge still more sociologists to contribute to the political process: "There are some issues which come before a legislature on which only a sociologist can provide expert knowledge."

THE SOCIOLOGIST AS PUBLIC OFFICEHOLDER

Arnold M. Rose

I HAVE LONG been puzzled about the paucity of books and articles describing the "inner life" of an elected public official. Those who seek and win legislative and executive positions in local, state, and federal government surely include some of the most articulate persons in the United States, and many of them are highly educated and skilled in writing. Of course, they are extremely busy men, who not only have to hold down a full-time job, but also "socialize" a great deal, campaign periodically to hold their jobs, and meet the never-ending requests of their constituents. But lack of time does not explain their failure to write, as they often are able to take on civic causes and some part-time business positions outside the call of duty. Often the busiest people are the ones most willing do "one more thing." Most politicians are also socially sensitive people, experienced in thinking through their role relationships to their fellow officeholders and to the more demanding among their constituents. But generally they do not write or talk about themselves, except in the most superficial terms.

I believe that being a sociologist helped me to understand my fellow politicians better and thus work more effectively with them to achieve common goals. I ran a very difficult race for the Minnesota House of Representatives in 1962, and served one session in the state legislature (I believe I could easily have won reelection, but academic and other commitments decided me against seeking office again). As far as I know, I am the only sociologist to have been a state legislator, although several others—including William Graham Sumner—have served in city councils and on local elective boards. I was definitely the first University of Minnesota professor to serve in the legislature, and I'm sure many of my colleagues both in the university and in the legislature did not know what to make of me.

It was obvious that I would have to overcome suspicions of me as a "highbrow" or "longhair" if I was to accomplish anything as a legislator. There are 135 representatives and 67 senators in the Minnesota legislature, and one has to persuade at least half of them of the "rightness" of one's position to get a bill passed. There was the additional handicap that I was in the minority party.

The first thing one learns is to distinguish among one's roles as an advocate of a cause, as a representative of one's constituents, and as a member of a working group. Many legislators—about 40 percent in Minnesota—are attorneys, and they have already learned this distinction before entering public office, as a necessary part of the practice of their profession. But some of my friends, including some legislators who had unusual difficulty in getting bills passed, failed to grasp this distinction; they would say something like "How can you stand so-and-so, he takes such an extreme position," or "he is a tool of the vested interests." For a group of men to work together in a legislature, each must distinguish the man from the public position he takes on an issue. The man is evaluated on the basis of his intelligence (sometimes called "shrewdness"), his knowledge of the issues, his willingness to work hard, his decency and agreeableness in interpersonal relations, his reliability when he gives his word. Every man sizes up every other man in these matters, and rates him. The public position a legislator takes on issues is something else—this, in the eyes of his fellow legislators, is his private personal conviction of what he must do to get reelected, either because his constituents demand it or because it is what his sponsoring interests expect of him in return for their sponsorship.

When it comes to voting on a bill, each legislator will ascertain first whether he has a public position to take on it—whether he has a personal conviction regarding it that he wishes to assert publicly, whether some of his constituents or sponsors have written or spoken to him about it, or whether his party or party legislative caucus has made it an issue. If he has no public position on the bill, he is likely to vote in terms of his own personal feelings in regard to the proponents (especially the chief sponsor) and the opponents of the bill. The latter is why the mutual ratings among legislators as men are so important for the passage or nonpassage of a bill and why a respected member of the minority party can get almost as many bills passed as the average member of the majority party. From one point of view, this process of voting in terms of mutual ratings as men can be called "logrolling" and many political scientists have derogatively called it that, because it implicitly means "I'll vote for your bill, if you later vote for one of mine." But the process is also based on two important facts—one does not have a public position on most bills, and one can have knowledge of the merits of only a small proportion of the legislation one has to vote on. Thus mutual confidence becomes the basis of voting on the majority of bills. One reason a legislator does not talk frankly about himself is that he does not wish to reveal his ignorance about most bills and his vote on these bills in terms of the logrolling process of personal confidence. If he has personal confidence in a member of the opposing party, party loyalty inhibits him from publicizing this high personal confidence because public endorsement of a member of the opposing party can be used in an election campaign against a member of one's own party.

Being a sociologist helped me to understand the role of leadership in a working group. A legislature has only a few formal leaders, and some of these may be merely stooges for the Executive (the governor in a state) or for some powerful figure who does not wish to assume the ceremonial or chore functions of a formal leader. So informal leadership emerges. It is, of course, part of the same process of making mutual ratings that I have already mentioned. Leaders are not only to be classified as formal and informal, but also as general and specific. The formal leaders have special powers—such as assigning of bills to committees by the speaker and taking up or not taking up a bill by a committee chairman—which the new legislator soon learns to respect. On the other hand, there may be informal leaders who are the "powers behind the throne," who can simply tell a formal leader how to use his powers on controversial matters. These top informal leaders, who by definition are the most respected men in the legislature, are general leaders—their expertise lies mainly in their knowledge of the legislative and political processes. There are also specialized leaders—legislators who know most about a particular area of legislation. In each party, these are the ones whose opinion is sought, even by the general leaders, when it comes to voting on a bill in the specialized area. Contemporary government is so complex that no legislator can be a specialist in more than a few of the many issues on which he is obliged to vote.

Even a freshman legislator can be a specialized leader, if he has expertise in certain areas of legislation. As a sociologist, I had specialized knowledge in the areas of education, health and welfare, and urban problems, and the speaker acceded to my request to be placed on committees dealing with these subjects. On these committees, I could be a leader both in introducing and in supporting legislation on which I had specialized knowledge beyond that of my seniors. For example, I introduced and secured the passage of a bill to make higher education available to youths whose parents were on relief and for whom no funds were otherwise available for a college education. The education committee specifically, and the legislature generally, were impressed with the facts I could present about the existence of some brilliant youngsters whose fathers were dead or incapacitated, and who, by existing law, had to turn their small earnings toward their personal support rather than toward higher education because the main support for their families came from public welfare funds. Another bill I introduced and secured passage for was one to remove the stigma of a distinctive birth certificate for illegitimate children not adopted into normal families. Information about vital statistics, the psychological consequences of social stigma, the frequency and procedures of name-changing played a significant role in getting this bill's acceptance. These were not "important" bills, and cost the state little or no money, so they could be accepted as nonpartisan bills on the basis of my evidence as to the need for them.

An "expensive" bill was introduced by a legislator from the majority party, at the behest of the Minnesota Medical Association, to provide medical care for elderly persons who had enough income to take care of their ordinary living costs but not enough money to pay for extraordinary medical costs. My cosponsorship was sought because I was known to be an "expert" in social gerontology and had led civic activities in behalf of the aging. Because the bill involved significant new expenditures for the state government, many legislators—especially from the majority party—were opposed to it. Because the minority party, my party, was supporting stronger *federal* legislation in this area, many legislators of the minority party were opposed to what they regarded as "stopgap" legislation on the state level. My support was sought in the hope that I could persuade my colleagues in the minority party to vote for the bill. I had relevant knowledge about the financial and medical needs of older people in the state, about the alternatives facing older people when they met catastrophic illness, about the various statutes which other states and countries had used to meet the problem. I used this knowledge in two ways: (1) to get a number of changes in the bill so as to make it into a more effective instrument of social policy for the benefit of a segment of older citizens; (2) to convince my colleagues in the minority party that the amended bill was a desirable one and that it was not contradictory, but was supplementary to the bill they favored (then pending before the federal Congress). Even though I could not be the chief sponsor of this bill, since it involved heavy expenditures and I was not in the majority party which assumes responsibility for state finances, I was the effective leader in shepherding the bill through the House of Representatives, because I was the legislator best informed about its complicated provisions.

Knowledge is effective even when a bill fails. Two bills that I introduced, fought for, and saw die were reintroduced into the next session
of the legislature and there gained stronger support. One was a bill to
improve the mass transit system of the metropolitan area of the state.
There were too many controversial aspects to the bill, and too little
public awareness of the long-run need for it to get it passed immediately.
I did persuade the committee chairman by my factual arguments to set
up a subcommittee to give the bill a thorough public hearing. The public
hearing, to which I could bring outside experts to testify as well as
present my own evidence, served the purpose of getting newspaper publicity and public interest in the problem. After two years of this, a modified bill could gain enough votes to pass the House. An identical bill
failed in the Senate, and I like to think that the public hearing in the
House so educated my colleagues there that they were in advance of
the senators and even of other public leaders. The second bill I authored
and saw fail—to remove an arbitrary limitation on dollar aid to the
indigent aged, which simply forced them into more expensive nursing
homes with no dollar limitation—was passed in the next session of the
legislature. The arguments that we proponents of the bill used—that the
existing law was a case of being "penny-wise and pound-foolish"—had a
cumulative effect and finally got through to enough legislators to pass
the bill.

Other examples could be added, but it should be obvious that knowledge is an asset in a legislature and sociological knowledge is relevant
to many issues that come before a legislature. I'll put it even more
bluntly: There are some issues which come before a legislature on which
only a sociologist can provide expert knowledge. Since few sociologists
testify at legislative committee hearings, this means that this area of
legislation lacks the expert hand which much other legislation (say, on
taxation or control of business) normally gets. Of course, some legislators
with a minimum of formal training in sociology make themselves amateur experts in sociology, and even the professional sociologist must
occasionally admire their accomplishments. Social workers frequently
testify at legislative hearings and help formulate much social legislation;
they usually provide a substitute for the sociologist. This is true not
only in the area of social welfare, but also in legislation dealing with
urban problems, crime, public health, recreation, youth opportunities,
and many other areas, in part or in whole. I'll wager that most sociologists
would be amazed to attend committee hearings and observe how much
"sociological" testimony is presented there and discussed by legislators.

I have suggested two general ways in which a sociologist finds his
training useful in a legislature: (1) To understand better the structure
and functioning of a certain type of social organization so as to work
more effectively in it; (2) to bring to bear certain specialized knowledge
from the discipline to relevant practical problems faced by the legisla-

ture, and thus to function as a specialized leader within it. A third way in which a sociologist finds his training useful in public life is as a perpetual campaigner: the academic student of public opinion can do a better job of selling himself to the voting public and can better influence the affairs-conscious public to support the legislation he favors. Of course, there are severe limits on a legislator in terms of the resources he has to reach the electorate, but a candidate for statewide or federal office has greater access through the mass media.

I have long held the theory that because of the difference between public opinion and mass opinion[1] there is a necessity for appealing to these two different entities in two quite different ways. Public opinion exists, I hold, when people are interested in and informed about an issue and are willing and able to discuss it. There is only mass opinion about an issue when interest in it is marginal, knowledge is superficial and next to nonexistent, and there is little discussion. It is important for a candidate to distinguish these two kinds of opinion and deal with them in different ways. Through a public opinion poll, formal or informal, he must identify the issues that have engaged public opinion. He must then inform himself thoroughly about these issues and come to a stand concerning them that he can defend before the public. When discussing such an issue in a public gathering, he should demonstrate his knowledge about *both* sides of the argument and present the side opposing his own with fairness and sympathy. In this way he can neutralize some of the antagonism likely to develop among those opposed to his stand and perhaps even win a few opponents to his position.

As to the issues in mass opinion, the candidate can pick and choose which ones he wishes to be identified with. He needs to be informed about a few of these so he can impress the small number of constituents who might be made interested. The candidate can bring these issues into the realm of public opinion only slowly, and he is not likely to gain many votes because of his stand on them, no matter how important he thinks they are. I have seen candidates appear to be duds when they discussed informatively or fervently an issue about which there was only mass opinion. (This was true even of Adlai Stevenson in the 1956 presidential election campaign, when he sought to argue the need for international control of nuclear explosions.)

Once the candidate is in public office, however, he can use the channels of publicity available to him as officeholder to help make the issue one for public opinion. The issue need not be presented to the mass with balanced and rational arguments to be effective. President Kennedy helped to *create* public opinion strongly in favor of international control

---

[1]Arnold M. Rose, *Sociology: The Study of Human Relations* (2d ed.; New York: Alfred A. Knopf, Inc., 1965), chap. 9; Arnold M. Rose, "The Study of the Influence of the Mass Media on Public Opinion," *Kyklos*, Vol. XV (2d issue, 1962), pp. 1-20.

of nuclear explosions, just as President Johnson helped to create public opinion in favor of an antipoverty program. But neither started with it as a campaign issue. During a campaign a candidate has to deal with the issues already before the public, unless his opponent simply forfeits the field and allows him to develop any issue he wishes to. During my campaign, I *had* to talk about tax matters, for which I had little background and about which I had to specially inform myself. I made little mileage in discussing some of the issues on which I was well informed and personally thought very important, such as some of the welfare problems and the need for mass transit. In getting these reactions from my future constituents, I brought added support to the hypothesis I had about public and mass opinion.

I can now return to the question with which I opened this essay—Why is there so little written by politicians on their own inner workings and personal experiences? I think the main part of the answer should be clear by now: Most successful and sensitive politicians who could write informatively and perceptively on these matters are "applied sociologists" and "social psychologists," without benefit of formal training. They find it as difficult and as embarrassing to explain to the public what they really do as the formally trained sociologist does. Besides, the politician faces the stereotyped image of himself as superficial in knowledge, shallow in conviction, and possibly venal in interests. (I don't say that some of this is not true, especially of some politicians, but it is much less true than the public thinks.) So the politician does not try to explain himself, but rather hides himself behind his smile and his public image. He has other motivations for not revealing himself frankly, of course: Seldom does any professional reveal the secrets of his trade to the public, the sociologist of the profession tells us, and the politician especially does not wish to reveal anything that would be embarrassing to his friends or useful to his opponents. So public officeholding, despite the apparent salience of its occupants, remains the least understood and least studied of all occupations. Perhaps we can say that to reveal the public officeholder as he really is is another way in which the sociologist as officeholder finds his training useful.

F̶ew accounts of sociology in action are as movingly and usefully told as the first-person account below of a long, uneven, and arduous personal effort in community rehabilitation. The writer, Mrs. Carla Eugster, has evolved over years of experience a very patient and understanding technique of wide transferability, a technique effective in creating or rebuilding hope and strength in previously "defeated" human beings. She recounts the deliberately slow process by which she allowed a nearby poverty-stricken community to get used to her, the indirect educational program she initially pursued, her pervasive concern with training leaders and transferring leadership away from herself, the heartache she felt over foolish rebuffs from the larger community, the rich pleasure she knew from local projects well done, and the earthy process by which her program was finally assimilated by the community. Throughout one knows himself in the presence of a strong and insightful woman, one whose dedication to strengthening others is so great as to leave the reader himself a "taller" individual for having known her.

FIELD EDUCATION IN WEST HEIGHTS:
EQUIPPING A DEPRIVED COMMUNITY TO HELP ITSELF*

Carla Eugster

IN THE SUMMER of 1958, I entered the deprived Negro area of West Heights in order to increase the ability of its residents to deal effectively with the problems of their environment. I had pursued this aim previously under trade union and union educational auspices. This time, however, I acted on my own. My volunteer status, as a neighbor housewife, did not appear to alter my task other than to create a slightly greater than normal bewilderment about my motives.

I am calling my work in West Heights, field education. This term would designate some of the functions now performed by several existing categories of professionals. These would include: union organizers,

---

*Reprinted here with permission of the author and *Human Organization*, from the issue of Fall, 1964.

union educators, public health nurses, rural demonstrators, group social workers, community organizers, adult educators, recreation workers, and church field workers. The intended work of the Peace Corps among underdeveloped peoples overseas, and the growing interest in the culturally deprived at home make it increasingly necessary to formulate the concept of field education as a unique profession. The purpose of this paper is to suggest the nature of field education processes with specific reference to what occurred in West Heights.

I

Four hundred Negroes live in West Heights. The area predates by two or more generations the wealthy white suburbia which now surrounds it. Although white residents are close by, a highway, a railroad track, and a strip of woods define the boundaries within which the people of West Heights live. Their homes range from shacks and trailers to good substantial houses. Most dwellings are overcrowded, provide only cold running water, and are poorly heated by coal, wood, or gas burners which stand in the living room. Employed adults work primarily as domestics and unskilled laborers. Many mothers, as the sole supporters of their families, must leave their children to fend for themselves during the day. Although less than a third of the residents attend church regularly, the area has both a Baptist and an AME Zion church, each governed possessively by a small group of trustees composed primarily of women. In 1955, the two-room schoolhouse of West Heights was closed. For some West Heights children, school integration marked the occasion of their first trip outside of West Heights.

Civic and religious leaders in the county had made sporadic efforts to alleviate the hardships of the West Heights community. They were in large measure responsible for the paving and lighting of West Heights streets, and the substitution of running water and toilet facilities for wells and outhouses.

I discovered the area tucked behind my own backyard with only a strip of woods between our separate worlds. I entered West Heights on my own impulse without seeking financial or moral backing from any group.

The field educator must first overcome the normal tendency of the culturally deprived to repress awareness of the painful realities which delimit them. Once needs can be openly discussed the field educator seeks to find one particular need toward which he can focus the attention and energies of the entire deprived community. This need may constitute a major or minor problem. It may affect health, housing, income, education, child care, or recreation. It must, however, offer a unifying point of interest around which a field program—a community plan of action—can be evolved.

In partnership with local leaders the field educator will then see the deprived community through a sustained community effort with its normal range of crises, defeats, and victories. If there are no clearly acknowledged indigenous leaders, he must bring together a small number of residents who, hopefully, in sharing responsibility with him, will become leaders. With time the field educator seeks to turn the entire moral and administrative responsibility for the field program over to the community and its leaders. The extent to which he succeeds will roughly measure the degree to which he has equipped this culturally deprived community to pursue its own political, social, or economic goals.

II

Communication, on many planes, is the field educator's first concern. Coming as a stranger, he must gain entrance to the deprived community. He must learn its language which, in proportion to its economic, social, or geographic isolation, will be unique: He must in turn convey some understanding of his mission. As he structures his introductory meetings in which members of the deprived community are brought together, communication remains his goal, but with a widening focus. He wants to help the residents to grope toward and to express some sense of themselves in relation to the larger culture.

Some field educators ring doorbells, stating at once a reason for their presence. Others seek an introduction through a local church or some other familiar channel. I prefer a slow-paced private exploration. Thus I walked into West Heights and wandered through its streets chatting to no apparent purpose with women hanging up the wash, men standing in front of the general store, or children playing in the streets. Sometimes I sat on church steps or porch stoops and simply watched and listened. Upon invitation I visited church services and "stopped in" for tea.

Within a few weeks I had acquired some sense of the mood of the community, the tempo of its life, and the unique accents of its idiom. I began to seek a more purposeful confrontation. A friendly woman agreed to bring neighbors together to meet me, but the appointed evening found her home locked and dark. Other similar efforts also aborted. Finally I asked the trustees of the Baptist Church to give me the use of their building for three educational programs. Their minister, Reverend Brown, urged them to agree.

Reverend Brown was only slightly more educated than the average West Heights resident. He was a messenger-clerk by day and minister by night. On this occasion he stated that anything which "enlightens the hearts and minds of the people is Godly work." He pointed out that education was greatly needed in West Heights, citing in evidence the dropping of empty beer cans on church property and a tendency of church members to split their infinitives. I demurred that the correction of these faults was not precisely what I had in mind.

The trustees were hesitant to make their church available to the middle-class white stranger. They had two fears, neither wholly unwarranted. The first was that I might constitute a threat to the power which they possessed over a segment of the community. The second was that I might revive a citizens association which was now defunct. For reasons not clearly stated, the community's experience with citizens associations had left a residue of bitterness. This is not, however, an uncommon result of grass-roots organization which precedes a workable grasp of organizational procedures. The trustees finally decided that I could use their church if I would limit my subject to the noncontroversial one of public speaking!

At the end of the three programs, Reverend Brown, with the acquiescence of his trustees, asked me to "keep on going." I agreed to conduct a monthly program on a variety of subjects if a small number of West Heights people would meet with me as an education committee to share planning and administrative responsibilities.

Committee members, which included Reverend Brown, did not at first understand that "committee" meant a specific group of people, the same people each time. Gradually, committee members became reliable participants at the monthly educational programs where they rotated the function of master of ceremonies. But their attendance at committee meetings, and their performance of delegated responsibilities, was always problematic. Meeting notices usually listed the wrong place, wrong time, wrong day, or were not issued at all. Oral announcements were vague and misleading. I once heard the secretary announce that the next program would take place

> either before or after the Thursday choir rehearsal either at the Baptist or Methodist church.

Programs were indifferently scheduled in conflict with other church activities. Bungling once into a banquet, Mr. Jenkins, our M. C. for the evening, bounded to the front of the church and said,

> Now folks, while you're sitting here waiting for your dinner, our committee is going to entertain you with a little education.

At monthly committee meetings my suggestions were passively accepted. Members had few of their own to offer. With time they began to gossip about themselves and their neighbors and to pose their own amused cynicism against my professed view in which Reverend Brown supported me that our monthly educational programs were justified if only one person derived some benefit. Gradually committee members began to consider with me how to attract more people to our programs, what topics we should discuss, and what the greatest needs of their community might be.

During the early months of our education program the white ministers and civic leaders from the surrounding community, who had previously assisted West Heights, made an independent effort to consider once again what they might do for the community. Despite their reiterated view that West Heightsians should help themselves, they were troubled by the continuing existence of West Heights as a deprived area. Uncertain where to begin they asked Reverend Brown to advise them, but he proved unable to formulate West Heights needs or to suggest the most effective way others could help. Somewhat anticlimactically, the group decided to provide money for West Heights church repairs. It also asked Reverend Brown to have West Heights "call on us any time we can be of help." Later West Heightsians tried to do so, but these county leaders were unable to recognize the plea for help when it came.

With erratic assistance from the education committee I proceeded with the monthly programs. Sometimes I presented a movie or invited a guest speaker, but the most important part of the program was the discussion period. Topics included Child Care, Health, Adolescents, Family Life, The Danger of Rumors, Children and the Schools, Looking for Work, Race Problems, Citizenship. On one occasion I showed a documentary film of a Southern Negro community similar to West Heights. Two women stated they didn't like to think about people who lived or acted "like that." One man said, "Those people live in nothing but a slum." Mrs. Davis, a member of the education committee replied, "That kinda brings it home, doesn't it?"

In a discussion of health it was heatedly revealed that the county provided no garbage or trash collection service for the West Heights area. This was cited as an instance of racial discrimination. There was no awareness of the more relevant truths that the residents of West Heights had no person or group who could speak in their name; that they had never formally requested garbage collection service; that they did not know how to ask, whom to ask, or, in the event that their suspicion of discrimination was confirmed, how to fight for this service. When I suggested they seek a lawyer's help one man replied, "Yes, why don't we pay a lawyer to tell us why, no matter how badly we need it, they won't give it to us!"

After a few months of adult education programs, West Heights children asked if they could not have a program too, a request which precipitated our first crisis. Youngsters of every age trooped into the children's program. They watched a movie quietly enough, but every effort to engage them in conversation was met by various kinds of obstreperous behavior: the adolescents sinking sulkily in their seats, smoking or necking in the back rows; preteens playing boogie-woogie on the church piano and tag in the aisles; babies crying, and eight- to ten-year-olds clamoring loudly to do what "teacher" wanted. The fiasco could have been simply funny had it not released and at last given justification for the latent uneasiness with which many in West Heights had viewed the education program from the first.

At the next meeting of the education committee, I waited alone on the steps of the empty and locked church, but no one came. This had happened before of course, but in the following days I could not reach committee members by telephone and no one seemed to know when to expect them. Community pressure had frightened committee members away, and I had finally to seek them out in their own homes, in an effort to woo them one by one back to the program. In place of the persons I had started to like and know, I was now confronted by strangers who gravely told me that they were terribly sorry, but they realized now that the education program was just a waste of time. The people were not really interested; there was no reason to bother with it anymore. The minimal aim of these encounters was to persuade the members to meet again as a committee if only to end the program by committee decision rather than individual defection.

When the committee reassembled, Reverend Brown took over the meeting. He stated there had been some misunderstanding and confusion over the education program and that the time had come to decide upon goals which committee members could explain to others. He had given the matter some thought, he said, and it was his belief that the committee should decide upon three objectives—what should they be? After some discussion these were written down:

1. To teach proper hygiene and care of children.
2. To improve the morals and manners of the people.
3. To lead the people to a better way of life.

Suddenly committee members became self-conscious. One of them said, "Here we are, talking and talking, and you haven't said a thing! After all, it's *your* program!"

Here was the first of the crucial moments for which a field educator waits: an opportunity to relinquish or transfer responsibility from himself to the culturally deprived people with whom he works. Thus I tried in my reply to convey my belief and gratification that if it ever had been *my* program it was so no longer.

Pressed to state my opinion I admitted my disagreement with the goals they had proposed, which seemed to imply that we could tell others how to live their lives and solve their problems. Our role, I thought, was to provide an opportunity for members of the community to come together in order to think about common problems—

Just stop there a minute, please [Reverend Brown broke in] Now how does this sound? I'm just tryin' this out. Miz Green comes up to me, she says Reverend Brown what *is* this education program, and I say Miz Green, its a *chance* to think together, a chance to *think* together, a chance to think *together!*

Around the table the phrase went, each committee member trying and testing, changing the inflections, pondering it. Yes, it was right. We did not need three objectives. One was enough and we had found it.

STRUCTURING A FIELD PROGRAM

Having brought about a monthly confrontation of community problems and having won from the education committee an identification with this limited aim, I began to move into the second phase of the field education process: to develop a plan of action—a field program—to alleviate one specific problem. In West Heights the specific problem was not difficult to choose. In one form or another it had crept into every committee or community discussion: the problem of the schoolchildren.

At the time of school desegregation, West Heights children were performing at levels of from one to five years behind those of white contemporaries. Now, four years later, the same disparity continued. Even kindergarten children were lagging behind. However much they had learned in their first five years, West Heights children, as they entered school, could not name colors, they could not count, they could not follow directions. They were ignorant of nursery rhymes. They could neither listen nor express themselves. They had never been to an art gallery, post office, library, or zoo. In kindergarten they learned, if nothing else, the unforgettable lesson that they were "dumb." Subsequent grades found them further behind their more privileged classmates than when they started.

School officials had not advised West Heights parents of the academic status of their children. Yet the parents were obsessively aware that something was wrong. Children were clearly unhappy and increasingly rebellious. In one of our early monthly educational programs the participants struck out blindly against the schools. I had asked, "How can you interest your children in school?"

I do the best I can [one woman angrily replied] I get my Johnny there if I have to beat him all the way. Why just this morning they called me again. I said he's there all right, I seen him through that door myself. They said, Well, he's not here now. I told them, see here, I do my job, I get 'im there, now you do *your* job and keep 'im!

I began to discuss with members of the education committee the academic deficiencies of West Heights children which underlay their unhappiness and delinquency. Here, I suggested, was a concrete problem with which we might deal. Committee members were skeptical. One mother said, "We're not educated ourselves. How can *we* help to educate the children?" My answer was to motivate them to overcome their cultural handicap by demonstrating that their home community valued their academic achievements. Committee members scoffingly contended that their fellow West Heightsians could not care less. Yet three new members came to the next committee meeting. The committee decided to meet more often.

Within a few weeks we had evolved the general outlines of the Home Study Program: to convert the West Heights community into an after-school place of study by establishing scheduled study sessions in West Heights homes and churches, and to invite educated volunteers from outside of West Heights to attend as tutors. Committee members freely predicted that no children would come, that volunteers, if I found any, would quickly quit, that no West Heightsians outside of the committee would give us the use of their homes. "The only people who would lift a finger are sitting in this room right now," Mrs. Davis said. Yet "the people sitting in this room" were clearly intoxicated by the thought that they might actually provide leadership in remedying the school problem.

I now decided to clarify my advisory role by asking the committee to elect its own chairman. I pointed out that I was not a committee member, that I did not vote, and that I should not be filling a role which properly belonged to an elected official. Committee members understood that I was asking them to accept central responsibility for our developing home study plans. "We know why you want us to do that, [Mr. Jenkins said] and that's exactly why we aint'a gonna do it!" But I insisted. Reluctantly the committee elected Mrs. Jones, the only member who was not present! She seemed the least likely candidate: a blind woman who was meek, soft-spoken, and acquiescent. Yet at our next meeting she began by administering a forceful rebuke:

In my opinion, [she stated] whenever people meet together, and for whatever purpose, they should open and close with prayer. We shall now pray.

Over succeeding months our new chairman emerged as a dedicated and determined leader. Before and after committee meetings we would privately review meeting procedures. For some months I phoned to her suggested agenda items. A day came when Mrs. Jones took the lead and phoned a tentative agenda to me. Eventually we ended our premeeting consultations.

Under the auspices of the new chairman we began to work on a letter to school principals advising them of our developing plans for a home study program and asking for guidance. For weeks committee members had discussed and modified my initial draft. At last they were ready to send it. Reverend Brown requested that a copy of this letter be sent to each of the ministers and civic leaders he had met, with a short note inviting suggestions or comments. The committee unanimously insisted that all 12 of these copies be signed by each committee member.

A normal business meeting was turned over to the "signing" which became a touching ceremony, letters circulating around the table in utter silence as members tensely affixed their signatures. It took courage to sign this letter, not only because the signees had never before addressed prominent community figures as one adult to another, but also because here was tangible evidence of their assumption of new responsibility.

The letters were mailed. Three days passed. There were no answers. Five days, ten, twenty; still no answers and the heart-sickening recognition there would be none. The committee's leap towards responsibility had been met by an unnerving silence. West Heights had asked for help but the addressees did not discern the request and failed to meet it, a failure all the more ironic in that the help they were asked to give was simply to understand and to acknowledge that an ambitious stab at self-help was about to begin.

At this point the home study plan almost foundered. Committee members intimated that I had led them out too far. I was myself surprised, indeed appalled when the addressees failed to answer our letter. I could, perhaps, have intervened personally to impress upon them its importance. But if the field educator is not to become institutionalized as the guardian angel of a deprived community, he must take care to remain in the background, to stand as inconspicuously as he can in unity with indigenous leaders. He helps the people of a deprived community to make themselves heard, but he does not interpret or speak for them. To the degree to which I mediated West Heights and the larger community, I could have won for West Heights temporary gains, but only to the detriment of its ultimate autonomy which was my aim. A culturally deprived community needs to be able to confront the outside world in its own right; but its ameliorative efforts can never depend upon winning the approval or cooperation of the outside world.

I now urged the West Heights committee to proceed with the home study program without the prior sanction of school principals[1] or evidence of moral support from the religious or civic leaders of the county. With considerable misgivings the committee members agreed to set the date for our first week of study sessions.

In the days immediately preceding the first study sessions the people of West Heights were clearly excited. When I entered the area children ran to greet me, clamoring to know if their nighttime "teachers" would be engineers, lawyers, or firemen. A man I did not know stopped me to state that if we needed a model to hold up to the children we could turn to him! Another ran off his porch, grabbed my hand, and said, "When I seen you pass I said to myself: there's Mrs. Lincoln!"

Study sessions started in January, 1960. We invited children of each grade level to attend three study sessions a week. Both West Heights churches and three private families had agreed to house study sessions. One West Heights adult stood by at each session as a community host to the children and visiting tutors. I had found 15 volunteer tutors from among personal friends and members of the Social Action group of the Unitarian Church. Defying all predictions the West Heights children re-

---

[1] Some months earlier, in private conversations with school principals and two school board members, I had broached the possibility of my helping the West Heights committee to initiate a home study program. It may be interesting to note the difference in their reactions. All doubted if the plan would succeed, but the school board members warmly encouraged the attempt, whereas the principals opposed it. Later the same principals became proponents for the expansion of the home study program within the school system.

sponded en masse necessitating the finding of more homes for study sessions, and many more volunteers.

Unintentionally we had backed into an enormous undertaking quite beyond the administrative competence of the West Heights committee. The simple time-place coordination of an expanding corps of volunteers meeting in a shifting number of places—all subject to last-minute cancellation due to eviction, illness, drunkenness, fire, or misunderstanding—was in itself a staggering task. But beyond this, tutors needed educational materials, moral support, and technical guidance. School principals were somewhat taken aback when the improbable scheme actually came to fruition. But they quickly encouraged West Heights children to attend study sessions and agreed to facilitate periodic meetings between schoolteachers and volunteer tutors. Practically every church in the county and numerous civic organizations offered help. West Heights children were suddenly invited to plays, concerts, tours of laboratories, picnics, the zoo, and the circus. Quantities of used clothes, toys, and books were dropped into our hands. A hastily assembled group of volunteer tutors agreed to share responsibility for these burgeoning aspects of the program.

The West Heights committee retained responsibility for urging children to attend study sessions, dealing with West Heights churches and families which were housing study sessions, finding additional West Heightsians to give us the use of their homes, continuing the monthly educational programs, and leading the West Heights community into broader, deeper, and more effective support of their children's schooling. It was now my task to share the administration of these field aspects of the home study program with local West Heights leaders in such a way as to qualify them to carry it alone.

SHARING AND TRANSFERRING LEADERSHIP

Shortly after the start of the study program, the education committee persuaded a few teen-age boys to construct an outdoor bulletin board where notices relevant to the expanding educational activities could be posted. The committee knew it must somehow protect the board and its displays from the inveterate vandalism of West Heights children. Initial discussion centered upon the possibility of buying unbreakable glass, or bigger and better padlocks, but I opposed this public demonstration of distrust. Reverend Brown suggested that the board be entrusted to the children by making it their bulletin board. Mr. Jenkins said that we should give it to them at a dedicatory ceremony. Thus one Sunday morning a religious service was held in the empty lot before the new bulletin board. With prayer and song and sermon the board was presented to West Heights children. It is four years later now. West Heights adolescents are still throwing rocks at street lights, breaking church windows, and writing dirty words on sidewalks, but the bulletin board has remained intact.

The volunteer tutors who came into West Heights tended as a socio-economic group to be more permissive with children than West Heights parents. The difference was exaggerated by the tutors' conception of their role as surrogate relatives or adult friends rather than as parents or teachers. Children, quickly sensing their security, responded with love, but also with behavior problems never seen in the schools. West Heights parents were puzzled and sometimes angered by the wide latitude which tutors gave to the children. The tutors became firmer in time, but not soon enough to avoid trouble with the AME church which, after the first few weeks of tumultuous and noisy study sessions, decided to end its relationship with the study program. In this case, in contrast with the Baptist church, the uneasiness of the ruling matriarchy was backed up by a minister who had always been distrustful of my presence in the area.

Inquiring committee members were told that children had been disrespectful of church property, that the study sessions were raising the heat bill, and church facilities should, in any event, be reserved for religious uses. The education committee was indignant, and quite prepared to advertise the church action as an indication of just where the Methodists stood when it came to aiding West Heights school children. I urged the committee to seek to unify the community, not to splinter it. The Methodist members of the committee agreed to reopen the question with their trustees. Mrs. Davis, of the committee, happened to be one of them. She described a part of the subsequent trustees meeting as follows:

The Minister said he'd wanted us to do something about the young people all along, but we wouldn't listen to him. Then the first white lady that comes along, we throw open the doors. Well I told him, "Reverend Wilson, she's qualified!" That got 'im mad and he said he didn't feel easy with folks of the opposite race. I said well neither do I Reverend Wilson, but that's a feeling you and I have to overcome!

When the issue came to a vote the minister abstained, and the trustees voted six to one to reopen the church to study sessions.

At the end of the school year I suggested that a ceremony be held to honor the efforts which the children had made. The notion was an alien one. At the next committee meeting, when the secretary read her minutes, the suggestion was reported as "a ceremony to thank the children for coming to study sessions." Mrs. Davis said no, my idea had been to thank the volunteers for tutoring the children. I suspect it was not until the honors program was actually taking place that West Heights adults understood that they were convening to pay tribute to their own children. In the act of honoring them, many parents for the first time understood that the children were doing something of which to be proud, and that the adults, by providing the occasion, the place, and the encouragement for their extra school efforts, also had a reason to be proud.

The honors program did, in fact, bind all the participants more closely to the home study effort. West Heights schoolchildren in their Sunday clothes, the predominantly white tutors, schoolteachers, and school officials, and the semiliterate Negro residents of West Heights all crowded into the small West Heights Baptist church for the ceremony. Reverend Brown officiated. The program began with church songs and prayer. The committee secretary narrated the history of the home study program. To my wry delight she gave only passing mention to my name, but spoke, at length, of what "we, in the education committee" had decided to do. Prominent citizens in the audience were recognized. They included representatives of embassies, the federal government, the County Council, and the State Board of Education. The chairman of the School Board gave a congratulatory address.. A group of volunteer tutors played a Haydn quartet. Each schoolchild was given a book picked specifically for him. Families which had housed study sessions were given a reproduction of a great masterpiece. The ceremony ended with everyone singing, "God Bless America."

At the start of the next school year, it was no longer difficult to persuade West Heights families to let us use their homes. Also, for the first time, senior high school students were willing to attend study sessions.

As a new approach to the school problems of culturally deprived children the home study program began to attarct widespread attention. Almost all of our publicity missed the field program context. Every news story, however flattering in intent, offended the people of West Heights. The most serious crisis of the entire field program was caused by a television broadcast.

Members of the education committee had voted CBS permission to film a five-minute news feature on the study program. But they had not anticipated the manner in which their poverty would be exaggerated and exposed, with close-ups of the only outhouse, the last remaining water pump, and the most dilapidated homes. West Heightsians turned angrily upon our committee members whose first impulse was to disclaim responsibility for the TV sequence and to join their critics in opposition to the entire home study effort. Mrs. Jones phoned to say that she had done all in her power to be of service, but there was no satisfying the people of West Heights and she was through. Despite her protestations that "it wouldn't be safe" I persuaded her to call an open meeting for the entire community. We ensured a large attendance by publicizing on posters the question: "Should We Permit More TV Features on Our Home Study Program?"

Bitter and angry statements were made at this meeting. One woman asserted that when her employer saw the primitive conditions in which she presumably lived, she had been fired. Another charged that we posed as people wanting to help, but all we did was bring trouble and pain. Residents from the better homes complained that they had lost face among their friends and work associates.

These statements were countered by newly articulated defenses of the home study program: children were staying out of trouble; parents knew where their children were at night, teachers and principals were agreed that children were benefiting from study sessions. One committee woman turned to the relatively better educated and wealthier members of the community and cried out,

You don't give us your homes for study sessions. You don't take part in the adult education programs. You don't work on our committee; the only time we *do* see you is when we've made a mistake! If you care anything at all about West Heights, why don't you help?

Discussion turned to the alleged purpose of the meeting: how to handle future TV requests. For the first time the people of West Heights contemplated the example they might be setting for other deprived communities. For the first time they weighed the probable hurt to their own feelings against the good they might do for others. The meeting closed with overwhelming sanction to accede to future requests to televise the study program.

A Mr. Hamlin came to the next committee meeting. He said that the community upheaval over the TV program had made him and his neighbors feel that there should be a general association which could speak for everyone. They had wondered if the education committee could help to get one organized. Thus the move for a citizens association, when it finally came, was inspired not by newly aroused concern over housing, health, or citizenship, but in defense against dangers, imagined or real, which seemed to flow from the field program itself!

The committee agreed to arrange the time and place of an organizational meeting, and to have Mrs. Jones officiate long enough to enable those present to choose their own chairman. I stated that I would not participate in this meeting.

The organizational meeting of the West Heights Citizens Association was well attended. Mr. Jenkins of our education committee was elected chairman. Other committee members were elected to the executive board together with what seemed to be at least one representative of every clique and faction within West Heights.

After one year of the home study program, school personnel noted improved school attitudes and performance; the probation officer reported a marked decrease in delinquency; the public health nurse reported improved upkeep of homes and higher family morale. Before the end of our second year we had 70 volunteer tutors. Among them were lawyers, physicians, musicians, biochemists, psychologists, mathematicians, economists, social workers, psychiatrists, businessmen, and housewives. A further group of 40 women were distributing cookies and fruit to all study sessions. Ninety percent of the West Heights schoolchildren were still attending study sessions, and 23 homes—or one out of every four homes in West Heights—had been made available to the study program.

In the same interval of time the West Heights Citizens Association (with which I had declined any connection) obtained garbage collection service and successfully fought, before the City Council, an effort, by a group of businessmen, to have part of the West Heights land rezoned for commercial use.

After two and one-half years of home study sessions, the School Board agreed to incorporate the home study program into the county educational system, and to hire two full-time field educators to continue and to expand the home study approach.

III

A field educator seeks to enable a deprived community to confront and to mitigate its needs. Before he can begin, he must learn, or at least gauge the degree to which he is dealing with, an alien tongue. Educated laymen seeking to aid a deprived community may well appreciate the difficulty of making themselves understood, but they tend to underestimate the more subtle problem of understanding the culturally deprived whose meanings are throttled by inarticulateness, altered by cultural idiosyncrasy, and masked by traditional lower-class forms, courtesies, and reticences.

Even when he achieves some flow of communication with the members of a deprived community, the field educator does not expect them to simply state their needs as the county leaders expected Reverend Brown to do for West Heights. For however obvious these needs may be to the outsider, if the people involved saw them with equal clarity it would be an invitation to despair, to madness, or to crime.

It is necessary to see facts if people are to change them. But the culturally deprived do not believe they have the power to change them. It is the apparent unalterability of the circumstances of their lives which render them too terrible to perceive. Consequently the culturally deprived repress or distort their awareness of these circumstances. We saw, for example, that the people of West Heights interpreted the absence of garbage collection service in their area as proof of racial discrimination. Yet once they acquired the ability to act, they discarded this interpretation and obtained the service by pursuing the normal channels which had been available all along.

The field educator mitigates the harshness of their needs by conveying, over a period of time, his faith that the members of a deprived community have, or can acquire, the power to alleviate them. Braced by his implied promise to transmit techniques of self-help, the culturally deprived finally do the painful thing which he requests: that is, they permit themselves to acknowledge, to see more clearly, and to name their needs.

Once the protective layers of resignation, cynicism and repression have been stripped away, the field educator has incurred a terrible responsibility. For to face the stark realities of their lives can be destructive to the members of a deprived community. The field educator, as the instrument of that confrontation, must now stick with these culturally deprived adults until he has successfully given over into their hands the ability to alter these realities. He must do this even though the potentially destructive energy he has loosed, when not turned inward, threatens himself. For he is both a member and symbol of the more privileged community and, at the same time, the one who has induced the members of the subculture to face and to suffer the full meaning of their deprivation.

Ambivalence is the inescapable psychological context of any field education effort. The field educator is alternately, or even at the same time, the object of love and hate. If he succeeds in bringing a field program into effect, he will find the deprived community very reluctant to let him withdraw from leadership. As Mrs. Davis of the West Heights committee said, when I asked the committee to choose its own chairman, "We like it fine, just the way you've been takin us." At this point it may also be tempting to the field educator to hang on to the small kingdom over which he now wields a certain power.

In impetus, conception, and administration, the field program may well begin as the creation of the field educator. If he is to give it into the possession of the culturally deprived he must:

1. Develop the field program so that it is rooted in or can become rooted in the peculiar ethos of the deprived community.

2. Inspire the courage and teach the skills which would enable members of the deprived community to accept moral and administrative responsibility for the field program.

Developing a Field Program Within the Ethos of the Deprived Community

If the field program remains alien to the unique modes of the subculture, native creativity is barred from it. The field educator encourages members of the deprived community to reconcile the program to their own ethos. A subtle two-stage process is involved. The first is to encourage the culturally deprived to transmit to field programs the coloration and accents of their community. The second is to win for the program centrality of focus within their culture. The progressive grafting of religious ritual on to home study meetings and ceremonies is one way in which West Heights residents have given to the program a familiar aura. But the second step has not been taken. The program's educational aims have not yet been made relevant to, nor incorporated within, their religious purposes. This is exemplified by Reverend Brown who, despite his devoted support of the home study effort, has yet to mention child or adult education within the context of a normal religious service.

The new field educator hired by the county school system initiated a rotating chairmanship in the West Heights committee. In recognition of the services already performed by Mrs. Jones, he arranged a ceremony to confer upon her the honorary title of chairman emeritus. The ceremony again illustrated our failure to bring home study aims into the center of the community's awareness. Reverend Brown had improvised a religious ritual during which, anointing Mrs. Jones' head with oil, he stated, "In the name of the Father, the Son, and the Holy Ghost I now pronounce you . . . ." In this moment he forgot the term "Emeritus," but he made an intuitive leap. "I now pronounce you Mother Chairman," he said triumphantly. Heads nodded and voices murmured approval. This was a concept everyone could understand, and suddenly the whole idea seemed right, and not a mocking incongruity brought in from the field educator's other world. But when the minister invited spontaneous eulogies from the congregation, one person after another rose to tell how this committee chairman comforted the bereaved, tended the ill, brought solace to those in trouble. No one commented upon the work for which she was being honored: upon the dedication and leadership she had shown in working with her neighbors to encourage children to set higher educational goals. And evidences of the children's progress, which West Heightsians had frequently enumerated, no one on this particular occasion thought to mention.

Preparing the Deprived Community to Accept Moral and Administrative Responsibility for the Field Program

The field educator transmits a technique, an ethic, and an image. The technique is reducible to the roles and functions of officers and members, and to basic organizational procedures. It is no accident that parliamentary procedure comes first in any union education program. Its inner meaning, to the organizationally illiterate, is a revelation: that ideas can be turned into acts, that recognition of problems can give rise to programs which alleviate them.

But in order to apply a modicum of organizational know-how, a culturally deprived community needs a concomitant ethic: to accept disagreement as necessary to the democratic process and to honor commitments even in the face of trouble.

In the first honors program, Mrs. Jones reported that committee members had not always agreed with one another.

Sometimes [she said] we just had to agree to disagree. But do you know, we are still meeting; and we are still friends!

Her surprise reflected the usual tendency of the uneducated to avoid or to mute conflict. They have learned that open disagreement brings violence, personal jeopardy, or long-lasting enmities. Within the context of group discussion and action it is necessary to say what you want and why, which means one must be able to oppose another with impunity. This is simply something to learn, as is the grace which permits acquiescence to the will of the majority.

Although it is gratifying to develop the power to alleviate their own problems, the culturally deprived never lose the recurrent wish to shed the somehow dangerous responsibilities they have assumed. Thus periodic defection will take place even when there is no crisis to trigger it. As the emerging leaders gain confidence, as they acquire status in their leadership role, as they develop a new image of themselves, these defections bcome less frequent. But initially crisis is a sure warranty of abdication.

The field educator will suggest that a leader is one who stands up to crisis. He will be able to transmit the courage to do so when he demonstrates, through the course of the program, that crises can be turned to advantage. Indeed one could view a field program as the climbing of a ladder, the steps of which are the crises which marks the ascent.

The crises I have described of the West Heights effort left the field program stronger, not weaker. In each instance they brought about an initial abdication followed by recommitment and growth. This is not, to be sure, their inevitable course. Crises can destroy a field program, and certainly will if the field educator or the emerging leaders mistake the initial abdication of the culturally deprived for their final judgment. A field educator turns a crises to advantage by making it the occasion for a conscious exercise of veto power. In the face of their abdication he assembles the leaders or members of the deprived community and thereby places the life or death of the field program in their hands. A formally structured moment of decision challenges the participants to make the "no" of their abdication explicit. If their intuitive judgment finds the program to be in their best interests they will say "yes" instead. But saying "yes" in the moment of crisis means they must fight for the field program if they are to save it, and in so doing they become even more committed to the effort in which they are engaged.

As the field educator teaches organizational procedures and an ethic to make them operative, he will slowly be giving the effective control of the field program over to the culturally deprived. But this is not a simple one-way progression. Effective control shifts erratically back and forth between the educator and the leaders of the deprived community. When, through loss of nerve, or temporary alienation, local leaders abdicate, the field educator bears residual responsibility. He must protect the field program and, if necessary, run it until the local leaders return. Despite its fluctuating reality, the field educator will foster the image of indigenous control. For the successful transfer of control rests in part upon a fiction which precedes and makes possible the fact: the fiction that the culturally deprived leaders are leading before they in fact lead; that they are controlling before they in fact control. At best the leaders of the deprived community will recognize this fiction as an idealized image of themselves which, if they wish, they can make true.

Thus, along with the program which he helps to shape, the field educator will be weaving its story, a romantic version of the reality which confers a maximum of meaning and makes possible a maximum of growth to the culturally deprived community. As increasing indigenous control is an important aspect of this story, he will underplay his residual administrative function. The leaders of the deprived community are not fooled. They know who is running things when they, in fact, are not. But as the trustee of a realizable goal, the field educator does not make an issue of their abdications. He keeps intact that idealized image which facilitates their return to responsibility and the ultimate realization of local autonomy.

In a program with the news appeal of the West Heights effort, an image with a shifting correspondence to reality becomes more difficult to nourish. Press, radio, and TV all share the general middle-class inability to conceive of meaningful problem-solving participation on the part of the culturally deprived. Whereas the field educator may, at times, overstate that participation, the mass communications media will always understate it, or not state it at all, self-help being somehow invalidated in their eyes if it takes an outsider's special knowledge to set it in motion. Thus, to the great detriment of the home study program, West Heightsians have been consistently portrayed in the press as passive objects of help, although from the start they were indeed indispensable partners to the effort.

The field educator will constantly seek ways to involve local leaders in acts or postures which enhance the image of their autonomy both in their own eyes, and in those of the outside world. The annual West Heights honors program idealizes the story of the home study program and the significance of the West Heights community in initiating it. In speech and song the community honors its children and the facilitating help of its residents. In the honors program the people of West Heights portray themselves to the world as firmly at the helm of the home study effort. The taste of that possession is sweet, and arouses a hunger to retain it.

CONCLUSION

With specific reference to the West Heights home study program I have defined a field educator's aim as the transfer of self-help tools and motivation, or the transfer of the effective control of a field program from the field educator to a culturally deprived community. A professional field educator knows this to be an enormously difficult task. His commitment is commensurate with its complexity.

Transfer of effective control takes place as a field program acquires the cultural aura of the community involved, as the program aims attain primacy of focus within the community, and as indigenous leaders acquire those techniques and codes which are prerequisite to the realization of a newly desired and larger image of themselves.

The War on Poverty is not going to be easily or quickly won—if it is won at all. Fundamental research questions presently remain unanswered: What types of poverty are there? How does elasticity for reform differ among the types? Which particular remedial tools work where, when, with whom, and with what effect? And what is life likely to be like beyond poverty? Applied sociology has a large role to play in securing answers, designing and appraising remedial efforts, helping transfer overlooked lower-class strengths into postpoverty life styles, and exploring middle-class resistances to lower-class gains. In the essay below I recount my own experiences in related action projects, trying thereby to interest many more sociologists in this new challenge to the social sciences —and this new and crucial test of our equalitarian democracy.

A SOCIOLOGIST IN THE WAR ON POVERTY

Arthur B. Shostak

MY ACTION role, one stretching back formally only two years, has thus far involved me in three major programs: the design and operation of a short-term residential Pilot Project for 100 male high-school dropouts; the design (and pending operation) of a long-term residential Job Corps Urban Training Center for 2,016 young men; and the design and implementation of an informal program of antipoverty "community consultation."[1] I plan here to review briefly all three, seeking, quite frankly, to draw some readers into "recruit" positions in what I consider to be the nation's greatest domestic struggle.

Pilot Project

In the spring of 1964 I was invited to associate on a part-time basis with the University of Pennsylvania's new Human Resources Program

---

[1] While my action role is recent my preparation is long and varied: In the fall of 1961, I worked part time in an ambitious, but unsuccessful effort to better prepare prisoners for job success while on parole. In the winter of 1963, I helped the city of Philadelphia design a research project in manpower retraining. In the summer of 1963, I advised the Philadelphia Navy Yard on problems in race relations, job training, and personnel evaluation. In the spring of 1964, I affiliated with HRP, an association I continue to the present.

(HRP). Having been instrumental in the formation of the three-man HRP (a unique administrative unit attached to the Office of the University President), and, being in full support of its mandate to fight urban and human blight in all of its forms, I accepted the invitation.

My first two-day-a-week assignment entailed locating and reviewing the widely scattered and characteristically uneven literature on the nation's several million high-school dropouts (or "holdouts"). At the request of HRP director Dr. Howard E. Mitchell, a clinical psychologist, I prepared a position paper evaluating what had been learned about the rehabilitation of dropouts, and charting the reform distance that lay ahead. My research helped us gain support inside the university for a six-week summer residential Pilot Project which the two of us, Dr. Mitchell and myself, designed for Philadelphia area dropouts. We also employed the literature review to buttress an application for financial support HRP submitted to the Federal Office of Education (Department of Health, Education, and Welfare).

I proceeded next to join with HRP's only other staff member, a graduate student in social planning, to help recruit, select, and orient a Pilot Project staff composed of ten college student counselors, two head teachers, two work directors, and two senior counselors. In addition to lecturing and conducting staff seminar discussions on culture, poverty, and school dropouts, I helped locate other training source people and I chose field sites for staff visits (e.g., the counselors spent one of five training days "hanging around" typical slum-area community centers). I also selected certain inexpensive and invaluable booklets that went to every staff member (e.g., studies of dropouts, delinquency, educational problems, job prospects for youth, etc.).[2] And finally, I ran practice sessions in the use of a dozen or so questionnaires, rating forms, and report sheets I had designed for different levels of staff (counselors kept a ten-point weekly "diary," one that focused on enrollee self-valuation, personal relationships, and classroom progress. Work supervisors submitted daily reports employing a five-factor evaluation of effort shown, skills practiced, cooperation offered, and so forth).

During my full-time employ in the hastily improvised six-week summer project, I played out of necessity many different roles (logistics aide, public relations aide, community relations aide, enrollee confidant, vocational counselor, etc.). Three roles in particular, however, especially involved my sociological training and action orientation: I helped implement impromptu program reforms; I mediated line-staff conflicts; and I pursued HRP's very considerable applied research interests.

---

[2]The review entailed of the poverty literature convinced me an anthology of timely, clear cut, and constructive essays was badly needed. I helped draw together a reader during the summer of 1964: A. Shostak and W. Gomberg (eds.), *New Perspectives on Poverty* (Englewood Cliffs, N.J.: Prentice-Hall, Inc., [Spectrum Books], 1964).

An example of the unanticipated program reforms in which I had a hand involved my learning early one morning that a shoving incident had combined with heated racial slurs and rumors of "hard" reprisals to heighten racial tensions between the project's 73 Negro and 27 white male enrollees. My informal investigation led me to endorse a suggestion made by some boys that we "air the whole mess" that very night. Working against time, rising tensions, and the serious misgivings of other project staff members, I lunched with five volunteer spokesmen for the boys, and helped focus the pending evening's panel program on three issues: Why this tension in the project? What was gained? And where did we go from here? Strong in the unprecedented voluntary attendance of every one of the 100 enrollees, the evening program eventually aired such topics as personal sensitivity to racial epithets, the aggrieved feelings of project whites who unexpectedly found themselves in the minority, and the association between the outside community's "long, hot summer" and our own project race tensions. Feelings were high and opinions ran strong, but accommodation was the theme the boys chose to develop (along with expressions of surprise—and gratitude—for the frankness and the fact of the evening's program).

As a mediator of line-staff conflicts, I drew on my training as an industrial sociologist to help the project director unravel communication foul-ups, sort out lines of responsibility, clarify questions of authority, investigate the state of morale, and resolve personality disputes. A typical conflict involved the question of whether the college counselors (line men) or the two work directors (staff men) had greater authority on our playlot community building sites. Under intense time pressure, I sought to resolve the conflict bluntly by identifying and transferring from the worksites those college counselors least able to cooperate with the (noncollege) work directors even as I "encouraged" the work directors to instruct the enrollees *through* the counselors present. Sympathetic discussions with both harried sides also went far to help resolve other similar conflicts.

HRP's considerable research interests involved me in auditing the questionnaires, rating forms, and report sheets I had earlier designed and distributed. To supplement written data I carried out a program of semiguided tape-recorded interviews with five gang "runners" (leaders) in our project and with several other project "types." With Dr. Mitchell's aid, I prepared scales of job satisfaction, measures of social adjustment, and indices of overall personal progress, frequently trading some refinement for necessary ease in instant reporting and action-taking. I welcomed volunteer research assistance from the ranks, and, after explaining social research in general and a questionnaire in specific, proceeded to gain considerable aid in hand-tabulations and analysis from 18-year-old boys with ninth-grade reading levels. Throughout the project's six weeks I sought every opportunity possible to discuss such sensitive research issues as personal values and goals with the boys, their street gang workers (occasional visitors), and their parents (still rarer visitors). After the project's conclusion in July, 1964, I helped Dr. Mitchell and others evaluate its significance, spread our new-found knowledge of male dropouts, follow the lives of our 100 enrollees, and transfer lessons learned to HRP's new concern, a Job Corps training center for 2,016 male adolescents.

Training Center

HRP was invited in the fall of 1964 to submit a proposal to operate a large Job Corps training center for the Office of Economic Opportunity.

As a member of the proposal planning team (and building on our summer's experience) I sought to help make more explicit crucial values of planning team members. For example, when one of our three sub-contractors, a business company interested in providing certain supplies for the Urban Center, naïvely recommended a high wire fence and a barred jail, I conducted a probing seminar with the entire planning team to help all realize what values underlay such a suggestion and where its implementation might lead. In this connection I prodded the entire group into touring a typical fenced and barred reformatory, believing this a necessary touchstone for our own value-laden design. (Similarly, I initiated and led planning team seminars that asked such crucial action-oriented questions as whether a dead-end dull job was better than none, whether dropping out of a Job Corps center would constitute a completely overwhelming "defeat" for many hapless young men, whether the government's insistence on a loyalty oath for Job Corps enrollees worked an undue hardship on the program, whether the middle class *really* wanted victory in the "War on Poverty," and whether we really knew with any clarity the kind of society we were preparing men for.)

As the only sociologist on the urban center planning team, I was assigned a wide and challenging range of problems: I was asked to help appraise the significance an outdoor country setting might have in the rehabilitation of urban dropouts. I was asked to help a professional educator design the social studies component for the center's remedial education program. I was asked to join psychologists in pondering the optimum size of living units, the locus of identification of enrollees (with the smallest living unit, or the center, or the university, or the Job Corps), and the significance of different program combinations of school, work, and leisure. I was asked to consult with economists who might help us predict the jobs most likely to exist for center graduates. I was asked to discuss with criminologists the implications of homosexual activities in all-male training centers, and I was requested to design a practical and relevant system of leaves and center social activities. I was also asked to design a practical program of student self-government for the center. Indeed I reviewed every facet of our pioneering design in terms of available insights into "contraculture," "peer-group allegiance," "status leverage," "relative deprivation," and so forth.

Community Counseling

At present, while the federal government proceeds with its review of our training center proposal, I work part-time on an unpaid, volunteer basis as a consultant with various neighborhood antipoverty groups.

Typical of this type of work is an effort I made recently to encourage three low-income community associations to endorse their own candidates for Philadelphia's unique Poverty Council elections (the only elections of its kind in America). I listened first to their deep-bred cynicism regarding local politics, self-appointed redeemers of the poor, and the federal "War on Poverty." In dialogue fashion, I explored with these men the possible costs and gains of still one more struggle, I discussed the relative freshness and sincerity of Sargent Shriver's associates in OEO, and I raised the question of the likely significance of city-wide apathy in the "showcase" election. After several reviews of the matter at successive meetings, all three groups chose to endorse candidates for the Poverty Council (354 candidates eventually contested 144 openings). Attending regular meetings of still another low-income neighborhood group, I discussed the merits of establishing a "well-heeled" board of directors, seeking "poverty dollars," switching the focus in its evening center from play-plus-learning to learning-plus-play, and locating new sources of volunteers.[3] Traveling to other cities, I have consulted with neighborhood groups anxious to understand more about Philadelphia's Poverty Council (the subject of two professional papers of mine),[4] the intricacies of local participation in the federal government's Community Action effort, and the real condition of the "War's" various parts (e.g., the Job Corps backlog of unaccommodated applications is staggering—some 250,000 in July, 1965).

Summary

I do not wish to make it all sound smooth and easy; it has not been that at all. There has been failure (ten boys had to be expelled from the summer project; nearly 15 are now in jail); there has been frustration (the government has stretched out our training center review many more months than originally envisaged); there has been disappointment

---

[3]Believing as a citizen and as a sociologist that much of the "War's" success or failure will hinge on the involvement of the poor, I have geared my consulting in a nondirective, option-exposing manner. My concern has been primarily with stimulating local participation and decision making, a task more difficult than the directive option, but one much more fundamental and significant.

[4]Arthur B. Shostak, "Containment, Co-Optation, and Co-Determination," *American Child*, November, 1965, pp. 15-19; Arthur B. Shostak, "Promoting Participation of the Poor," *Social Work*, January, 1966.

(the overtaxed Office of Economic Opportunity has not paid full attention to our Pilot Project findings).

But to counter these disappointments there has also been the unforgettable thrill of attending the irregular "graduation" of the project's 90 remaining enrollees—boys who had never before in their lives successfully completed anything. There has been the unforgettable feeling of accomplishment when the last word of a two-volume 600-page proposal for a practical "utopia" was finished, for a Job Corps Urban Training Center that one hopes (knows!) will make a deep and far-reaching difference in rehabilitation efforts. And there has finally been the invaluable lesson in human worth available when a group of low-income citizens one works with shakes off the lead weight of apathy, and stirs and acts with newfound self-esteem.

D eveloping countries require as much sociological aid as they can possibly get, and they are not getting enough. Particularly needed is the
kind of encompassing applied project described below by its designer,
Dr. Marshall B. Clinard. Among other things, the New Delhi project gave
practice to citizens in local self-determination, helped develop a feeling
of community, eased the successful introduction of modern tools and
ways, and required "upper and lower castes to sit at the same table and
Muslim women in purdah to attend meetings with Hindu women." The
successful conduct of such projects requires clear understanding of refined
issues in the transmission, adaptation, diffusion, and evaluation of cross-
cultural change experiments.

THE SOCIOLOGIST AND SOCIAL CHANGE IN
UNDERDEVELOPED COUNTRIES*

Marshall B. Clinard

ONE OF THE objectives of the Society for the Study of Social Problems
is to link scientific knowledge to concrete social problems; another is to
contribute to the solution of crucial social problems and formulate social
policies. No policy restricts our concern exclusively to the social problems
of America. Our focus this year is on "Social Problems in International
Perspective" in the hope that our members might become more concerned
with social problems in other countries and by so doing make possible
a comparative theory of social problems and social policies.

Accordingly, I should like to make some comments on the role of sociologists, particularly in our society, in helping to deal with the social
problems of Asia, Africa, and South America, those underdeveloped
continents which loom in the foreground of today's news. What I have
to say may be equally applicable to our members from other disciplines.

Since zero meridian passes through Europe, most maps show that

---

*Presidential address, Society for the Study of Social Problems, Washington, D.C.,
August 28, 1962. Reprinted with permission of the author and *Social Problems*, from
the issue of Winter 1963.

continent as the center of the world. This is an unwarranted assumption to many Asians whose civilization goes back thousands of years. A Swiss economist has said: "The conception of Europe as the center of the world was still so much a matter of course right up to the Second World War that we never gave a thought to the cartographical expression of the fact. From our point of view, this map of the world with Europe as its centre was profoundly and historically justified."[1]

The massive and always depressing problems of underdeveloped countries—illiteracy, extreme poverty, over-population, poor housing and sanitation, high rates of disease and death, and lack of recreational and cultural amenities—are not the same as the important social problems of the Western world today—high rates of crime and delinquency, mental disorders, and alcoholism. Their problems might be looked upon as characteristic of those of American and Western European nations of one to three centuries ago, and they might well be expected more closely to approximate the problems of the Western world as they become more highly industrialized and urbanized countries.

Problems of underdeveloped nations are regarded today as being primarily based upon economic factors or upon inadequate exposure to Western ways of life. From an economic viewpoint the situation is due to low income and inadequate capital formation. Consequently, Western policy makers have assumed that massive amounts of foreign capital will alleviate the conditions of such countries as India. The fallacy of the "economic man," which sociologists helped to root out, has been replaced by the myth of the economic nature of social problems in underdeveloped countries.[2]

It has been argued by others that social change is produced by contact with the more advanced ideas and methods of the West; where Western ideas intrude, change will follow. This is far too simple an explanation; mere contact with other more scientific ways of living does not necessarily lead to their adoption. There is "no reason to assume that when a traditional society is disrupted the disruption will leave it more desirous than before of adoption of the way of life of technologically advanced societies."[3] It may instead become even more antipathetic to Western ways of life, as was certainly the case in many instances of European colonialism. In some countries great social change has not occurred after long periods of contact; Indonesia, for example. Moreover, non-

---

[1] Friedrich Traugott Wahlen, "Our Responsibility towards Economically Developing Countries," in Toni Hagen, Friedrich Traugott Wahlen, and Walter Robert Corti, *Nepal: The Kingdom in the Himalayas* (Bern: Kummerly and Frey, Geographical Publishers, 1961), p. 14.

[2] Also see Leo Schnore, "Social Problems in Underdeveloped Areas," *Social Problems*, Vol. 8 (Winter, 1960-61), pp. 182-201.

[3] Everett E. Hagen, *On the Theory of Social Change: How Economic Growth Begins* (Homewood, Illinois: The Dorsey Press, Inc., 1962), p. 19.

Western societies cannot always simply adopt procedures; they must devise new ones better fitted to their norms, values, and social structure. The basic issues in underdeveloped countries cannot be explained so simply, for they involve issues of sociological and social-psychological concern as well. Rural community development programs involve not merely such economic problems as supplying adequate fertilizers and seed grains or providing new agricultural techniques: the peasant farmer must want to change his practices.[4] For example, the Japanese method of paddy culture was introduced into India over ten years ago, yet it has not been generally accepted and India's rice yield remains the lowest in the world. Measures to induce relevant social change are called for which are as planned, precise, calculated and integrated in manner as economic change. A basic difficulty of rural community development in India is, as has recently been pointed out, that the tailor-made government program has not sufficiently recognized the individual differences in the values and norms of the 550,000 villages.

It is not only in their attitude to manual work that the peasant communities differ. There are significant differences also in respect of other traits and aptitudes, such as thrift, industry, mobility and readiness to exploit economic opportunity, which makes the problem of planning even more complicated. It is clear from the many prevailing value systems which determine not only a community's pattern of production and consumption, of farm management, marketing and even housing, but also its primary attitudes and wants. These vary greatly from one community to the next, within groups in the same region and even locality otherwise enjoying in all respects equal resources and opportunities.[5]

Other illustrations could well be cited such as the adoption of family planning methods and the adoption of sanitation practices and improved health and hygiene techniques.[6] The mere availability of birth control devices in India by no means guaranteed their adoption. While there appears to be little opposition from the Hindu religion on theological grounds, there is the complication of the importance of sons as part of religious and caste duties tied to the belief in reincarnation; the high child death rate; the dependency of women on children for their status; the important role of the mother-in-law; the social isolation of women and difficulties in intimate communication with their husbands; the absence of a social security system except through sons and many other factors as well. Moreover, the problem involves effective communication of the idea and techniques of birth control to a highly heterogeneous

[4]Bert Hoselitz, "Problems of Adaptng and Communicating Modern Techniques to Less Developed Areas," *Economic Development and Cultural Change*, Vol. 2 (January, 1954), pp. 249-69.

[5]Kusum Nair, *Blossoms in the Dust: The Human Element in Indian Development* (London: Gerald Duckworth & Co., Ltd., 1961), p. 191.

[6]Kingsley Davis, "Institutional Patterns Favoring High Fertility in Underdeveloped Areas," *Eugenics Quarterly*, Vol. 2 (March, 1955), pp. 33-39.

society, as Bogue and Lionberger have pointed out.[7] Somewhat similar problems, although less involved, are faced in the area of introducing new sanitary and health practices. In a recent study of 1254 families in 25 villages of India, only 10 percent knew that water could be purified by boiling.[8] Nearly half of them attributed common dysentery to excessive heat. Only 3 percent had latrines, and only a third of them used them regularly, the men objecting to their use because of the distance from the fields and the women because of their desire to stroll in the fields and gossip with other women. The problem of changing caste practices and attitudes toward untouchability are even more involved.

THE SOCIOLOGIST AND SOCIAL CHANGE

The sociologist has always had an interest in, and has advanced many general theories of, social change. The new and old countries of Africa, Asia, and South America require rapid social change today, and presumably the sociologist should be able to help meet their age-old problems and the new ones created by industrialization and urbanism. Underdeveloped areas furnish a comparative situation in which to test important sociological generalizations based on a highly industrialized American culture.

What can the sociologist contribute to social change and the solution of social problems in underdeveloped countries? He has several roles, namely research, teaching, and as a consultant on action policies. Sociology is a new science in most countries, and it is still a newer one in developing countries where the number of sociologists is small, their teaching loads heavy, and often their research training inadequate. Probably a basic need of most developing countries is the analysis and systematization of knowledge about the culture and society, the institutions and values. In India, for example, the study of the ancient culture of the age-old Veddas does not necessarily tell us much about the nature of modern urbanism and the influence of Western culture on urban society, contemporary caste relations, the power structure, class ways of life, the rights of women, and religious practices as they are today. There is need for research on the extent and nature of delinquency, crime, and mental disorder.

Such research not only contributes to scientific knowledge but also

---

[7]See Donald J. Bogue, "Some Tentative Recommendations for a 'Sociologically Correct' Family Planning Communication and Motivation Program in India," (Unpublished paper, 1962), "Experiments in the Use of Mass Communication and Motivation to Speed Adoption of Birth Control in High Fertility Populations," (paper discussed at the annual meeting of the Sociological Research Association, Washington, D.C., August, 1962); and Herbert F. Lionberger, "Some Observations Regarding the Nature and Scope of Action-Research in Family Planning" (Unpublished paper, May 20, 1961).

[8]The Ford Foundation in India, *Roots of Change*, New York, November, 1961.

helps to build up a body of data for social planning and social action. Too rapid social change could upset existing local or national institutions and thus create chaos rather than orderly change. If the sociologist could foresee some of the imbalances or conflicts which might develop from a course of action, underdeveloped countries would benefit immensely. In India, for example, a basic task is to discover how to integrate values of a technological and materialistic Western world with those of a theological, prescientific and feudalistic society. On the basis of an appraisal of existing aims, aspirations and values, the sociologist might furnish insights and perhaps predict developments from the introduction of a new social program.

Sociologists who do research in underdeveloped countries should work as much as possible with their foreign counterparts and students to help them improve their assessments of social processes and problems in a scientific manner. All too often Western social scientists wish to take credit and exploit a research situation for their own professional advantage.

Most American sociologists who have gone to underdeveloped countries have held teaching posts, some under the Fulbright program, while others have been under the auspices of the Ford Foundation and the Agency for International Development. Where they have been effective and have been permitted to be so they have also contributed to social change through the knowledge they transmit and their influence on younger scholars. The foreign teacher is working within the framework of the local culture and university rather than teaching foreign students in America far removed from their own culture.

The sociologist has also had the role of consultant in governmental action programs in underdeveloped countries. In comparison with the consultants in economics, their number has been small. Most have been involved in programs of rural community development, but others have been consultants in such programs as urban community development, urban planning, and family planning. A sociologist acting as a consultant in underdeveloped countries has several functions:

(1) He helps conceptualize problems, formulates basic assumptions, and brings together existing and needed data to make policy decisions. He helps shape policy decisions but does not make the final decisions.

(2) By designing and carrying out needed action-research programs he helps provide material on which a policy decision can be made.

(3) Often he can introduce a sociological approach into a problem which has been considered basically, for example, an economic or public health one.

(4) He communicates knowledge and research materials available from other countries which have been either unknown or overlooked.

(5) As a foreigner, he has a fresh approach to a local situation which may

have been overlooked by local workers whose long association has conditioned them to a particular view and even inertia. Once, for example, as a consultant I suggested what was thought by others to be a novel idea, namely, if Indian cities did not have the daily visits of the municipal sweeper to the alleys and lanes, they might remain freer of filth, my point being that the use of the cen-turies-old sweeper tended to destroy citizen responsibility and was a cause of the unsanitary practices rather than the conventional Indian viewpoint that what was needed was more and better sweepers.

(6) The consultant from a developed country is able to present an image of what things could be, particularly if similar conditions once existed in his own country. All too often persons in charge of social action in such countries feel that the situation has always existed and thus cannot be changed.

(7) As an outsider the foreign consultant can deal more frankly with per-sons higher in the often rigid bureaucratic structure of the government hier-archy.

(8) Sociologists working as consultants in underdeveloped countries can contribute much in the evaluation of action programs. This work often re-quires greater scientific ingenuity, elaborate research design, and professional judgment than is found in many a conventional research study, although some do not call it research because it is action-oriented. This work resembles typical basic research programs in many ways, with the important exception that the research hypotheses become goals or objectives, and there is an attempt to measure the progress of an action program against certain norms and standards of performance. Moreover, the sociologist is expected to submit proposals for changes in administrative procedures and plans of action. It is assumed that if these changes are made the subsequent evaluation will show improved results.

(9) Finally, as President Heald of the Ford Foundation has indicated, the role of innovator is expected of a consultant:

The best consultants are prized not so much for their specialized knowledge but for their broad viewpoints and analytical powers.. Though skilled in quenching fires and rescuing foundering operations, they function uniquely by extricating problems from traditional and organizational straitjackets. The con-sultant is a specialist with a 360 degree sweep. He penetrates the underbrush and identifies the heart of the problem. He suggests avenues toward solution distilled from long and varied experience. Although his solution must be sound and practical, they are apt to be creative and unconventional.

SOCIAL CHANGE AND THE INDIAN SLUM: A CASE STUDY

These ideas on the role of the consultant in bringing about social change in underdeveloped areas have been derived, in part, from my experiences in an action program in India, as a consultant on urban community development to the Ford Foundation and the Delhi Municipal

Corporation.[9] In this pioneer project we have tried to stimulate rapid social change in the way of life of the slum dwellers of Delhi. I should like to discuss the project as an actual example of similar possibilities for sociologists to apply their knowledge and approach in other areas and in other countries.

The Problem. The project grew out of the problems created by the recent rapid urbanization of India which has had its counterpart in other Asian countries as well as Africa and South America.[10] In all underdeveloped areas the cities carry a heavy burden as centers of government, commerce, transportation, and increasing industrial development. In India the cities have been growing at a rate twice as great as the general population. Today a fifth of the Indian population lives in cities, making an urban population of 75 million which exceeds the total populations of all but six countries in the world today. Kingsley Davis estimates that by the year 2000 the percentage of population living in cities will be 30.8, or 300,000,000 persons living in the cities of India.[11] Unless the living conditions of these urban people can be rapidly improved it will be difficult for them to maintain their political stability or to function properly in an increasingly industrialized setting. The situation may even become more difficult unless immediate social changes are instituted.

Like many other Indian cities, Delhi has experienced a fourfold growth in its population, from 700,000 in 1941 to 2,600,000 in 1961. The density of Delhi is 136,000 persons per square mile, with some areas with as many as 400,000 per square mile, as compared with 76,000 in Manhattan with its multi-storied apartment buildings. Delhi's slum population lives in a squalid chaos of tenements, hovels, shacks, and bazaar stalls scattered through narrow congested streets, alleys, and lanes, where open drains are often blocked with refuse, garbage, and excreta. Many areas lack adequate amenities such as latrines, water taps, or electric outlets. The infant mortality rate is one of the world's highest, and the death rate from dysentery, cholera, typhoid fever, and tuberculosis is also high.

---

[9]Marshall B. Clinard and B. Chatterjee, "Urban Community Development in India: The Delhi Pilot Project," in Roy Turner, (ed.), *India's Urban Future* (Berkeley: University of California Press, 1962), pp. 71-94; Marshall B. Clinard, "The Delhi Pilot Project in Urban Community Development," *International Review of Community Development*, No. 7, (1961), pp. 161-70; and B. Chatterjee and Marshall B. Clinard, *Organizing Citizens' Development Councils* (Delhi: Department of Urban Community Development, Municipal Corporation of Delhi, 1961). B. Chatterjee is the Director, Department of Urban Community Development, Delhi Municipal Corporation. A second pilot project in urban community development was started with a Ford Foundation grant in Ahmedabad in 1962.

[10]UNESCO, *The Social Implications of Industrialization and Urbanization* (Five Studies in Asia, Research Centre on the Social Implications of Industrialization in Southern Asia), (Calcutta, India, 1956); UNESCO, *Social Implications of Industrialization and Urbanization in Africa South of the Sahara*, (1956); and Philip M. Hauser, (ed.), *Urbanization in Latin America* (New York: Columbia University Press, 1961).

[11]Kingsley Davis, "Urbanization in India: Past and Future," in Turner, *op. cit.*, pp. 3-27.

Health services are generally inadequate, but even if they were adequate many urban persons would not avail themselves of modern medical care. Because of lack of scientific knowledge, as well as reliance upon folk and religious beliefs, they either do not seek medical care or rely upon quacks who charge exorbitant rates. In a situation where written communication is widely needed, the urban areas of India have high illiteracy rates, and furthermore many adults see no reason to become literate or even encourage their children to become literate.

Over all hangs the deadly air of apathy and the absence of civic responsibility. The urban population, even in local areas, is increasingly a heterogeneous one, and there is little or no neighborhood feeling. There is little cooperation between persons of different castes, religions, and regional origin. In some cases there is a semblance of former local population unity, but the increasing migration and housing pressures are breaking this down. By themselves the government of India and the municipal governments can do little to change a situation which affects in all of India at least 50,000,000 slum people.

The Application of Sociology to an Action Program

Various sociological principles and concepts have been applied to the solution of such a problem. Rather than looking at the problem primarily as an economic one, certain objectives were proposed for the project: (1) to stimulate, foster, and establish common associations to promote community consciousness and integration on the basis of shared concerns and shared projects; (2) to identify and prepare natural leadership in order to enable local areas to meet their day-to-day problems on a mutual-aid and self-help basis; (3) to inculcate pride and a sense of belonging to their places of residence; and (4) to pave the way for tackling civic services on a decentralized basis.

In the design, as well as in later evaluation of this action program, certain principles have been developed: the group rather than the individual is the unit for social action; new forms of consensus must be established to integrate persons of diverse status around new goals; local beliefs and the existing power structure should be understood, while avoiding caste, religious, and political considerations by subdividing the larger group; new leadership patterns should be developed; a new self-image among slum dwellers should replace feelings of apathy and futility, through the use of new symbols of prestige; the Indian woman's desire for higher status, and the desire of caste and religious minority groups for equality, should be utilized; age generation conflicts should be recognized and reconciled; competition for status should be fostered as a motivating force in self-improvement; the role of patterns of communication should be studied; and the need for and acceptance of constant evaluation of assumptions and procedures should be kept constantly in mind.

Some basic principles of change have been observed, such as the following:

(1) The need for change must be perceived by the group.

(2) Optimum use should be made of local values. Their destruction might well lead to severe strains and, in extreme cases, to anomie and social disorganization.

(3) The needs felt by people as opposed to those felt by the innovator represent one of the most important factors in the acceptance of an innovation in any particular case.

(4) Changes which people readily see as desirable usually achieve a more rapid and widespread acceptance than changes of long-term or not easily understood benefits.

(5) An effort must be made to single out the person or persons who are most appropriate carriers of the innovation.[12]

The Group as the Unit

Slum life is largely a product of group practices, many of them centuries old. If changes are to be brought about the agent must be the group concerned. Permanent change must proceed through a process of self-help in which the slum people as a group see the need and develop the ability to change. For example, family planning classes in the project areas have been conducted in the lanes and alleys for groups of interested women, with the approval of the Executive Council. Rather than going individually, as is customary to clinics, slum women, as a group, are thus able to face any opposition from their mothers-in-law or husbands.

The problem is primarily not an economic one or merely exposure to scientific ways. Nor are the conditions of health and sanitation found in an Indian city primarily products of the Indian culture, as similar conditions characterized Western Europe two or three centuries ago and more recently parts of America, as Sjoberg has indicated.[13]

Establishing New Goals and Forms of Consensus

Community relationships based on territorial ties mean little to most Indians of the slum whose allegiance is largely to family, caste, religion, occupation, and region. A further complication is the weakening or

---

[12]Also see Charles J. Erasmus, "An Anthropologist Views Technical Assistance," in Lyle W. Shannon, *Underdeveloped Areas* (New York: Harper & Bros., 1957), pp. 295-308, and Walter R. Goldschmidt, "The Inter-relations between Cultural Factors and the Acquisition of New Technical Skills," in Bert F. Hoselitz (ed.), *The Progress of Underdeveloped Areas* (Chicago: The University of Chicago Press, 1952), pp. 149-51.

[13]Gideon Sjoberg, *The Preindustrial City: Past and Present* (New York: The Free Press of Glencoe, Inc.)

destruction in the city of old unities such as kinship, caste, or occupational bonds which have been basic to unity in India for ages past.[14]

If peoples' attitudes and practices are to be changed, some change is required in the people's general living situation. Some type of new local community areas had to be created artificially out of the dense, heterogeneous mass of the city. These have been created by specially trained community organizers who have tried to develop self-help and citizen participation among these slum people. An experimental situation was designed to discover the differences in response to the idea of territorial organization as well as differences in necessary techniques. Various types of experimental groups of 2,000-4,000 persons were artificially delimited in the densely populated slum areas. The 37 experimental groups, involving 50,000 persons, varied in caste, religion, occupation, income, and political composition, as well as in the physical nature of the areas. Some groups serve as control groups and in addition it is possible to compare these areas with the unorganized parts of the slum.

The basic organizational unit has been the Vikas Mandal or citizen development council, a formal organization with its own constitution, and a dues-paying membership with their own elected representatives. Each project has a women's counterpart or auxiliary which recognizes the separate status of Indian women by giving them a semi-independent organization. In a general way the organization was able to utilize some of the principles of neighborhood organization worked out by American sociologists Shaw, McKay, Burgess, Alinsky, Mel Ravitz, and others.

This new type of social organization, the territorial unit, has enabled forces of change to be unleashed in other areas such as in caste relations and the status of women. The organizational nature of the project requires upper and lower castes to sit at the same table and Muslim women in Purdah to attend meetings with Hindu women.

Where new local issues have come under discussion, such as the cooperative paving of a lane, providing new latrines, keeping an area clean, and mass vaccination campaigns, it has been possible to get a high degree of unity among people with diverse caste, regional, religious, and occupational backgrounds. Coleman's studies of community conflict and organization around issues such as fluoridation and urban renewal in the United States suggest the same thing.[15] The continued association, organization, participation in, and sharing of project goals has contributed to the security of religious minority groups and promoted intercaste, linguistic, and regional harmony. To develop a feeling of community, self-help activities have included common bulletin boards, paving lanes, community latrines and water facilities, whitewashing areas, cele-

---

[14]"Nature and Extent of Social Change in India," *Sociological Bulletin,* Vol. XI, March and September, 1962. Symposium of the Indian Sociological Society held at Mysore October 19-21, 1961.

[15]James S. Coleman, *Community Conflict* (New York: The Free Press, 1957).

bration of Independence Day, community singing, and sports programs for children.

Subunits to Avoid Power Groups

In Indian cities there is always the possibility that exploitation of caste, religion, or political differences could destroy any unity based on territorial grounds. Therefore, instead of having a general election, representatives are elected at the level of 15 to 40 families. Here such considerations are relatively significant, the small size of the unit making it hardly worth the manipulation. By gerrymandering the small unit, it has been possible to get various minority groups represented on the council.

Diversity of Local Beliefs and the Power Structure

Any attempts to change prevailing practices must be preceded by recognition and familiarity with local beliefs. Each area must be carefully studied. A detailed community research profile is prepared in order to understand the social characteristics of the population with emphasis on its main divisions, the power structure, the role of the women, the family and age composition of the people, and the prevailing attitudes and opinions of the constituents toward health, sanitation, and other conditions. As a project is started and interviewers ask questions, great hostility and suspicions are initially encountered, for the nature of the project is difficult to understand. Rumors are rampant: the purpose is really to raise rents, collect taxes, move the people to new housing colonies, ration food, or attempt to restrict the number of people. The first successful self-help project in an area seems to stop these rumors by diverting the concerns of the people to new areas of consensus.

Creation of New Leadership

Emphasis has been placed on devising criteria for identifying and developing potential new leadership rather than relying on formal traditional leaders who might resist change. Leadership was not sought among caste, religious, and political leaders whose interest might lie in other objectives rather than in changing the local community. Also important has been the identification of potential hostile leadership in the power structure. The new leaders were more representative, being largely of the same social status background. It was assumed, for example, that illiterate persons could more readily motivate illiterate persons. Consequently, two-thirds of the council executive committee members have never before been leaders, over one-fourth are from lower castes, nearly half have had no formal education, and several council presidents can neither read nor write.

Although it is often assumed in the Western world that illiteracy is a serious handicap for local community leadership, in the Delhi project, people with less education are more likely to be elected. They are thought to reflect more of their own feelings and aspirations and thus more likely to work energetically for community betterment. Although in some project areas educated persons are available, slum people generally select leaders from the less educated group. One out of 20 of 351 executive committee members of 21 councils were totally illiterate; almost half were either illiterate or semiliterate. Compared to "voluntary" citizen groups in the slums who were not elected, it has been found that the percentage with little education is twice as great. Consequently, the conclusion has been drawn that the real "grass roots" origin of an organization might well be judged by the educational level of its leaders.

Development of a New Self-Image by the Use of Prestige

Apathy and lack of confidence in the possibility of self-help by people of low economic and social status has characterized most projects in the beginning. The creation of a new self-image has provided a possible motivating force for slum people to change their practices. Stimulating the new and novel idea of self-help in the face of great apathy, however, has required much ingenuity. One way to stimulate an awareness of self-help possibilities has been the skillful presentation in the initial interview of the question, "What problems do you think the people in this area could solve for themselves?" Few can suggest anything, but the question arouses much discussion among the area residents about the strange idea of their being thought able to do or change things themselves. Out of it seems to come awareness of self-help and a new consensus about themselves.

Whether one wishes to term the situation "status need" or some form of conspicuous consumption which Erasmus has recently elaborated into a general theory of cultural development, the desire for status has been useful in changing the self-image.[16] One of the first cooperative self-help projects, for example, desired by slum people has often been the numbering of their shacks, sometimes even adding names and whitewashing the area. Since there are far more pressing problems and many cannot read, it seemed evident that they wished to have some feeling of identity and importance in an urban setting comparable to that of middle- and upper-class areas with their names, numbers, and neatly whitewashed flats and homes.

On this principle a number of devices have been adapted to enhance their prestige image of themselves. It has been our hope and expectation that the people will try to live up to this new image of themselves. All 37 projects have letterhead stationery printed with the name of each group in Hindi, Urdu, and English. The stationery, even though few

---

[16]Charles J. Erasmus, *Man Takes Control: Cultural Development and American Aid* (Minneapolis: University of Minnesota Press, 1961).

can read or write, together with a small office for which furniture is supplied, makes them feel important. With a new feeling of prestige it is likely that other changes will follow such as improved sanitation, literacy, and better care of the children. Other devices have included cooperative visits to historical and cultural centers and community picnics, all to enhance their middle-class conceptions of themselves.

While the project is a part of municipal government, full credit is given to the local leadership in order to build up confidence, responsibility, and facilitate social change. Local elected leaders of each project appear in the council chambers to report directly to the highest city officials on what has been done in their areas. They become the agents of social change rather than the community organizers.

The Status of Women and a New Self-Image

Slum women are more likely to be motivated to work for social change than men. Considering their low status this came as quite a surprise. After a closer look at the situation, it has been concluded that this very position of lower status in traditional family and community situations has made them assume greater responsibility for change within the framework of a new type of organization based on territorial ties. Such changes reflect a deep desire on the part of women to demonstrate their social equality. Slum women have participated so little in an all-male society that they are more likely to be enthusiastic rather than skeptical in working for the removal of centuries-old slum problems. For example, to change their image of themselves and their status, traditional Kertans or singing and devotional groups are first organized among Hindu women, and recitation of ancient Urdu poetry among Muslim women. Then attempts are made to interest the women in these groups in a new conception of themselves through such activities as child care, family nutrition, family planning, and community sanitation.

Minority Status and Social Change

The Muslim minority appears to be the most difficult to change largely because of their traditional religion, close in-group relations, seclusion of women, and the very difficult sanitary conditions which have developed. Contrary to expectations, Muslim projects have turned out to be the most successful. Part of this can be explained by their minority status and the desire to improve their image in the eyes of the Hindu community. Other factors have been their incipient dissatisfaction with traditional practices which a new organizational structure can possibly change through the growth of new and more progressive leadership.

Age Generation Conflict

Age generation conflict has presented a serious problem in attempting social change. On the one hand is the political zeal, enthusiasm, and determination of younger persons while on the other is the stable maturity and relative inaction of many persons who because of their age occupy a position of high status in India. There is disagreement in values, in priority, and in speed of implementing social change. In facing this problem attempts have been made to build more effective channels of communication and at the same time interpret each group, and its needs, to the other.

Competition Among Groups for Status

Competition for status among local groups has been effectively used to increase the unity, pride, and involvement of slum dwellers. Regular athletic competitions such as volley ball and cricket between the children and young people of the various councils have been successful in stimulating local pride. Area cleanliness competition between different groups has been fostered, as have contests for babies who exhibit the best personal and nutritional care. There have also been frequent gatherings of the officers of the various citizen councils, a two-day camp-out of officers, visits of officers of one project to those of another, and such exchange of gifts as giving a name plate to another organization.

Lines of Communication

Experience has been gained in extending the lines of communication among people living under densely crowded conditions. The width of a road or lane often determines the nature of communication; if the lane is narrow communication flows more easily along and across it than if it is wide. The flow of an open drain may determine the relationships of people near it. Communication between those living on upper floors of two-storied buildings and those living below is rare and makes the discussion of community issues difficult. In general the more crowded the living conditions the more favorable the situation is for the development of effective community ties and self-help. Density promotes association and communication; the impact of each other's problems and difficulties seems to motivate them to deal with common concerns.

Evaluation Studies

A number of evaluation studies have been undertaken, particularly to determine variations among the 37 different experimental councils. These have included studies of self-help activities and contributions, leaders' reactions, and changes in women's attitudes. Among the indices used to measure performance have been percentage of membership, attendance at executive committee meetings, and effectiveness of leadership. For example, a group of 21 councils in the first two years engaged in 531 self-help activities, of which three-fourths were equally divided among health and sanitation, cultural and recreational, and physical improvements and basic amenities.[17] The total value of the self-help activities by these councils is estimated at 123,000 rupees.

CONCLUSION

Although the opportunities for American sociologists to act as consultants on foreign programs of social change and on problems in their own country are increasing, are sociologists capable or willing to submit to the test of social action? Thousands of research papers by professional sociologists are available today. While most of them characteristically call for future needed research, seldom does one either call for social action or suggest the problem-solving implications of the research.

While it is likely that sociologists may increasingly be asked to serve as consultants both here and abroad, probably few will come forward and of them only a small number will be successful. One reason for this situation is that when the sociologist is asked to propose a practical solution for some issue falling within the supposed area of his personal competence he usually asks for more research money. In fact, few sociologists would ever admit that the area had been so sufficiently "researched" that the time had come to suggest social action.

Other sociologists might feel that, being pure scientists, they should not sully their professional reputation with anything so degrading as social action which is often regarded as a form of intellectual "prostitution."[18] It might be argued that such an approach is not followed by countless economists, political scientists, anthropologists, and others who do so without endangering their reputations as scientists. Hundreds of academic economists, for example, have been associated with planning the fiscal and monetary policies of underdeveloped countries under United Nations and other auspices. Countless economists have been associated with overseas economic development programs of the United States government during the past six years, but only some 25 sociologists have served as consultants during this period.

One can easily understand the sociologist's reluctance to make practical suggestions. In the first place, he is afraid that, despite his verbiage and claims that his discipline should be recognized as the equal of the physical sciences, he is really not in a position to undertake the prepara-

---

[17]*Evaluation Study of The Vikas Mandals* (Citizens' Development Councils) (New Delhi: Department of Urban Community Development, Municipal Corporation of Delhi, March, 1962).

[18]"Five years ago when a plea was made at the annual meeting of another equally reputable social science fraternity for help in finding qualified men, the reaction was quick and certain. It would be virtual professional prostitution for a social scientist to become identified with a Government action program for as long as two years. Social scientists could not move away from theory and research or the academic world if they were to ascend the professional ladder." Quoted in Louis Miniclier, "ICA Experience with Anthropologists," paper presented for the annual meeting of the American Anthropological Association, Philadelphia, November 19, 1961.

tion of analyses that may lead to social action. As Zetterberg has put it, "The fact that the social scientist says, 'Let's do research about,' signals his common inability to draw upon codified knowledge when faced with a new practical problem. We have competent researchers but hardly any competent consultants."[19]

Second, he is fearful of being associated with what might be termed social work, with which he was so long associated and more often still confused. Rather than seeing the direction of other behavioral sciences he has developed false images of the scientist forever detached and aloof from the world of practical reality. He is fearful that he will receive no professional recognition for any action work from his colleagues who conceive of his role as writing and research within an academic community.

Third, despite elaborate theory building and preoccupation with quantitative techniques which he feels will give him scientific respectability, the sociologist has probably had less first-hand experience with the actual data of his science than any other. Not really knowing about human beings, social institutions, and communities at first hand he obviously feels ill-equipped to devise action programs that may have considerable immediate consequences. It has been my observation that sociologists working in underdeveloped countries become much more familiar at first hand with human situations and this has a salutary effect upon them and their work.

Fourth, unlike the economist whose basic theory and concepts are better organized for application to social practice, the sociologist's knowledge in such situations is often diffused and unorganized. He is often not sure what he can do. The practical application of social theory may help to improve basic theoretical sociology. "It forces theorists to be at least reasonably precise; to stay in close contact with reality; and to have more than a technical vocabulary to offer when talking about social events."[20]

Despite the sociologist's rationalizations of being a pure scientist, of not being interested in social action and similar verbalizations, the frank fact is that he is seldom asked today to help as a policy consultant. It is true that more and more sociologists are being employed in research capacities by various agencies and even businesses, the result of which makes many swell with academic pride. Yet their opportunity for social action is limited and they remain well down in the power structure in this regard.

In spite of the problems of our age today, few sociologists are in a position in government to make or even draw up policy decisions. There

---

[19]Hans L. Zetterberg, *Social Theory and Social Practice* (New York: The Bedminister Press, 1962), p. 17.
[20]*Ibid.*, p. 189.

is no sociological equivalent to the President's Council of Economic Advisors. While economists, historians, political scientists, and others are brought in to serve on advisory commissions in government, the sociologist continues to be left out. For them the phone from those in high places seldom rings.

There are countless problems that need sociological insight. The services of more sociological consultants are needed in America today in designing and evaluating programs involving urban neighborhood councils, delinquency control, mental health, race relations, and in countless other areas. Zetterberg has recently described in detail how a sociologist, as a consultant, even designed a program to increase audience response to museum activities.[21] The control of the economy of the nation involves a host of sociological factors.

By not being concerned with social action in such situations as those provided in underdeveloped countries, sociologists miss an important scientific opportunity; the opportunity to test their points of view and knowledge through immediate application to programs of social control. No one has ever stated this better than Sutherland: "This concern with practical programs is justified, in part, as experimentation which may be valuable because of its immediate results but at any rate will be valuable in the long run because of the increased knowledge which results from it. If practical programs wait until theoretical knowledge is complete, they will wait for an eternity, for theoretical knowledge is increased most significantly in the efforts at social control."[22]

---

[21]*Ibid.*, pp. 135-78.
[22]Edwin H. Sutherland, *Principles of Criminology* (4th ed.: Philadelphia: J. B. Lippincott Co., 1947), pp. 1-2.

■■

An apprenticeship for a career in applied sociology is now available through the nation's foreign and domestic Peace Corps. More structured than a year "on the road," more meaningful than a Boswellian or Cook Agency "Grand Tour," and more challenging than most graduate curriculums or postdoctoral years, these two corps offer the sociologist a unique opportunity to gain and give simultaneously. Dr. A. Paul Hare frankly admits that at the start he was not sure sociology had much to offer the foreign Peace Corps; the record of his year in the Philippines should dispel this misgiving. In addition, his own gains as a sociologist appear considerable—as illustrated by the reality lesson experienced while observing Philippine funeral processions. Finally, the stress Dr. Hare places on having a particular project-related experience before one attempts a research or consultative role with the project is very well taken, although previously difficult to achieve. Hopefully, the new opportunity presented by the Corps for an "apprenticeship" in participation and consultation will help implement this change.

■■

PLANNING FOR UTOPIA—A SOCIOLOGIST IN THE
PEACE CORPS*

A. Paul Hare

WHAT DOES A sociologist do in the Peace Corps? When I was asked to join the Corps staff shortly after its formation in 1961, I was frankly not sure about the relevance of my sociological background for the role of an overseas administrator. However, after a year's experience with the Corps in the Philippines (1961–62) I have concluded that I was at least as well equipped as other Corps staffers with backgrounds in political science, economics, history, or the like; indeed, as a sociologist, I was perhaps a little better equipped to work in an active way with problems in developing countries. Three examples of the kind of thing I did as a Peace Corps sociologist should help make this clear: the first entailed

---

*This article is based in part on a paper presented at the meetings of the Pennsylvania Sociological Society, Chambersburg, Pennsylvania, October, 1962.

analysis and construction, the second, analysis and assignment, and the third, analysis, prediction, and evaluation. In all three cases a background of study concerning the whole of society proved invaluable.

The Training Affair

During my first few weeks in the Philippines, before any of the Corps volunteers had arrived, I was asked to work out the details of an additional eight weeks of prefield training for the volunteers. The Corps had previously arranged to hold the training on the campus of an agricultural college near Manila, but, for some unknown reason, the crucial lecturers, all staff members of the government's Bureau of Public Schools, were decidedly reluctant to participate.

Determined to unravel the matter, I initiated an informal investigation that was not long in revealing that the Bureau of Public Schools was the traditional rival of the college faculty. The Bureau men in general were older and had worked up through a national hierarchy of primary and secondary education. The agricultural college faculty members were younger men who had higher prestige in the society. To make matters even worse, the Bureau had its own educational training center in a mountain rest area, a center which had been proposed for Peace Corps training but had been rejected as being too far from Manila. Now, the Bureau officials were being asked to carry out a training program on their rival's home base. They would not even come to committee meetings to make further plans.

With the problem's analysis sufficiently complete, my next task as a sociologist was that of constructing a "bridging group," an appropriate social invention in cases where the problem is largely one of institutional rivalry.[1]

The original plan for the Corps training program had called for a training chairman from one or the other of the rival groups. I tackled this first, believing that a settlement here would set the tone for ensuing and similar settlements of otherwise contentious issues. In short order, a new training committee (or "bridging group") was established, complete with equal representation of the Bureau of Public Schools and the agricultural college—and chaired by a Peace Corps staff member. This stress on "getting the job done" while preserving the status of parties embroiled in institutional rivalries won new support for the Corps, and likely contributed to the success of the training mission.

The Household Affair

A second example of my use of sociology occurred near the end of the in-country training for the Corps' first group of volunteers.

---

[1] H. A. Thelen, *Dynamics of Groups at Work* (Chicago: University of Chicago Press, 1954).

We were faced with the task of dividing the 128 volunteers into households of four volunteers each, either men or women. Volunteers wanted to express their own choices for future housemates and we proposed to consider their choices as one part of the selection process (a first round of choices had actually been made before they left the United States). Overall, we were determined to do the assigning in as scientific and effective a way as possible.

A first check on the character of the choices made by the volunteers was suggested by my previous work in small-group sociology. Since I knew from small-group studies that the growth of friendships is often associated with proximity, and since I was aware that the volunteers had been assigned roommates on an alphabetical basis during stateside training, I anticipated an alphabetical pattern in household choices. To test this hypothesis, I prepared a chart showing who had chosen whom among the volunteers. This took the form of a matrix with the names of the volunteers listed alphabetically along two sides of the chart, a check mark indicating a choice in the appropriate row and column and as anticipated, most of the choices lay along the diagonal, the A's having chosen the A's, the M's the M's, and so on.

Since the first set of household choices turned out to reflect proximity more than compatibility based on personality characteristics, we asked the volunteers to make new choices near the end of the in-country training. By that time they had known each other longer ("barrack-type" accommodations also meant many occupied the same sleeping area), and we expected the effect of proximity would be less marked. In any event, we already had useful sociological evidence that volunteers would tend to say they "liked" their housemates no matter with whom they might be assigned since "proximity" would once again likely have its effect.

To this "new choice" material I added additional data available from the two "personality" tests I had asked the volunteers to take. After scoring the tests on an IBM computer in Manila, I further combined the sociometric choice and personality data with certain social background information gathered during the recruitment and selection of every volunteer—and moved from this to recommendations of household groupings.

The Prediction Affair

We employed the sociological material mentioned above not only as part of an attempt to produce "compatible" four-man households of volunteers but also in an effort to predict the success of volunteers in the field. Returning to the IBM computer in Manila, I later compared our first-run predictions with ratings given by regional Corps administrators after the volunteers had taught for three months in the field. At the end of their two years of service, more ratings were obtained for the volunteers, and this made possible the further analysis I have reported else-where in a technical paper.[2]

Post-Corps Experience

The examples of analysis, construction, assignment, prediction, and evaluation are drawn from my one-year stay in the Philippines, but, in fact, my role as a sociologist with the Peace Corps did not end, but only took a new turn with my return to the States.

To begin with, I was asked by the Corps to help code the open-ended answers to a Corps questionnaire given by the first group of volunteers to complete a full two-year term. Since I had had actual Corps field experience, the Corps assigned me a set of answers to an open-ended question which asked volunteers to identify up to three occasions overseas when they felt depressed or had low morale. The volunteers were asked when these periods in the field had occurred, how they felt at the time, and what they did about them. It was necessary, therefore, to develop codes for types of stress, reactions to stress, moods, and agencies of intervention. Using these data, I was able to test several hypotheses drawn from the social-psychological literature and from Corps field reports about "culture shock" and reactions to stress. As the results of this research will appear shortly in an official Peace Corps publication, I will not go into them here: the important point for "sociology in action" is rather that several opportunities for systematic research presented themselves once I had had actual Peace Corps field experience.

I also worked on the well-publicized readjustment challenge that confronts returning Corpsmen. My own return after a year with one of the first Corps groups left me in a position to anticipate some of the readjustment problems of two-year veterans of the field. These include the "culture shock" of reentering an impersonal, fast-paced society, and the feeling that one's contemporaries have little knowledge of or concern for the problems of developing nations. Perhaps most telling is the loss of the feeling of total commitment to one's work that is present in the Peace Corps. One really did feel like a pioneer on the "new frontier."

To document some of the feelings and experiences of returning Corpsmen, I joined with a fellow returnee, Dr. Lawrence Howard, a political scientist who had also been a staff member in the Philippines, and the two of us organized a privately financed (Danforth Foundation) conference for volunteers who had been back in the States six months.

Using the "group interview" technique I had explored some years earlier in a study of a college culture, we held a residential two-day interview at Pendle Hill, a Quaker center for adult education located in

[2]A. Paul Hare, "Factors Associated with Peace Corps Volunteer Success in the Philippines," *Human Organization* (in press). Paper presented at the meetings of the Eastern Sociological Society, New York, April, 1962.

Pennsylvania.[3] The group consisted of a sample of about 30 men and women from different types of Corps projects around the world. Since this was the first conference of its kind to be held, a summary we prepared of the two-day "group interview" was widely circulated among the Peace Corps staff and was published in both the *Peace Corps Newsletter* and a social science journal in the Philippines. Our conference summary helped give volunteers and staff a chance to anticipate some of the problems of adjustment that they would face on return to the States, and, for Dr. Howard and me, it provided a rewarding and satisfying episode of "action research."

Summary

What does a sociologist do in the Peace Corps? A great variety of things. I have described some of these already, and will only briefly in conclusion cite a personal reward, and offer a personal guideline—both of special significance to the interested sociologist.

I have failed thus far to call adequate attention to the reward in "reality stress" available to the sociologist in Corps participation. In many ways one "takes" much, even as one "gives" much while a Corpsman. In my own case, I found that many social facts which had existed for me only as bare statistics came alive during my year of Corps field work. To cite just one example: I had heard much about the population explosion and knew something of the world's vital statistics, but until I reached the Philippines and saw the large number of schoolchildren who had to be turned away from school each year, the statistics did not come alive. I had also heard of high death rates in developing countries, but again, the real content of such rates was first demonstrated for me by the high incidence of Philippine funeral processions, often with the group bearing a small coffin.

Finally, I would call attention to the fact that both a great need *and* an opportunity for social scientists exists in the Peace Corps. Here, perhaps more so than with other older, established institutions, I would strongly encourage you to be a participant before you become an observer. This guideline is generally more honored in the breach than in the observance, but it is no less meaningful for that: Having "been there," I do not hesitate to urge you to pursue "sociology in action" *initially* through field experience. Planning for a Utopia merits nothing less than such participation—and requires fully as much, somewhere along the way, if the endeavor is to be a successful one.

---

[3]A. Paul Hare and J. S. Davie, "The Group Interview: Its Use in the Study of Undergraduate Culture," *Sociology and Social Research*, 1954, pp. 81-87.

PART THREE

PROSPECTS

W hat are the prospects for applied sociology? They turn in large part
on our ability to better understand the reasons that lead many social
scientists to currently avoid involvement in social action programs. According to Dr. Frank Riessman and Dr. S. M. Miller, the authors of the unusual
essay below, the lingering power of an ideology that call "the psychiatric world view" serves at present as a constraining and privatizing
force." Unfortunately seen as sophistication, the "psychiatric world view"
is in fact increasingly ill-suited to society's needs and to the possibilities
of the social sciences. It remains to be seen whether we will grow beyond
it: if we do, considerable credit will probably be owed the Riessman-
Miller kind of social analysis—and action prescription.

SOCIAL CHANGE VERSUS THE "PSYCHIATRIC WORLD VIEW"*

Frank Riessman and S. M. Miller

THE NEW center-city poor are generating a series of crises for the
school, mental hospital, and social agency with their established middle-
class outlook, traditions, and structure. The poor have long been alienated from the teacher, the psychiatrist, and the social worker but a new
element has emerged to force change. Today's poor have a number of
potentially power-producing qualities that make them more difficult to
ignore: They are concentrating in heavy proportions in the suburb-segre-
gated metropolis and they are "colored," fusing together on ethnic as well
as economic issues.

This potential might is only beginning to be appreciated by social
scientists and other intellectuals. For example, Michael Harrington's pes-
simistic notion of a "culture of poverty" led him to conclude that the poor
are a self-defeated minority, socially invisible, politically impotent, and
completely ignored.[1] Perhaps this was true when he started his book, but

*To stimulate thought on the 1964 Annual Meeting theme, "Orthopsychiatric
Responsibility in Social Change," the Editorial Board and the Program Committee
of the Association invited Dr. Riessman and Dr. Miller to prepare this paper for the
Journal. Copyright by the American Orthopsychiatric Association, Inc., reprinted
by permission of the authors and the American Journal of Orthopsychiatry, from the
issue of January, 1964.
[1] See Michael Harrington, The Other American (New York: Macmillan Co., 1962).

in the current period poverty is receiving a tremendous amount of attention. We find:

1. Fourteen "grey cities" projects concerned with educational programs similar to that of Higher Horizons, specifically directed toward the deprived;

2. An array of community projects similar to Mobilization for Youth, concerned with increasing opportunities for the urban poor. (The President's Mental Health Bill may open up a comparable potentiality in psychiarty);

3. Five major books dealing with poverty and inequality within the past year;

4. Central domestic discussions revolving around questions closely related to urban poverty, for example, housing, discrimination, unemployment, education;

5. Most important of all, the Negro revolution, which is powerfully challenging established social and economic practices as well as fashionable liberal intellectual styles.[2]

Intellectuals are not awakening the poor; the poor are awakening intellectuals.

What will this awakening bring? Social scientists can play an extremely important role during this period, charting new paths, developing programs, and providing active support and leadership. While it is too early to assay their role in relation to the Negro movement, it is already clear that they are certainly generally supportive but apparently not actively involved. Little of the passionate and pervasive commitment that characterized their involvement in the labor revolution of the '30s has appeared. This hesitation is surprising because the Negro revolution promises shifts in the entire political fabric of society, shifts that seem congruent with the interest of large numbers of intellectuals in progressive social change.

For a better understanding of this lack of involvement in the most important social upheaval of two and one-half decades, it may be useful to examine the intellectual atmosphere of the '40s and '50s, particularly the psychiatric world view emerging in those years. Despite the partial decline of this world view, it has considerable lingering power and serves, we contend, to curtail ardor, involvement, and commitment. Moreover, some of its defects are precisely those displayed by many intellectuals in

---

[2] At least six major factors propel the poverty movement: The powerful challenges being raised by both wings of the Negro movement (the integrationists and the nationalists); the stagnation in economic growth, unemployment, and the increasing failure of military expenditures to buoy up the economy; the prospect of automation and the concomitant decline in the need for unskilled labor; the continued migration of the poor to the cities; the Supreme Court decision regarding reapportionment of governmental representation and its significance for urban-rural power distribution; and the considerable interest of the Kennedy administration in one of its main sources of power, namely, the urban vote.

their dealings with the larger world and may be instructive for that reason. In today's rapid social change and intellectual hesitation, we may be ripe for a self-critical analysis of this psychiatric world view, preparatory to deeper participation in the social changes that lie ahead.[3]

THE PSYCHIATRIC WORLD VIEW

Formerly, authoritarian thinking and behavior were considered in political and ideological terms; in the '50s they came to be described in terms of the "authoritarian *personality.*"

Crime and juvenile delinquency were seen mainly as reflections of family instability and personality maladjustment. Criticism of basic features of the society was formulated in terms of the neurotic conflicts of our times." Communist bureaucracy and political rebelliousness alike were analyzed as reflections of distorted relationships to parents. Segregation and discrimination were viewed largely in terms of their pathological *personality* effects upon the Negro. Learning problems of children were attributed to psychological conflicts or emotional blocks.[4]

Psychiatric categories functioned as both cause and effect, as independent variable and dependent variable alike. Discrimination *caused* personality problems while educational difficulties were the *result* of need conflicts. At times it almost seemed as if discrimination and prejudice would have been acceptable had they not produced deleterious *personality* consequences!

So ran thought in the age of psychiatry, which defined almost everything in psychological terms. Although it may not have been clear that we had a neurotic culture, it became increasingly evident that we were living in "psychiatric culture."[5]

---

[3]It should be noted that the phenomenon of the intellectual engagé was not completely absent in the '50s; witness C. Wright Mills. Mills, however, was relatively isolated (although not ignored!) in social science circles.

[4]See for example: T. W. Adorno, *et al.*, *The Authoritarian Personality* (New York: Harper & Bros., 1950). D. Bingham, "Problems of Personality Development Among Negro Children," in *Nature, Society and Culture*, C. Kluckhorn and H. Murray (eds.), (New York: Alfred A. Knopf, Inc., 1953). P. Blanchard, "Cases Illustrating Psychoanalytic Contributions to the problems of reading disabilities," in *Outside Readings in Psychology* (eds.), E. Hartley, H. Birch, and R. Hartley (New York: Thomas Y. Crowell Co., 1955). K. Horney, *The Neurotic Personality of Our Time,* (New York: W. W. Norton & Co., Inc., 1939). A. Johnson, "Juvenile Delinquency" in *American Handbook of Psychiatry*, S. Arieti (ed.), (New York: Basic Books, Inc., 1959, pp. 840-55). On page 855 is cited a list of references reflecting a psychiatric view of delinquency, including the works of A. Eichhorn, K. R. Eissler, K. Friedlander, M. Griffin, W. Healy, S. A. Szurek, and E. Weiss. A. Kardiner and L. Ovesey, *The Mark of Oppression* (New York: World Publishing Co., 1951). G. H. J. Pearson, *Psychoanalysis and the Education of the Child* (New York: W. W. Norton & Co., Inc., 1954).

[5]Strictly speaking, "psychological terms" is an incorrect formulation, because psychodynamic, psychoanalytic explanations emphasizing unconscious causes became the vogue. In this paper, the word "psychiatry" covers the gamut of psychoanalytical orientations. While we later refer to processes in psychotherapy, our major concern is with inappropriate generalization of these basically psychological views to the society at large.

All kinds of problems—social, medical, educational, political—were interpreted through the new psychiatric world view. Problems were not searchingly examined to determine their variable causes or whether and how psychological causes might play a role. Rather, presumed psychological diagnoses were readily given and typically went unquestioned.

This world view was costly in at least two ways: It deflected analysis and action away from nonpsychodynamic (for example, social) approaches and it often contaminated the original problem by introducing inappropriate modes of attack.[6]

But it did much more: It sponsored new values, new goals, new models of man.

THE NEW HERO AND THE PATHOLOGY OF MODERATION

A new hero emerged in the age of psychiatry. He had a number of interesting attributes. He was expressive and calm, free and well-balanced, self-actualized and moderate, autonomous and cooperative. He was neither intense nor overemotional; a good team man, he was a productive being. He evidenced his ability to work, love, and relate to people. Through it all, he was an individualist—not a conformist.

The new hero was thoughtful, knew and accepted himself, and possessed just the right amount of extroversion and introversion. He cared about people and society. He was democratic, antiauthoritarian, and antibureaucratic. He had a mild interest in politics, and strongly rejected the masses and mass culture—one of his few strong feelings. He was not too overtly competitive, disliked conspicuous consumption, and favored sex equality. He preferred relatively permissive—although currently more balanced—child rearing and education.

Our new hero did not get burningly angry, nor was he known for his passionate conviction or intense ardor. He was, in sum, the new well-adjusted middle-class man.[7]

Contemporary psychiatry in the U.S. typically questions extreme, intense behavior. This questioning arises, in part, out of psychiatry's fundamental concern with pathological self-damaging behavior, which is often extreme. On the other hand, many healthy urges of the patient are underdeveloped and therefore unlikely to manifest themselves in intense form. Thus, unwittingly, psychiatry has come to look with suspicion on very strongly held beliefs and urges, often characterizing them as resistances or reaction formations.

---

[6]An important question not addressed in this article concerns the *appropriate* use of psychological levels of explanation in analyzing various problems, including social problems.

[7]The passionate commitment of many intellectuals to Adlai Stevenson in 1952 and 1956 is an interesting exception. As the political symbol of much of the new hero ideology, standing in contrast to the old-fashioned traditional style of Eisenhower, Stevenson overcame many intellectuals' reluctance to be political believers.

In practice this stress on equilibrium—the middle road—has led to a number of difficulties that would be more obvious were this orientation less compatible with today's bias in favor of moderation.

Frank Barron, in a fascinating article on the psychology of imagination,[8] pointed out that, judged by the criteria for health prescribed by modern psychiatry, a large number of creative scientists and artists would be abnormal. Much of the behavior of many creative people is characterized by intensity, turbulence, and lack of calm.

Barron notes "the apocalyptic rages of Beethoven, the savage indignation of Jonathan Swift, the terrible loneliness of Van Gogh, the criminality of Rimbaud, the shameless preenings of Baudelaire, the stoical despair of Emily Bronte, the excruciating physical and spiritual pain endured by Heine," and asks, "Could it be that these creative people had been in need of psychotherapy?" He further observes that, in the typical criteria offered for mental health, he heard "warmth mentioned, but not heat; spontaneity, not passion. No one had spoken of willfulness, fierce self-assertion, hatred of an established order."

An important criticism that can be leveled at twentieth century psychiatry is that it has not sufficiently developed a high order of creative people. More often it has produced "balanced" people, who have rid themselves of their earlier neurotic intensities, but have not replaced them by new constructive zeal.[9]

Too often the implicit advice is to avoid soaring for "unrealistic" heights. Better never to have tried and lost than to have tried at all seems frequently to be the implicit motto.

WHICH MOTIVES ARE QUESTIONED?

One of the most subtle avenues through which the new hero values penetrate through the psychiatric milieu to the public at large is that of the questioning of some motives and the unquestioning of others.

In psychotherapy, patients express various ideas, feelings, impulses, attitudes, many of which are implicitly or explicitly questioned by the therapist who encourages the patient to delve beneath the surface and

---

[8]Frank Barron, "The Psychology of Imagination," *Scientific American*, September, 1958, pp. 151-66.

[9]Psychiatry has not fully faced the enormous problem of developing energy, intensity, fervor in people. The underlying assumption is that, if the neurotic conflict tying up the energy is removed, then the person will be able to go on fairly easily to be productive. This assumption is actually a derivative of Freud's libido theory, which has been rejected by most modern schools of therapy. According to this theory the individual had just so much energy, and this constant amount is either bound up in conflict or available for constructive sublimation. Unfortunately, insufficient attention has been focused on how to redirect the energy after it has been released from conflict. Much more crucial, however, is the slight concern for methods of increasing the total energy of the individual, because the traditional libidinal model, with its constant energy assumption, has tacitly remained.

uncover the motivational origins of these feelings, preparatory to changing them. A large number of feelings and beliefs would typically be
questioned and analyzed: intense ambition, authoritarian views, strong
anticapitalist leanings, most traditional middle-class values, prejudice,
hostile feelings, and the like.

But when an individual, whether he is in therapy or not, expresses a
need to develop himself, or a democratic impulse, or any of the attributes of the new hero, the motives underlying these feelings are not
typically sought for or uncovered. Their acceptability is usually considered self-evident. Motivational reductions are lest apt to be made than
if, by contrast, an individual were to express a revolutionary wish, an
authoritatrian tendency, a deep belief in religion, or, for that matter, any
highly conservative, well-established middle-class value.

True, democratic, cooperative, warm feelings are not always interpreted as genuine motives but as disguises for other kinds of motives.
However, if they are seen as an individual's true motives they are not
inspected further, whereas authoritarian, revolutionary, and traditional
beliefs would not be accepted as genuine motives. Not only are the personality attributes and motives of the new hero unprobed, his values remain unchallenged.

This value bias is one of the most important ways in which psychotherapy has been incorporated into our middle-class world view. Our
quarrel with the value penetration of psychotherapy is its unconscious
projection of the values of the middle class. Many *may* be intrinsically
related to psychological well-being, but this must be carefully demonstrated, not tacitly assumed. Furthermore, because these values are unconsciously projected, there is little if any consideration of the possibiilty
that a wide variety of other values might be consistent with psychological
health. A pluralistic outlook is not part of the psychiatric world view.

THE "NEW IDEOLOGY"

The psychotherapeutic world view was intimately related to a number of trends and movements extremely popular in the '40s and '50s and
cannot be fully understood apart from them. Those trends included progressive education, the child-rearing movement, the sexual "revolution,"
the high regard for creativity, and the great interest and sway of the
writings of Riesman, Fromm, and Whyte.[10] Hereafter these trends will
be referred to as the "new ideology."[11]

---

[10]In the '60s David Riesman and Erich Fromm have become intensely concerned
with issues of peace. It is their earlier work to which we refer.

[11]An interesting related trend that can only be alluded to here was developed in
the late '50s in the "end of ideology" thesis of Daniel Bell and Seymour Lipset. This
trend was part of the same pattern reflecting the "end" of: involvement, strong belief,
intensity, far-ranging goals, and deep social criticism. It was a philosophy of accommodation, consensus, and pragmatism.

Instead of analyzing each of these views separately, it is useful to investigate their social origins as a group. Such a sociological analysis of the rise of the new ideology as a whole may provide clues to the extrascientific reasons for its flourishing development.[12]

While it may be difficult to place precisely, it seems fairly evident that the new ideology arose after the Great Depression and spread rapidly with the end of World War II. This new world view had its greatest appeal in intellectual professional circles, and from there spread to large portions of the middle class, particularly the *new* middle class of professionals and managers.

A number of *traditional* middle-class ideals were seriously challenged, one of the first being the Protestant Ethic, with its emphasis on hard work and repressive control of emotion as the keystone of success. Criticism of traditional education with its emphasis on discipline, authority, and order was no longer restricted to a narrow group of Dewey's disciples. (Just as psychoanalysis began with Freud some years before it captured the American middle class, so progressive education arose long before it became an institution in the 1940's.)

This period brought with it the emphasis on child rearing not for the child's sake alone but, in Orlansky's phrase, a "revolution in the nursery"— an important instrument of social change and the key to future adult happiness and productiveness. New methods of child rearing developed, accenting permissiveness and expression and deemphasizing discipline and the control of emotion.

This era was also marked by a great stress on sex education, an attack on traditional morality, and ultimately by demands by more extremist wings (Wilhelm Reich, Paul Goodman) for a "sexual revolution" as the key to change.

The psychodynamic world view was part of the same picture. It attempted to weaken the traditional superego values of the old middle class on the grounds that a good deal of neurotic difficulty stems from an overly severe superego. It espoused greater emotional expression, self-acceptance, and self-actualization. *It was primarily concerned with individual, nonsocial methods of change.*

All these movements had much in common. They represented a rejection of certain traditional middle-class mores, especially discipline, industriousness, diligence, and emotional control. The old middle-class values of freedom and individualism were reformulated as demands for emotional expression and permissiveness. Creativity, self-actualization, and autonomy became the key goals, rather than competitive success.

---

[12]The social origins and social functions of a system cannot reductionistically be employed as tests of its validity. Our concern with the social basis of the new ideology is rather to illuminate the specific extrascientific reasons for the uncritical acceptance of these ideas. For example, the institutionalization of psychotherapy has been little affected by the generally unfavorable scientific evidence regarding its value.

The new ideology also tended to favor introspection and strength through consciousness, knowledge, awareness. Thus, with regard to sex, there was more concern with providing information (sex education) than with solutions or guides to the morality issues. The attack on secrecy, the appearance of the Kinsey Report, were part of the same trend. The preference for "talking things out" and "accepting yourself" fits in here. Parlor psychoanalysis with its public self-examination served the same need. Consciousness was equated with power and control. To understand one's problems gave a measure of control, and all the movements comprising the new ideology reflected this need for control, more particularly ego control.

SOCIAL ROOTS

What social variables contributed to the sweep and power of this new world view with its ardorless hero and its accent on nonsocial, individual etiology of social phenomena? Why did it arise in the '40s and '50s, rather than the '30s?

The Great Depression stimulated much social thinking of a radical bent. American capitalism itself was questioned and the Soviet Union was looked upon with some interest in intellectual quarters. The realization of the moral and democratic failure of the Soviet world coincided with the end of the depression and the resurgence of American capitalism. At the same time capitalism no longer had the vitality and forward march that had marked its historic rise. The values necessary in capitalism's earlier days that propelled the old middle class—"pull in your belt," "work hard," "don't fool around"—were no longer indispensable to modern bureaucratic, sales-oriented capitalism. The problem of traditional capitalism was production; the problems of modern capitalism are distribution and organization. The values that characterized the former were no longer useful; in fact at times they were downright inconvenient.

Along with this change came the decline in importance of the old middle class of small businessmen and independent farmers and the concomitant rise of the new middle class, with two different segments and two somewhat different value orientations. On the one hand was the organization man and the sales group, on the other, the professoinal intellectual strata.

These two groups required values quite alien to the old entrepreneurial middle class, and, to some extent, different from each other. Riesman's and Fromm's categories neatly describe the different orientations of these strata: the inner-directed man is the old middle class with what Fromm describes as a compulsive dedication to work, the hoarding orientation, and the accompanying superego values of the Protestant Ethic; the other-directed man is the new salesman and the organization man portrayed by Fromm as the "exchange," market-focused personality, conforming not to basic traditions but to trends and other people. And then there is the autonomous man, Riesman's Lochinvar, Fromm's productive character type, Maslow's self-actualized man, the new hero of the intellectual professional, searching to be free. Autonomous man opposes equally the stuffy compulsiveness of the old tradition-bound middle class and the new conformism of the bureaucratic salesman. He chooses instead the values of creativity, freedom, self-development, expression; at times these values have merged with permissiveness, anarchy, *laissez faire*, rampant individualism. A de-emphasis on organization, discipline, and inhibition emerged because organization and order, after all, can easily become identified with bureaucratic regulation and pedantic compulsivity.

BUREAUCRACY'S NEED FOR CREATIVITY

Despite the constrictions upon freedom and creativity emanating from "bureaucracy," there was, surprisingly enough, a great need for creativity and some measure of freedom on the part of the industrial bureaucracy itself. This is what the new ideologists such as Riesman, Fromm, and Whyte failed to grasp adequately.

They appeared to think that the call for creativity, which is a crucial feature of the new ideology, simply reflected social criticism and was basically an antibureaucratic complaint. Permissiveness, expressiveness, political ardorlessness contribute to the kind of creativity required today by the corporation and the professions. The tasks facing these occupations require ingenuity, a facile shifting from one activity to another, getting along with others without being completely trammeled by cooperation, a capacity to grapple with the new. And it is not only the 2 percent of the labor force in research who face such tasks; both business executives dealing with great technological changes and swiftly changing markets and professionals grappling with rapidly evolving skill demands and increasingly employed in large-scale bureaucracies have these problems.[13]

The new ideology with its stress on individual flexibility and creativity is functional, then, for occupational success. No wonder the cries of Fromm, Whyte, Riesman, and others for nonconformity were warmly and easily accepted. Some corporation presidents wrote of their desire to employ mavericks; college presidents demanded nonconformist students (but not on their campuses!); slick magazines published attacks on the cult of conformity. Rigid conformity may be all right for clerks but not

---

[13]At the same time that it requires creativity and imagination, modern bureaucracy also attempts to limit and control them both consciously and unconsciously, and herein lies the clash with the intellectual. Thus the new ideology reflects bureaucracy's need for creativity and at the same time struggles against the anticreative, restrictive controls of bureaucracy, which have become identified with discipline, authority, and conformity per se.

for executives and professionals. Consequently, a variety of groups in society assault conformity and praise creativity and independence.

The new ideology replaced the old individualism with a tempered and psychologized new individualism. Independence, self-development (the modern displacement for success striving) are still the core, although the individual recognizes that he may have to cooperate to be acceptable. The individualist shows imagination with the tasks he is assigned but does not deeply question the institution that assigns them. He is more concerned with his family's emotional health than before and carefully allots time for his family. He abhors injustice and violence, but they are not his responsibility. He is a busy citizen involved in the complex of suburban committees because he wants to feel that he has some control over the events directly impinging on his family; the local tax rate and the obsessive concern regarding education for his children are more compelling issues than racial equality.

True, some criticism still lingered, but more and more it became a rather vague criticism of "society," and "the culture." More important, a quiet presumption grew that, whatever was wrong with it, the society was a given entity. Adjustments would have to be made within its basic framework, even if the starting point of analysis was a criticism of the "contradictions of the culture." The ills of society had to be cured without basic reorganizations. More individualistic solutions such as psychotherapy became popular. If social change was impossible, it was best to concentrate on individual improvement. The age of psychologism was born. Child development and education took on enormous importance because they were a form of action, seemingly under the individual's control, which could bring great improvement without raising the question of societal change.

THE NEW UNCONSCIOUS

Despite the psychological self-consciousness of the architects of the new ideology, they have not developed an awareness of their own role in society and how it contributes to the shaping of their value preferences. Thus, the neo-Freudians as well as the progressive educators talked a great deal about man's needs for self-expression, creativity, and the like, with very little awareness that they were expressing their own special needs in a particular historical period, out of their own specific position in relation to the bureaucratization of society. *In ethnocentric fashion, without perspective, they supposed their own needs and values represented a universal model of man or human nature.* Unwittingly, for the rejected life and death instincts of Freud, they substituted the "basic needs" for productivity, creativity, self-actualization, autonomy. They committed the age-old error of intellectuals so well exemplified by Mannheim in "Ideology and Utopia"—the error of assuming that, although other ideas may be socially produced, their own were pure and above cultural influence. The extrascientific factors that might be affecting them, their own professional bias and particular experience, were not scrutinized carefully.

The absence of perspective among the new ideology makers provides a key to understanding many of their difficulties, as well as the distortions and abuses that have arisen as their ideas have been put into practice. The abuses of the age of psychiatry are shown in a new light. The tendency to psychologize problems, the parlor psychoanalysts, the new models of human nature with the projected middle-class needs of creativity and self-expression (with self-actualization at the apex), the alienation of lower socioeconomic groups from psychotherapy, the failure to seek for nonpsychiatric methods of change—all these and many more are far easier to comprehend if the psychiatric movement is seen, not only as a mode of treatment, but as one expression of the ideology of the new middle class.

Progressive education also illustrates the impact of implicit assumptions. Critics have decried the excesses and distortions of progressive education. Excesses are often related to unexamined assumptions, and in this instance the assumptions are best understood in connection with what progressive education deemphasized, namely, discipline, authority, tradition, routine hard work—values increasingly alien to the new middle class in its frantic search for the much-demanded creativity. In contrast it emphasized expression, freedom, intrinsically satisfying work—values increasingly important to the new middle class. No wonder then that, as progressive education was experienced by more and more middle-class people, the values it deemphasized tended to be neglected, although they had not been entirely ignored in the original writings of progressive educators. *Those values that were peripheral in the original system of progressive education were neglected or distorted in later practice,* because the hidden social meaning—the congeniality with new middle-class needs —came more into play as the system became an institution. The seeds of the late errors can be found in part in the original ideology, but if the movement had had greater social self-awareness, many of its excesses might have been discarded long before the sputnik so dramatically, and perhaps excessively, revealed them.

CONCLUSION

The psychiatric world view arose in the '40s with the postdepression resurgence of the American economy and was propelled forward by the rapidly expanding and increasingly powerful professional stratum. This view was linked to other ideological movements (the New Ideology) such as child rearing, progressive education, and sex education. All were basically ego-centered philosophies with a powerful emphasis on ego control. Placing less hope in broad societal change than was done in the '30s, the new middle class focused on those elements that seemed subject to direct individual control: the family, child rearing, sex behavior, education, development of the self (through self-understanding), and emotional expression. Moreover, the flexibility that derives from ego control is more useful for the development of the creativity needed by the professional than would have been the inhibiting, binding control of the tradition-bound superego.

The psychiatric world view and the new ideology reflect the occupational and advancement needs of the professional stratum in a period of retreat from broad social change and passionate political involvement.

These world views, while perhaps well-adapted to the occupational aspirations of the professional, are not suited to the possibilities of social change in the present period.

This context, we believe, furnishes a framework within which to comprehend the halting involvement of social scientists and intellectuals in currently developing social changes. The blinders acquired during the age of psychiatry in the '40s and '50s still limit intense commitment and the search for far-reaching social change. Since the limitation of commitment is seen as sophistication, wholehearted involvement is withheld. The psychological mode of thinking has not developed a vocabulary of social change, let alone a theory. For example, the intricate writings on prejudice and discrimination with their heavy psychological bent have been made largely irrelevant by recent events. These hesitations and blinders are residues of the past intruding into the swiftly changing American political landscape with its new needs for the contributions of intellectuals.

We do not believe that their contribution requires direct participation in social movements (they need not march on Washington). Nor does it require the anarchistic total rejection that characterizes the radicalism of Paul Goodman, for example.[14]

We do believe that the professional's most significant contribution is likely to lie in the application of his skills (analysis, research, conceptualization) to the problems of social change, thus linking his professional interests and his social conscience. *Here the great danger stems from professional parochialism,*[15] whereby particular professional formulations, rather than the problem at hand, dominate in shaping the nature of the contribution. One would hope that the professional's contribution would

---

[14]Goodman's impractical radicalism allows for an excellent discharge of feeling against the system and its absurdities; but, because many of his specific remedies are so unlikely, unrealistic, and unhistoric, they represent no real threat to the system and call forth no serious action on the part of enthusiastic adherents. It is not surprising that Goodman can be the "court jester" to the establishment.

[15]We think that some of the involvement of social scientists in the peace movement has been characterized by this parochialism: e.g. the psychologists who are very much concerned with showing how their specific conflict-reducing paradigms might be beneficial in reducing world conflict.

be conditioned more by the requisites of social change than by particular professional inclinations and that the professions will themselves change so that they will be increasingly relevant to the central domestic issues of our time.[16]

In essence, we need intellectual involvement with a problem-centered technology, rather than method-centered, prestige-oriented professionalism.

---

[16]A fascinating area for study would be the Negro revolution, with its variety of leaders rather than one charismatic all-powerful leader, its all-class character, its remarkable tactics, slogans, organization, and discipline, and the relationship between the integrationist and nationalist trends.

W hat are the prospects for applied sociology? They turn in large part on our ability to clearly distinguish between the legitimate and the self-deceiving demands of our role as scientist and between the natural and the artificial demands of our scientific method. Some would have us pursue a value-free sociology that others label a cruel myth; some would have us restrict ourselves to something they call "pure" or basic, while others, like the writer below, warn such a restriction "leads frequently to hypocrisy, irresponsibility, pretentiousness, and sometimes to evasion or outright dishonesty." The writer, Dr. Alfred R. Lindesmith, reviews this and several related controversies in his brief essay, advancing bold and often brow-arching resolutions for many perplexing matters. Especially intriguing is his notion of the likely developments on an academic Day of Judgment, developments that leave us all, theorists and practitioners, much to ponder.

SOCIAL PROBLEMS AND SOCIOLOGICAL THEORY*

Alfred R. Lindesmith

MEMBERS AND friends of the Society: I want tonight to make a brief statement of the reasons which cause me to believe in and support this society and to hope that it will continue to prosper. In doing so I shall perhaps somewhat overstate and oversimplify my case in order to emphasize my point and for the sake of brevity. I trust that whatever this talk lacks in wit and wisdom will be to some degree compensated for by its brevity.

As I see it, there is a sharp and categorical difference between the concern with social problems and the interest in sociological theory. The former involves applied or practical research and the attempt to influence policy. It is almost always a many-sided, multidisciplinary matter, and involves committing oneself on questions of value or morality, as when legal reform is advocated for the sake of justice or when police reform is urged to protect or restore civil liberties.

In contrast, the task of theory construction is, and probably must be,

*Presidential address to the Society for the Study of Social Problems delivered on August 28, 1960, New York. Reprinted with permission of the author and *Social Problems*, from the issue of Fall, 1960.

the concern of single disciplines which focus their attention on particular aspects of human social behavior concerning which they seek to formulate valid and significant generalizations. To qualify for the honorific designation of "scientific" these formulations must satisfy a number of requirements which, in the study of human behavior, are especially hard to meet. It is not enough that the writer be careful and exact, that he use numbers rather than words, that the generalizations have no practical implications, or that they be couched in complicated and abstruse language. To qualify as scientific, generalizations of the social scientist must measure up to those standards and specifications which are reasonably clearly established and formulated in the tradition and literature of modern Western science.

In this concern with the development of theory it is desirable and inevitable that the sociologist concentrate on sociological rather than social problems. In his scientific role he is concerned merely with what things are, not with what ought to be. He seeks to be detached, dispassionate, objective, and impartial. When he has his scientific hat on he avoids the ethical commitments and value judgments involved in social policy and, I am inclined to think, he is usually not qualified as a scientist to speak authoritatively on social problems. I say this because such problems are not exclusively sociological but are compounds of many diverse elements which are not the exclusive concern of any single discipline.

Having said these things it may appear that the argument leads logically to the conclusion that the sociologist ought not be concerned at all with social problems as such. There was a time when I thought that this was so and I am still inclined to agree that, insofar as he is a scientist, the sociologist's central concern is not with social problems. The dilemma of the sociologist who wishes to be a scientist and who is at the same time vitally concerned with matters that are the subject of controversy on the practical policy level, is most properly handled, in my opinion, not by renouncing one's civic responsibilities but by accepting them and keeping them separate from one's scientific responsibilities. There are risks in whatever one does, but I think the risks here are greatest when the sociologist sets himself apart from his society and tries to limit himself, so far as his public functions are concerned, to being a "pure" and "basic" scientist.

This attempt to be "pure" and "basic" is all too often stultifying and leads frequently to hypocrisy, irresponsibility, pretentiousness, and sometimes to evasion or outright dishonesty. To use an illustration from a field in which I am especially interested, there are those who do scientific studies of drug addiction and refuse, in the name of science, to commit themselves on the policy question. This seems hypocritical and evasive to me when the individual concerned, from his dealings with addicts, has acquired some ideas on policy with respect to them. If one has such views and conceals them, this is simply a lack of frankness and has nothing to do with science. The scientific pose that is regularly assumed is that more money should be spent on research before we can know what we ought to do. This attitude tends to maximize the flow of research funds, but it also often puts the investigator on the side of the *status quo*. The more miserably and ineffectively the drug problem is handled the more money will be spent investigating it. The effects of a change in policy can never be exactly predicted and if reform must wait until we are sure of the future it will wait forever.

Another aspect of this matter is to ask whether the scientific theories for the sake of which sociologists renounce their civic responsibilities are worth it. Despite the optimistic and constructive attitudes which we tend to assume publicly when we face our undergraduate classes or the members of other disciplines which are as vulnerable as we are, I think most of us privately realize that we have not traveled far enough along the path of science to take ourselves too seriously in this respect. Much of what passes as theory is not really that. More often it is common sense dressed up in fancy verbiage and sometimes it is just verbiage. Much of what is taken as progress consists of the substitution of new words for old ones and many allegedly original ideas turn out to be merely a reflection of inadequate familiarity with the contents of libraries.

While I think that progress is being made in creating a more scientific sociology, I also feel that one has only to read our journals to realize that many investigators are trying to join the scientific family by sneaking in the back door without credentials. One feature of this attempt is to make a virtue of the impracticality of what one does, the assumption being that since it is impractical it must be scientific. Much of the research for which such claims are made falls between two stools, and, being neither practical nor scientific, has no significance at all. One wonders if it would not be better to drop the scientific pretension which is not backed up by the substance of science and limit oneself to enterprises which at least have the virtue of practical relevance. I would not go so far as to advocate this as the goal of sociology. All I want to emphasize is that it is not a sin for a scientist to be concerned with the social problems of his community or society; it is closer to a sin for him not to be so concerned.

Another of the diseases of our discipline which is connected, I think, with our attempt to divorce ourselves from the practical concerns of our society is an excessive preoccupation with techniques at the expense of subject matter. This has led to what has been called the "trivialization" of research in which answers having the appearance of great precision are sought for questions which hardly seem to matter, or in which the self-evident is substantiated within an inch of its life. The image of the sociologist from this viewpoint appears to have become that of a clever technician, available for hire, flitting from one problem to another as research subsidies become available. The criteria for the selection of projects appears to be, not the importance of the problem, but availability of funds and of data amenable to certain types of treatment.

The experiences connected with being involved in and concerned with social problems is, I think, an excellent counterirritant to the tendency of academicians to become oversubtle, overtheoretical, overpretentious and overconfident of their own verbal and numerical formulations. It is a good thing, even vital, for example, for the criminologist who analyzes crime with IBM machines to visit or know about courts, law, prisons, and the police and to be actively concerned with the reform of these institutions when they need it. Association with people of diverse backgrounds and professions who share a common interest in social policy tends to keep one humble and gives one roots in the society which nurtures and supports him. Without this touchstone I think there is a tendency for research to come to be regarded as a racket or merely a convenient way to acquire a reputation, get promotions, and make a living.

Thus, while it seems that it is the central job of the sociologist to advance theoretical knowledge I will venture that he should, as a protection against the involutional disorders of excessive academic isolation, maintain as an avocation at least an interest in at least one problem area. In this area I think he should be an expert and an activist, seeking to know not only what pertains to his discipline but everything that he can learn and to exert influence on policy. Properly conceived and managed I believe that this kind of an interest serves to correct some of the typical academic diseases and ultimately serves the cause of scientific advancement.

One wonders how long it will be before there will come an academic Day of Judgment when, perhaps, the long-suffering patient subjects who fill out our questionnaires and submit themselves for interviews will get the idea they are being exploited and demand an accounting. Perhaps those who pay the bills will sometime add up all the money and man-hours expended in "pure" research, balance it against the results, and wonder whether it has been worth it. Certainly it is reasonable to expect that there eventually will be some kind of payoff in the form of public disillusionment and disenchantment for the present halcyon days of easy money. When this payoff comes I am convinced that the sociologist who will come off the best will be the one who has not written exclusively for other sociologists and who has not washed his hands of all practical affairs.

The therapeutic effects of practical interests and activities arise in the main, I think, from communicating with persons who are not sociologists, social scientists, or academicians. Scientific results must, after all, be communicated. Just as the standards by which scientific conclusions are judged are not derived from a single discipline, so also must these conclusions be disseminated and judged beyond the confines of single disciplines and beyond the confines of the academic world. It is a valuable but often chastening experience to try to tell the hard-headed intelligent layman or administrative official what the latest sociological discoveries have been in the field of his competence. Not being able to use the specialized language of our discipline we often find that when compelled to resort to straight-away English some of the glamour and originality of the ideas seems to vanish. One would hardly, for example, use that magic French word anomie in talking to nonsociologists but when this concept is expressed in ordinary English words, as it can be, it seems to lose much of its charm and much of its explanatory potency. I do not think that it can be contended that sociology is so advanced today that its solid achievements cannot be formulated in language which an intelligent layman can grasp. We need to communicate in this manner with people outside our fields in order to maintain our own health.

One of the unformulated assumptions which we are led to make by the desire to be regarded as scientists even if we are not is that research is an end in itself, and that it is a noble enterprise per se to spend government or foundation money in doing it. This assumption is manifestly false. Carried to its extreme it sometimes leads to the exploitation of human subjects for personal aggrandizement and to the perversion of the scientific spirit. The goal becomes simply that of securing funds. The more problems there are and the more ineffectively they are dealt with, the greater the flow of subsidies. Under such circumstances it is easy to accept the rationalizations which keep one out of controversy, which do not jeopardize the sources of funds, and which support the status quo.

To use drug addiction as an illustration again, the greatly increased prevalence of addiction, especially of young persons after the late war, was a blessing for those looking for research funds. By and large the money that has been put into the study of this problem was probably put into it for practical objectives, to further the understanding of addiction in order to improve the methods of controlling and dealing with it. The proper methods of control are, it happens, the subject of bitter controversy between conflicting schools of thought, between those who advocate reform and those who oppose and often have something to lose from it. In the studies of addiction that have been made since it became a popular subject, remarkably little attention has been given to the crucial aspects of the problem which are the issues in this popular debate and on which policy is based. Without in any way disparaging what has been done, it seems more than a coincidence that so few researchers have looked into what might be called the "hot" aspects of the subject.

There is, in short, serious danger of being corrupted by those who give us money, and the danger is increased by the attractiveness of the rationalizations by which this seduction is effected. The investigator who unwittingly, perhaps, comes to put the securing of funds in first place, necessarily thereby loses some of his scientific objectivity and independence and often neglects important aspects of his subject. A vital participating interest in problems is, I think, some protection, at least, against this kind of perversion, and helps to keep us honest and independent by reminding us of our responsibilities to our subjects, our society, and our principles. It is in this spirit, rather than in that of an artificial and radical detachment, that the solid accomplishments of the social sciences are likely to be made.

This society represents to me both a protest against some of the trends which I have mentioned and a means of giving organized opportunity to the desire to express oneself freely and participate more fully in controversial matters of public policy. Because I feel that this activity should be kept distinct from the scientific function, I hope that this society does not become simply another sociological society in which these functions are not separated and in which nonsociologists are not at home. This society is an interest group or association of interest groups rather than a professional association. As such I think it has already had a significant effect as a gesture of protest and in providing an avenue of expression for interests and a point of view that for a time were close to being outlawed by the advocates of "purity."

As I said at the beginning, I have probably overstated my case. I do not wish to imply that there is nothing to be said for pure and basic social science or for sociological theory. On the contrary, I think there is much to be said for them, but there is little point in saying it here because this concern is not currently threatened, and has in fact been oversold. It seems to me that there is perhaps too much energy being expended in this direction on what has been called "grand theory." Some of this seems to me like working on the tower of a structure which still lacks an adequate foundation. In any case, scientific purity is not assured by the negative acts of refusing to participate in community affairs or of not committing oneself on questions of value or public morality. It is more likely to be assured, as I have indicated, by a judicious balancing of the detached theoretical attitude and that of active participation in the process of change, provided that this combination is coupled with an understanding of the differences between these two orientations. Each has its special risks, limitations, abuses, and biases and these need to be analyzed and guarded against. To a considerable extent these two perspectives serve as correctives for each other with the practical attitude constantly checking the abuses and excesses of the theoretical, and the theoretical giving depth and historical perspective to the practical.

I think it is futile to renounce the practical concern, because, from the very fact that we live in a society, we are committed to its values and norms. The assumption of a purely detached theoretical attitude means only that one does not recognize this commitment and the responsibilities it imposes, and that without knowing it, one aligns oneself by default with the opponents of reform. I think that this society was established with something like this in mind and I think it represents the views of many more people than its membership might indicate. I trust that it will in the future realize its goals and define its special functions even more fully than it has in the past.

What are the prospects for applied sociology? They turn in large part on our creativity in adapting academic institutions to the challenge. Dr. Ronald Lippitt describes below a pioneering, ongoing effort at adaptation, the Center for Research on the Utilization of Scientific Knowledge (University of Michigan). This large-scale, interdisciplinary, and sophisticated organization shows the way: universities everywhere have a model here for immediate emulation. Even as the inventor has left his backyard garage for the research laboratory, so is it time for social science practitioners to supplement their one-man operations through affiliation with new, resource-rich university centers for applied social science.

THE PROCESS OF UTILIZATION OF SOCIAL RESEARCH
TO IMPROVE SOCIAL PRACTICE*

Ronald Lippitt

MY OBSERVATIONS in this paper are based on some brief, but varied experiences with problems of science utilization encountered at our Center for Research on the Utilization of Scientific Knowledge at the University of Michigan. Our staff teams of sociologists, psychologists, and others are involved with such social problems as delinquency, illegitimate pregnancy of teen-agers, the educational motivation of culturally deprived children, the lack of creative teaching practices, leisure-time programs for central-city girls, the pathology of communication between parents and teen-agers, and the mental health and productivity problems of work groups in government and industry. In each project a special effort is made to focus on the process by which scientific knowledge and personnel can help develop and validate significant improvements in educational and social practice.

Patterns and Research Utilization Processes

I want especially in this paper to distinguish between three patterns

*Adapted with permission of the author from a much longer paper in the *American Journal of Orthopsychiatry*, Vol. XXXV, No. 4, 1965, pp. 663-69. Copyright, the American Orthopsychiatric Association, Inc. Reproduced by permission.

of research utilization which bring into the "science consumer system" new knowledge and validated practice from outside, and three other patterns which develop scientific knowledge within the system and then utilize it as a basis for improvement of practice.

1. In the first pattern, the scientist consultant in collaboration with a practitioner or practice group identifies and defines a problem of practice. This definition is used in retrieving research knowledge helpful in deriving both action implications and the design for an improvement of practice or the invention of new practice.

For example, a recent one-day consultation conference focused on the problem of how the several million citizens of a metropolitan area could be involved in the development of plans for the metropolitan region. A team of professional and political leaders from the metropolitan area spent the first half of the day interviewing invited resource people. Some of the outside resources were familiar with research and theory in this field and three of the outsiders were leaders of similar projects in other metropolitan areas. With a predeveloped schedule of research retrieval probes the host team conducted a guided conversation with the visiting resource people. All this retrieved information was tape-recorded. During the second phase of the day's activities the local leadership took active initiative in attempting to formulate implications of this inquiry for the development of a program for their own metropolitan situation, and they began to project the elements of a design for action that drew from the implications both of previous research and previous practice innovations. The next steps of developmental work were also clarified and agreed on.

A second example started from the definition by elementary school personnel of their problem of "the in-betweeners." These were defined as primarily older elementary school acting-out boys who were too disruptive to be acceptable in the classroom or other educational facilities of the school, but too young and not seriously delinquent enough to be appropriately in the hands of the police and the court. A "knowledge retrieval" session of school people and scientists from child development, educational psychology, social psychology, and sociology identified a variety of relevant research findings and then focused on producing a series of statements about the possible implication of the findings for "things that should happen to the clients" in order for a signficant process of resocialization and education to be achieved. These statements of implications from research findings were used as a springboard for a brainstorming session with the practitioners about program design that might deal with the problem. An action design for reeducation emerged which was quite different from anything which either the researchers or the practitioners had visualized originally. This design was later tested for feasibility in two schools, evaluated as successful, and subsequently diffused to other schools.

2. The second pattern for importing knowledge from outside the system entails conducting an extra-system feasibility test of a design procedure to meet some social practice issue. This test is conducted by the applied science team under controlled conditions, and, if the test proves successful, the newly developed model for improved social practice is demonstrated and recommended for adoption by the target system.

An example here concerns the development by our staff of the so-called cross-age socialization design. From our previous research we hypothesized that one of the major potentials in most educational and socialization situations was going unused, namely, the potential influence of older peers on younger peers. We decided to test experimentally the feasibility of training ten-, eleven-, and twelve-year-olds to function as educational aids and socialization agents with five-, six-, and seven-year-olds. The experimental settings were a camp and an elementary school where teams of scientists and social engineers controlled the experimental programs. Results indicated it was feasible to train the older peers to assume creative teaching functions. There was very significant response on the part of the young, and the older children showed great personal growth in their own attitudes and achievement because of their experience of responsibility in collaboration with adults and their learning from the training seminars. It was possible thereafter to present this evidence to a school system concerned about the problems of achievement and motivation in young pupils. The school system adopted our model on a tryout basis and later made several creative adaptations in the process of carrying out and evaluating the design.

3. The third pattern of importation is a very exciting one to me. This is the process of identifying creative innovations invented by practitioners someplace else and developing procedures for getting appropriate documentation about these social inventions so that their relevance to local needs can be considered and the essential features of the practice adopted or adapted. One of the great tragedies in American education and social practice is that a large proportion of the creative inventions which are in line with good research and theory never become visible and are never appropriately transmitted from one setting and one practitioner to another. What dissemination does take place is of such low quality that successful high-quality adoption is usually impossible.

An example of a model for coping with this problem is illustrated in a current Center project with a state teachers association. All teachers in a selected school system now have an opportunity to fill out a "Teaching Practice Nomination Sheet" identifying their invention of a teaching practice to cope with a particular type of educational problem (for example, stimulating more motivation to learn) or the invention of a colleague. These nomination sheets go to a screening committee which reviews the conceptual and research relevance, the practical significance, and the potential adoptability of each practice. This experiment seeks to discover the kinds of practices that can be communicated by this written form, the kinds that require additional steps of observation, and the types that require more intensive training and consultation. Above all, we have developed a procedure for identifying, describing, and importing new models into the system which have been developed by practitioners in other communities, agencies, or organizations.

Let us turn now to three patterns of utilization of scientific resources which differ from the foregoing in emphasizing the *local* development of the resource knowledge to be utilized.

1. The first pattern has the organization or agency contract with the scientist team to collect diagnostic data relevant to some problem, analyze the data, and feed the data back for the sponsor's use. A brief example will illustrate this pattern:

The Center's action research team recently conducted an intensive city-wide study of a sample of delinquents and matched nondelinquents to assess factors related to the development and maintenance of delinquent behavior. They also conducted an interview study of key educational and socialization policy leaders concerning their conceptions of delinquency and its prevention. These data were analyzed by the scientist team and were reported back to the community leaders in a series of community seminars to which the key community leaders were invited. Staff members were available during these seminars to provide interpretation of the findings and to react to the generalizations and implications formulated by the community leaders.

2. The second pattern has the outside applied researchers supervise a self-study process within the sponsoring organization or community or agency, training local staff members to collect information and to participate in the processing of data, interpretation of findings, and the spelling out of implications for the development of change.

Our classroom teaching study is an illustration of this pattern of science utilization. Thirty teachers from seven school systems volunteered to work with us on a diagnostic self-study of their classroom education climate and the possible implications for changes in their teaching practice. During the spring the action-research team provided the teachers with questionnaires to inquire into their own attitudes and orientations, and with rating and questionnaire tools to use in eliciting information from their classroom group concerning orientation toward learning, toward the teacher, toward each other, and many other aspects of classroom dynamics. During the summer the teachers met regularly with the staff to help tabulate and analyze the data, to develop the concepts needed to work on interpretation, and to think through the implications of the findings for possible changes in their own teaching role in the fall. Consultation was provided in this thinking-through process, and in clarifying the plans for the use of new teaching procedures.

3. The third and final pattern of internal mobilization is quite different from the other two. It focuses on the idea that the practitioner needs

training in learning how to be a consumer of scientific resources before he can be a utilizer of scientific knowledge.

a. One of our activities in this connection is focused on training teachers in the techniques of social science problem-solving and providing them with a tool kit of diagnostic tools and conceptual orientations to assist them in collecting appropriate information and using it to solve their problems of classroom management.

b. In another project we have developed a laboratory course in behavioral science for elementary-school children. The students have an opportunity to discover who the behavioral scientists are and how their resources can be used, as well as to learn to carry through their own inquiry projects on various problems of human relations. (It seems clear that part of the current negative orientation toward scientific resources, in mental health, education, and social welfare, is because of a serious lack of any such education about the nature and the utility of social research and the social scientists.)

The Roles and Training of the Social Research Utilization Agent

From our studies we have come to conceive the research utilization function of our staff as requiring them to be *linking agents* at various points in the flow of research utilization. We have to develop new skills of retrieving and organizing research-based knowledge so that it links up to the needs of the social practitioner or client population. Helping the practitioner to clarify his resource needs is, of course, another aspect of this linking responsibility. And there is a necessary linkage function in helping the practitioner work through the implications of new knowledge.

As I have noted in several examples, still another function of the research utilization agent is to serve as inquiry consultant or trainer, assisting the client population in carrying through its own diagnostic research and working through the meaning of the findings for changes of practice. We must also find effective and appropriate ways of linking creative innovations to their colleagues to facilitate the spread and successful adaptation of new practice.

Our own experience with graduate seminars and practicums has revealed that there are significant numbers of students, both in the behavioral science departments and in the professional schools, who are eager to explore these new roles. These students seek new skills quite different from the research production skills typically taught in behavioral science departments and from the skills of operating practice taught in the professional schools. Certainly the training of research utilization agents requires a grounding *both* in behavioral science discipline and in professional values and technology. This obviously puts a new strain on the fairly segregated curriculum designs and training sequences which still exist in most of our graduate programs. The challenge is great—*and* surmountable.

-- ■--■--

What are the prospects for applied sociology? They turn in large part on the matter of our ethics as practitioners—a vital and underdiscussed subject. Because I could not find an explicit, essay-length discussion in the literature of sociology, I take the liberty below of borrowing an exceptional related essay from the literature of social work. Dr. Halleck's unsettling arguments have applicability far beyond the situation he analyzes between clinical worker and adolescent: all too many projects involve all too much duplicity—the reasons often going deep into the most fundamental orientations of the practitioner. Dr. Halleck does us all a service in raising the delicate, sensitive, and fundamental matter of our truthfulness—its uses and abuses—in our budding applied science.

■--■

THE IMPACT OF PROFESSIONAL DISHONESTY ON

BEHAVIOR OF DISTURBED ADOLESCENTS*

Seymour L. Halleck

ADULT WORKERS in all the clinical behavioral sciences tend to lie to their adolescent patients. The lying may at times be on a fully conscious basis; at other times it may be more or less beyond awareness.[1] The net effect of this behavior is to confuse and at times infuriate the adolescent, which in itself may produce greater rebellion, more symptoms, and more pain—or exactly the opposite of the original goals. As is true for most dynamic situations, whether one is dealing with individuals or with groups, positive growth must often follow a painful appraisal of less acceptable behavior and motivations. A realistic examination of dishonest behavior on the part of professional workers can then be considered a painful but necessary procedure that may encourage freedom to develop new and more effective techniques.

This discussion is focused primarily on the interaction of professionals

*Reprinted here with permission of the author and of the National Association of Social Workers, from *Social Work*, Vol. 8, No. 2 (April, 1963), pp. 48–56.

[1] *The Myth of Mental Illness: Foundations of a Theory of Personal Conduct* (New York: Paul B. Hoeber, 1961).

with adolescents who are either institutionalized or who are involved with community agencies. This group certainly constitutes the great majority of adolescents who come into contact with psychiatrists, psychologists, sociologists, and social workers. In some instances, particularly in private practice, when the worker may function only as the patient's —or at most the family's—agent, some of the aspects of dishonest behavior may not apply, and these exceptions will be noted. There are at least seven areas in which adolescent clients are deceived either through conscious fabrication or through subtle and unconscious communication of attitudes to which professional workers do not adhere.

THE LIE OF ADULT MORALITY

In confronting the chaotic sexuality and poorly controlled aggressiveness of the adolescent, most professional workers tend to communicate the possibility of a world in which such impulses are resolved easily. They imply that adults control their impulses and that success in the world is dependent upon such restraint. To a limited extent this is certainly true. Too often, however, they present a picture of the world that is far removed from reality and does not take cognizance of the social usefulness of certain kinds of aggressive and sexual behavior. The adolescent boy knows that aggressiveness, and sometimes unscrupulous aggressiveness, may be a prerequisite for success. He knows that the interviewer sitting behind the desk has probably struggled aggressively to gain the status of a professional position. The sexually promiscuous adolescent girl knows (even if she has not read the Kinsey report) that on a statistical basis the professional person with whom she intereacts has probably at some time in his life been guilty of the same behavior for which she is being punished.

It may be unrealistic to communicate readily the worker's own deficiencies and therefore provide the adolescent rationalizations for disturbed behavior. There is a frequent tendency, however, to err in the other direction. Professionals communicate a picture of themselves and their world as one in which only the highest type of values and moral standards prevail. The adolescent cannot understand this. His personal experiences, his observational powers, and his intuitiveness tell him that something is wrong. He wants to like and to identify with adults, but he is painfully aware of an inconsistency or basic dishonesty in their approach. He may then come to believe that adults are incapable of being anything but "phony" and react by rebellious behavior or isolation from the adult world.

This type of dishonesty is seen with considerably less frequency in private psychotherapeutic interactions, especially with adults. Here the worker tries to produce a climate in which the universality of antisocial impulses is accepted and usually discussed freely. An unwillingness to extend this same honesty to a large portion of adolescent patients is a serious error. The adolescent is struggling to understand the adult world. He will learn the truth about it whether he is told or not.

THE LIE OF PROFESSIONAL HELPFULNESS

The professional worker who confronts adolescents in the courtroom, the community clinic, or the state institution serves a dual role, as an agent of the community and as a helping person. The community wants him to control, attenuate, or in some way modify the behavior of an individual who is causing it some distress. The worker is also interested in his client; he feels some wish to make the disturbed adolescent a more comfortable and effective person. It is important to understand, however, that in the majority of these situations (there are exceptions in private practice) the worker does not function as an agent of the adolescent patient. His salary is paid by the community. When the community's needs conflict with the adolescent's needs, it is the community that must be obeyed and decisions are not always made entirely in the patient's interest. It is still possible within the limitations of this role for the worker to maintain an honest identification as someone who wants to help the adolescent. If he does not communicate, however, that one of his most basic roles is other than help oriented, he is being dishonest.

Most adolescents do not seek help; they are sent. For example, take the case of an adolescent boy who has been a behavior problem in school and has been referred to the school psychologist. The boy is told that he must see a professional person and that the psychologist will try to help him. He knows, however, that the school is somewhat provoked with him and that its officials are going to act to prevent him from being an annoyance. He does not know what will be done. He does know that the school psychologist, functioning as the agent of the community, may exert a tremendous amount of power over him. As a result of his interaction with this professional worker he may be removed from school, forced to attend special classes, or even removed from his home and sent to an institution. No matter how benign a person the school psychologist then turns out to be, it is very difficult for the adolescent to perceive him as a helping person.

As long as the worker and the adolescent are aware of the fact that the professional may be participating in mutually antagonistic roles, effective communication is possible. The situation is complicated, however, when the worker pretends that his only motivation in seeing the adolescent is to help him. The adolescent realizes that this is obviously untrue. He then perceives the adult worker as dishonest, which only makes him want to be dishonest in return. Experienced workers have learned that the word "help" rarely evinces a positive response from the adolescent. He experiences it as a kind of "Kafka"-like doubletalk. In many settings, then, the word "help" is perceived by the adolescent as an unreliable and perhaps dangerous word.

THE LIE OF CONFIDENTIALITY

The issue of confidentiality is closely related to the problem of helpfulness. Most case-workers, psychologists, and psychiatrists have been taught that the model for a professional helping relationship is derived from the psychotherapeutic situation. In traditional forms of psychotherapy the communications of the patient or client to the worker are considered private material to be shared with no one outside the treatment situation. Many of the techniques professional workers use in interviewing, evaluating, diagnosing, or counseling the adolescent are derived from what they were taught about psychotherapy. Often the worker behaves as though the adolescent is entitled to expect confidentiality and as though it were going to be provided. It is extremely rare for the adolescent to be told directly who is going to see the report the worker writes, who is going to read it, and with whom the case is going to be discussed.

The issue here, as with helpfulness, is that the worker cannot guarantee confidentiality to the patient since he is not the agent of the patient. The worker has obligations to the child's family, his clinic, his agency, or his institution. Even if after submitting an initial diagnostic report he begins to see the adolescent in a more traditional psychotherapeutic relationship, complete confidentiality can rarely be promised. While it is true that useful communication can take place between the worker and the adolescent without the guarantee of confidentiality, it is also true that to imply that this guarantee is extended, or to extend it with the full knowledge that it is not meant to be kept, can result in development of situations that inhibit communication. It does not take a very clever adolescent to understand that the worker has primary responsibilities to his agency and to the community. He may fully understand that whatever information he gives will be shared with others and can be used in making important decisions about him. If professionals do not let him know this, he will perceive their behavior as dishonest, and his communications to the adult world will be effectively diminished.

THE LIE OF REWARDS FOR CONFORMITY

The necessity of conforming to adult standards is most often communicated to adolescents whose behavior deviates from the norms of the community. To this sizable proportion of disturbed adolescents, professional workers seem to be saying, "Your behavior is unacceptable, it produces more difficulty and leads you to experience more pain. It is to your own infinite advantage to be passive, to conform, to obey." There is ample evidence, however, that in attacking the behavioral defenses of the adolescent, workers remove character armor, leaving him more susceptible to anxiety. There is really little in the way of pleasure that can be promised to the adolescent if he risks giving up characterological defenses. This has been discussed previously in terms of the problems imposed on the criminal when he is viewed as a "patient."

Society and the psychiatrist in particular may be imposing an almost intolerable burden on the delinquent in asking him to exchange the "bad" role for the sick role. It is not surprising that the criminal looks upon the usual rehabilitation program with cynicism and distrust. Only when those in charge of treatment searchingly ask themselves what they are trying to do to the delinquent when they try to make him into a conforming citizen and are able to appreciate what he is giving up in accepting the sick role can therapy be successful.[2]

It is always a moving, sometimes an overwhelming, experience to see an adolescent abandon behavioral expressions of conflict for a more introspective way of life. This is never accomplished without considerable pain and sometimes despair. If the adolescent is told that the simple expedient of conforming to adult standards produces pleasure, he is told a lie. Conformity on the part of the adolescent certainly meets the immediate needs of the community; whether it meets the needs of the individual adolescent is questionable. When workers pretend to him that it does, they encounter only confusion and anger, especially when he experiences the inevitable anxieties that come when he attempts to control his behavior.

DENIAL OF LIMITATIONS

The majority of adolescents who come to the attention of community agencies are from troubled homes and lower socioeconomic groups. Many of them have been subjected to severe psychological and economic deprivations. Their educational experiences have been limited. Psychiatric studies have produced data which indicate that the effects of early emotional deprivation are to a certain extent unmodifiable.[3] Deficiences in early educational experiences may also seriously limit potentialities for achievement in the world.

The average professional worker comes from a middle-class background, which in our culture implies a far greater potentiality than that

---

[2] Seymour L. Halleck, "The Criminal's Problem with Psychiatry," *Psychiatry*, Vol. 23, No. 4 (November, 1960).

[3] J. Bowlby, "A Note on Mother-Child Separation as a Mental Health Hazard," *British Journal of Medical Psychology*, Vol. 31, No. 3-4 (1958), pp. 247-48; G. Engel, F. Reischsman, and H. Segal, "A Study of an Infant with Gastric Fistula in Behavior and the Rate of Total Hydrochloric Acid Secretion," *Psychosomatic Medicine*, Vol. 18, No. 5 (October, 1956), pp. 374-98; H. Harlow, "The Nature of Love," *The American Psychologist*, Vol. 13 (1958), pp. 673-85.

seen in most adolescent clients. (Here we must, of course, exclude selected disturbed adolescents of superior intelligence, of middle-class
background, or from reasonable well-integrated homes.) Many workers
fail to see that with a few exceptions they are dealing with people of
limited potential who will never be like them. Failing to realize this fact,
the worker may then encourage identifications, ambitions, and achievements that are not possible for his client and which leave the adolescent
with a feeling of frustration.

Few workers are guilty of consciously pushing their clients to achieve
beyond their limits. Many of them, however, repeatedly deny the impressive limitations of some of their patients and assure them that the
development of certain identifications and goals is entirely possible. This
is a type of unconscious dishonesty that may produce considerable harm.
The adolescent may righteously say to himself, "Who is this guy kidding?
Is he trying to reassure me or reassure himself? Maybe he's trying to
humiliate me by throwing my inadequacies in my face. He'll never understand me."

"OPEN UP; TRUST ME; ALL WILL GO WELL"

A close relationship is a foundation of any successful therapeutic
interaction. Experiencing closeness to another person leads to the possibility of examining one's behavior in such a way that unfavorable
personality defenses can be modified or exchanged for more useful ones.
Most professional workers leave school with the feeling that they will
be successful with clients if they can persuade them to be open and close.
The adolescent, however, especially the disturbed adolescent, frequently
is struggling with some of the negative aspects of closeness that he experiences as stultifying or smothering. He has begun to find certain types
of relationships among his peers that provide him with a feeling of considerably more safety. To abandon movement in this direction and again
attempt to develop a close relationship with an adult involves grave
risk-taking for him. He is well aware that the little freedom he has gained
may have to be surrendered if too much closeness develops.

If the worker realizes this, he can gently, tactfully and with some
humility gradually allow a meaningful, nonsymbiotic relationship to
develop between him and the child. In a healthy close relationship between adolescent and adult, the adolescent is allowed certain kinds of
independence, dignity, and, of course, distance when he wants it. The
social structure in which most professional workers function makes it
extremely difficult to provide this kind of relationship. They usually begin
in settings in which they have tremendous power over the adolescent,
who is thrown into a forced dependency. The adolescent is often forced
into a relationship that he, at least on a conscious level, has not sought.
The possibility of prolonged relationships is often limited by the fact

that both professionals and their clients are extremely mobile, frequently changing responsibilities, jobs, and geographical locations. A sustained, intensive relationship is not a common occurrence in most situations developed in community agencies.

Professional workers are guilty, nevertheless, of continuously exhorting the adolescent to "open up; trust me; if you rely on me and share things with me, all will go well." But the disturbed adolescent knows that this is not true! He knows that the person who is pleading with him to expose himself may be a person with whom he will have only limited future contacts and whom he can see few reasons for trusting. He is further aware of the possibility that he can lose much in such a relationship and that the worker may not really be offering a true intimacy between equals. To the adolescent it seems like a poor bargain. He feels that the worker is dishonest in offering this type of bargain and he reacts with fear. distrust, and cynicism.

"WE LIKE YOU BUT NOT YOUR BEHAVIOR"

Anyone who has spent much time with adolescents knows that their behavior can be provocative, frustrating, and at times infuriating. It is distressing to see how few professional workers are willing to admit honestly how angry they get with their adolescent clients. This anger frequently is rationalized with statements to the effect that "I like you but not your behavior." Sometimes the worker's anger is totally denied but comes out only through his behavior toward the adolescent. In these types of situations workers sometimes tell the adolescent that they are not really angry with him but they feel that he must be disciplined for his own good, and that by depriving him of privileges or changing his situation, they are really trying to help him. Frequently this anger is displaced onto the parents or onto other professional workers. Anyone who works with adolescents in a community or institutional setting is painfully aware of the extreme rivalry and sometimes open animosity between individual professionals and their groups. The fact is that it is almost impossible to work with adolescents for any period of time without becoming periodically angered.

It is dishonest and unfair both to the worker and to the adolescent to deny, rationalize, or displace this anger. It belongs in the therapeutic situation and should be communicated with as much restraint, tact, and honesty as the worker is capable of providing. To do less than this establishes a basically dishonest pattern of interaction and precludes the possibility of the adolescent experiencing positive emotional growth. He knows that adults at times find him intolerable and cannot be expected to cooperate or communicate with people who are unwilling to admit this fact.

PREREQUISITES TO AN HONEST APPROACH

By the time the professional worker comes to his first meeting with the adolescent he is encountering a child who has probably been lied to repeatedly by his parents and relatives. If the adolescent has also had experiences with welfare agencies this situation may have been compounded through dishonest behavior on the part of professional workers. The child may by this time have learned a variety of techniques of resistance to cope with what he perceives to be the "phoniness" of adults. This situation is one of the most important contributing factors to the sullen inertia and negativism so often found with adolescent clients. A good portion of the malignant effects of this factor can be ameliorated through a change in techniques and attitudes on the part of the worker directed toward a more honest interaction. When efforts are made toward more scrupulous honesty with adolescent patients it is almost invariably gratifying to discover a child who is more open, talkative, and willing to discuss areas of life that are not ordinarily communicated. The child seems almost delightfully surprised to discover that he can talk to an adult in a free and easy manner.

The methods of developing an honest approach to an adolescent patient or client are uncomplicated and straightforward. They are based on a conviction on the part of the worker that he is going to be scrupulously honest with himself and the child when he discusses or implies attitudes toward the seven areas considered earlier. It is only necessary for the worker to be aware of any tendency to convey untrue attitudes and ideas and to make a constant effort to avoid doing so. A useful illustration can be obtained through outlining the behavior and attitudes of a professional who is trying to avoid the pitfalls previously discussed. The techniques and attitudes employed by this hypothetical worker in his interactions with adolescent patients will be described. These techniques, whether utilized by youth workers, teachers, or parents, can effectively increase communication between adults and adolescents.

With respect to the "lie of adult morality" no effort is ever made by the worker to criticize, disparage, or in any way condemn the adolescent's antisocial behavior. Rather, it is considered as something the community (rightly or wrongly) will not tolerate if done openly and, most important, as something that *has not served the social or personal needs* of the adolescent. A routine and essential part of an initial interaction with any adolescent consists of a careful assessment of the net gains and losses caused by his behavior. The social usefulness of certain kinds of aggressive behavior is never disparaged. No attempt is made to discuss behavior in terms of right or wrong, neurotic or normal, or good or bad. The worker will attempt at times to communicate his own moral standards, which may or may not be more stringent than those of the patient.

These are always clearly labeled as the worker's personal beliefs and it is made clear that they may not be relevant for the patient.

The lies of professional helpfulness and confidentiality are handled directly by explaining the evaluator's own position as precisely as possible during the initial interview. The child is told who is employing the examiner, what the examiner's responsibilities to his employer are, what kind of report will be written, and exactly who will see and discuss it. Contrary to what might immediately be expected most adolescents respond favorably to such an approach. When the rules of the "game" of interviewing are wholly apparent to them, there is little need for defensiveness or negativism. The sheer surprising impact of having an adult be so direct with them often in itself produces a favorable effect that encourages them to be more open.

To avoid taking the stand that conformity or adjustment to adult standards breeds comfort and contentment the worker must have a deep and thorough understanding of the role of antisocial behavior in maintaining the adolescent's equilibrium.. He must be thoroughly able to empathize with the "fun" and at times pleasure associated with behavior that flaunts rules. He must also realize that such behavior may be all that stands between feelings of hopelessness and despair. Adjustment to the adult world is not presented as something that necessarily brings pleasure but rather as a necessary and sometimes unpleasant requisite to survival. At times the worker might even openly discuss conformity as a burden and warn the patient as to some of the dangers of such behavior. Such an approach provides leverage when the issue of the adolescent's rigid conformity to his own peer group inevitably arises during a prolonged relationship.

Avoiding the communication that most adolescent clients have the same potential as the professional worker involves a careful attention to not confusing the worker's own needs with those of the child. Our hypothetical worker freely discusses with adolescents the problems of moving from one social class to another and makes no effort to pretend that class distinctions do not exist. The barriers to advancement which minority group adolescents profess are more often accepted as realities than interpreted as projections. The adolescent boy who has a long police record and who has missed out on many educational opportunities is not deluded into believing he can "be anything he wants." The girl who may have had one or more illegitimate children is not assured of her potential for making a favorable marriage. The worker's general attitude is that this can be a "tough world" in which only a determined few manage to overcome the deprivations of their early background.

While the worker may firmly believe that a relationship with an understanding and skilled adult promulgates favorable personality change all efforts are made to let the adolescent develop the relationship at his own pace and without extravagant, implied promise of its value. The patient is told exactly when and for how long the worker will be available. Full attention is paid to the risks the client takes in developing a relationship; sometimes these risks are actually spelled out. Strenuous efforts are made to deal with the adolescent's fear of being swallowed up in his dependency needs. "Openness" is encouraged as a necessary prerequisite to gaining understanding but is not held out as a "cure-all" or as a goal in itself. Exhortations to trust the worker are avoided rigorously. Rather, the adolescent is told that he will have to decide himself about the worker's trustworthiness on the basis of his own experience.

Perhaps the most outrageous dishonesty perpetrated against adolescents by professionals involves their tendency to cover up their own angry feelings, which invariably develop toward the patient. It is surprisingly easy to tell an adolescent when he is annoying and such communications, when presented in a restrained but straightforward manner, rarely have a negative effect upon the relationship. A communication such as "I find your behavior during this interview extremely difficult and I'm having trouble keeping from getting annoyed myself" may in many instances be preferable to "What's bothering you?" or "How can I help?" or even to passive acceptance of provocative behavior. The adolescent appreciates this kind of straightforwardness. It tells him where he stands and enables him to look at his behavior without having to deceive either himself or the adult.

CONCLUSIONS

Anyone who has reared children knows that occasional dishonesty is essential if the child is to grow up with a reasonable degree of security. The truth to children, if understood, may be unbearable. If an orderly, sane, and relatively nonchaotic way of life is to be maintained, it is essential that children at times be deceived or at the very least kept in the dark as to issues they are not yet ready to master. In the treatment of adults there are clear landmarks for the worker to follow. Adults who enter psychotherapy are greeted with an atmosphere that not only condones but puts a premium on truthfulness on the part of all participants. Exceptions are made only when it is felt that the patient is too seriously ill to comprehend or tolerate the impact of truth. In these cases various deceptive practices may be used for the patient's benefit.

If one could argue convincingly that the great majority of disturbed adolescents were similar to children or to the severely disturbed adult, there would be considerable justification for withholding truth and practicing deception for the adolescent's own gain. Anyone who works with adolescents, even seriously disturbed ones, however, is quickly aware that such a comparison is invalid. Adolescents are extremely open to learning. They are in the process of discovering new aspects of the world around them, and are also increasingly preoccupied with their own inner world. Even the most disturbed adolescent has rarely developed a fixed pattern of rigid personality defenses that preclude being able to look at the truth in a reasonably open way.

The professional worker knows that the adolescent is capable of serious volatile impulsive behavior and does not have available to himself the controls that most adults have learned. Perhaps much of the explanation for an unwillingness to be honest with adolescents is related to a fear that they will not be able to tolerate the truth and that it will be used in a destructive, unhelpful way. One can also speculate that dishonest behavior might be related to the frightening impact of aggressive and sexually provocative adolescent behavior that touches upon areas of our own problems which have not been completely understood or worked through. When we present a dishonest picture of the world to our clients, we may really be trying to avoid the despair of facing the frightening world in which we live and thereby to reassure ourselves.

To interact honestly with an adolescent, all interested adults must believe that the growth of useful personality traits is more likely to take place in an atmosphere of truth than of dishonesty. This involves a willingness to take the risk of presenting communications that temporarily disturb the adolescent and a tolerance of the possibility that many of these disturbances will be directed against the adult. Any adult who wishes to communicate effectively in this manner must of course come to terms with self-deceptions in his own life so that they do not interfere with his ability to face reality with others.

What are the prospects for applied sociology? They turn in large part on our ability to do more with what we now know and in so doing advance both theory and practice. Progress here requires the kind of imaginative mixing of elements represented below by Dr. Ray Elling's prescription for public health improvements. His work combines insights into organizations drawn from industrial sociology, insights into health care from medical sociology, and insights into social-class correlates from the sociology of stratification. This kind of cross-fertilization, with its demand for considerable breadth in knowledge, constitutes a formidable challenge—even as it is an indispensable ingredient in the progress of applied sociology.

THE DESIGN AND EVALUATION OF PLANNED CHANGE
IN HEALTH ORGANIZATIONS

Ray H. Elling

THE UNNATURAL conflict between sociological theory and contribution to valued human endeavor *can* be resolved. I will argue here that theory and contribution to human well-being can be "melded" through the engagement of a well-prepared sociologist, along with practitioners, clients, and policy level supporters,[1] in the creation of new forms of social organization and in comparative measurement of their effects. Later in this essay I will offer an example of such an hypothesized organization for the delivery of preventive health and medical care services.

Background

Etzioni[2] has not confronted the central issue by asking the sociologist to become knowledgeable about, involved in, and a

---

[1]Howard E. Freeman, "The Strategy of Social Policy Research," *The Social Welfare Forum* (1963), pp. 143-60.

[2]Amitai Etzioni, "Social Analysis as a Sociological Vocation," *American Journal of Sociology*, Vol. 70 (March, 1965), pp. 613-22. Reprinted in an abridged version elsewhere in this volume.

teacher of, social issues. I agree with him and with others[3] who contend it is the intellectuals' heritage to examine social issues critically— such matters as armaments and nuclear policy, international aggression, development and population, adequate health care for all, integration and democratic participation, meaning and beauty in a gadget-oriented junkyard society, etc.—and, in so doing, to help guide the society to reasonable alternatives. The important thing, however, is not that we stand on the sidelines and carp but that we engage in *change*.

While sociological findings and perspectives are useful in examining social issues, the maximum challenge to sociological expertise lies in doing something about them. For this effort, the very best theories and methods are required, and they in turn will require amendments and retesting as one designs, effects, and measures desired changes in social organization.[4]

Preconditions

The first condition for effective design and study of new forms of social organization involves a moral principle and capable people. The principle is the promotion of human well-being in the long run *and* the short run. To resort to any other value stance would be to foster immoral types of social change. Naturally, there will be legitimate disagreements as to what specific changes will foster human well-being in the short run and the long run. But the principle should not therefore be abandoned.

We must develop as well a cadre of able social scientists well prepared in theory, methods, and research processes and techniques; a cadre enthusiastic about a career devoted to the advancement of social science through contribution to human well-being. In addition to expertise in the discipline, adequate preparation implies that the social scientist will acquire an intimate working knowledge of the subcultures, organizations, roles, and occupational groups in the area in which he hopes to improve social organization. Thus, if his contribution is to be in the health field, it will be improved by immersion in the social organization of hospitals, health departments, schools of the health professions, clinical and laboratory research settings, etc.

Other preconditions involve the characteristics of problems in the solution of which the social scientist can fruitfully become engaged. As Merton and Devereux have pointed out:

---

[3]George B. de Huszar (ed.), *The Intellectuals* (New York: The Free Press of Glencoe, Inc., 1960), Part IV, "Role of Intellectuals."

[4]Social organization is one of the primitives of our framework. We might attempt to define it as patterned human behavior which depends, at some point, upon symbolic interaction with other humans. Thus the limiting case of a person talking to himself is an example of social organization, for his social self has arisen through symbolic interchange with significant others. Anselm Strauss, *The Social Psychology of George Herbert Mead*, (Chicago: University of Chicago Press, 1956).

At least three essential elements are jointly involved in the emergence of any practical problem:

1) A *perceived discrepancy* between some existing (or future) external situation, on the one hand, and the values or goals of an individual or organization, on the other;

2) A feeling of a *need for adjustive activity* or for corrective action of some sort;

3) A "puzzle element"—an *awareness of ignorance or doubt* about at least some of the facts and relationships believed to be relevant to a decision about what, if anything, should be done.[5]

Depending on the nature of the problem, the creation of change may involve an initially small group of social scientists and others in activities to create among wider and wider circles (1) a perceived discrepancy, (2) a feeling of need for adjustment and (3) a recognition that knowledge is not adequate to achieve the adjustment.

The usual variety of sociological research—the study of "what is" or "what has been"—may be a necessary first step to the design of change. One must understand the structure of the internal system, the relations of this system to external sources of control and support, and the orientations and behaviors of the target population; but often "the returns are in" regarding the structure of a discrepant situation, and enough knowledge is on hand to suggest that the design of change be undertaken instead of yet another descriptive study.[6]

An invitation for the social scientist to design a new form of organization is highly desirable.[7] At the very least, the groups warranting change must then accept and take part in it. Similarly, while colleagues, professionals, and policy makers are involved in any planned change, groups may also be involved in early phases of change. In any case, the clients must ultimately be involved since they have to accept the product if the effort is to succeed. Thus, the new form of organization and the evaluation of it must be designed with four groups in mind: *social scien-*

---

[5]Robert K. Merton and Edward C. Devereux, Jr., "Practical Problems and the Uses of Social Science," *Trans-action,* Vol. 1 (July, 1964), pp. 18-21.

[6]Still, I caution against the easy statement "we all know that variable X is directly related to and affects variable Y" unless considerable evidence has been gathered which actually suggests this. The great difference between what is suggested in this paper and normal administrative practice is that usual assumptions may need to be established or challenged by descriptive research before planned change can be adequately designed and entered upon. Of course time and resources are limited and many "best guesses" of informed persons may have to be built into the design.

[7]In discussing the necessary involvement of persons other than the social scientist and his peers, Howard Freeman has given particular attention to the needs and orientations of the operating system and those of the policy system. Freeman *op.cit.,* "[What is] advocated here, is that the social researcher accept the commitment and obligation to be primarily responsible for the development of the research design and the selection of variables in applied studies, and that his obligation includes orienting his research to the operating and policy system as well as to the peer system."

tists who can contribute theoretical ideas and methods, offer reflection, and serve as "change agents";[8] *workers* internal to a health service or other system who must implement changes; *control-supporters* external to the system; and *participant-recipients* of the service and/or other products.[9]

THEORETICAL CONSIDERATIONS

The choice of relevant variables must be left to the design of change in a specific case. But there are some general points I would like to make about theory. The first has to do with the possible size of the social unit; the second with the problem of the extent to which a system can be isolated for planned change; the third with whether any hierarchization of change-relevant variables is possible; and the fourth with knowing the extent to which predictions regarding single variables can be entertained.

1. I envision *no* theoretical limit to the size of the social unit within which planned change can be undertaken. It seems natural to consider these units as progressing from the change of behavior and attitudes of individuals to the restructuring of a society, or even some international order. In a given institutional segment, such as a health establishment, changes would tend to be undertaken at the levels of individual health behavior and attitudes; adoption of innovations by a health organization; introduction of a new health service organization into the stream of history; reordering of the exchange relations among health and welfare organizations in a community; design of a new division of labor among health occupations in a set of organizations, possibly in a community or region as a whole; development of public opinion regarding health practices and services; and other problems. Consideration of the design of change on the societal or larger level—as in the President's physical fitness campaign—would be rare, but not beyond possibility.

2. Only in the researcher's laboratory (and possibly not even there since laboratory experiments have a way of developing a subculture related to the surrounding culture in patterned ways) is it possible to isolate a social system for study. This problem exists alike for traditional sociological investigations and for those of the action-oriented type proposed here. The only solution which now seems possible is for the re-

---

[8]For a discussion of this role see Chapter 5 of Ronald Lippitt, Jeanne Watson, and Bruce Westley, *The Dynamics of Planned Change* (New York: Harcourt, Brace, 1958).

[9]"In the last analysis the health of the community is based upon the ideas, ideals, attitudes and behavior patterns of the individual and his family, for these determine what he will or will not, can or cannot, expect or accept from those who make health their professional concern." Earl L. Koos, *The Health of Regionville* (New York: Columbia University Press, 1954), as cited in Kurt W. Deuschle, "Organizing Preventive Health Programs to Meet Health Needs," in *Meeting Health Needs by Social Action, The Annals*, Vol. 337 (September, 1961), p. 45.

searcher to be aware that external influences are likely to be involved, and for him to gather data with regard to them. This, of course, is at best a partial solution; the problem deserves continuing consideration.

3. The strict structural-functionalist approach implies that the parts of a system are so closely interdigitated that *no* statement regarding a hierarchy of "explanatory power" among variables is possible. Note, however, the following challenge:

> Interrelatedness and reciprocity do not necessarily mean . . . that all factors are of the same weight, that there is no primacy, 'no place where the thread begins.' It is not unscientific to speak of a *basic* structure, if, in fact, there are some institutional areas which play a relatively determining and directing role in social change. Besides, it is inescapable in actual research and explanation of the facts collected to choose a starting-point.[10]

I would add that most empirical researches find that while more than one independent variable is related to some dependent variable of interest, some independent variables "explain" more of the variance than do others.

4. The design and evaluation of planned change will usually involve a prediction of a desired effect occurring when a set of independent variables are altered. Thus, it will usually *not* be possible, even with several before-after and experimental-control group comparisons, to know which variables had the greatest effect or which failed to operate on a dependent variable. If enough situations could be studied so as to vary the alteration of independent variables from place to place or time to time, it might be possible to examine independent and interaction effects. At this point, I can only recognize that this is one of many humbling theoretical and methodological challenges which confront us in the design and evaluation of change.

A PROPOSED ACTION PROGRAM

By way of example of an approach, I will propose a change in health organization and a way of evaluating it. I might choose an example on the individual level—say smoking or eating behavior. Here the work of Lewin

---

[10] Behice, Boran, "Sociology in Retrospect," *American Journal of Sociology*, Vol. 52 (January, 1947), p. 320. The "internal pressure for functionalism to find a rationale for all things" and careful consideration of other problems and possibilities of the approach are given in Melvin Tumin, "The Functionalist Approach to Social Problems," *Social Problems*, Vol. 12 (Spring, 1965), pp. 379-88. See also Don Martindale (ed.), *Functionalism in the Social Sciences: The Strength and Limits of Functionalism in Anthropology, Economics, Political Science, and Sociology* (Philadelphia: The American Academy of Political and Social Science, 1965).

on the change of food habits would be revelant,[11] as would the work of Festinger with the theory of cognitive-dissonance and the development of attachment to a group,[12] and the work of others.[13] On a broader level, one might attempt to design a planning system which would solve the problem of coordination among health agencies and occupational groups. Here, work on community power systems and their relation to support and control of health agencies would be important.[14] Study of the strategies and means by which individual agencies gain support would be relevant[15] as would studies of the conditions related to exchanges among agencies,[16] and other work.[17] Space limits me however, to the consideration of a problem at the intermediate level of organization-client relations.

The problem I will consider here is the well-established gulf between "middle" class dominated, bureaucratically organized health agencies and

---

[11]Kurt Lewin, "Forces Behind Food Habits and Methods of Change," Bulletin CVIII (Washington, D.C.: National Research Council, 1943).

[12]Eliot Aronson and Judson Mills, "The Effect of Severity of Initiation on Liking for a Group," Journal of Abnormal and Social Psychology, Vol. 59 (1959), 177-81.

[13]Work on the concept of commitment seems central. This may best be pursued through social-self role analysis. See Howard S. Becker, "Notes on the Concept of Commitment," American Journal of Sociology, Vol. 66 (July, 1960), pp. 32-40; and "Personal Change in Adult Life," Sociometry, Vol. 27 (March, 1964), pp. 40-53. Also Hans L. Zetterberg, "Compliant Actions," Acta Sociologica, Vol. 2 (1957), pp. 179-201.

[14]L. Vaughn Blankenship and Ray H. Elling, "Organizational Support and Community Power Structure: The Hospital," Journal of Health and Human Behavior, Vol. 3 (Winter, 1963), pp. 257-69; Robert G. Holloway, Jay W. Artis, and Walter E. Freeman, "The Participation Patterns of 'Economic Influentials' and Their Control of a Hospital Board of Trustees," Journal of Health and Human Behavior, Vol. 4 (Summer, 1963), pp. 88-99; W. V. D'Antonio, et al., "Institutional and Occupational Representatives in Eleven Community Influence Systems," American Sociological Review, Vol. 26 (June, 1961), pp. 440-46.

[15]Ray H. Elling, "The Hospital-Support Game in Urban Center," Chapter 3 in Eliot Freidson (ed.), The Hospital in Modern Society (New York: The Free Press of Glencoe, Inc., 1963).

[16]Sol Levine and Paul White, "Exchange as a Framework for Interorganizational Analysis," Administrative Science Quarterly, Vol. 5 (March, 1961), pp. 583-601; Eugene Litwak and Lydia F. Hylton, "Interorganizational Analysis," Administrative Science Quarterly, Vol. 6 (March, 1962), pp. 395-420; Walter J. McNerney and Donald C. Riedel, Regionalization and Rural Health Care, An Experiment in Three Communities, (Ann Arbor: Bureau of Hospital Administration, University of Michigan, 1962).

[17]Inventories of external influence agencies and their control and inspirational functions in the health field are helpful. Milton I. Roemer and Helen McClanahan, "The Impact of Governmental Programs on Voluntary Hospitals," Public Health Reports, Vol. 75 (June, 1960), pp. 537-44; "The Hospital's Relation to Prepaid Group Practice," pp. 108-17 in Proceedings of the Tenth Annual Group Health Institute, Chicago Group Health Association of America, 1961. Also work which deals with networks of organizations and the planning process seems important; Robert Morris, "Basic Factors in Planning for the Coordination of Health Services," American Journal of Public Health, Vol. 53 (February and March, 1963), pp. 248-59 and 462-72.

"lower" class patients who now have no alternative to these organizations for the receipt of adequate preventive and treatment services.[18]

This problem seems particularly acute and well established in the area of prenatal care. Here the United States holds the dubious distinction of having slipped between 1950 and 1962 from sixth to eleventh place among the nations of the world in infant mortality.[19] That availability and receipt of adequate care is important in this problem and that the problem is concentrated in "lower" class areas is suggested by the following:

In America's pockets of poverty, the infant death rate is well above the national average and, in a few cities like New York and Washington, D.C., the situation is growing worse rather than better. In parts of New York's Harlem, a poor and predominantly Negro and Puerto Rican area, 41.7 babies in each 1,000 die at birth or during the first year. In Flushing, a predominantly white middle-income area less than 10 miles away, the rate is one-third that— 13.5 deaths per 1,000. Mississippi, with the lowest per capita income in the nation, has the highest state infant mortaility rate—40 deaths per 1,000 or 60% above the U.S. average. Among all U.S. Negroes and non-whites, average infant deaths are 43.2 per 1,000, nearly double the national figure for whites. . . .

A study of 57,657 births by the Obstetrical Cooperative, an organization reporting statistics for 16 U.S. hospitals, shows a dramatic correlation between medical checkups during pregnancy and a child's chances of living.

Babies of mothers who had no medical care during pregnancy had a high death rate of 133 per 1,000 during the "pre-natal" period defined as the period roughly from early pregnancy to 28 days after birth. But when the mother had four to six examinations during pregnancy, only 33 in 1,000 babies died during that period. And, with seven to nine examinations, mortality dropped to 18 per 1,000. . . .

Federal health experts are concerned especially with the relationship between infant deaths and care in charity hospitals which treat most indigent mothers and their babies. In maternity clinics of many such hospitals, patients

[18]August B. Hollingshead and Fritz C. Redlick, *Social Class and Mental Illness* (New York: John Wiley, 1958), chap. IV; Jerome K. Myers, Lee L. Bean, and Max P. Pepper, " Social Class and Mental Illness: A Ten Year Follow-up of Psychiatric Patients," *Connecticut Medicine*, Vol. 28 (May, 1964), pp. 355-59; Edward A. Suchman, "Social Patterns of Illness and Medical Care," *Journal of Health and Human Behavior*, Vol. 6 (Spring, 1965), pp. 2-16; Robin Badgley and Robert W. Hetherington "Medical Care and Social Class in Wheatville," *Canadian Journal of Public Health*, Vol. 53 (October, 1962), pp. 425-31; Charlotte Muller, "Income and Receipt of Medical Care," *American Journal of Public Health*, Vol. 55 (April, 1965), pp. 510-21; "Medical Care, Health Status, and Family Income," National Health Survey, U.S.P.H.S. Pub. No. 1000 Series 10, No. 9, 1964; section on "Low Income Behavior" in Frank Riessman, Jerome Cohen, and Arthur Pearl (eds.), *Mental Health of the Poor* (New York: The Free Press of Glencoe, Inc., 1964).

[19]"Second National Conference on Public Health Training, Aug. 19-22, 1963," Public Health Service Publication No. 1087, Table 6, p. 47; "Helping Babies Live; High Infant Mortality Among Poor Spurs New Efforts to Reduce Rate; Pre-Natal Clinics Will Get New U.S. Funds; Brooklyn Hospital Cuts Exam Delays; Many Other Lands Do Better," *Wall Street Journal*, July 3, 1964, p. 1 ff.

must wait long periods without appointments, sometimes returning a second day before seeing a doctor. Such delays may discourage many women from seeking care, officials say.[20]

A perceived discrepancy exists: there is a feeling of need for adjustment on the parts of professionals and others, there is an air of puzzlement in the situation since it is known that various tinkering efforts (prepayment, appointments instead of waiting lines, brightening up present clinics, etc.) have not adequately succeeded, and indications are that change here would clearly be directed toward the improvement of human well-being. In short, the preconditions for the design and evaluation of significant change in health organization seem to be present in this situation.

It must be admitted that some details of "lower" class culture in general are unknown. Also, there are important variations in way of life according to ethnic group, religion, specific occupation, urban-rural residence, etc. But I hypothesize, the broad essential outlines are known:[21]

1. There is a sense of deprivation and powerlessness.

2. There is an actual relative lack of material means and life is unpredictable; there is a relative lack of control over the environment.

3. The life space of the individual is relatively unified and based predominantly on face-to-face validation of experience from close, significant others, rather than on specialization and emphasis on secondary relationships as in the "middle" class.

4. Closely related to the above, if not a part of the same element, relations are predominantly informal.

5. There is a concentration of life interest and identity in a given locality—an area, a neighborhood.

6. The time perspective is present-oriented rather than past or future-oriented.

7. Kin and friendship ties extend for the spreading of risk, but the single marriage may not be as firm as in the "middle" class.

---

[20]While this quotation suggests the efficacy of prenatal care in fostering the health of the infant and the mother, it should be noted that some work questions this with respect to at least one specific health problem: Samuel Schwartz and John H. Vinyard, Jr., "Prenatal Care and Prematurity," *Public Health Reports*, (March, 1965), pp. 237-48.

[21]Our emphasis here is on the urban "lower" class. These characteristics represent the generally common elements reported in a number of studies. Important among these sources are: Albert K. Cohen and Harold M. Hodges, "Characteristics of the Lower-Blue-Collar Class," *Social Problems*, Vol. 10 (Spring, 1963), pp. 303-34; Hollingshead and Redlick, *op. cit.*, chap. IV, Herbert Gans, *The Urban Villagers* (New York: The Free Press of Glencoe, Inc., 1962); Elizabeth Herzog, "Some Assumptions About the Poor," *Social Science Review*, Vol. 27 (December, 1963), pp 389-402; Edward Suchman, "Sociomedical Variations Among Ethnic Groups," *American Journal of Sociology*, Vol. 70 (November, 1964), pp. 319-31; Ray H. Elling and Gustavo Iacona, "Participation Patterns Among Italian Males in a 'Lower' Class Urban Area," paper in preparation.

8. Self-attitudes may be negative and disparaging where standards of community authorities are concerned (doctors, nurses, social workers, and other health workers fall in this category along with ministers, policemen, teachers, and others).

9. Education is low and anti-intellectuality abounds; as a consequence, authoritarianism may prevail and there is an attachment to toughness and the concrete feeling or event.[22]

10. There is a search for "instant status" through luck at gambling, purchase of prestige symbols on time, etc.

Contrasted with this we have the characteristics of a bureaucracy—the usual form of organization (clinics, hospitals, etc.) through which care is offered:[23]

1. There is an attempt to order human relations rationally. This involves an emphasis on logic and order.

2. There is an elaborate, but centralized, hierarchy of authority and decision making.

3. There is a complex specialization in the division of labor, and tasks are routinized.

4. Formality and written rules govern or affect much of the action.

5. Relationships are often secondary, through records, memos, copies of letters, etc.; thus persons are classified according to a system of labels re-ecting the flow of work and system of authority.

6. A spirit of formalistic impersonality guards against personal favor and special interests.

7. Appointments, rewards, and punishments are accorded for merit in pursuit of organizational goals.

8. Things are run on a schedule and the time perspective is future-oriented.

In comparing the cultural assumptions of these two forms of social organization, the lower-class- and the middle-class-dominated bureaucracy, we see a nearly complete mismatch. By making such a comparison we are in a position to suggest a new form of health service organization which

---

[22]For example, Suchman's data, *op. cit.*, 1964 and 1965, shows that those most tied in with a local, informal network tend to feel that treatment is required only if there is pain. Preventive concepts are generally discounted. A treatment not felt to be working will quickly be discarded in favor of a home remedy if pain does not subside very soon. We should also recognize that preventive orientations may be disease or situation specific. See Howard E. Freeman and Camille Lambert, Jr., "Factors Affecting Utilization of Public Health Dental Clinic," *Journal of Health and Human Behavior* (Fall, 1965).

[23]Again this is a composite picture. Weber's ideal type statement is followed closely as it tends to highlight the elements involved. Gerth and Mills, *op. cit.*, chap. VIII, "Bureaucracy." Victor A. Thompson, *Modern Organization* (New York: Alfred A. Knopf, Inc., 1961), chap. 2, "Bureaucracy." Any actual organization has important modifications. For example, formal rules may be relaxed as a matter of "strategic leniency." Peter Blau, *Bureaucracy in Modern Society* (New York: Random House, Inc., 1956).

we can hypothesize will be more effective in gaining the participation of "lower" class patients.

This new form of health service organization should be prepaid through tax funds or other community support to make it economically available; it should be locally based, preferably on the street of the people to be served; and it should be run informally, the personnel involved being willing to sit on the doorstep and "pass the news of the day." This may imply a lack of emphasis on elaborate records and forms.

The personnel should have an intimate knowledge of sociocultural aspects of behavior, particularly of the lower class. This should include knowledge of local politics. They should also have a thorough enough grounding in medical and health sciences to offer adequate care. The care itself should be general and focused on the family or household unit; it should not be a specialty-oriented service, even when a particular problem like prenatal care is uppermost in the minds of health professionals. Closely related to the last point, the general health advisor (this may be a general physician, a specially prepared public health nurse, or other specially prepared health worker) must be willing to consult on a wide range of troubles and aid persons in their searches for help.

Local residents (prospective patients) should have final authority over the general organization of service, professionals serving in an advisory service capacity only. There should be firm connections in terms of power, authority, and transportation with a health center and other health agencies where the full armamentarium of medical care and preventive services would be available. The general health adviser would lend important confidence to the client, assuring him that he would not be lost or mishandled in a strange, bureaucratic maze. Finally, there must be adequate support for the endeavor from community leaders and, to the extent possible, professional associations.

Evaluation of this form of care would begin with a careful survey of morbidity and care patterns in at least one experimental and one similar control area before any change in service is provided.[24] The service would be set up and social science observers would keep a running field diary of the events which mark the introduction of this new organization into "the stream of history." A series of surveys would be conducted to yield

---

[24] Only the bare logical outlines of the evaluation methods and procedures are mentioned here. This general design was employed on the community level in the Vicos project in Peru. See Allan R. Holmberg and Henry F. Dobyns, "The Process of Accelerating Community Change," *Human Organization*, Vol. 21 (Summer, 1962), pp. 107-24. For a full treatment of evaluation see the forthcoming book by Edward Suchman, Jack Elinson, and George James, *Evaluation in Public Health*. Another approach, the ideal-type method of evaluation, is discussed by Otto Pollak, "Design of a Model of Healthy Family Relationships as a Basis for Evaluative Research," *Social Service Review*, 31:4 (December, 1957). A general consideration of methods and other problems is given in A. W. Gouldner, "Theoretical Requirements of the Applied Social Sciences," *American Sociological Review*, Vol. 22 (February, 1957), pp. 92-102.

panel data on change in morbidity and health care participation patterns. The original design would be modified after at least two waves of survey data show that success is less than it theoretically should be. This implies modification and contribution to theory, and, not incidentally, to human well-being.

What are the prospects for applied sociology? They turn in large part on our ability to spread the successful application of sociology into previously untapped areas. Sociology has much to contribute in the struggle to make sense of this nation's "surfeit of honey," its "feminine mystique," its "pursuit of excellence," and so forth. Sociology has recently been successfully introduced into the organized effort to help keep the peace. Dr. Theodore Olson's account is intriguing for his intimate knowledge of this development, his plans for strengthening sociology's contribution, and his stress on the special contribution sociology alone of the social sciences can make to the movement. In possibly no other area do the prospects of applied sociology—and the prospects of mankind—so intimately relate.

THE NEW PEACE EFFORT: SOCIOLOGY OVERCOMING IDEOLOGY

Theodore Olson

THERE HAS BEEN an important recent shift in private work for peace away from the assumptions and style of an ideological movement toward a sociologically conditioned interpretation of the task of peacemaking. Reflecting on my participation in this process, I focus in particular upon developments in the training of peace effort personnel.

I

There has been a "peace movement" of one sort or another in the United States for over 300 years. The term is elastic,[1] but its core refer-

---

[1] Ranging from the Strategic Air Command's Orwellian slogan, "Peace is Our Profession," to the withdrawn fruit-and-nut communitarians. For the most useful survey of the entire period up to World War II, see Merle E. Curti, *Peace or War: The American Struggle*, 1636–1936 (New York: W. W. Norton & Co., Inc., 1936). No comprehensive study exists of the postwar period, but studies evocative of various trends include the following: the symposium, "Is There Another Way?" *Progressive*, October, 1955; Presentation #3, "Development of the Peace Effort's Hard Core After World War II," following p. 209 in Theodore Olson, *Peace and the American Community* (New York: Turn Toward Peace, 1963); Roy Finch, "The New Peace Movement," Parts I and II, *Dissent*, Winter and Spring, 1963; and Arthur Herzog, *The War-Peace Establishment* (New York: Harper & Row, 1964).

ence has always been to those who believe that war must be put away as a permissible recourse for public policy.[2] The peace movement, though small and fragmented, has often enjoyed an influence quite disproportionate to its size. Yet the story of the peace movement is a story of failure, repeated and utter failure. Whole phalanxes of "committees for . . ." and "councils against . . ." seem not to have altered public policy in periods of crisis. Each time, with the approach of war, the whole imposing apparatus of propaganda, pledges, and campaigns has come ingloriously unstuck. The recurring verdict of the populace has been that reality has overtaken what was at best premature and at worst a fanatical delusion. Even the known effects of nuclear weapons have not caused significant public enrollment in the traditional peace movement.

The traditional forms of the peace movement—personal witness pacifism and the "cause" organization—bear the marks of their ideological origin and nurture. That is, their understandings of basic reality and of public events are determined by a prior set of beliefs that form a privileged structure not itself open to inspection or question. Thus the peace movement's response to its own staggering reverses has also been ideological: "The trouble is not in here; it is out there. Our perception of the nature of our task is quite in order. In fact, the crisis or war would not have occurred had the nation been acting on the basis of peace movement strategy. If any fault lies in us, it is that we have not been sufficiently dedicated. We must therefore try harder. The future is ours—or there is no future."

The growth during the 1950's of an in-group ethos in the peace movement did not alienate the career-committed, the marginal, or those with a positive need for a simplified universe. But many others began to experience the peace movement as confining, where once it had been liberating. As a result, in the early 1960's the rate of attrition from significant participation in the peace agencies reached crisis proportions. Some of the disillusioned were from the "cause" organization wing. Others were frustrated "sitters-in" or "sailors-to," worn down by the realization that to do the same thing again would make no more difference than it

---

[2]Within this historic core, getting rid of war has been pursued in two chief ways, both deeply expressive of basic American understandings of politics. The first can be called political moralism, in which the achievement of a national no-war policy was viewed as the imperative yet natural and inevitable extension into our institutional life of the truths expressed in personal pacifism and "common morality." Historically, this has meant that the problem of conscientious objection has received a disproportionate emphasis and that the nation of the future was conceived as a corporate conscientious objector.

The other impulse is that of voluntaristic rationalism. War, whatever its merits in the moment of crisis, impedes the growth of a rational society based on meeting "men's needs." It destroys much of the social rationalization already achieved. Therefore the more rationally we proceed, the less scope is provided for future outbreaks of disastrous violence. In the end, a rational international system will banish war quite as naturally as proper drains have checked diphtheria.

had this last time. The rate of attrition in direct action projects, always high, now effectively exhausted the reservoir of potential actionists.[3]

Most cruel of all was the bewildering contrast between the failure of the nonviolent peace movement and the increasing effectiveness of those same tactics and principles in the nonviolent civil rights movement. Indeed, some key civil rights workers were "on loan" from the peace movement.

Perspective on these problems could only be supplied by asking different questions, by stepping behind the *how* and turning attention to the *what:* to data, to ideas verified by observations about the ways men function in groups and societies—in a word, to sociological questions and procedures. Accordingly, from approximately 1959 to the present there has been a discernable shift in work for peace away from the movement style and into the milieu of community sociology. While it may be too early to speak of a triumph, clearly the shift can be described as sociology in the process of overcoming ideology. And though restructuring has been accomplished across the entire spectrum of what is now styled "the peace effort," nowhere I believe has this been more marked or more indicative for the future than in the recruiting and training of new personnel.

In the ideological movement phase of the recent past, two recruitment methods were used, both fitting easily into the moralistic ethos. The organizational side of the movement was set up on a "good cause" basis. The like-minded or "concerned" banded together on the pattern of the standard American voluntary organization (i.e., one convinced people and brought them into membership, one wrote letters, lobbied, listened to speakers, and attempted in general to be the local organizational voice of those concerned for peace). In this way the "peace group" took its place in the community spectrum of good cause and special interest groups: YM/YW, literary, businessmen's, religious, women's, mental health, planned parenthood, NAACP, juvenile delinquency, court and prison reform, etc.[4] It was thus a tidy part of the middle-class way of life in the Northern states.

The second recruitment tradition differed dramatically from the first. Built into any peace agitation group is a potential parting of the ways.

---

[3]For the exemplary concept of direct action, the problem was specially cruel. Devoted to the sub-Christian notion that "unmerited suffering" would produce "spiritual power" and the conversion of their opponents, some now began to see that, as John Braine put it in reflecting on his own experience, "If I had an enemy, if I genuinely thought of someone as being a menace to my country's security and even to peace, I'm afraid that nothing would please me more than for him to go to prison. If he virtually sent himself there, so much the better." In the anthology, David Boulton (ed.), *Voices From the Crowd: Against the H-Bomb* (London: Peter Owen, 1964), p. 184.

[4]Yet these other groups were usually far more functional than the local peace agency chapters. These were not often producers of programs, but rather mere consumers of programs produced by their own organizational bureaucracies.

When a war comes, some youths fight in the war; others, together with their elders, fight against the war itself. The direct action wing of the peace movement extended this principle to the between-war periods. Many actionists identified sub-Christian doctrines about the efficacy of sacrifice and the power of purity with the essence of nonviolence. They declared that the peace movement would grow as the populace saw "the power of nonviolence" in action against the nation's war machine or war potential. One by one or en masse, men and women would be converted, themselves becoming part of a chain reaction that in the end would make it impossible for the United States to maintain a war posture. In the same way, the American example of national conscientious objection would produce other national converts and so bring world peace. And even if it did not, it were far better for us to die nobly than to kill.

Psychologically, the whole enterprise was a doomed exercise in autarchy, an attempt to do the whole job oneself out of one's own inner resources. The conscious attempt to recruit a mass peace movement was sabotaged by a deeply held notion of the power of the individual person or individual nation to "make it happen." Here too one was recruited into an established pattern of behavior and attitude. One did not need to be trained to have a conscience. Indeed one's recruitment was the sign that one had already qualified for full participation.

Beginning in 1959, steps were taken by peace movement professionals to experiment with new ways of achieving a world without war, new ways that required a totally different notion of recruitment and training. These experimenters no longer looked on the traditional peace groups as the center whose increment would establish peace. Instead, they looked at the whole panorama of American voluntary organizations, and they asked: What roles do various volunteer groups play at the national or symbolic level? What role at the community level? What role do they play for their membership, which includes most Americans? How many of them already have a program relation of some kind to war/peace problems? How can they be aided to enrich and focus their own programs? How can they be coordinated in such a way as to make their weight felt and their voices coherent and persuasive to the body politic? "Function" and "role," standard sociological concepts, became key terms. It became clear that the nexus of work for all these efforts was the local community. The emphasis therefore shifted to one of degrees of achievement along a spectrum, rather than the grandiose apocalyptic or legislative fiat that would bring peace.

Initial work in the new area was begun in Berkeley under the direction of Robert Pickus, formerly an influential theoretician and program leader in the American Friends Service Committee. The Berkeley program, called Acts for Peace, indicated in its very name a shift to discrete, bite-sized, yet coordinated individual actions along a broad front of community affairs. Its dramatic success in breaking out of the pacifist and good-cause ghettos and in achieving continuing relationships with "the real world" led to the creation in 1962 of Turn Toward Peace.

Turn Toward Peace was a national coordinating agency, including the traditional peace agencies, but designed specifically to involve the whole continuum of national voluntary organizations. Each was assumed to have a role in originating or disseminating relevant information and program and in helping to provide the climate for acceptance of the TTP goal: "a disarmed world under law, in which free societies can grow and flourish." TTP structure was elaborated nationally and locally to aid and to take maximum advantage of the contributions offered by participating unions, veterans' groups, social service, religious, political and social action agencies. It was made specifically nondoctrinal and, within the stated goal, open-ended, so that still other bodies and segments of the national and local communities could readily participate.[5]

If it was to function at all, this highly articulated and sophisticated structure required trained personnel at every level. "Coordinators" would have to be sent from national organizations or developed and trained if "organization for peace" were to replace that "organization for war" which TTP saw as characterizing the American city and society as a whole.

But the very notion of sending in coordinators—of using and combining existing resources of diverse and even conflicting kinds—made plain the fact that "the man with the message," the ideological zealot, would not do in this work. The ideological approach had largely been parasitic upon the congealed state of the mid-century American social process. The movement's "mass" tactics were the articulation of a deeply felt frustration with this condition. When, instead, experimentation was begun with ways of unfreezing this process, a radically different leadership style was required: men and women who were cognizant of basic social science research techniques, oriented toward data and servicing procedures, toward the development of sophisticated techniques—mass techniques if necessary—capable of use in changing local and ultimately national reality.[6]

In the summer of 1962, a Quaker agency, New York Friends Group, authorized a long-term feasibility study, looking toward the establish-

---

[5]The best single short exposition of this concept was published as "Disturber of the Peace: An Interview with Robert Pickus," *Mademoiselle*, December, 1961. See also Herzog, *op.cit.*, pp. 235-37. For a somewhat differently stressed programmatic outline of a "new" peace effort, see Amitai Etzioni, *The Hard Way to Peace* (New York: Collier, 1962). Though the initiators of the new emphases combined solid social science training with peace organization experience, it must be emphasized that the largely autodidactic leadership of the traditional peace agencies made it possible in the end to sustain the new work. It was with their aid that the first attempts were made to think through the requirements for training field workers in the peace and related social action efforts.

[6]Civil rights and urban problem agencies were beginning to experience the same needs and to feel the same desperate pinch for trained field leadership.

ment of a full-time educational institution for the training of this needed new leadership. The initial focus was to be on the peace effort. As director of the new program, I initiated curriculum conferences and other meetings with experts in the content, the techniques, and the business of training itself. The resulting data, though abundant, were still not centered on the specific problem at hand. It was clearly necessary to experiment, to prove out possible directions, assumptions, and techniques before we could approach institutions, foundations, prospective faculty, and organizations.

With this in mind, we began a pilot seminar in the spring of 1963 with interne-trainees and junior staff from several social action agencies. The questions were many. Was it possible to teach these ideas and skills in an ordered manner? Could a "peace-effective" orientation be taught objectively and not merely caught by a kind of organizational osmosis? Would the race and social service groups be ready to participate? And more important, would there be jobs for graduates of the course?

Students in this first group were thoroughly representative of the complex transition described earlier. They had not been recruited but were supplied to us out of current stock by interested agencies: The American Friends Service Committee, Turn Toward Peace, the Committee for Nonviolent Action, National Research Council for Peace Strategies, and New York Friends Group itself. Educationally, they ranged from second-year undergraduates to M.A.'s. Some were personal witness pacifists. Others were newly alienated from both pacifism and imperial mid-century America. Gratifyingly, most others were there because the new peace effort made rational sense to them in terms of vocational choice. Unlike the others, their vocational commitment connected them to the ordinary processes of our society instead of alienating them from normal life.

On the basis of our experience in this seminar with the curriculum given us by consensus of the conferences, I was able to expand this outline nearly to the size of the Sears catalog. This volume was issued by Turn Toward Peace as *Peace and the American Community*. It was designed as an instructor's manual for a combined work and study program for internes that would be carried on over the full academic year in four TTP regions across the country. The New York seminar for the fall was also geared more specifically to the needs of TTP's central staff interne-trainees. We were now in a position to offer an integrated program of seminars, study, and tests to go with the acquisition of skills and general orientation.

The work was devoted initially to orientation and the acquisition of information, then afterward to the development and demonstration of research skills. Finally, the trainees were introduced to organizational and technical skills. Tension at the start was acute between the necessity of supplying background information and the trainee's "need to know" certain skills important in the "work" side of his work and study program.

Typical of the background information we presented was the historic and intellectual roots of the peace movement, which we carried forward in the United States on a stimulus-response model centered on the various war crises up through the Cold War and the breakup of the bipolar phase of that conflict.[7]

In many respects the single most important part of the seminar (despite its being marked with tension) was our attempt to provide trainees with tools for analysis of the organizations among which they would be working. We sought to move beyond folklore: what "everybody knew" about X organization. We sought to provide the basis for insight as well as for information gathering, and we sought to enable trainees themselves to train others in these analytical operations.

The first part of this work, called "description," saw the facts gathered on origin, constituency, effective outreach, form of organization, finance, publication, major personalities, and associations with other groups. For example, under "forms and finance" the following questions were asked: "Is it a membership group? If so, is it organized on the national level or does it have regional and local horizontal organization? Is it set up by chapters like the Women's International League for Peace and Freedom? Or is it not a membership group at all, but set up on the committee-constituency pattern, like the American Friends Service Committee? In either case, how does the structure work? How large a group, gathered from what places, does the decision making? Is it the expression of one man's concern or not? Is it mainly a letterhead or does it actually carry on program work? How much money is involved, on the national and local levels? How much is it collected: contributions, dues, subscriptions, campaigns keyed to issues? What accounting is there to members or to the public? What percentage goes to staff salaries and what to program?"[8] This information proved difficult to obtain, even from present organizational leadership.

Even more difficult to extract were materials useful in building up what we called a "profile." Here we asked of an organization: 1) what does it believe causes war or peace; 2) what dynamic or vision sustains

---

[7]Of particular importance here was the distinction, necessary to draw since before World War II, between aligned and nonaligned work for peace. Here we treated as one all peace activity done from within the framework of the Cold War, whether on behalf of the United States or for the Soviet Union. Nonaligned peace work was that done by groups, wherever based, which criticized the Cold War itself and assessed critically the plans and actions of their own government. By these tests, the official peace statements of the AFL-CIO and those of the Communist-dominated World Council of Peace both fell in the aligned category. But the distinction was not intended to establish sheep and goats on a new bipolar basis. It was put forward as a means of evaluation on a "how much" basis, rather than a black-and-white "whether" basis. In nearly every case the aligned/nonaligned framework proved most easy to grasp by those from the mainstream of the nonideological fifties. It was resisted most tenaciously by the survivors of the ideological peace movement.

[8]Olson, *op.cit.*, p. 386.

the group and what is its time perspective; 3) how does the group understand social change as taking place and what is its notion of the role of conflict, of power; 4) what is its picture, if any, of the good society; 5) to what extent does the group accept a bipolar ˚view of the Cold War, no matter what the group's value commitment; 6) what are the group's policy proposals; 7) what does the group do in pursuit or implementation of its policy proposals; 8) what is the group's role as self-defined; 9) what is the group's role or image as seen by others; 10) how do or do not the following dichotomies apply: expressive/instrumental, conventional/radical, vanguard/plodders, beat/square, crisis-oriented/long-range, religious/secular, old/young, shoestring/substantial operation?[9]

It was against demanding analytical work of this type that many participants reacted strongly. Some, by reason of poor prior training, were unable intellectually to cope with it. Many complained of a time squeeze between this work and their other labor as internes. Some resisted strongly any deep probe of organizational motivation. To be "for peace" was to have a privileged motivational sanctuary. And organizationally —as personally?—much would therefore be forgiven that would be given short shrift if attempted in other fields. The analytical approach produced malaise precisely as it was professional or businesslike in attitude. "After all, you can't sell peace like soap." Participants often displayed remarkable ingenuity in defending an ideological virginity. Still others resisted learning "petty details" and the more mundane aspects of office life, on the theory, apparently, that they were in some sense executive trainees who were above all this.

Throughout, the major focus of the program remained its study of the community, community organization, and how to work within community structures for changes in those structures and in the community. The study assumed the trainees' acquaintance with the various theories of community and centered on sources of cohesion and identity, on lines of communication and control, and on the role of the local community in sustaining or changing a war- or defense-oriented society. The unique role in the U.S. of the voluntary organization was stressed. The program presented a range of possible structures for a community-based peace effort, without itself recommending any single structure. It did bear down heavily on the need for a low-keyed, "listening" approach to beginning community organization for peace.

All this paid off in the concrete business of actual program planning and execution. Here the study and work sections of the interne program operated in close harmony. Program areas were laid out: community opinion leaders, voluntary organizations, mass media, work with children, youth, and women. Trainees helped to develop supply services for these

---

[9]*Ibid.*, pp. 390–95.

programs: literature, speakers, film-and-discussion programs, art and display. The full range of public issues-centered work was reviewed with much attention given to example. Seminar leaders were veterans of everything from letter campaigns and meeting promotion to nonviolent direct action. Ten channels for continuing programs were set forth, from businessmen to farmers to students. The program also laid stress on procurement and development of a wide range of specific materials for all these programs. It closed with a section on the logistics of such a continuing community peace program based broadly on achieving "a disarmed world under law, in which free societies can grow and flourish."

The ability to marshal data, to take a nonideological approach to problems of organization and outreach, to work with an extended time perspective on complex tasks—all these were prime characteristics of the men and women we sought. For the first time we had a means of probing for, developing, and evaluating potential personnel in relation to these abilities. No longer would right belief and moral fervor suffice.

II

Beyond the immediate results of the seminars themselves, the feasibility study was considered to have demonstrated the need and the ability to move ahead into concrete institutional form. Peace, civil rights, and social service agency heads expressed the keenest interest, and funds became available. Leaders of the Crozer Foundation, an educational philanthropy in Chester, Pa., were involved at an early date, and, in September, 1965, Upland Institute, a graduate-level professional school of social action leadership training opened. It was to be one of a growing complex of institutions on the Crozer campus concerned with somatic and mental health, theology and urban development, as well as with social action leadership training. The institute's governing board of fellows includes such significant names in U.S. social science and social action as: Keneth Boulding, Harold Taylor, Robert Gilmore, Bayard Rustin, and Benjamin Mays, among others. The initial class of students numbered twenty-four.

In the end, it may be false to speak of the triumph of sociology here. The great imperialists within the discipline have not had much relevance to the work described in this paper. The most useful sociological contributions have come from issue-concerned scholars and teachers. But the "triumph" is perhaps the more impressive because so few sociologists have been involved at all: I am qualified in theology and my successor in political science. It has been a unique experiment in which the leadership of a movement was driven by hard experience, not to new extremes of ideology, but, instead, to a change in the very basis of their own self-understanding. It has been found that the tools most useful in this reconstruction have been sociological in nature.

This is perhaps not surprising to those whose professional lives have been spent in the discipline. But much of the rest of the world looks upon psychology or religion or political science or even the military sciences as the chief peace-relevant fields of study. It has been our experience that so long as this was so, the peace effort was confused and confined within a small segment of the populace. Now, without loss of what is pertinent in these other disciplines, sociology has given us a significant boost toward a disarmed world under law, in which free societies can grow and flourish.

EPILOGUE

It seems to me
that those of us
who have knowledge
about our society,
especially
if we are aware of threats
to that part of the society
we would prefer
to perpetuate,
must engage in social action.
By becoming a part
of the world,
we may change its direction
or otherwise contribute to
man's appreciation of man
as a human being.
With effort,
and by taking some risks,
we may prevent
the emergence of some serious
and dire outcomes. But if we
fail to act, or fail in the acting —
"KAPOW" —
right in the collective kisser.*

ROY G. FRANCIS

---

*Adapted with permission from "Kapow!! An Argument and a Forecast," by Roy G. Francis, from *Social Problems,* Winter, 1965.

APPENDIX

SOCIAL ANALYSIS

Success as an applied sociologist requires a prior mastery of, and a life-long interest in, social analysis. Mills advises in this connection that "the social sciences are becoming the common denominator of our cultural period, and the sociological imagination is becoming our most needed quality of mind." Social analysis is the route to the acquisition of a "sociological imagination," a quality of mind necessary if one is to achieve a lucid summation of what is going on in the world and what may be happening within oneself. Social analysis is also the route to an intelligent choice of a social problem to work on, to preparation of an intelligent design and implementing a reform project; and to an intelligent, unsparing appraisal—and redesign—of the evolving project. Much of this is illuminated in the three essays that follow: Professor Amitai Etzioni explores the promise and problems of social analysis, while Professor Irving L. Horowitz offers two excellent examples of this sociological form.

SOCIAL ANALYSIS AS A SOCIOLOGICAL VOCATION*

Amitai Etzioni

WHAT IS lacking in American sociology is *social analysis,* the *systematic* exploration of societal issues, that is, concern with the methodological questions of sociological analysis of the great issues of our age, which invariably involves the study of macroscopic units.

The subject of social analysis, though, is the issues, not the sociological units or building stones; the focus is on the instruments to be utilized to elevate the analysis of societal issues, to improve on amateur, intuitive, or journalistic sociology. Traditional training in sociology is no more a preparation for social analysis than training in biophysics or biochemistry is a substitute for medical training. Social analysis requires special training as well as distinct methods, knowledge, and a professional tradition. Social analysis requires more than a simple application of an existing

*I am indebted for comments on an earlier version of this article to Martin Wenglinsky, Ethna and Edward Lehman, Charles Kadushin, and in particular to William J. Goode. The present version has been abridged with permission by Dr. A. Shostak, editor of this volume, and is reprinted from *American Journal of Sociology,* March, 1965, by permission of the University of Chicago Press.

body of knowledge to the study of a set of problems; it is also a question of studying the problems that application of sociology engenders. When sick, one would hardly exchange treatment by one M.D. for that of two Ph.D.'s in biology.

Hence, the call for social analysis as a new element of sociological training is a call for *the professionalization of sociology*—for adding to sociology as a science, as the institutionalized desire to know, the systematic concern with application of knowledge, the institutionalized desire to help.[1]

The *subject matter* of social analysis is all of substantive sociology; but social analysis as a discipline is not to replace the fields of political sociology, race relations, or the study of stratification, but is to deal with *the generic methodological, intellectual, and professional problems which the substantive sociologies raise.* Each of the substantive fields combines—in addition to information about the subject matter—three and not two essential elements. To study politics one had best know something about politics, draw on a general theory and methodology, *and* be prepared to handle the generic problems of substantive analysis. The same problems would reappear if you were to study other substantive fields, for example, the sociology of religion or criminology, but would not arise if you were engaged in sociological theory per se or pure methodology.

What is the substance of social analysis and what generic problems does its study raise? The focus of social analysis, and its *raison d'être,* are the problems of the age, the application of sociology to the understanding of society, its major subcollectives, and a society's place in more encompassing communities. Sociological theory and research slice society into social systems, role sets, and reference groups; social analysis is concerned with applying such concepts to the evolution of a world community, the redistribution of social wealth, efforts to advance the growth of civil rights, the development of "have-not" countries, etc. Sometimes the transition from sociological theory to social analysis is fairly straightforward and simple, often it is not; but always the problem of applying our fragmented knowledge to social action needs to be systematically studied.

Obviously I do not share the feeling, expounded by C. Wright Mills in this context, that our investment in methodology was largely wasted or that our bets on general theory are misplaced.[2] On the contrary, it seems to me, our efforts are starting to pay off handsomely and *hence* we are more ready than we ever were to apply our theories and methods to major societal issues and to be systematically concerned with the problems such application raises.

A hardly novel historical approach to sociology serves to emphasize

---

[1] Talcott Parsons, "Some Problems Confronting Sociology as a Profession," *American Sociological Review,* Vol. XXIV (August, 1959), pp. 547-59.

[2] C. Wright Mills, *The Sociological Imagination* (New York: Grove Press, 1957), esp. p. 50 and pp. 74-75.

this point.[3] We started with grand social theories, formulated in emotion-laden terms (e.g., progress), covering no more and no less than all of history and all of mankind; we began by flying so high on the verbal trapeze that most of our propositions could not be pinned down; and those that could be often did not withstand empirical tests. Our grandiose designs collapsed.

Then, we foreswore high jumps; we preferred to advance step by step, even if it should take us a hundred years to learn to walk firmly, rather than engage again in breathtaking but also neck-breaking gymnastics.[4] We sharpened our tools on the radio listening of housewives and focused our concepts by observing small groups of college sophomores chatting before a one-way mirror. *Such a concentration was essential for a transition period;* but behavior which is quite suitable for student days becomes an adolescent fixation when it dominates the behavior of a mature man. Sociological theory ought to be further extended and methods of collecting and analyzing data improved, but our wings have sprouted; we are now ready to fly. It would be an overreaction to our earlier misadventure to remain earthbound to a restrictive interpretation of our discipline, to delay a new test flight of social analysis.

Another reason we, as a profession, shy away from social analysis is our fear of value judgments which, we sense, are more rampant in social than in sociological analysis. Weber's bequest to us, we keep telling generations of students, is the separation of understanding from criticism, which is the basis of all rational, and hence scientific, analysis. But—we do not always remember to add—Weber carefully distinguished between a *wert-frei* and a *wert-los* approach (between one free of values and one without values or literally valueless). A *wert-frei* sociologist holds his values in abeyance while he follows the guidelines his data reveal, allowing them to speak rather than imposing on the data the findings his heart desires. Thus he is "free" from values while engaging in the procedural act of science. But this is not to imply that the work of the very same sociologist needs to be *wert-los*, either in his professional or his citizen role.

In his professional role, the sociologist, like any other scientist, must choose his research topic by nonscientific, normative criteria. I say "must" because there are no intrinsically scientific criteria for this selection. One might say we are out to fill in the lacunae of sociological theory, chart the unknown areas left on the map; we do not know what we shall find, we only know where the uncharted areas lie. But our map has more unknown than known spots, and how is one to tell, on what scientific consideration, which to chart first? Moreover, since so much of our charting is tentative, rechecking the known is as important as exploring the unknown. Hence

---

[3] Cf. Ralf Dahrendorf, "Toward a Theory of Social Conflict," *Journal of Conflict Resolution,* Vol. XI (1958), pp. 170-83.

[4] Lewis Anthony Dexter, "A Note on Selective Inattention in Social Science," *Social Problems,* Vol. VI (Fall, 1958), pp. 176-82.

the list of topics a sociologist can legitimately choose from for his study is as long as the list of topics there are. Our selection is thus invariably determined by intellectual curiosity, aesthetic values, fads, career interests, availability of funds, leadership of senior colleagues, and what not. But there is nothing intrinsic in sociology as a discipline that makes the study of macroscopic units less respectable than microscopic ones, now that we are equipped with the basic skills and tools necessary to handle both kinds of units.

But social analysis requires macroscopic analysis. Most of the problems of the age are those of large collectivities or are directly affected by them; in issues such as accelerated desegregation, redistribution of the national income in favor of the underprivileged, or averting nuclear war, the federal government and the national society play a critical role. The infrequency with which social analysis topics are selected derives not from any inner light that sociology sheds on research but from largely extrinsic shadows. It arises in part from the tendency to award more status to basic than applied research, and in part from the hangover of poor social analysis, the pangs of which are still with us. Actually by now social analysis could be fully respectable; the taste of past generations' brew should no longer hinder our distilling a new one.

Two more arguments in favor of sociology as it is (and the *status quo* in sociological training) need to be examined. It is said that sociologists, by learning to walk, will find out how to fly. You can learn from the fruit fly, it is correctly suggested, new laws of genetics that apply to all animals and plants. Similarly, we can derive from sophomores' chitchat universal laws of interaction which enrich our understanding of social behavior in general. But while it is true that in this way we can learn the "universal" elements of our theory—all the universal chemical characteristics of water are represented in any drop—we cannot study the emergent properties of complex units in noncomplex ones.[5] We will not learn much about the anatomy of elephants by studying that of fruit flies. Hence, while we ought to continue to study small groups for their own sake and for the light they cast on social behavior in general, *we ought to invest more of our resources in macroscopic sociology.*

But, it is said, as a second line of defense in favor of our present low investment in social analysis, you cannot direct scientists and tell them what to study. If sociologists find race relations an unrespectable subject, unless it can be used to perfect survey methods or to redefine the concept of prejudice, what can we do? What we can do is to realize that the distribution of scientific resources is not random, does not follow a *laissez-faire* pattern, and is "interfered with" regularly anyhow.[6] The distribution

[5] This point is elaborated in Amitai Etzioni's *A Comparative Analysis of Complex Organizations* (New York: The Free Press of Glencoe, Inc., 1961), pp. xii ff.

[6] See Robert Gilpin and Christopher Wright, *Scientists and National Policy-Making* (New York: Columbia University Press, 1964). See also Amitai Etzioni, "National Guidance of Science," in *The Moon-Doggle* (Garden City, N.Y.: Doubleday & Co., 1964), pp. 42-70.

of sociological manpower is directly affected by the advantage of required courses, which as a rule include theory and research techniques over optional courses; by Ph.D. committees that approve and encourage some subjects and discourage others; by foundations and federal agencies—which we advise—who support some subjects to the neglect of others; and by space awarded in our journals, as well as attention granted at regional and national professional meetings, to some subjects over others. All these are occasions where theory and methodology are celebrated while social analysis is given, at best, second-class citizenship.

The institutions of sociology are lagging in this matter far behind many leading sociologists. Our journals are a case in point. They are the major windows through which, month after month, we display our hardware before prospective clients, competitive stores, and one another. Even a brief perusal of the *American Sociological Review* and the *American Journal of Sociology* of the last decades will show that theoretical and methodologically oriented articles are predominant; social analysis is little dealt with. Not that sociologists have not written outstanding essays on the issues of the day, without using them to redefine concepts or demonstrate correlations. But these essays did not find their way into our professional journals. Thus Parsons' article on McCarthyism was published in the *Yale Review;* Riesman's "Abundance for What?" in the *Bulletin of the Atomic Scientists;* Gans's studies of our urban problems in *Commentary;* Shils's insights into the role of intellectuals in new nations appeared in *World Politics;* Merton's classic "The Self-fulfilling Prophecy" in *The Antioch Review;* etc., etc.

One might ask, are not these journals precisely the place where such articles ought to be presented? Is it not the function of publication in these journals to bring sociology to the attention of well-educated segments of society? While this is of course true, the almost exclusive publication of such articles in lay journals puts them in danger of being lost to sociological tradition and training. They are not readily available to most members of our profession and are not easily encountered by new students or members of other disciplines who skim our journals. Nor are the disciplinary problems raised by these essays systematically explored; in short, they are only indirectly a part of sociology, rather than in the front row.[7]

Probably the loyal sociologist will find it hard to accept, as I do, that our discipline devotes less energy, time, and means to social analysis than do other social sciences. Industrial development, for instance, is a major preoccupation of economists, while sociologists, who have at least as much to contribute to this field, have devoted comparatively little atten-

---

[7]My practical suggestion is that some space in our journals be given to social analysis essays; there is really no danger that the nonprofessional publications will be deprived. Similarly, social analysis books written by sociologists (or on subjects sociologists ought to write about) should be systematically reviewed, and review essays—dealing with the generic problems they raise—be invited.

tion to it. Similarly, psychologists have made major contributions to the study of war and peace (see for instance the work of Charles Osgood, the recent president of the American Psychological Association). We have at least as much to give this vital area as our colleagues in psychology, but here again we have given little.[8]

Finally, sociological scientism is revealed in the aloof attitude toward social action of many members of our profession. This is a severe case of elephantiasis in which the professional role of the sociologist has made deep inroads into his role as a member of the educated elite of the community. This is not just a question of being a bad citizen but of not living up to a special social obligation we have as persons who know society expertly.

To indicate more clearly what I have in mind, let me point to another helpful (for social as well as sociological analysis) term, that of role pairs. Role pairs are roles which appear frequently together in a society, in the sense that they are carried out by one and the same actor. The importance of such combinations is that they provide the most effective means of communication known between two roles—personal union. They also allow economy of resources, such as that found in the housewife-mother pair, security and elevator-boy combination, teacher-researcher, doctor-medical professor, etc.

The role pair of sociologist-intellectual is a particularly effective one. Not that all sociologists were ever intellectuals or vice versa, but there seems to have been a much higher degree of overlap in earlier generations. The growing tendency to disassociate the two roles is particularly regrettable because the virtue of such role combination is greater now than it used to be in the days when it was more common, for now we command a body of theory and methodology as well as a store of validated knowledge about man-in-society which can provide much-needed background for speculation about society.[9] The social analysis of Daniel Bell, Lewis Coser, Nathan Glazer, David Riesman, Dennis Wrong, and other contemporary sociologists who fill this role pair is much more hard-headed, soundly based, and politically sophisticated than that provided by earlier generations of social analysts or by their former college mates who majored in English literature and still interpret the American scene

---

[8]Marvin B. Sussman, "The Social Problems of the Sociologist," *Social Problems*, Vol. XI (Winter, 1964), pp. 215-25.

[9]For discussion, from various perspectives, of how the role pair of sociologist and social analyst operates, or fails to operate, see Alvin W. Gouldner, "The Myth of a Value-free Sociology," *Social Problems*, Vol. IX (Winter, 1962), pp. 199-213; and Alfred R. Lindesmith, "Social Problems and Sociology Theory," *Social Problems*, Vol. VIII (Fall, 1960), pp. 98-101.

For discussion of how the two roles inform one another, see Robert K. Merton, "Social Problems and Sociological Theory," in Merton and Robert A. Nisbet (eds.), *Contemporary Social Problems* (New York: Harcourt, Brace & World, Inc., 1961), pp. 697-737, and Robert K. Merton, *Mass Persuasion* (New York: Harper & Bros., 1946), pp. 185-89.

in the light of moods revealed in *Moby Dick* or "understand" the Soviet Union because they suffered with Dostoevsky and Pasternak.

As a discipline, however, we do not encourage, or at least do not train for, the sociologist-social-commentator pairing of roles. In earlier days the clergy and radical movements provided the sparks that fused sociological training with social concern. Today, in the age of specialization, more and more sociologists feel that what is proper behavior in their role as scientists is the proper behavior in their community role as well; the only way they face a social problem is through the lenses of theory and methodology. Civil defense, for example, becomes a subject for a study of attitudes ("people who fear war more are also more in favor of fallout shelters") or an occasion to try out a new computer program in mass dynamics.[10] The sociologist's scientific role is pre-empting time, energy, and resources that belong to his role as intellectual, as one who is committed to societal issues and expresses his concern about them more effectively than other observers since he knows more than they about the society he is commenting upon. Thus he not only is against nuclear war, but applies his knowledge of society to understand why nations become inflexible in the face of such a danger and freeze rather than act, and shares his analysis with those who seek to reduce the danger through political action but lack the benefits of the sociologist's training and expertise.

Social analysts are, in essence, those trained to apply the tools and findings of sociology to society, a task now left to outsiders, neither trained nor equipped to crack our codes, or to insiders with little systematic training in the methods of application in general and of social analysis in particular.

---

[10]Robert S. Lynd, *Knowledge for What?* (Princeton, N.J.: Princeton University Press, 1939); and Peter L. Berger, *Invitation to Sociology* (Garden City, N.Y.: Doubleday & Co., 1963), esp. chap. IV.

THE LIFE AND DEATH OF PROJECT CAMELOT*

Irving Louis Horowitz

IN JUNE of this year—in the midst of the crisis over the Dominican Republic—the United States Ambassador to Chile sent an urgent and angry cable to the State Department. Ambassador Ralph Dungan was confronted with a growing outburst of anti-Americanism from Chilean newspapers and intellectuals. Further, left-wing members of the Chilean Senate had accused the United States of espionage .

The anti-American attacks that agitated Dungan had no direct connection with sending U.S. troops to Santo Domingo. Their target was a mysterious and cloudy American research program called Project Camelot.

Dungan wanted to know from the State Department what Project Camelot was all about. Further, whatever Camelot was, he wanted it stopped because it was fast becoming a *cause célèbre* in Chile (as it soon would throughout capitals of Latin American and in Washington) and Dungan had not been told anything about it—even though it was sponsored by the U.S. Army and involved the tinderbox subjects of counter-revolution and counter-insurgency in Latin America.

Within a few weeks Project Camelot created repercussions from Capitol Hill to the White House. Senator J. William Fulbright, chairman of the Foreign Relations Committee, registered his personal concern about such projects as Camelot because of their "reactionary, backward-looking policy opposed to change. Implicit in Camelot, as in the concept of 'counter-insurgency,' is an assumption that revolutionary movements are dangerous to the interests of the United States and that the United States must be prepared to assist, if not actually to participate in, measures to repress them."

By mid-June the State Department and Defense Department—which had created and funded Camelot—were in open contention over the project and the jurisdiction each department should have over certain foreign policy operations.

On July 8, Project Camelot was killed by Defense Secretary Robert McNamara's office which has a veto power over the military budget. The decision had been made under the President's direction.

*Reprinted with permission from *Trans-action*, Vol. 3, No. 1 (November/December, 1965), a publication of the Community Leadership Project, Washington University, St. Louis, Mo.

On that same day, the director of Camelot's parent body, the Special Operations Research Organization, told a Congressional committee that the research project on revolution and counter-insurgency had taken its name from King Arthur's mythical domain because "It connotes the right sort of things—development of a stable society with peace and justice for all." Whatever Camelot's outcome, there should be no mistaking the deep sincerity behind this appeal for an applied social science pertinent to current policy.

However, Camelot left a horizon of disarray in its wake: an open dispute between State and Defense; fuel for the anti-American fires in Latin America; a cut in U.S. Army research appropriations. In addition, serious and perhaps ominous implications for social science research, bordering on censorship, have been raised by the heated reaction of the executive branch of government.

GLOBAL COUNTER-INSURGENCY

What was Project Camelot? Basically, it was a project for measuring and forecasting the causes of revolutions and insurgency in underdeveloped areas of the world. It also aimed to find ways of eliminating the causes, or coping with the revolutions and insurgencies. Camelot was sponsored by the U.S. Army on a four to six million dollar contract, spaced out over three to four years, with the Special Operations Research Organization (SORO). This agency is nominally under the aegis of American University in Washington, D.C., and does a variety of research for the Army. This includes making analytical surveys of foreign areas; keeping up-to-date information on the military, political, and social complexes of those areas; and maintaining a "rapid response" file for getting immediate information, upon Army request, on any situation deemed militarily important.

Latin America was the first area chosen for concentrated study, but countries on Camelot's four-year list included some in Asia, Africa, and Europe. In a working paper issued on December 5, 1964, at the request of the Office of the Chief of Research and Development, Department of the Army, it was recommended that "comparative historical studies" be made in these countries:

Latin America. Argentina, Bolivia, Brazil, Colombia, Cuba, Dominican Republic, El Salvador, Guatemala, Mexico, Paraguay, Peru, Venezuela.

Middle East. Egypt, Iran, Turkey.

Far East. Korea, Indonesia, Malaysia, Thailand.

Others. France, Greece, Nigeria.

"Survey research and other field studies" were recommended for Bolivia, Colombia, Ecuador, Paraguay, Peru, Venezuela, Iran, Thailand. Preliminary consideration was also being given to a study of the separatist movement in French Canada. It, too, had a code name: Project Revolt.

In a recruiting letter sent to selected scholars all over the world at the end of 1964, Project Camelot's aims were defined as a study to "make it possible to predict and influence politically significant aspects of social change in the developing nations of the world." This would include devising procedures for "assessing the potential for internal war within national societies" and "identify(ing) with increased degrees of confidence, those actions which a government might take to relieve conditions which are assessed as giving rise to a potential for internal war." The letter further stated:

> The U.S. Army has an important mission in the positive and constructive aspects of nation-building in less developed countries as well as a responsibility to assist friendly governments in dealing with active insurgency problems.

Such activities by the U.S. Army were described as "insurgency prophylaxis" rather than the "sometimes misleading label of counter-insurgency."

Project Camelot was conceived in late 1963 by a group of high ranking Army officers connected with the Army Research Office of the Department of Defense. They were concerned about new types of warfare springing up around the world. Revolutions in Cuba and Yemen and insurgency movements in Vietnam and the Congo were a far cry from the battles of World War II and also different from the envisioned—and planned for—apocalypse of nuclear war. For the first time in modern warfare, military establishments were not in a position to use the immense arsenals at their disposal—but were, instead, compelled by force of a geopolitical stalemate to increasingly engage in primitive forms of armed combat. The questions of moment for the Army were: Why can't the "hardware" be used? And what alternatives can social science "software" provide?

A well-known Latin American area specialist, Rex Hopper, was chosen as director of Project Camelot. Hopper was a professor of sociology and chairman of the department at Brooklyn College. He had been to Latin America many times over a thirty-year span on research projects and lecture tours, including some under government sponsorship. He was highly recommended for the position by his professional associates in Washington and elsewhere. Hopper had a long-standing interest in problems of revolution and saw in this multi-million dollar contract the possible realization of a life-long scientific ambition.

THE CHILEAN DEBACLE

How did this social science research project create a foreign policy furor? And, at another level, how did such high intentions result in so disastrous an outcome?

The answers involve a network spreading from a professor of anthropology at the University of Pittsburgh, to a professor of sociology at the

University of Oslo, and yet a third professor of sociology at the University of Chile in Santiago, Chile. The "showdown" took place in Chile, first within the confines of the university, next on the floor of the Chilean Senate, then in the popular press of Santiago, and finally, behind U.S. embassy walls.

It was ironic that Chile was the scene of wild newspaper tales of spying and academic outrage at scholars being recruited for "spying missions." For the working papers of Project Camelot stipulated as a criterion for study that a country "should show promise of high pay-offs in terms of the kinds of data required." Chile did not meet these requirements—it is not on the preliminary list of nations specified as prospects.

How then did Chile become involved in Project Camelot's affairs? The answer requires consideration of the position of Hugo G. Nutini, assistant professor of anthropology at Pittsburgh, citizen of the United States and former citizen of Chile. His presence in Santiago as a self-identified Camelot representative triggered the climactic chain of events.

Nutini, who inquired about an appointment in Camelot's beginning stages, never was given a regular Camelot appointment. Because he was planning a trip to Chile in April of this year—on other academic business—he was asked to prepare a report concerning possibilities of cooperation from Chilean scholars. In general, it was the kind of survey which has mild results and a modest honorarium attached to it (Nutini was offered $750). But Nutini had an obviously different notion of his role. Despite the limitations and precautions which Rex Hopper placed on his trip, especially Hopper's insistence on its informal nature, Nutini managed to convey the impression of being an official of Project Camelot with the authority to make proposals to prospective Chilean participants. Here was an opportunity to link the country of his birth with the country of his choice.

At about the same time, Johan Galtung, a Norwegian sociologist famous for his research on conflict and conflict resolution in underdeveloped areas, especially in Latin America, entered the picture. Galtung, who was in Chile at the time and associated with the Latin American Faculty of Social Science (FLACSO), received an invitation to participate in a Camelot planning conference scheduled for Washington, D.C., in August 1965. The fee to social scientists attending the conference would be $2,000 for four weeks. Galtung turned down the invitation. He gave several reasons. He could not accept the role of the U.S. Army as a sponsoring agent in a study of counter-insurgency. He could not accept the notion of the Army as an agency of national development; he saw the Army as managing conflict and even promoting conflict. Finally, he could not accept the asymmetry of the project—he found it difficult to understand why there would be studies of counter-insurgency in Latin-America, but no studies of "counter-intervention" (conditions under which Latin American nations might intervene in the affairs of the United States). Galtung was also deeply concerned about the possibility of European scholars being frozen out of Latin American studies by a inundation of sociologists from the United States. Furthermore, he expressed fears that the scale of Camelot honoraria would completely destroy the social science labor market in Latin America.

Galtung had spoken to others in Oslo, Santiago, and throughout Latin America about the project, and he had shown the memorandum of December, 1964, to many of his colleagues.

Soon after Nutini arrived in Santiago, he had a conference with Vice-Chancellor Alvaro Bunster of the University of Chile to discuss the character of Project Camelot. Their second meeting, arranged by the vice-chancellor, was also attended by Professor Eduardo Fuenzalida, a sociologist. After a half-hour of exposition by Nutini, Fuenzalida asked him point-blank to specify the ultimate aims of the project, its sponsors, and its military implications. Before Nutini could reply, Professor Fuenzalida, apparently with some drama, pulled a copy of the December 4 circular letter from his briefcase and read a prepared Spanish translation. Simultaneously, the authorities at FLACSO turned over the matter to their associates in the Chilean Senate and in the left-wing Chilean press.

In Washington, under the political pressures of State Department officials and Congressional reaction, Project Camelot was halted in midstream, or more precisely, before it ever really got under way. When the ambassador's communication reached Washington, there was already considerable official ferment about Project Camelot. Senators Fulbright, Morse, and McCarthy soon asked for hearings by the Senate Foreign Relations Committee. Only an agreement between Secretary of Defense McNamara and Secretary of State Rusk to settle their differences on future overseas research projects forestalled Senate action. But in the House of Representatives, a hearing was conducted by the Foreign Affairs Committee on July 8. The SORO director, Theodore Vallance, was questioned by committee members on the worth of Camelot and the matter of military intrusion into foreign policy areas.

That morning, even before Vallance was sworn in as a witness—and without his knowledge—the Defense Department issued a terse announcement terminating Project Camelot. President Johnson had decided the issue in favor of the State Department. In a memo to Secretary Rusk on August 5 the President stipulated that "no government sponsorship of foreign area research should be undertaken which in the judgment of the Secretary of State would adversely affect United States foreign relations."

The State Department has recently established machinery to screen and judge all federally-financed research projects overseas. The policy and research consequences of the Presidential directive will be discussed later.

What effect will the cancellation of Camelot have on the continuing rivalry between Defense and State departments for primacy in foreign policy? How will government sponsorship of future social science research be affected? And was Project Camelot a scholarly protective cover for U.S. Army planning—or a legitimate research operation on a valid research subject independent of sponsorship?

Let us begin with a collective self-portrait of Camelot as the social scientists who directed the project perceived it. There seems to be general consensus on seven points.

First, the men who went to work for Camelot felt the needs for a large-scale, "big picture" project in social science. They wanted to create a sociology of contemporary relevance which would not suffer from the parochial narrowness of vision to which their own professional backgrounds had generally conditioned them. Most of the men viewed Camelot as a bona fide opportunity to do fundamental research with relatively unlimited funds at their disposal. (No social science project ever before had up to $6,000,000 available.) Under such optimal conditions, these scholars tended not to look a gift horse in the mouth. As one of them put it, there was no desire to inquire too deeply as to the source of the funds or the ultimate purpose of the project.

Second, most social scientists affiliated with Camelot felt that there was actually more freedom to do fundamental research under military sponsorship than at a university or college. One man noted that during the 1950's there was far more freedom to do fundamental research in the RAND corporation (an Air Force research organization) than on any campus in America. Indeed, once the protective covering of RAND was adopted, it was almost viewed as a society of Platonist elites or "knowers" permitted to search for truth on behalf of the powerful. In a neoplatonic definition of their situation, the Camelot men hoped that their ideas would be taken seriously by the wielders of power (although, conversely, they were convinced that the armed forces would not accept their preliminary recommendations).

Third, many of the Camelot associates felt distinctly uncomfortable with military sponsorship, especially given the present United States military posture. But their reaction to this discomfort was that "the Army has to be educated." This view was sometimes cast in Freudian terms: the Army's bent toward violence ought to be sublimated. Underlying this theme was the notion of the armed forces as an agency for potential social good—the discipline and the order embodied by an army could be channeled into the process of economic and social development in the United States as well as in Latin America.

Fourth, there was a profound conviction in the perfectibility of mankind; particularly in the possibility of the military establishment performing a major role in the general process of growth. They sought to correct the intellectual paternalism and parochialism under which Pentagon generals, State Department diplomats, and Defense Department planners seemed to operate.

Fifth, a major long-range purpose of Camelot, at least for some of its policy-makers, was to prevent another revolutionary holocaust on a grand scale, such as occurred in Cuba. At the very least, there was a shared belief that *Pax Americana* was severely threatened and its future could be bolstered.

Sixth, none of them viewed their role on the project as spying for the United States government, or for anyone else.

Seventh, the men on Project Camelot felt that they made heavy sacrifices for social science. Their personal and professional risks were much higher than those taken by university academics. Government work, while well compensated, remains professionally marginal. It can be terminated abruptly (as indeed was the case) and its project directors are subject to a public scrutiny not customary behind the walls of ivy.

In the main, there was perhaps a keener desire on the part of the directing members of Camelot not to "sell out" than there is among social scientists with regular academic appointments. This concern with the ethics of social science research seemed to be due largely to daily confrontation of the problems of betrayal, treason, secrecy, and abuse of data, in a critical situation. In contrast, even though a university position may be created by federally-sponsored research, the connection with policy matters is often too remote to cause any *crise de conscience*.

THE INSIDERS REPORT

Were the men on Camelot critical of any aspects of the project?

Some had doubts from the outset about the character of the work they would be doing, and about the conditions under which it would be done. It was pointed out, for example, that the U.S. Army tends to exercise a far more stringent intellectual control of research findings than does the U.S. Air Force. As evidence for this, it was stated that SORO generally had fewer "free-wheeling" aspects to its research designs than did RAND (the Air Force-supported research organization). One critic inside SORO went so far as to say that he knew of no SORO research which had a "playful" or unregimented quality, such as one finds at RAND (where for example, computers are used to plan invasions but also to play chess). One staff member said that "the self-conscious seriousness gets to you after a while." "It was all grim stuff," said another.

Another line of criticism was that pressures on the "reformers" (as the men engaged in Camelot research spoke of themselves) to come up with ideas were much stronger than the pressures on the military to actually bring off any policy changes recommended. The social scientists were expected to be social reformers, while the military adjutants were expected to be conservative. It was further felt that the relationship between sponsors and researchers was not one of equals, but rather one of superordinate military needs and subordinate academic roles. On the other hand, some officials were impressed by the disinterestedness of the military, and thought that far from exercising undue influence, the Army personnel were loath to offer opinions.

Another objection was that if one had to work on policy matters—if research is to have international ramifications—it might better be conducted under conventional State Department sponsorship. "After all," one man said, "they are at least nominally committed to civilian political norms." In other words, there was a considerable reluctance to believe that the Defense Department, despite its superior organization, greater financial affluence, and executive influence, would actually improve upon State Department styles of work, or accept recommendations at variance with Pentagon policies.

There seemed to be few, if any, expressions of disrespect for the intrinsic merit of the work contemplated by Camelot, or of disdain for policy-oriented work in general. The scholars engaged in the Camelot effort used two distinct vocabularies. The various Camelot documents reveal a military vocabulary provided with an array of military justifications; often followed (within the same document) by a social science vocabulary offering social science justifications and rationalizations. The dilemma in the Camelot literature from the preliminary report issued in August 1964 until the more advanced document issued in April 1965, is the same: an incomplete amalgamation of the military and sociological vocabularies. (At an early date the project had the code name SPEARPOINT.)

POLICY CONFLICTS OVER CAMELOT

The directors of SORO are concerned that the cancellation of Camelot might mean the end of SORO as well in a wholesale slash of research funds. For while over $1,000,000 was allotted to Camelot each year, the annual budget of SORO, its parent organization, is a good deal less. Although no such action has taken place, SORO's future is being examined. For example, the Senate and House Appropriations Committee blocked a move by the Army to transfer unused Camelot funds to SORO.

However, the end of Project Camelot does not necessarily imply the end of the Special Operations Research Office, nor does it imply an end to research designs which are similar in character to Project Camelot. In fact, the termination of the contract does not even imply an intellectual change of heart on the part of the originating sponsors or key figures of the project.

One of the characteristics of Project Camelot was the number of antagonistic forces it set in motion on grounds of strategy and timing rather than from what may be called considerations of scientific principles.

The State Department grounded its opposition to Camelot on the basis of the ultimate authority it has in the area of foreign affairs. There is no published report showing serious criticism of the projected research itself.

Congressional opposition seemed to be generated by a concern not to rock any foreign alliances, especially in Latin America. Again, there was no statement about the project's scientific or intellectual grounds.

A third group of skeptics, academic social scientists, generally thought that Project Camelot, and studies of the processes of revolution and war in general, were better left in the control of major university centers, and in this way, kept free of direct military supervision.

The Army, creator of the project, did nothing to contradict McNamara's order cancelling Project Camelot. Army influentials did not only feel that they had to execute the Defense Department's orders, but they are traditionally dubious of the value of "software" research to support "hardware" systems.

Let us take a closer look at each of these groups which voiced opposition to Project Camelot. A number of issues did not so much hinge upon, as swim about, Project Camelot. In particular, the "jurisdictional" dispute between Defense and State loomed largest.

State vs. Defense. In substance, the debate between the Defense Department and the State Department is not unlike that between electricians and bricklayers in the construction of a new apartment house. What "union" is responsible for which processes? Less generously, the issue is: who controls what? At the policy level, Camelot was a tool tossed about in a larger power struggle which has been going on in government circles since the end of World War II, when the Defense Department emerged as a competitor for honors as the most powerful bureau of the administrative branch of government.

In some sense, the divisions between Defense and State are outcomes of the rise of ambiguous conflicts such as Korea and Vietnam, in contrast to the more precise and diplomatically controlled "classical" world wars. What are the lines dividing political policy from military posture? Who is the most important representative of the United States abroad: the ambassador or the military attaché in charge of the military mission? When soldiers from foreign lands are sent to the United States for political orientation, should such orientation be within the province of the State Department or of the Defense Department? When undercover activities are conducted, should the direction of such activities belong to military or political authorities? Each of these is a strategic question with little pragmatic or historic precedent. Each of these was entwined in the Project Camelot explosion.

It should be plain therefore that the State Department was not simply responding to the recommendations of Chilean left-wingers in urging the cancellation of Camelot. It merely employed the Chilean hostility to "interventionist" projects as an opportunity to redefine the balance of forces and power with the Defense Department. What is clear from this resistance to such projects is not so much a defense of the sovereignty of the nations where ambassadors are stationed, as it is a contention that con-

ventional political channels are sufficient to yield the information desired
or deemed necessary.

Congress. In the main, congressional reaction seems to be that Project
Camelot was bad because it rocked the diplomatic boat in a sensitive
area. Underlying most congressional criticisms is the plain fact that most
congressmen are more sympathetic to State Department control of foreign affairs than they are to Defense Department control. In other words,
despite military sponsored world junkets, National Guard and State Guard
pressures from the home State, and military training in the backgrounds
of many congressmen, the sentiment for political rather than military
control is greater. In addition, there is a mounting suspicion in Congress
of varying kinds of behavioral science research stemming from hearings
into such matters as wire-tapping, uses of lie detectors, and truth-in-pack-
aging.

Social Scientists. One reason for the violent response to Project Camelot, especially among Latin American scholars, is its sponsorship by the
Department of Defense. The fact is that Latin Americans have become
quite accustomed to State Department involvements in the internal affairs of various nations. The Defense Department is a newcomer, a dangerous one, inside the Latin American orbit. The train of thought connected to its activities is in terms of international warfare, spying missions,
military manipulations, etc. The State Department, for its part, is often a
consultative party to shifts in government, and has played an enormous
part in either fending off or bringing about *coups d'état.* This State Department role has by now been accepted and even taken for granted.
Not so the Defense Department's role. But it is interesting to conjecture
on how matter-of-factly Camelot might have been accepted if it had
State Department sponsorship.

Social scientists in the United States have, for the most part, been publicly silent on the matter of Camelot. The reasons for this are not hard to
find. First, many "giants of the field" are involved in government contract
work in one capacity or another. And few souls are in a position to tamper
with the gods. Second, most information on Project Camelot has thus far
been of a newspaper variety; and professional men are not in a habit of
criticizing colleagues on the basis of such information. Third, many social
scientists doubtless see nothing wrong or immoral in the Project Camelot
designs. And they are therefore more likely to be either confused or angered at the Latin American response than at the directors of Project
Camelot. (At the time of the blowup, Camelot people spoke about the
"Chilean mess" rather than the "Camelot mess.")

The directors of Project Camelot did not "classify" research materials,
so that there would be no stigma of secrecy. And they also tried to hire,
and even hired away from academic positions, people well known and
respected for their independence of mind. The difficulty is that even
though the stigma of secrecy was formally erased, it remained in the

attitudes of many of the employees and would-be employees of Project Camelot. They unfortunately thought in terms of secrecy, clearance, missions, and the rest of the professional nonsense that so powerfully afflicts the Washington scientific as well as political ambience.

Further, it is apparent that Project Camelot had much greater difficulty hiring a full-time staff of high professional competence, than in getting part-time, summertime, weekend, and sundry assistance. Few established figures in academic life were willing to surrender the advantages of their positions for the risks of the project.

One of the cloudiest aspects to Project Camelot is the role of American University. Its actual supervision of the contract appears to have begun and ended with the 25 percent overhead on those parts of the contract that a university receives on most federal grants. Thus, while there can be no question as to the "concern and disappointment" of President Hurst R. Anderson of the American University over the demise of Project Camelot, the reasons for this regret do not seem to extend beyond the formal and the financial. No official at American University appears to have been willing to make any statement of responsibility, support, chagrin, opposition, or anything else related to the project. The issues are indeed momentous, and must be faced by all universities at which government sponsored research is conducted: the amount of control a university has over contract work; the role of university officials in the distribution of funds from grants; the relationships that ought to be established once a grant is issued. There is also a major question concerning project directors: are they members of the faculty, and if so, do they have necessary teaching responsibilities and opportunities for tenure as do other faculty members.

The difficulty with American University is that it seems to be remarkably unlike other universities in its permissiveness. The Special Operations Research Office received neither guidance nor support from university officials. From the outset, there seems to have been a "gentleman's agreement" not to inquire or interfere in Project Camelot, but simply to serve as some sort of camouflage. If American University were genuinely autonomous it might have been able to lend highly supportive aid to Project Camelot during the crisis months. As it is, American University maintained an official silence which preserved it from more congressional or executive criticism. This points up some serious flaws in its administrative and financial policies.

The relationship of Camelot to SORO represented a similarly muddled organizational picture. The director of Project Camelot was nominally autonomous and in charge of an organization surpassing in size and importance the overall SORO operation. Yet at the critical point the organizational blueprint served to protect SORO and sacrifice what nominally was its limb. That Camelot happened to be a vital organ may have hurt, especially when Congress blocked the transfer of unused Camelot funds to SORO.

Military. Military reaction to the cancellation of Camelot varied. It should be borne in mind that expenditures on Camelot were minimal in the Army's overall budget and most military leaders are skeptical, to begin with, about the worth of social science research. So there was no open protest about the demise of Camelot. Those officers who have a positive attitude toward social science materials, or are themselves trained in the social sciences, were dismayed. Some had hoped to find "software" alternatives to the "hardware systems" approach applied by the Secretary of Defense to every military-political contingency. These officers saw the attack on Camelot as a double attack—on their role as officers and on their professional standards. But the Army was so clearly treading in new waters that it could scarcely jeopardize the entire structure of military research to preserve one project. This very inability or impotence to preserve Camelot—a situation threatening to other governmental contracts with social scientists—no doubt impressed many armed forces officers.

The claim is made by the Camelot staff (and various military aides) that the critics of the project played into the hands of those sections of the military predisposed to veto any social science recommendations. Then why did the military offer such a huge support to a social science project to begin with? Because $6,000,000 is actually a trifling sum for the Army in an age of multi-billion dollar military establishment. The amount is significantly more important for the social sciences, where such contract awards remain relatively scarce. Thus, there were differing perspectives of the importance of Camelot: an Army view which considered the contract as one of several forms of "software" investment; a social science perception of Project Camelot as the equivalent of the Manhattan Project.

WAS PROJECT CAMELOT WORKABLE?

While most public opposition to Project Camelot focused on its strategy and timing, a considerable amount of private opposition centered on more basic, though theoretical, questions: was Camelot scientifically feasible and ethically correct? No public document or statement contested the possibility that, given the successful completion of the data gathering, Camelot could have, indeed, established basic criteria for measuring the level and potential for internal war in a given nation. Thus, by never challenging the feasibility of the work, the political critics of Project Camelot were providing back-handed compliments to the efficacy of the project.

But much more than political considerations are involved. It is clear that some of the most critical problems presented by Project Camelot are scientific. Although for an extensive analysis of Camelot, the reader would, in fairness, have to be familiar with all of its documents, salient general criticisms can be made without a full reading.

The research design of Camelot was from the outset plagued by ambiguities. It was never quite settled whether the purpose was to study counter-insurgency possibilities, or the revolutionary process. Similarly, it was difficult to determine whether it was to be a study of comparative social structures, a set of case studies of single nations "in depth," or a study of social structure with particular emphasis on the military. In addition, there was a lack of treatment of what indicators were to be used, and whether a given social system in Nation A could be as stable in Nation B.

In one Camelot document there is a general critique of social science for failing to deal with social conflict and social control. While this in itself is admirable, the tenor and context of Camelot's documents make it plain that a "stable society" is considered the norm no less than the desired outcome. The "breakdown of social order" is spoken of accusatively. Stabilizing agencies in developing areas are presumed to be absent. There is no critique of U.S. Army policy in developing areas because the Army is presumed to be a stabilizing agency. The research formulations always assume the legitimacy of Army tasks—"if the U.S. Army is to perform effectively its parts in the U.S. mission of counter-insurgency it must recognize that insurgency represents a breakdown of social order. . . ." But such a proposition has never been doubted—by Army officials or anyone else. The issue is whether such breakdowns are in the nature of the existing system or a product of conspiratorial movements.

The use of hygienic language disguises the anti-revolutionary assumptions under a cloud of powder puff declarations. For example, studies of Paraguay are recommended "because trends in this situation (the Stroessner regime) may also render it 'unique' when analyzed in terms of the transition from 'dictatorship' to political stability." But to speak about changes from dictatorship to stability is an obvious ruse. In this case, it is a tactic to disguise the fact that Paraguay is one of the most vicious, undemocratic (and like most dictatorships, stable) societies in the Western Hemisphere.

These typify the sort of hygienic sociological premises that do not have scientific purposes. They illustrate the confusion of commitments within Project Camelot. Indeed the very absence of emotive words such as revolutionary masses, communism, socialism, and capitalism only serves to intensify the discomfort one must feel on examination of the documents—since the abstract vocabulary disguises, rather than resolves, the problems of international revolution. To have used clearly political rather than military language would not "justify" governmental support. Furthermore, shabby assumptions of academic conventionalism replaced innovative orientations. By adopting a systems approach, the problematic, open-ended aspects of the study of revolutions were largely omitted; and the design of the study became an oppressive curb on the study of the problems inspected.

This points up a critical implication for Camelot (as well as other projects). The importance of the subject being researched does not *per se* determine the importance of the project. A sociology of large-scale relevance and reference is all to the good. It is important that scholars be willing to risk something of their shaky reputations in helping resolve major world social problems. But it is no less urgent that in the process of addressing major problems, the autonomous character of the social science disciplines—their own criteria of worthwhile scholarship—should not be abandoned. Project Camelot lost sight of this "autonomous" social science character.

It never seemed to occur to its personnel to inquire into the desirability for successful revolution. This is just as solid a line of inquiry as the one stressed—the conditions under which revolutionary movements will be able to overthrow a government. Furthermore, they seem not to have thought about inquiring into the role of the United States in these countries. This points up the lack of symmetry. The problem should have been phrased to include the study of "us" as well as "them." It is not possible to make a decent analysis of a situation unless one takes into account the role of all the different people and groups involved in it; and there was no room in the design for such contingency analysis.

In discussing the policy impact on a social science research project, we should not overlook the difference between "contract" work and "grants." Project Camelot commenced with the U.S. Army; that is to say, it was initiated for a practical purpose determined by the client. This differs markedly from the typical academic grant in that its sponsorship had "built-in" ends. The scholar usually *seeks* a grant; in this case the donor, the Army, promoted its own aims. In some measure, the hostility for Project Camelot may be an unconscious reflection of this distinction—a dim feeling that there was something "non-academic," and certainly not disinterested, about Project Camelot, irrespective of the quality of the scholars associated with it.

THE ETHICS OF POLICY RESEARCH

The issue of "scientific rights" versus "social myths" is perennial. Some maintain that the scientist ought not penetrate beyond legally or morally sanctioned limits and others argue that such limits cannot exist for science. In treading on the sensitive issue of national sovereignty, Project Camelot reflects the generalized dilemma. In deference to intelligent researchers, in recognition of them as scholars, they should have been invited by Camelot to air their misgivings and qualms about government (and especially Army sponsored) research—to declare their moral conscience. Instead, they were mistakenly approached as skillful, useful potential employees of a higher body, subject to an authority higher than their scientific calling.

What is central is not the political motives of the sponsor. For social scientists were not being enlisted in an intelligence system for "spying" purposes. But given their professional standing, their great sense of intellectual honor and pride, they could not be "employed" without proper deference for their stature. Professional authority should have prevailed from beginning to end with complete command of the right to thrash out the moral and political dilemmas as researchers saw them. The Army, however respectful and protective of free expression, was "hiring help" and not openly and honestly submitting a problem to the higher professional and scientific authority of social science.

The propriety of the Army to define and delimit all questions, which Camelot should have had a right to examine, was never placed in doubt. This is a tragic precedent; it reflects the arrogance of a consumer of intellectual merchandise. And this relationship of inequality corrupted the lines of authority, and profoundly limited the autonomy of the social scientists involved. It became clear that the social scientist savant was not so much functioning as an applied social scientist as he was supplying information to a powerful client.

The question of who sponsors research is not nearly so decisive as the question of ultimate use of such information. The sponsorship of a project, whether by the United States Army or by the Boy Scouts of America, is by itself neither good nor bad. Sponsorship is good or bad only insofar as the intended outcomes can be pre-determined and the parameters of those intended outcomes tailored to the sponsor's expectations. Those social scientists critical of the project never really denied its freedom and independence, but questioned instead the purpose and character of its intended results.

It would be a gross oversimplification, if not an outright error, to assume that the theoretical problems of Project Camelot derive from any reactionary character of the project designers. The director went far and wide to select a group of men for the advisory board, the core planning group, the summer study group, and the various conference groupings, who in fact were more liberal in their orientations than any random sampling of the sociological profession would likely turn up.

However, in nearly every page of the various working papers, there are assertions which clearly derive from American military policy objectives rather than scientific method. The steady assumption that internal warfare is damaging disregards the possibility that a government may not be in a position to take actions either to relieve or improve mass conditions, or that such actions as are contemplated may be more concerned with reducing conflict than with improving conditions. The added statements about the United States Army and its "important mission in the positive and constructive aspects of nation building . . ." assumes the reality of such a function in an utterly unquestioning and unconvincing form. The first rule of the scientific game is not to make assumptions about friends and enemies in such a way as to promote the use of different criteria for the former and the latter.

The story of Project Camelot was not a confrontation of good versus evil. Obviously, not all men behaved with equal fidelity or with equal civility. Some men were weaker than others, some more callous, and some more stupid. But all of this is extrinsic to the heart of the problem of Camelot: what are and are not the legitimate functions of a scientist?

In conclusion, two important points must be clearly kept in mind and clearly apart. First, Project Camelot was intellectually, and from my own perspective, ideologically unsound. However, and more significantly, Camelot was not cancelled because of its faulty intellectual approaches. Instead, its cancellation came as an act of government censorship, and an expression of the contempt for social science so prevalent among those who need it most. Thus it was political expedience, rather than its lack of scientific merit, that led to the demise of Camelot because it threatened to rock State Department relations with Latin America.

Second, giving the State Department the right to screen and approve government-funded social science research projects on other countries, as the President has ordered, is a supreme act of censorship. Among the agencies that grant funds for such research are the National Institutes of Mental Health, the National Science Foundation, the National Aeronautics and Space Agency, and the Office of Education. Why should the State Department have veto power over the scientific pursuits of men and projects funded by these and other agencies in order to satisfy the policy needs—or policy failures—of the moment? President Johnson's directive is a gross violation of the autonomous nature of science.

We must be careful not to allow social science projects with which we may vociferously disagree on political and ideological grounds to be decimated or dismantled by government fiat. Across the ideological divide is a common social science understanding that the contemporary expression of reason in politics today is applied social science, and that the cancellation of Camelot, however pleasing it may be on political grounds to advocates of a civilian solution to Latin American affairs, represents a decisive setback for social science research.

THE IDEOLOGY OF HEMISPHERIC MILITARISM

Irving Louis Horowitz

GENERATING analysis of Latin-American military establishments is made difficult by differences of opinion and contrasting stereotypes held by militarists and sociologists. The militarist often thinks the sociologist a kinsman to the socialist, while the sociologist often thinks the militarist some kind of intrinsic, purple-sashed reactionary. Like most stereotypes, these have some basis in truth. It is the case, particularly in underdeveloped areas, that the sociologist tends to be politically Left, and tends also to have a less than flattering view of the military. It is also true that the militarist oftentimes does perform right-wing roles, and tends to protect and save, rather than to advance or build. However, with the current availability of new analytic tools, the sociologist, whatever his values, is in a good position to examine problems of the military. Similarly, with the rise of a new type of military man, "the national redemptive type," the old stereotypes about militarists are becoming less accurate than formerly.

All policy-oriented social researchers, including myself, continue to struggle with the problem of making policy recommendations which, at the same time, are scientifically viable. In this connection the following analysis of Latin military affairs is made in an attempt to clear away the debris of inherited ideological notions inhibiting a meaningful tension between science and policy.

The most significant contribution a sociologist can now make to the study of military establishments in the Third or Neutralist World, especially in Latin America, is a close scrutiny of conventional arguments for the necessity of present military postures. Consider, for example, the typical arguments and rationalizations of high military aid:

Boomerang thesis: It is argued that if the United States does not supply arms to them, rulers will turn elsewhere for weaponry and we will have made enemies out of friends. This is the most frequently applied rhetoric, and, to the best of my knowledge, it has been openly challenged within government circles only by Senator Wayne Morse.[1]

The basic fallacy in the argument is that the command position of our nonmilitary assistance could easily curb any propensity to purchase

---

[1] See Wayne Morse, "Report on a Study Mission," (Report to the Committee on Foreign Relations, U.S. Senate), (Washington, D.C.: U.S. Government Printing Office, 1960).

Furthermore, it is not true that all Latin-American rulers are thirsting for additional arms. Over the past several years, Juscelino Kubitschek of Brazil, Jorge Alessandri of Chile, and Lleras Camargo of Colombia have made strong appeals to the United States to move more funds into economic development programs and less into military assistance programs. Thus, the boomerang argument is without support even among many of those whom it is intended to serve.

Bulwark thesis: It is argued that the Latin-American military is the best defense the United States has against communism. The argument has been put most recently and most forcefully by John J. Johnson,[3] who arms elsewhere—with penalty of forfeiture of all U.S. economic assistance.[2] maintains that without the military every government in the Latin-American orbit would be further to the left than it is now and the matter would be one of degree.

Ignoring the assumption that this resistance to any and all Left tendencies is a good thing, what real evidence is there for this statement? Very little; military tyrants such as Fulgencio Batista, Perez Godoy, Juan Perón, and Rafael Trujillo had little trouble with the communist Left. Nor did the Communists have difficulties with the military regime.[4] It is the noncommunist Left, men like Juan Bosch of the Dominican Republic and Miguel Arrais of Brazil, who most often suffer at the hands of the entrenched military. On the other hand, in Guatemala and in Chile the military stimulated Left tendencies as part of a Nasserist or Bonapartist ideology. Thus, the "bulwark" argument lacks weight, either as a policy or as a value.

Hemispheric thesis: It is argued that the arms supply and training of military cadres is part of the overall United States strategy for defense of the Western Hemisphere in the event of attack. This argument is now heard with increasing frequency.

However, since no Latin-American military establishment could withstand a major conventional invasion, much less a thermonuclear attack, it is plain that the military are being trained for internecine counterinsurgency attack. This is obvious from the types of armaments shipped to Latin America by the United States—portable weapons, flame throwers, defoliation hardware—and from the rise in ideological "training."[5] This

---

[2] This is the argument of two former State Department officials in their recent book on Latin America. See Karl M. Schmitt and David C. Burks, *Evolution or Chaos: Dynamics of Latin Government and Politics* (New York: Frederick A. Praeger, 1963), pp. 36-38.

[3] John J. Johnson, *The Military and Society in Latin America* (Stanford, Calif.: Stanford University Press, 1964), pp. 143-44. See also my critique of this position, "The Military of Latin America," *Economic Development and Cultural Change*, January, 1965, pp 238-42.

[4] Cf. Robert J. Alexander, *Communism and Latin America* (New Brunswick, N.J.: Rutgers University Press, 1957).

[5] Cf. Schmitt and Burks, *op.cit.*, p. 38; also see David Galula, *Counterinsurgency Warfare* (New York and London: Frederick A. Praeger, 1964).

makes the notion cherished by many hemispheric-minded government officials that the military can be uniformly relied upon as a stabilizing agency simply preposterous. The "hemispheric defense" argument is the old "spheres of influence" doctrine spruced up to meet the increasing amount of guerrilla activity.

Developmental thesis: It is argued that the military can perform all sorts of civic actions. The army, by virtue of its unique level of discipline and organization, can take part in essential projects for economic and social development—everything from public works to health and sanitation programs. A further aim of civic action is to counter claims that the army is by nature and function an antipopular instrument. "As the interdependence of civil and military matters is increasingly recognized, the social and economic welfare of the people can no longer be considered a non-military concern."[6]

Leaving aside the fact that such civic action often turns into anticivil action, into conspiratorial acts against legitimately constituted governments, there are other grounds for declaring this latest and most sophisticated approach pernicious as well as unrealistic. First, the costs of the military are exorbitant with respect to the minimal possible contribution they may make to the general welfare. Second, the character and structure of the conventional armed forces of Latin America make them peculiarly ill-suited, in size and training of the officer corps, in temperament of the enlisted men, and in the outlook of the entire military organization to perform legitimate economic roles. They are what they are by virtue of their political roles; it is difficult to understand why or how or under what compulsion they should become developmentally oriented. The myth of middle-class salvation has given way to the myth of military salvation. But as long as either sector remains unaltered structurally, the developmental hopes pinned on either force are pipe dreams. Finally, civic action and developmental programs have the effect of making the military more political and less professional in their concerns. To the extent that they become policy involved, they must become policy oriented. And this means a deepening cleavage between the Army and the people; between political and professional roles.[7]

It is clear that these four rationalizations for maintaining and expanding militarism in the hemisphere are differentially put forth. While each of the Latin-American military establishments might employ these theses to justify its own behavior, basically they represent supposed United

---

[6]See U.S. Department of Defense, "Civic Action: The Military Role in Nation-Building," in *Armed Forces Information and Education: For Commanders,* January 15, 1964, pp. 1-3.

[7]For a critical evaluation of the developmental thesis, see Mario H. Orsolini, *La Crisis Del Ejercito* (Buenos Aires: Ediciones Arayu, 1964); also see Morus Janowitz, *The Military in the Political Development of New Nations* (Chicago: University of Chicago Press, 1964).

States needs in the area. This, in itself, is the most decisive aspect of the present situation—the breakdown of neocolonialism and its replacement with colonialism of a more classic vintage. Simply put, the present turn to counterinsurgency as a style of politics marks a return to military solutions of economic problems, rather than to economic solutions of military problems.

The form of colonialism may be classical, but its content is quite new. Marxian notions concerning the economic bases of imperialism seem quite outmoded and far-fetched given the economic costs and penalties of the present military actions undertaken or underwritten by the United States, military actions with scant chance for an economic "payoff" even in the distant future. Thus, while the form of colonialism has gone back to an earlier model, the substance of this colonialism is political rather than economic.

In consequence, the age of Latin-American *coups d'etat* may very well have come to an end. They are no longer allowed to unfold naturally, because even the most conservative of them may have unanticipated political consequences unfavorable to the metropolitan center. What has taken place by increasing degrees is the external, foreign management of internal conflicts in Latin America.

The Organization and Ideology of Hemispheric Militarism

To be sure, conflicts are still likely to be generated by the internal conditions within each of the Latin-American states; but they can rarely, if ever, long remain local in character. The tendency is increasingly to transform local conflicts into international tests of power. Power *golpes* were shaped by *both* internal and external forces. National and imperial forces performed a vital service of mutual reinforcement in overthrowing the regimes of Perez Jimenez, Juan Perón, Fulgencio Batista, Manuel Odria, etc. But it was clearly understood that the external influence had self-imposed limits, that is, that the *internal* interests would be responsible for providing the "ideology" and the "organization" of the new system of government. With the rise of overall strategies on a grand scale, with the assertion that the basic purpose of American national policy is to promote and secure a structure of world relationships compatible with the values of the United States and the free world, such historic forms as local control, idiosyncratic regimes, and classical Latin strong men can no longer be considered compatible with our master plan for a *Pax Americana*.

This nation's emphasis on overall design has also led to a higher degree of planning and coordination of hemispheric military activities. Accordingly, chinks in the armor of design have become intolerable. The Dominican Republic obviously poses no threat to the United States or to the free world per se. It does threaten the *gestalt* of the grand design. And, after all, the much feared and much vaunted domino effect can take place only when there are those wishing to build complete stable edifices with a broken deck of cards.[8]

The decisive variable has become foreign, rather than domestic; it has become centralized power, rather than autonomous authority. Perhaps this is what Juan Bosch, the former president of the Dominican Republic, was thinking about when he poignantly said of the recent Dominican crisis: "This was a democratic revolution smashed by the leading democracy of the world, the United States. That is why I think my time is over. I belong to a world that has ended politically."[9]

The following ninefold chart will perhaps clarify the "external" characteristics of North American involvement in Latin America. The key item here is economic development.[10] Another way of stating this is that the doctrine which asserts the legitimacy of "limited war" also, and parenthetically, asserts the need for unlimited intervention. And it is here that the issue of colonialism and development is joined in its full fury.

Without wishing to indulge in philosophic debate over the nature of determinism or causality, it is evident from the social science perspective that some variables can explain a greater degree of variance than others. The political apparatus of sixteenth-century Italy and the economic foundations of eighteenth-century England are obvious cases in point. It is my belief that the military apparatus of twentieth-century civilization has the same kind of "deterministic" properties—though to be sure, like any system of determinants, it has its limits, and perhaps even its deficiencies, as an explanatory system. In my estimate, the current rise of military establishments in underdeveloped countries, as well as the vigorous pursuit of counterinsurgency techniques and weapons among the major powers, together represent a readiness to generate social and economic advances through military means rather than through conven-

---

[8]Much earlier than the occupation of the Dominican Republic, the Department of Defense issued a statement to President Leoni of Venezuela requesting permission for the installation of naval bases at two sites in Venezuela, Paria and Goajira. The statement illustrates the sort of global military determinism which is becoming increasingly standardized policy. "The grave fact that a considerable sector of the Armed Forces have been seduced by ideologies dangerous to the national interests of Venezuela compels us to look forward to that time in the future when our own forces will have to guarantee the defense of the country; in support of perhaps that weak and small sector of the military which has not succumbed to the seductive voices of oppositional sirens." (Department of Defense, Request to the Commander of the Venezuelan Navy to Install Naval Base, P-2, 16-2-65, Series 009, Printed in *March*, Vol. 26, No. 1248 [March 26, 1965], p. 15). In this same issue see Gregorio Selser, "El Pentágono conmina a Leoni."

[9]*New York Times*, May 8, 1965, p. 8.

[10]For the final design of this ninefold table, I am indebted to the work of Seymour J. Deitchman, whose model of a limited-war matrix is surprisingly parallel to my own attempts at linking modern nonnuclear war and the level of the developmental process. But given the priority of publication of Deitchman's book, no less than its formal precision, I have adopted his model, with some serious modifications. See *Limited War and American Defense Policy* (Cambridge: The M.I.T. Press, 1964), esp. pp. 103-7.

TYPES OF PHYSICAL ENVIRONMENT (E)

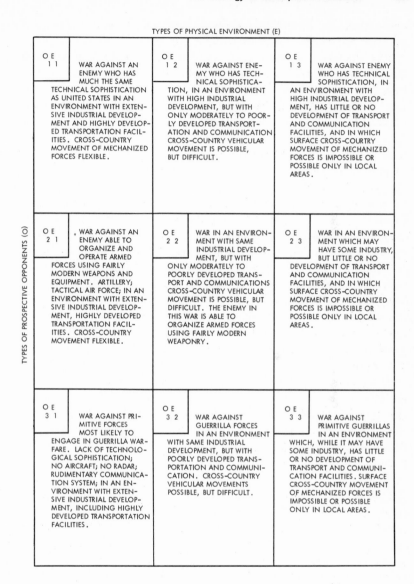

O E 1 1	WAR AGAINST AN ENEMY WHO HAS MUCH THE SAME TECHNICAL SOPHISTICATION AS UNITED STATES IN AN ENVIRONMENT WITH EXTENSIVE INDUSTRIAL DEVELOPMENT AND HIGHLY DEVELOPED TRANSPORTATION FACILITIES. CROSS-COUNTRY MOVEMENT OF MECHANIZED FORCES FLEXIBLE.	O E 1 2	WAR AGAINST ENEMY WHO HAS TECHNICAL SOPHISTICATION, IN AN ENVIRONMENT WITH HIGH INDUSTRIAL DEVELOPMENT, BUT WITH ONLY MODERATELY TO POORLY DEVELOPED TRANSPORTATION AND COMMUNICATION CROSS-COUNTRY VEHICULAR MOVEMENT IS POSSIBLE, BUT DIFFICULT.	O E 1 3	WAR AGAINST ENEMY WHO HAS TECHNICAL SOPHISTICATION, IN AN ENVIRONMENT WITH HIGH INDUSTRIAL DEVELOPMENT, HAS LITTLE OR NO DEVELOPMENT OF TRANSPORT AND COMMUNICATION FACILITIES, AND IN WHICH SURFACE CROSS-COURTRY MOVEMENT OF MECHANIZED FORCES IS IMPOSSIBLE OR POSSIBLE ONLY IN LOCAL AREAS.
O E 2 1	WAR AGAINST AN ENEMY ABLE TO ORGANIZE AND OPERATE ARMED FORCES USING FAIRLY MODERN WEAPONS AND EQUIPMENT. ARTILLERY; TACTICAL AIR FORCE; IN AN ENVIRONMENT WITH EXTENSIVE INDUSTRIAL DEVELOPMENT, HIGHLY DEVELOPED TRANSPORTATION FACILITIES. CROSS-COUNTRY MOVEMENT FLEXIBLE.	O E 2 2	WAR IN AN ENVIRONMENT WITH SAME INDUSTRIAL DEVELOPMENT, BUT WITH ONLY MODERATELY TO POORLY DEVELOPED TRANSPORT AND COMMUNICATIONS CROSS-COUNTRY VEHICULAR MOVEMENT IS POSSIBLE, BUT DIFFICULT. THE ENEMY IN THIS WAR IS ABLE TO ORGANIZE ARMED FORCES USING FAIRLY MODERN WEAPONRY.	O E 2 3	WAR IN AN ENVIRONMENT WHICH MAY HAVE SOME INDUSTRY, BUT LITTLE OR NO DEVELOPMENT OF TRANSPORT AND COMMUNICATION FACILITIES, AND IN WHICH SURFACE CROSS-COUNTRY MOVEMENT OF MECHANIZED FORCES IS IMPOSSIBLE OR POSSIBLE ONLY IN LOCAL AREAS.
O E 3 1	WAR AGAINST PRIMITIVE FORCES MOST LIKELY TO ENGAGE IN GUERRILLA WARFARE. LACK OF TECHNOLOGICAL SOPHISTICATION; NO AIRCRAFT; NO RADAR; RUDIMENTARY COMMUNICATION SYSTEM; IN AN ENVIRONMENT WITH EXTENSIVE INDUSTRIAL DEVELOPMENT, INCLUDING HIGHLY DEVELOPED TRANSPORTATION FACILITIES.	O E 3 2	WAR AGAINST GUERRILLA FORCES IN AN ENVIRONMENT WITH SAME INDUSTRIAL DEVELOPMENT, BUT WITH POORLY DEVELOPED TRANSPORTATION AND COMMUNICATION. CROSS-COUNTRY VEHICULAR MOVEMENTS POSSIBLE, BUT DIFFICULT.	O E 3 3	WAR AGAINST PRIMITIVE GUERRILLAS IN AN ENVIRONMENT WHICH, WHILE IT MAY HAVE SOME INDUSTRY, HAS LITTLE OR NO DEVELOPMENT OF TRANSPORT AND COMMUNICATION FACILITIES. SURFACE CROSS-COUNTRY MOVEMENT OF MECHANIZED FORCES IS IMPOSSIBLE OR POSSIBLE ONLY IN LOCAL AREAS.

TYPES OF PROSPECTIVE OPPONENTS (O)

tional industrial processes. The sheer capacity of military power to cancel any and all "processes of history" by canceling society entitles us to employ the term "military determinism" in describing the present era.

The Latin-American complex offers an excellent laboratory for showing the extent to which the military determine the game of politics in the "Third World." This is measurable by the fact that in the present decade eight countries have experienced one or more military coups (Argentina, Peru, Ecuador, Guatemala, Dominican Republic, Honduras, and Brazil); in three additional countries the military have continued their preeminence from the previous decade (Nicaragua, Paraguay, and Haiti); in one country a guerrilla army has been transformed into the regular army (Cuba); in another country its essentially pacifist civilian-oriented militia has been transformed into paramilitary, counterinsurgency units (Costa Rica).

Then there are nations in which the military perform backstage pivotal roles—an omnipresence rather than a simple presence (Venezuela, El Salvador, and Colombia). Mexico, Chile, and Uruguay are the only nations in which the military determination of policy is severely limited. They also are probably the only ones in which guerrilla insurgency units are nonexistent.

The rise of guerrilla activities throughout the "Third World" has been spectacular. Yet, it might well be the irony of hemispheric affairs that counterinsurgency units precede in time the formation of insurgency units. This, at any rate, seems to have been the sequence of events in the Dominican Republic. When the legitimate aspirations of the people are frustrated by military action, and when newly formed, foreign-sponsored counterinsurgency units spearhead the ouster of legitimate regimes, then a rise in guerrilla action is likely to follow. The exact causal sequence is important. If it is the case that counterinsurgency precedes the formation of insurgency units, then the self-fulfilling prophetic aspects of United States foreign policy may well turn into self-destructive actions.[11]

It is possible that for ecological, sociological, and political reasons, insurgency forms of revolutionary activity will either be unsuccessful or simply unfeasible. The patent failure of insurgency in the big nations of the hemisphere, particularly in Brazil and Argentina, makes it clear that insurgency warfare on the models outlined by Mao Tse-tung or Ernesto Guevara are not necessarily operational in highly urbanized and industrialized sectors.[12]

On the other hand, it must also be borne in mind that the deployment of regular troops, either of a home-grown or colonial-imported variety, does little to resolve fundamental demands made by revolutionary movements. If it takes between 20,000 and 30,000 troops to maintain a cease-fire agreement in one small Caribbean nation, it becomes evident that it would take at least 100 times that number to maintain an equilibrium

---

[11]Again, it should be noted that this is not an attempt to deny multicausality. Without a certain level of industrial production, modern armies are impotent. But even this basic shibboleth may be restricted to national armies. It does not seem so for guerrilla forces. Further, without a certain level of legal codes, armies tend to militarize civilian populations. But is this true in developing Third World regions? Questions like this compel a reconsideration of what variables in social analysis should or should not be considered as central. And whether changes in time and place do not necessitate a radical shift in the variables considered decisive.

[12]See on this the recent work by Edwin Lieuwen, *Generals vs. Presidents: Neomilitarism in Latin America* (New York: Frederick A. Praeger, 1964), esp. pp. 7-9, 126-29, 136-41.

in the face of revolutionary tides and sentiments. All of which should provide sober food for thought to those devotees of *realpolitik* who still believe that any who would rely upon international, legally sanctioned organizations are dazed romantics.

The ideology of hemispheric militarism, whether promoted by the United States or by indigenous military elites, assumes that every movement for reform or revolution must either have official *étatist* sanction or be vigorously opposed—by force if necessary. In the long run, such an inflexible ideology when translated into policy, erodes the foundation of pragmatic settlements or evolutionary solutions. In the name of combating conspiracy, present "hard-line" approaches make compromise impossible.

LIST OF CONTRIBUTORS

BAILEY, JOYCE. Miss Bailey is a junior at the University of California (Berkeley).

BERELSON, BERNARD, Ph.D. Currently vice-president of the Population Council (NYC), Dr. Berelson is coauthor (with Dr. Gary Steiner) of *Human Behavior: An Inventory of Findings* (New York: Harcourt, Brace & World, Inc: 1965).

BLUMBERG, LEONARD, Ph.D. Dr. Blumberg is a professor of sociology at Temple University, Philadelphia. He is also a codirector of research of the University's Diagnostic and Relocation Center (along with I. Shandler and T. E. Shipley, Jr.).

BUGENTAL, J. F. T., Ph.D., Diplomate in Clinical Psychology, A. B. E. P.-P. Dr. Bugental is affiliated with Psychological Service Associates (Los Angeles, Calif.).

BYNDER, HERBERT, Ph.D. Dr. Bynder is an assistant professor of sociology, and the director of the NIMH Training Program in the sociology of Medicine and Mental Health at the University of Colorado.

CLINARD, MARSHALL B., Ph.D. Dr. Clinard is a professor of sociology at the University of Wisconsin. His latest book is *The Slum and Urban Community Development: Experiments in Self-Help* (1965).
During 1958-60 and 1962-63 Dr. Clinard served as a consultant on urban community development to the Ford Foundation in India. Past president of the Society for the Study of Social Problems, Dr. Clinard is the current president of the Midwest Sociological Society.

ELLING, RAY H., Ph.D. Dr. Elling is an associate professor of sociology affiliated with both the Department of Sociology and the Department of Public Health Service at the University of Pittsburgh. He has contributed essays to *Sociology in Use* (Valdes and Dean, eds., [New York: MacMillan Co.] 1965), *The Hospital in Modern Society* (Freidson, ed., 1963), and *Sociology and Medical Care* (Scott, ed., n.d.).

ETZIONI, AMITAI, Ph.D. Dr. Etzioni is an associate professor of sociology at Columbia University. He is the author most recently of *The Moon-Doggle, Winning Without War, Modern Organizations, The Hard Way to Peace: A New Strategy,* and several other works. With Eva Etzioni he recently coedited *Social Change: Sources, Patterns, and Consequences* (New York: Basic Books, Inc., 1964).

EUGSTER, CARLA, M.A. A consultant, Mrs. Eugster has worked for many years and in many contexts—union, government, and educational—as a field educator. She is currently writing a play at her home in Baltimore, Md.

FANTINI, MARIS D., Ed.D. Dr. Fantini is presently a program consultant with the Ford Foundation (NYC).

FELDMAN, DAVID, Ph.D. Dr. Feldman is a staff member of the American Federation of Teachers (AFL-CIO). He was previously an assistant professor with the Department of Sociology, San Diego State College.

FREEDMAN, JONATHAN. Mr. Freedman is a senior research analyst in the Community Action Training Program, and a lecturer in the School of Social Work at Syracuse University.

FUKUYAMA, YOSHIO, Ph.D. Dr. Fukuyama is the secretary for research of the United Church Board for Homeland Ministries (NYC).

GILLETTE, THOMAS L., Ph.D. Dr. Gillette is an assistant professor with the Department of Sociology, San Diego State College.

GOLDSTEIN, RHODA L., Ph.D., Dr. Goldstein is a lecturer on sociology at Douglass College, Rutgers—The State University (New Brunswick N.J.). She has been active in local organizations concerned with integration in medicine, education, and housing.

HALL, RICHARD H., Ph.D. Dr. Hall is an assistant professor of sociology at Indiana University.

HALLECK, SEYMOUR L., M.D. Dr. Halleck is an associate professor of psychiatry with the University of Wisconsin Medical School. He is presently completing a study of psychiatry and criminology for publication by Harper & Row.

HARE, A. PAUL, Ph.D. Dr. Hare is an associate professor in the Department of Sociology and Anthropology at Haverford College. Previously he had spent several years doing "action"-research in the field of preventive psychiatry.

HOIBERG, OTTO G., Ph.D. Dr. Hoiberg is a professor of sociology and the director of the Community Development University Extension Division of the University of Nebraska.

HOROWITZ, IRVING LOUIS, Ph.D. Dr. Horowitz is an associate professor with the Department of Sociology-Anthropology at Washington University. He is the editor of *Power, Politics, and People: The Collected Essays of C. Wright Mills* (New York: Ballantine; 1963) and *The Anarchists* (New York: Dell Publishing Co. [Laurel Editions:] 1964).

JOHNSON, C. DALE, Ph.D. Dr. Johnson is an assistant professor with the Department of Sociology, San Diego State College.

KEY, WILLIAM H., Ph.D. Dr. Key is chairman of the Department of Sociology of Washburn University (Topeka, Kans.). He is also a project director and research associate with the Menninger Foundation.

KILLIAN, LEWIS M., Ph.D. Dr. Killian is a professor of sociology at Florida State University. He is the coauthor with Dr. Charles M. Grigg of *Racial Crisis in America: Leadership in Conflict* (New York: Prentice-Hall, Inc.; 1964).

KIRK, JEROME, Ph.D. Dr. Kirk is a research associate with the Graduate School of Industrial Administration of the Carnegie Institute of Technology.

LANG, KURT, Ph.D. Dr. Lang is an associate professor with the Sociology Department of the State University of New York at Stony Brook.

LEGGETT, JOHN C. An assistant professor in the Department of Sociology, University of California (Berkeley), Dr. Leggett has contributed to *Blue-Collar World* and to various journals.

LIPPITT, RONALD, Ph.D. Dr. Lippitt is a professor of sociology and psychology at the University of Michigan. He is also a director of the university's Research Center for Group Dynamics, the Institute for Social Research, and the Center for Research on the Utilization of Scientific Knowledge. He has served as president of the Society for the Psychological Study of Social Issues, and as editor of the *Journal of Social Issues*.

LOWRY, RITCHIE P., Ph.D. Dr. Lowry is a senior research scientist and an associate professor of research with the Special Operations Research Office of The American University (D.C.). He is the author of *Who's Running This Town? Community Leadership and Social Change* (New York: Harper & Row: 1965).

MARTON, GUNILLA. Miss Marton is a research and reading assistant at the University of California (Berkeley).

MILLER, S. M., Ph.D. Dr. Miller is a professor of sociology and senior research associate at Syracuse University. He is affiliated with the university's Youth Development Center, and coeditor (with Dr. Alvin W. Gouldner) of *Applied Sociology* (New York: The Free Press of Glencoe, Inc., 1965).

MORLAND, J. KENNETH, Ph.D. Dr. Morland is professor and chairman of the Department of Sociology and Anthropology at Randolph-Macon Woman's College. He is the author of *Millways of Kent* (Chapel Hill, N.C.: University of North Carolina Press).

NEWMAN, DONALD J., Ph.D. Dr. Newman is an associate professor of social work and a fellow in law at the University of Wisconsin. He is the author of *Conviction: The Determination of Guilt or Innocence Without Trial* (Boston: Little, Brown and Co., 1965), and is coauthor of *Sociology of Crime* (1960) and *Juvenile Delinquency* (1958).

OLSON, THEODORE, Ph.D. Dr. Olson has combined the Presbyterian ministry with nonviolent action and teaching. After a 1962 Ph.D. in this "amalgam," he directed a two-year research project that resulted in the establishment in 1965 of the Upland Institute (Crozer Theological Seminary, Upland, Pa.), a school he presently directs.

OPPENHEIMER, MARTIN, Ph.D. Dr. Oppenheimer is a lecturer in sociology at Bryn Mawr College. He is coauthor (with George Lakey) of *A Manual for Direct Action* (Chicago: Quadrangle Books, Inc., 1965).

PITTMAN, DAVID J., Ph.D. Dr. Pittman is a professor of sociology and director of the Social Science Institute at Washington University. He is the coauthor (with C. W. Gordon) of *Revolving Door: A Study of the Chronic Police Case Inebriate* (New York: The Free Press of Glencoe, Inc., 1958), has edited *Alcoholism: An Interdisciplinary Approach* (Springfield, Ill.: Charles C. Thomas, 1959), and has coedited (with Dr. Charles R. Synder) *Society, Culture, and Drinking Patterns* (New York: Wiley John & Sons, Inc., 1962).

RIESSMAN, FRANK, Ph.D. Dr. Riessman is a member of the Department of Psychiatry at the Albert Einstein College of Medicine (NYC). He is the editor, with Arthur Pearl and Jerome Cohen, of *Mental Health of the Poor* (New York: The Free Press of Glencoe, Inc., 1964); and the coeditor, with Arthur Pearl, of *New Careers for the Poor* (New York: The Free Press of Glencoe, Inc., 1965).

ROBBINS, RICHARD, Ph.D. Dr. Robbins is an associate professor of sociology at Wheaton College (Mass.), and a lecturer in sociology at Boston College. He is the author of *Racial and Ethnic Relations* (New York: Dodd, Mead & Co., 1965).

Rose, Arnold M., Ph.D. Dr. Rose is a professor of sociology at the University of Minnesota, and has authored or edited 17 books. Currently vice-president of the American Sociological Association, he has served as president of the Midwest Sociological Society and was founding member and president of the Society for the Study of Social Problems.

Saroff, Jerome R., Mr. Saroff is the state director of Planning and Research, Office of the Governor, Juneau, Alaska. He has an M.A. in City Planning from the Massachusetts Institute of Technology.

Schwartz, Michael, Ph.D. Dr. Schwartz is an assistant professor of sociology at Indiana University.

Schwartz, Morris S., Ph.D. Dr. Schwartz is a professor of human relations and the chairman of the Sociology Department at Brandeis University. He is the coauthor (with Dr. A. H. Stanton) of *The Mental Hospital* (New York: Basic Books, Inc., 1954).

Shostak, Arthur B., Ph.D. Dr. Shostak is an assistant professor of sociology at the University of Pennsylvania. He is coeditor, with William Gomberg, of *Blue-Collar World* (Englewood Cliffs, N.J.: Prentice-Hall, 1964), and *New Perspectives on Poverty* (Englewood Cliffs, N.J.: Prentice-Hall, 1965). He has contributed to *Frontiers of Management Science, The Negro and Employment Opportunity,* and *The Impact of Business,* along with a dozen professional and popular journals.

Sussman, Marvin B., Ph.D. Dr. Sussman is a professor of sociology and department chairman at Western Reserve University. He has also served as president of the Society for the Study of Social Problems and is currently editor of the *Journal of Marriage and Family Living.*

Tannenbaum, Robert, Ph.D. Dr. Tannenbaum is a professor of personnel management and industrial relations at the University of California (Los Angeles). He is also vice-chairman of the Department of Business Administration, head of the Human Relations Research Group, and research behavioral scientist with the Institute of Industrial Relations. Dr. Tannenbaum is the coauthor of *Leadership and Organization: A Behavioral Science Approach* (New York: McGraw-Hill Book Co., Inc., 1961).

Weinstein, Gerald M., Ed. Mr. Weinstein is presently director of the Elementary Teaching Project of the Fund for the Advancement of Education (NYC). He has previously served as associate director of the Urban Teacher Preparation Program at Syracuse University.

ANNOTATED BIBLIOGRAPHY

Action sociologists are fortunate in the rich literature available to guide and support their projects. The 33 books described below constitute a small, though representative, sample of the many excellent resources available, resources that include, in addition to hard-cover books, such outstanding journals as *Social Forces, Social Problems, the Journal of Applied Behavioral Science, Trans-Action,* and others. Together the particular books and journals substantially further the efforts of those who would build with, rather than simply mull over, the insights contained in the printed page.

ABRAHAMSON, JULIA. *A Neighborhood Finds Itself.* New York: Harper & Bros., 1959. 334 pp. Appendices. Bibliography. Index.

The author, an officer of the community agency involved, tells the story of a pioneering effort in a declining Chicago community to "fuse the challenges of Negro in-migration and conservation into the excitement of creating a fine interracial community." The writer seeks as well to "provide a possible guide to other communities faced with similar problems." Especially valuable is her very frank review of the various mistakes made by the largely successful Hyde Park-Kenwood Community Conference.

ARENSBERG, CONRAD M., AND NIEHOFF, ARTHUR H. *Introducing Social Change: A Manual for Americans Overseas.* Chicago: Aldine Publishing Co., 1964. 204 pp. Bibliography. Index.

The authors are concerned with lifting the insights we employ in cross-cultural interaction above the level of intuitive judgment. They discuss the basic cultural factors which should be understood for the successful introduction of new ideas or techniques. Major attention is paid to the local customs into which innovations can best be blended.

BATTEN, T. R. *Communities and Their Development: An Introductory Study with Special Reference to the Tropics.* London: Oxford University Press, 1957. 231 pp. Bibliography. Index.

A British overview of community development techniques employed throughout the Commonwealth, strong in the fact that over 150 officers from some 30 tropical and subtropical countries "have in some way or another contributed to the ideas it contains."

BENNIS, WARREN G.; BENNE, KENNETH D.; AND CHIN, ROBERT (eds.) *The Planning of Change: Readings in the Applied Behavioral Sciences.* New York: Holt, Rinehart and Winston, Inc., 1961. 764 pp. Index.

The largest collection of its type, this classic volume brings together 84 essays in four sections: "The Roots of Planned Change"; "Conceptual Tools for the Change-Agent: Social Systems and Change Models"; "Dynamics of the Influence Process"; and "Programs and Technologies of Planned Change." Especially valuable is the unique stress placed on the cooperative and collaborative aspects of personal relationships implicated in change—as well as the scientific findings related to change.

BERELSON, BERNARD, AND STEINER, GARY. *Human Behavior: An Inventory of Scientific Findings.* New York: Harcourt, Brace & World, Inc., 1964. 667 pp. Bibliographic index. Subject index.

An ambitious collection of 1,045 scientifically supported hypothess about human behavior, rare in its endeavor and its succinct, nontechnical presentation. No applied sociologist should be without it.

BIDDLE, WILLIAM, AND BIDDLE, LOWREIDE J. *The Community Development Process: The Rediscovery of Local Initiative.* New York: Holt, Rinehart and Winston, Inc., 1965. 277 pp. Appendix. Annotated 250-item bibliography. Index.

The book presents in case-study form the development process in two communities, a mining county in rural Appalachia and a deteriorating neighborhood in a northern industrial city. The research design is outlined and an attempt is made to clarify the relatedness of community development to various academic disciplines and helping professions. A preliminary identity is given the active community developer, who is essential to the process."

BOGUSLAW, ROBERT. *The New Utopians: A Study of System Design and Social Change.* Englewood Cliffs, N.J.: Prentice-Hall, Inc., 1965. 204 pp. Index.

This path-breaking challenge to social scientists and "social engineers" warns that modern system designers are embracing the most fundamental errors of early Utopian designers and are substituting "efficiency" for "humanitarianism." The sociologist-author calls on social scientists to abandon the role of bystander and exert new influence inside system design efforts.

BRUYN, SEVERYN T. *Communities in Action: Pattern and Process.* New Haven: College & University Press, 1963. 157 pp. Appendix. Bibliography. Index.

A sociologist analyzes the outcome of university-aided citizen efforts to solve pressing local problems in four Illinois communities. He later advances an ideal model of social action both practical and flexible enough to guide others in a wide range of situations.

ETZIONI, AMITAI, AND ETZIONI, EVA (eds.). *Social Change: Sources, Patterns and Consequences.* New York: Basic Books, Inc., 1964. 497 pp. Index of Names.

Fifty-five essays are divided into six sections: "Sources and Patterns of Change: Classical Theories," "Modern Theories," "Spheres of Change: The Modern Society," "Modernization," "Levels of Change," and "Processes of Change." Especially valuable is the collection's unique stress on social change on an international level.

GIBBONS, DON C. *Changing the Lawbreaker: The Treatment of Delinquents and Criminals.* Englewood Cliffs, N.J.: Prentice-Hall, Inc., 1965. 299 pp. Index.

The sociologist-author explains in his preface: "This book is intended to be several things simultaneously—an inventory and assessment of recent theories and research findings regarding causal processes in crime and delinquency, an overview of social patterns in correctional organizations, a theoretical venture in 'applied sociology,' and a contribution to correctional practice theory." Careful attention is paid such forms of treatment as individual depth psychotherapy, group psychotherapy, client-centered psychotherapy, and environmental change.

GOULDNER, ALVIN W., AND MILLER, S. M. (eds.). *Applied Sociology: Opportunities and Problems.* New York: Free Press of Glencoe, Inc., 1965.

A collection of 35 essays, many especially prepared for this volume, by sociologists in and outside of academia. Sections deal with the clinical approach in applied sociology, the practioner and his clients, race relations, criminology and delinquency, the community, the family, the international situation, the law, the contribution of applied sociology to general sociology, the contribution of applied sociology to public policy, and issues in applied sociology.

GROSSACK, MARTIN M., (ed.). *Understanding Consumer Behavior.* Boston: The Christopher Publishing House, 1964. 321 pp. Subject Index.

An attempt to show how the different behavioral sciences may be used to study market behavior, this collection of 20 reprints is edited by an applied psychologist who conducts research for consumer firms, banks, and advertising agencies. Essays of interest to the sociologist include: "Working with Behavioral Scientists" (Newman), "Sociological Reflections on Business" (Lazarsfeld), "Risk Handling in Drug Adaption" (Bauer), "Basic Dimensions of the Corporate Image" (Spector), and "Husband-Wife Interaction in Decision-Making" (Kenkel).

HOROWITZ, IRVING LOUIS (ed.). *The New Sociology: Essays in Social Science and Social Theory in Honor of C. Wright Mills.* New York: Oxford University Press, 1964. 488 pp. Index.

Twenty-eight essays pay tribute to the late C. Wright Mills by honoring his call for a passionate sense of significant problems and a passionate concern with solving them. Typical are essays by Edel on "Social Science and Value," Miller on "Poverty, Race, and Politics," Powell on "Reform, Revolution, and Reaction," and Germani on "Social Change and Intergroup Conflict." A powerful introduction by the editor sets the tone with its declaration that "sociology which rests on 'descriptive studies involving random ratlike movements' has had its chance — an opportunity fudged by the anti-humanism of its sociological assumptions, and by cowardice described as modesty."

KING, CLARENCE (ed.). *Working with People in Small Communities: Case Records of Community Development in Different Countries.* New York: Harper and Bros., 1958). 128 pp. Index.

A collection of reprints, now ten or more years old, recording in dramatic narrative fashion actual cases of community development in the United States, Korea, Mexico, Egypt, Greece, India, Nigeria, New Zealand, Thailand, and Puerto Rico. Each case is analyzed on its own merits as well as in relation to the others.

LEEDS, RUTH, AND SMITH, THOMASINA (eds.). *Using Social Science Knowledge in Business and Industry: Report of a Seminar.* Homewood, Illinois: Richard D. Irwin, Inc., 1963. 73 pp. Bibliography.

This report of a 1962 seminar covers such topics as establishing a stable working relationship between social scientist and businessman, recognizing the limitations of social science, and techniques of implementation of social science knowledge. Terse and plain-spoken, the book features a case study concerned with intergroup conflict.

LIKERT, RENSIS, AND HAYES, SAMUEL P., JR., (eds). *Some Applications of Behavioural Research.* New York: UNESCO Publications Center, 1957. 333 pp.

Seven essayists work from UNESCO-sponsored, research-reporting seminars; Likert discusses applied projects in general, Seashore discusses leadership training, Peter reviews human factors in research administration, Pelz considers research laboratory leadership, Bourne writes about group influence in marketing and public relations, Morrisett discusses psychological surveys in business forecasting, and Lesser and Peter review the impact of visits by foreign nationals.

LYND, ROBERT S. *Knowledge for What: The Place of Social Science in American Culture.* New York: Grove Press (Evergreen Black Cat Edition), 1964. 250 pp. Index.

An indispensable classic — both in terms of its appraisal of American culture in the late 1930's (the time of its original publication) and its critique of focus and methods in social science research. The chapters deal with "Social Science in Crisis," "The Concept of Culture," "The Pattern of American Culture," "The Social Sciences as Tools," "Values and the Social Sciences," and "Some Outrageous Hypotheses." As Max Lerner puts it, the book stakes out "the most spacious claims for the possibilities of social thinking — nothing short of the reconstruction of our culture."

MEYER, HENRY J.; BORGATTA, EDGAR F.; AND JONES, WYATT C. *Girls at Vocational High: An Experiment in Social Work Intervention.* New York: Russell Sage Foundation, 1965. 217 pp. Index.

An interdisciplinary team of two sociologists and a professor of social work reports on a six-year effort to prevent the "inevitable" delinquency of problem girls at a New York vocational school. The book is unique for its very frank appraisal of certain discouraging results, and the provocative questions it raises about the appropriateness of social casework as an exclusive approach to predelinquent problems. Cottrell, Jr., in the foreword, expresses his hope that "more persistent and systematic collaboration of social work and social science theorists should emerge from such enterprises as the one here reported."

MICHAEL, DONALD N. *The Next Generation: The Prospects Ahead for the Youth of Today and Tomorrow.* New York: Random House, Inc., 1965. 207 pp. Appendices. Index.

Action-oriented sociologists concerned to know where various trends current in our society appear to lead will find this book invaluable. Terse and engaging chapters discuss the economy, technological developments, organized efficiency; marriage, sex, and the family; education, work, leisure, and values and viewpoints. The author suggests in conclusion, that "regardless of the great personal pain it will entail, we must explore, more honestly and intensively than most of us ever do, which of the values and goals that we hold dear are appropriate to inculcate in youth for living in tomorrow's world — or for ourselves to live in planning for and guiding them."

MILLS, C. WRIGHT. *The Sociological Imagination.* New York: Oxford University Press, 1959. 226 pp. Index.

Likely the most significant critique of contemporary sociology, the book characterizes "Grand Theory" and "Abstract Empiricism," two dominant sociological styles, as approaches which help to insure "that we do not learn too much about man and society — the first by formal and cloudy obscurantism, the second by formal and empty ingenuity." Action-oriented sociologists will be especially interested in the applied counterparts of these dominant academic styles, namely, Liberal Scatter and Illiberal Practicality. Mills concludes with various prescriptions for reform, including a unique appendix on "intellectual craftsmanship." Sociology has not been the same since.

OBLER, PAUL C., AND ESTRIN, HERMAN A. (eds.). *The New Scientist: Essays on the Methods and Values of Modern Science.* Garden City, N.Y.: Doubleday & Co., Inc. (Anchor Books), 1962. 312 pp. Bibliography.

Among other things, the 17-essay collection explores the scientist's impact on society and the nature of his quest. The sociologist-activist might profit especially from "Science and People" by Warren Weaver, "The Social Responsibilities of Scientists" by Bertrand Russell, "Science and Public Understanding" by Dael Wolfle, and "The Moral Un-Neutrality of science" by C. P. Snow. The editors conclude: "The great lesson here is that we need not fear science nor should we idolize it; we should open ourselves to what it has to tell us and integrate it into our lives and societies."

OPPENHEIMER, MARTIN, AND LAKEY, GEORGE. *A Manual for Direct Action.* Chicago: Quadrangle Books, Inc., 1964. 123 pp. Appendices. Index.

Two sociologist-activists offer a practical training manual for nonviolent direct action. Sociological insights are plentiful, even as jargon and formalism are happily absent. The book is a model not only for nonviolent protestors, but for action-oriented, communications-conscious sociologists as well.

PAUL, BENJAMIN D. (ed.). *Health, Culture and Community: Case Studies of Public Reactions to Health Programs.* New York: Russell Sage Foundation, 1955. 477 pp. Index.

Sixteen essays, six by sociologists, deal with success and failure in health programs operating at the community level in a dozen or so countries. Sharply focused on the meeting of medicine and community, the book's six sections concern "Reeducating the Community," "Reaction to Crises," "Sex Patterns and Population Problems," "Effects of Social Segmentation," "Vehicles of Health Administration," and "Combining Service and Research." Taken as a whole, the editor concludes, the 16 case studies "indicate that a combination of social action and social research can be mutually beneficial."

RIESSMAN, FRANK; COHEN, JEROME; AND PEARL, ARTHUR (eds.). *Mental Health of the Poor: New Treatment Approaches for Low Income People.* New York: The Free Press of Glencoe, Inc., 1964. 648 pp.

Fifty-eight essays are divided into four sections: "Poverty, Mental Illness, and Treatment," "Low Income Behavior and Cognitive Style," "Psychotherapeutic Approaches for Low Income People," and "Rehabilitation of the Criminal, the Delinquent, and the Drug Addict." Action-oriented sociologists will find especially valuable the essays dealing with Highfields, Halfway Houses, Provo, "Open Hospitals," and the like.

ROSENBERG, BERNARD; GERVER, ISRAEL; AND HOWTON, F. WILLIAM (eds.). *Mass Society in Crisis: Social Problems and Social Pathology.* New York: The Macmillan Co., 1964. 663 pp.

The 64 essays have in common the belief of the authors that "human sensibility is under fire; we are threatened on every side," and, there is an additional serious threat in overconfidence in the efficacy of social science. The action-sociologist will profit especially from sections on sociologism, knowledge, cause and cure, expert and polity, ends and means, and action and nonaction. Korn's essay, "The Private Citizen, the Social Expert, and the Social Problem: An Excursion through an Unacknowledged Utopia," is "must" reading.

SANDERS, IRWIN T. *Making Good Communities Better*. Revised. Lexington, Ky.: University of Kentucky Press, 1953. 197 pp. Topical Index.

The author declares early that his handbook "has no axes to grind, no great inspirations to instill. The literature on the community is full of tracts, of documents with deep spiritual insight, and of article after article urging people to do this or do that if humanity is to survive. But we can assume that you — the reader . . . have the urge to do something, but need some guide to help you decide where to take hold, how to do a better job."

SPENCER, JOHN; TUXFORD, JOY; AND DENNIS, NORMAN. *Stress and Release in an Urban Estate: A Study in Action Research*. New York: Humanities Press, 1964. 335 pp.

A British study of a 1955-61 Bristol experiment in blending casework, group work, and community organization—the endeavor guided throughout by sociology and psychiatry. The book offers valuable insights into the use of indigenous workers, citizen participation, political systems, and other key elements in current antipoverty efforts here and abroad.

STEIN, MAURICE, AND VIDICH, ARTHUR (eds.). *Sociology on Trial*. Englewood Cliffs, N.J.: Prentice-Hall, Inc., 1963. 181 pp.

The volume's 11 essays, concerned as they are with the sociology of sociology, constitute "an expression of conscience for sociology as a whole." Part I explores "The Ethos of American Sociology"; Part II, "Value Neutrality as Disguise and Defense"; Part III, "The Suppression of Historical Concerns"; and Part IV, "The Rediscovery of Sociology: Some Straws in the Wind." Contributors include Mannheim, Mills, Gouldner, and ten others; all are determined to expose and reverse the trends that currently render sociologists "collaborators in the very processes that our theories tell us are likely to destroy us all."

VALDES, DONALD M., AND DEAN, DWIGHT G. (eds.). *Sociology in Use: Selected Readings for the Introductory Course*. New York: The Macmillan Co., 1965. 505 pp. Topical Index

A paperback collection of 50 essays generally first printed in the 1950's in sociological and anthropological sources. Chapters are devoted to culture, role, socialization, the small group, stratification, social organization, social and cultural change, public opinion, population and ecology, and prospects and problems of applied sociology.

WARREN, ROLAND L. *Social Research Consultation: An Experiment in Health and Welfare Planning*. New York: Russell Sage Foundation, 1963. 141 pp. Appendices. Index.

A frank account by a sociologist of his experimental introduction of a research service into an ongoing health and welfare agency, the book deals with three years' worth of successes and difficulties in some 30 instances of research consultation. Chapters discuss "The Research Consultant Role," "Social Research Projects as Social Action Episodes," "Goal Setting and Goal Displacement," and "Goal Attainment and Goal Failure." Especially interesting to action-oriented sociologists will be the author's preference for a service-oriented, rather than an academically oriented, model of the research consultant.

WHYTE, WILLIAM FOOTE, AND HAMILTON, EDITH LENTZ. *Action Research for Management: A Case Report on Research and Action in Industry.* Homewood, Illinois: The Dorsey Press, Inc., 1964. 222 pp. Appendices. Index.

The book reports in considerable detail a pioneering project in directed change conducted 15 years ago in a large hotel and kept from the literature until now by issues of confidentiality. Unique in its industrial setting, the project helped develop a new role for the hotel's personnel man — a role as applier of social science research findings. Especially valuable for the action-oriented sociologist is a long closing chapter, "On the Theory and Practice of Action Research."

WILKINS, LESLIE T. *Social Deviance: Social Policy, Action, and Research.* Englewood Cliffs, N.J. Prentice-Hall, Inc., 1965. 276 pp. Appendices. Index.

This work of a British UN expert attempts to provide a communications link between social researchers and administrators concerned with social action. Among other things, the author discusses strategies for social work and research, "general social accounting," and decision-making networks. An attempt is made to relate research methods to deviant behavior and juvenile delinquency, all in service to the author's guiding belief that "social administrator, social worker, and social scientist must get together and make a concerted attack upon the problems of the one world."

WOOTON, BARBARA, ASSISTED BY SEAL, VERA G., AND CHAMBERS, ROSALIND. *Social Science and Social Pathology.* London: George Allen & Unwin, Ltd., 1959. 339 pp. Appendices. Bibliography. Index.

A sweeping and critical review of criminological knowledge, the book is especially valuable to the action-oriented sociologist for its exposé of theories which direct attention away from social conditions toward the deficiencies of individual personality. Similarly healthy and irreverent questions are raised about our practice of inventing new institutions rather than improving the old, our practice of allowing classifications of clients to prematurely harden into administrative structures, our self-defeating preoccupation with segregated treatment of "maladjusted types," and the like.

ZETTERBERG, HANS. *Social Theory and Social Practice.* New York: The Bedminster Press, 1962. 190 pp.

A popular pioneering work, the book is divided into five sections: "The Problem," "The Knowledge of Social Practitioners," "The Knowledge of Social Theorists," "The Practical Use of Social Theory through Scholarly Consultations," and "On the Uses of Consultations." Especially valuable is the author's compact summary of the knowledge of the social sciences, his model for handling assignments, his case study of an actual consultation with the staff of an art museum that wanted to increase museum attendance, and his support of a novel venture, "applied social theory."